Wonderland

STORY & ART BY
Yugo Ishikawa

5

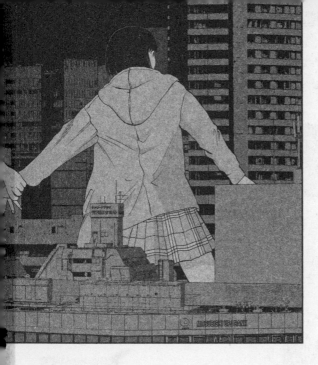

Alice, the ultimate weapon, can transform everything into nothing. She holds "the power of God" in her hands.

Story

Humanity's next evolutionary leap—the ability to manipulate matter itself—has wreaked havoc across the city.

For Yukko, a high schooler who's gotten caught up in all of this—and lost her parents because of it—and for Alice, Yukko's strange companion, this is just the latest in a series of mysteries... and all of it is Alice's fault. It is Alice, after all, who holds the ultimate power over all matter: the ability to change the mass of any object or creature.

She is the perfect weapon in the eyes of the SDF—and so, with the help of Iosif (also a human weapon, though with his own power), they are desperately pursuing her, trying to capture her for their own devices. But they're not the only ones hunting Alice: a pair of male twins with telekinesis have also joined the chase.

To evade their pursuers, Alice transformed herself and Yukko into giants, but have they really escaped...?

Characters

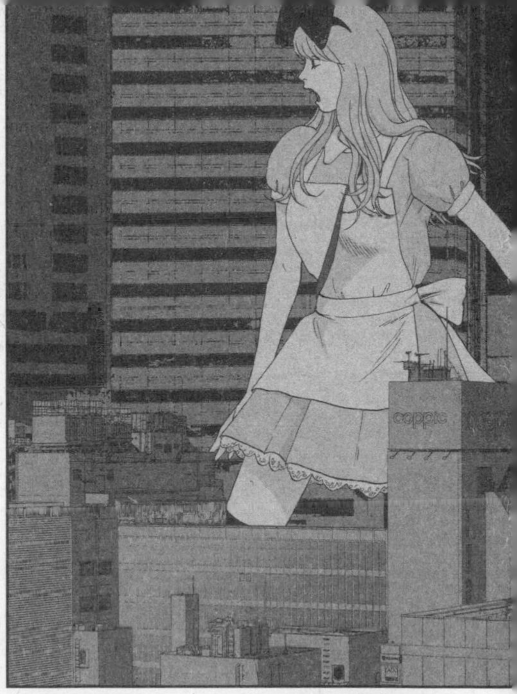

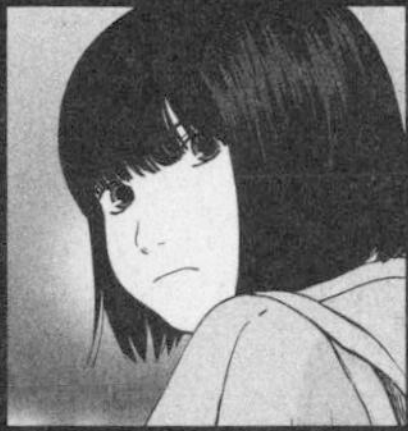

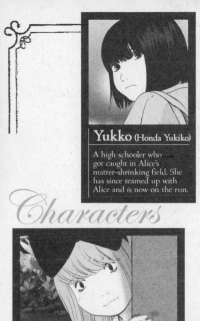

Yukko (Honda Yukiko)

A high schooler who got caught in Alice's matter-shrinking field. She has since teamed up with Alice and is now on the run.

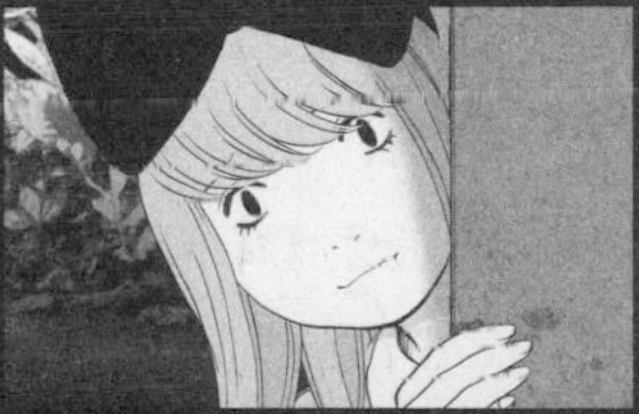

Alice

A foreign girl who's considered the "ultimate weapon." She holds the power of matter manipulation—the ability to shrink or enlarge mass and matter itself.

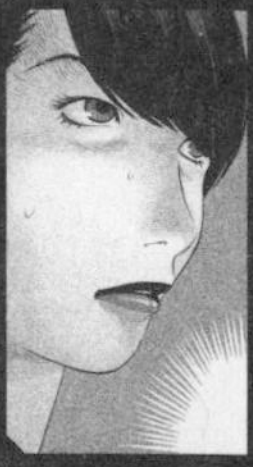

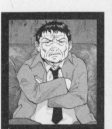

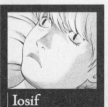

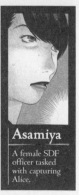

Asamiya

A female SDF officer tasked with capturing Alice.

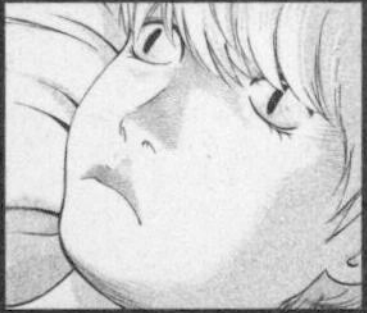

Iosif

A foreign boy who grew up with Alice in the same lab and is now helping the SDF find her. He can possess the minds of babies and small animals, and can see through their eyes.

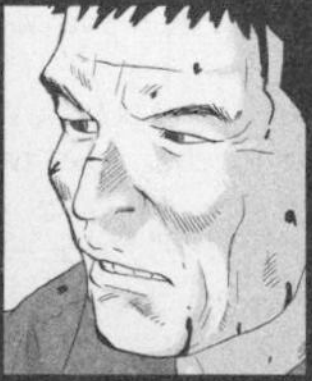

Taki

A man who got caught up in Alice's matter-shrinking field. Has mysteriously reappeared...

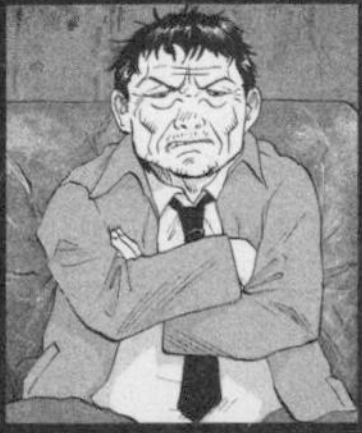

Genda

A regular guy who also got caught in Alice's matter-shrinking field. Helped save Alice and Yukko when they were on the run.

Contents

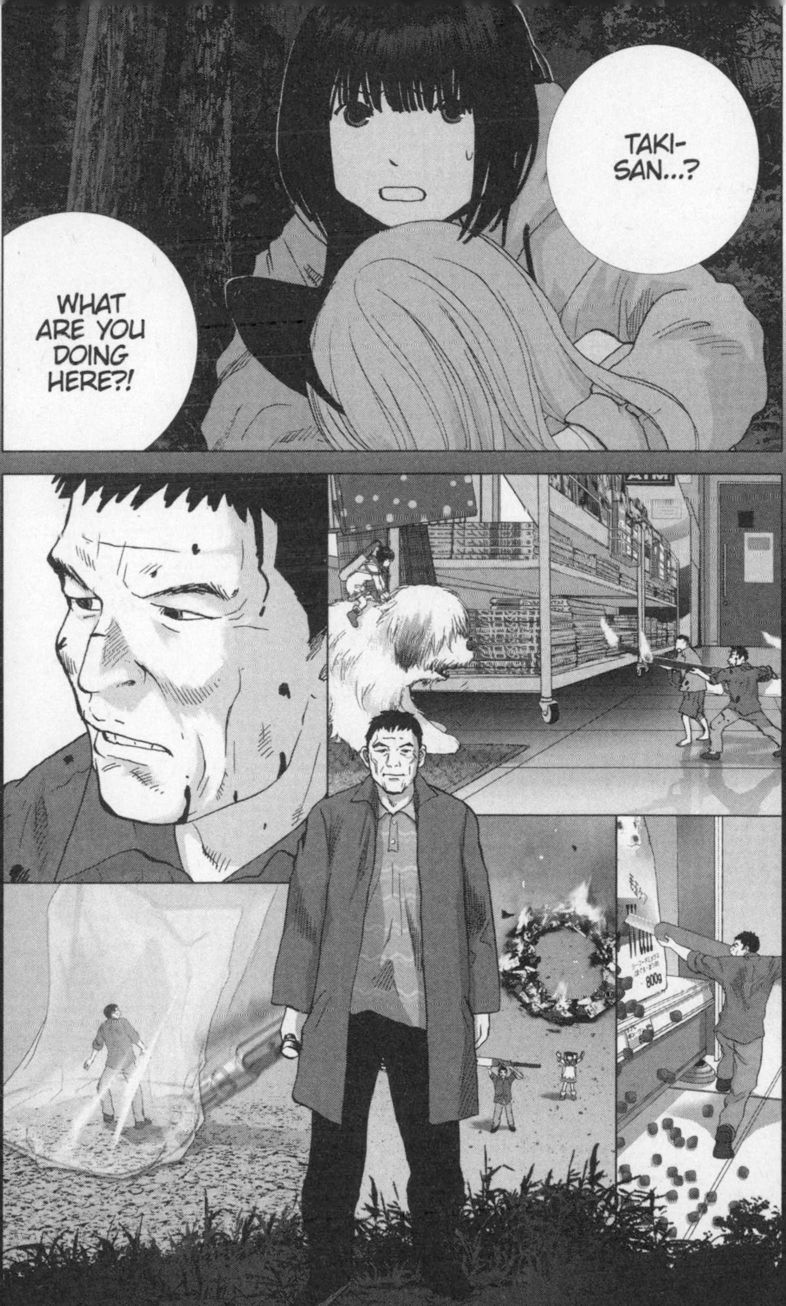
TAKI-SAN...?
WHAT ARE YOU DOING HERE?!
ATM
800g

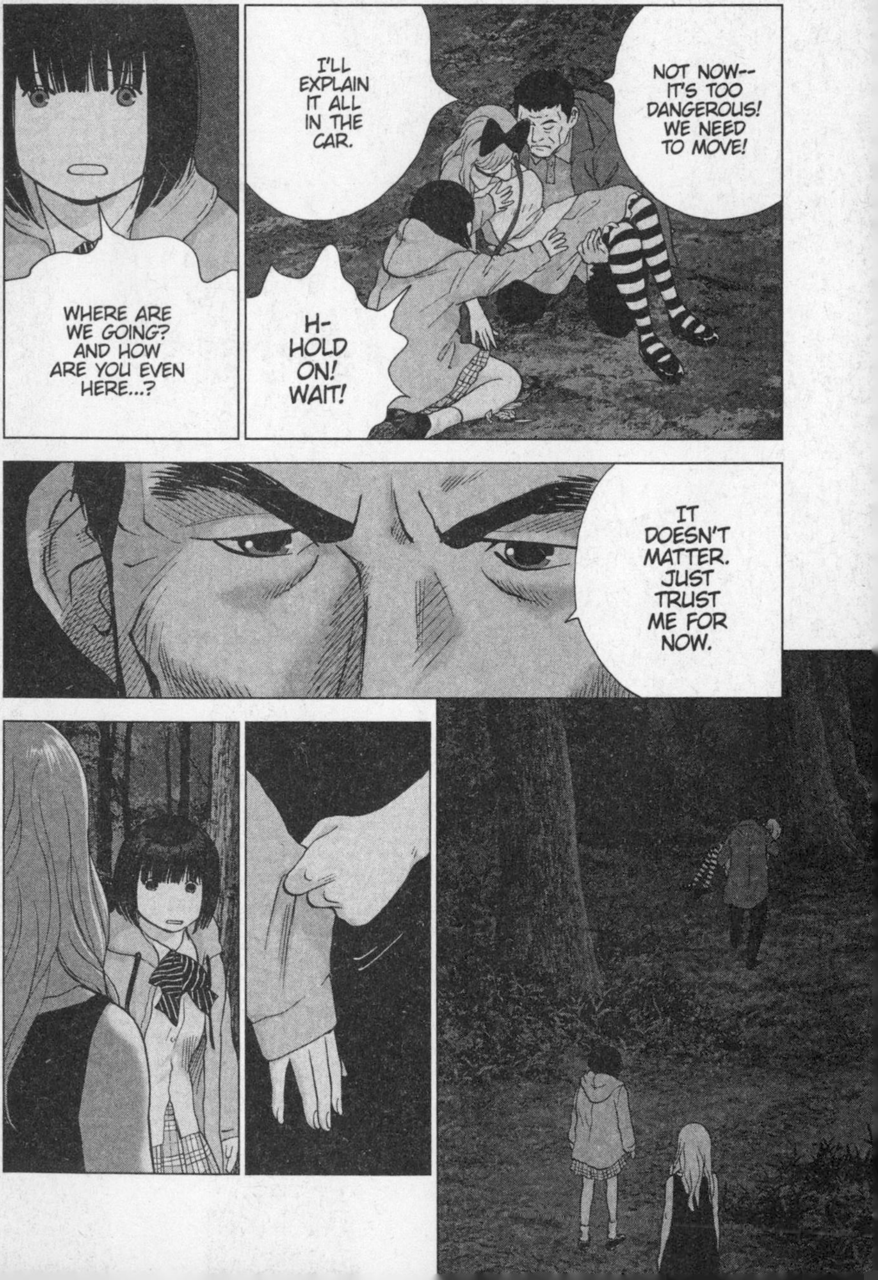
NOT NOW-- IT'S TOO DANGEROUS! WE NEED TO MOVE!
I'LL EXPLAIN IT ALL IN THE CAR.
H- HOLD ON! WAIT!
WHERE ARE WE GOING? AND HOW ARE YOU EVEN HERE...?
IT DOESN'T MATTER. JUST TRUST ME FOR NOW.

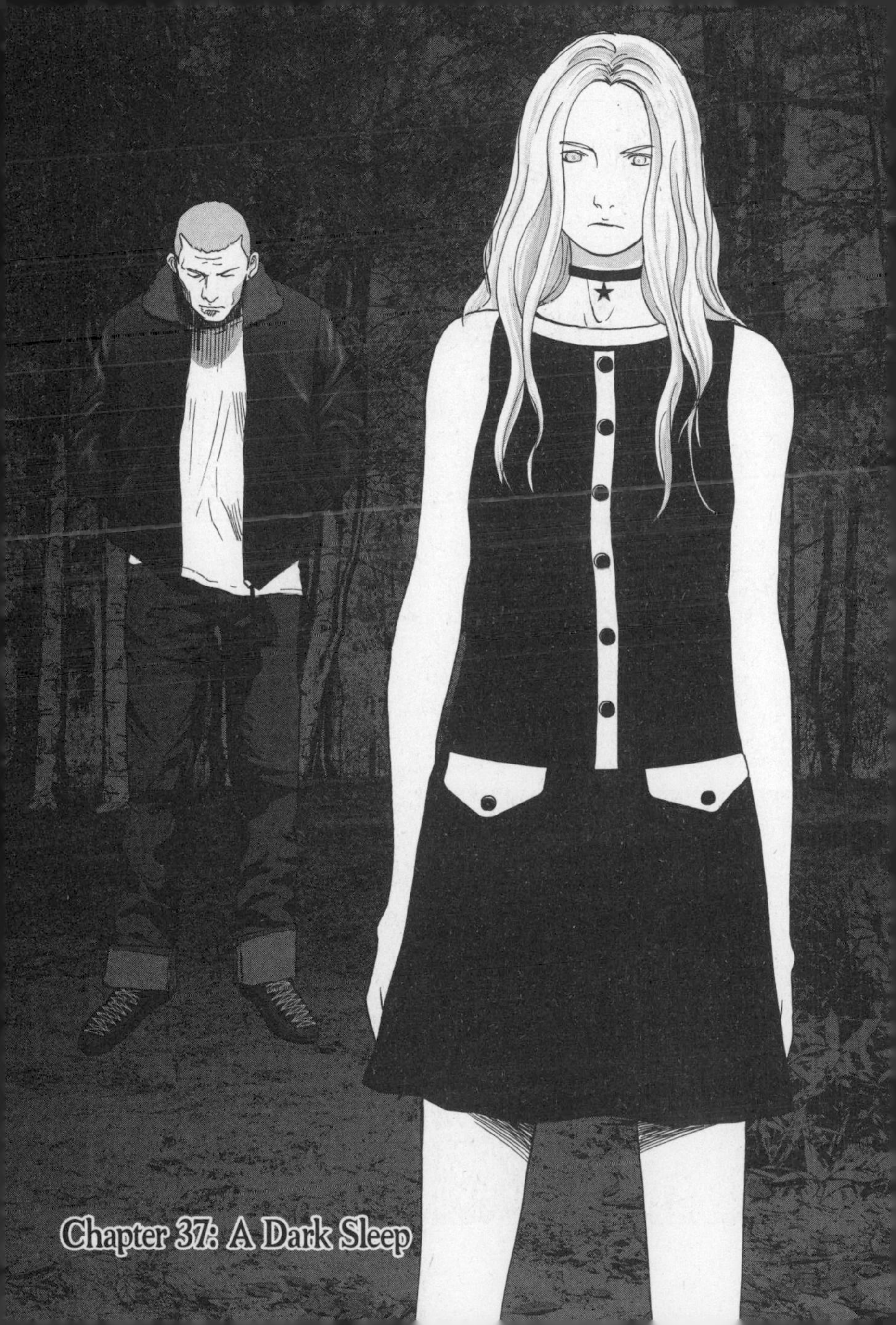
Chapter 37: A Dark Sleep

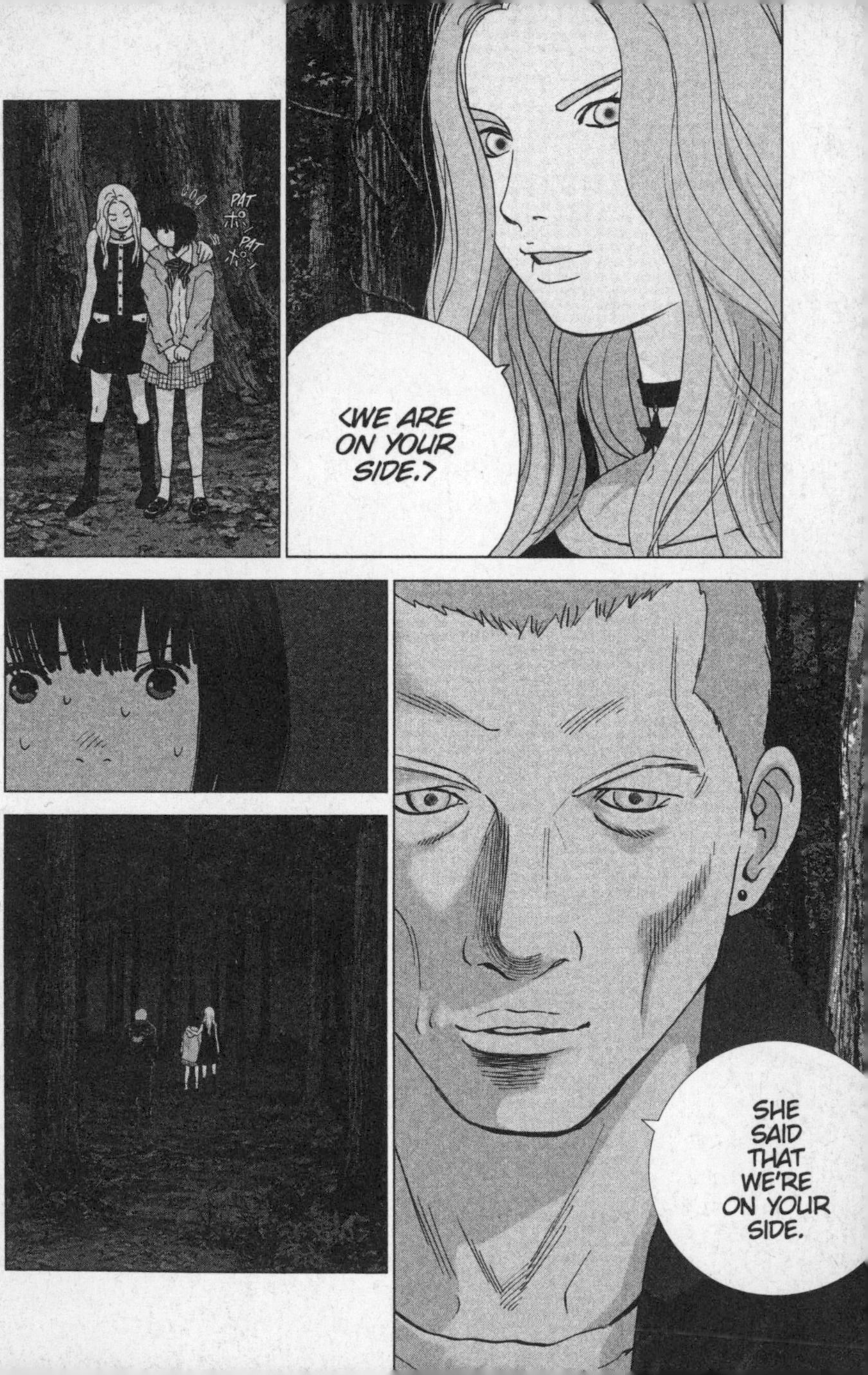
<WE ARE ON YOUR SIDE.>
PAT
PAT
SHE SAID THAT WE'RE ON YOUR SIDE.

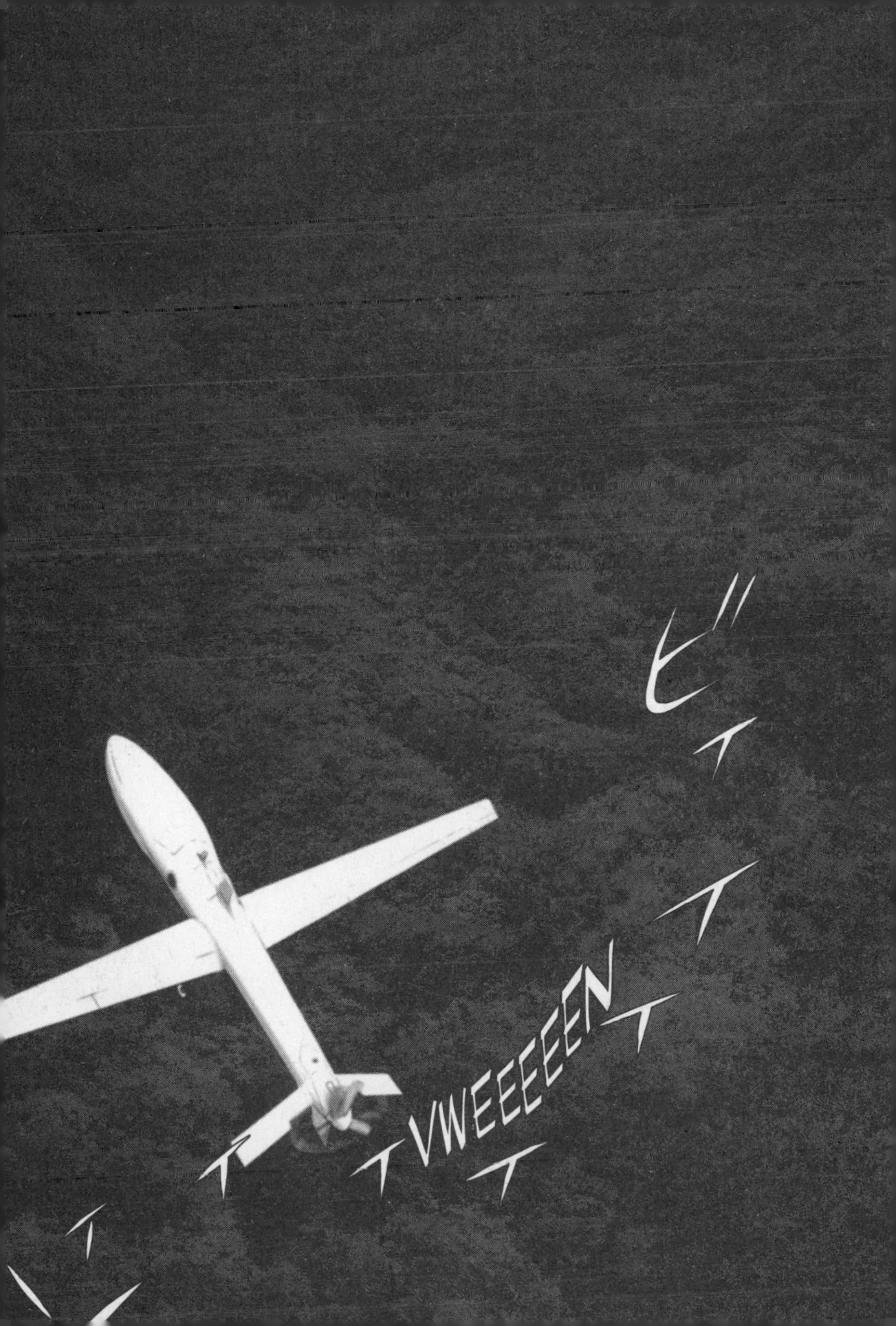
VWEEEEEN

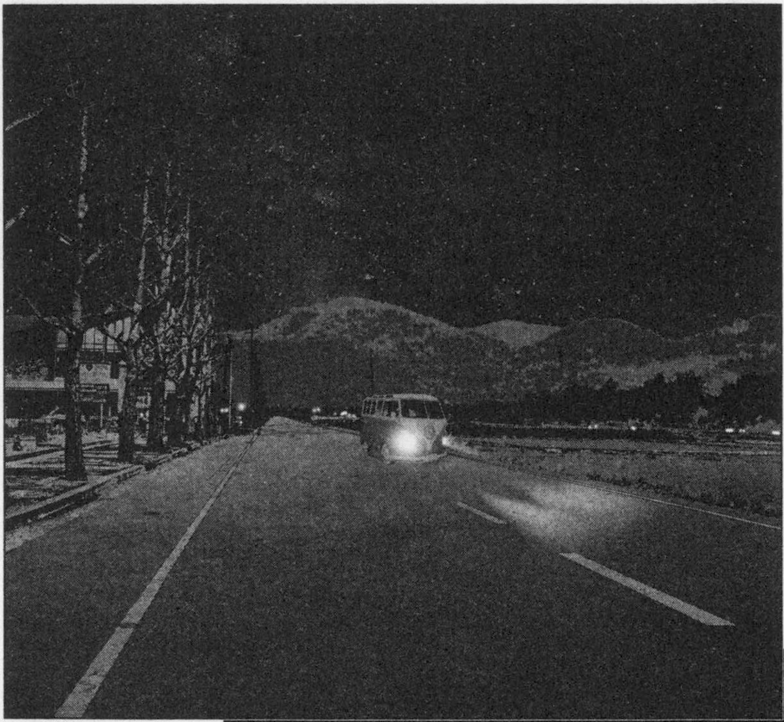

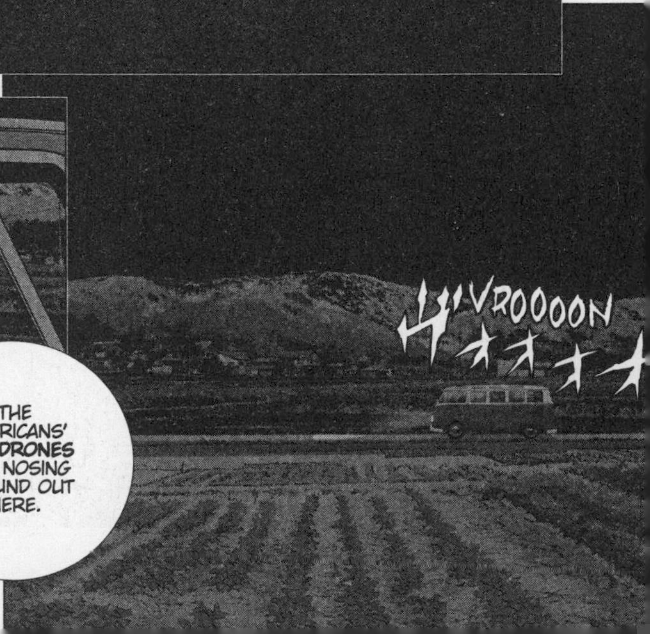
ヴオオオオ
VROOOON

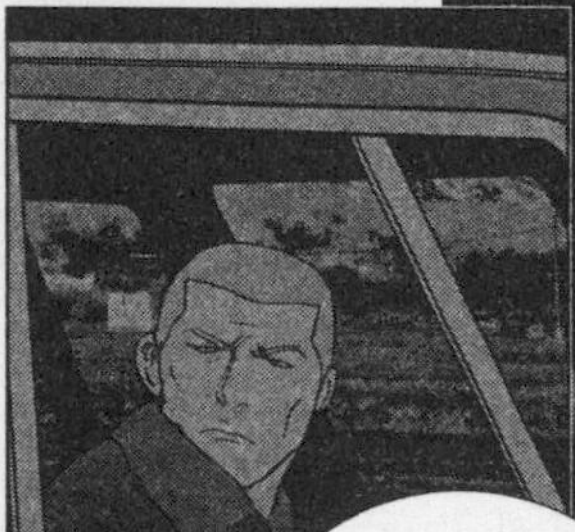
THE AMERICANS' PET DRONES ARE NOSING AROUND OUT HERE.

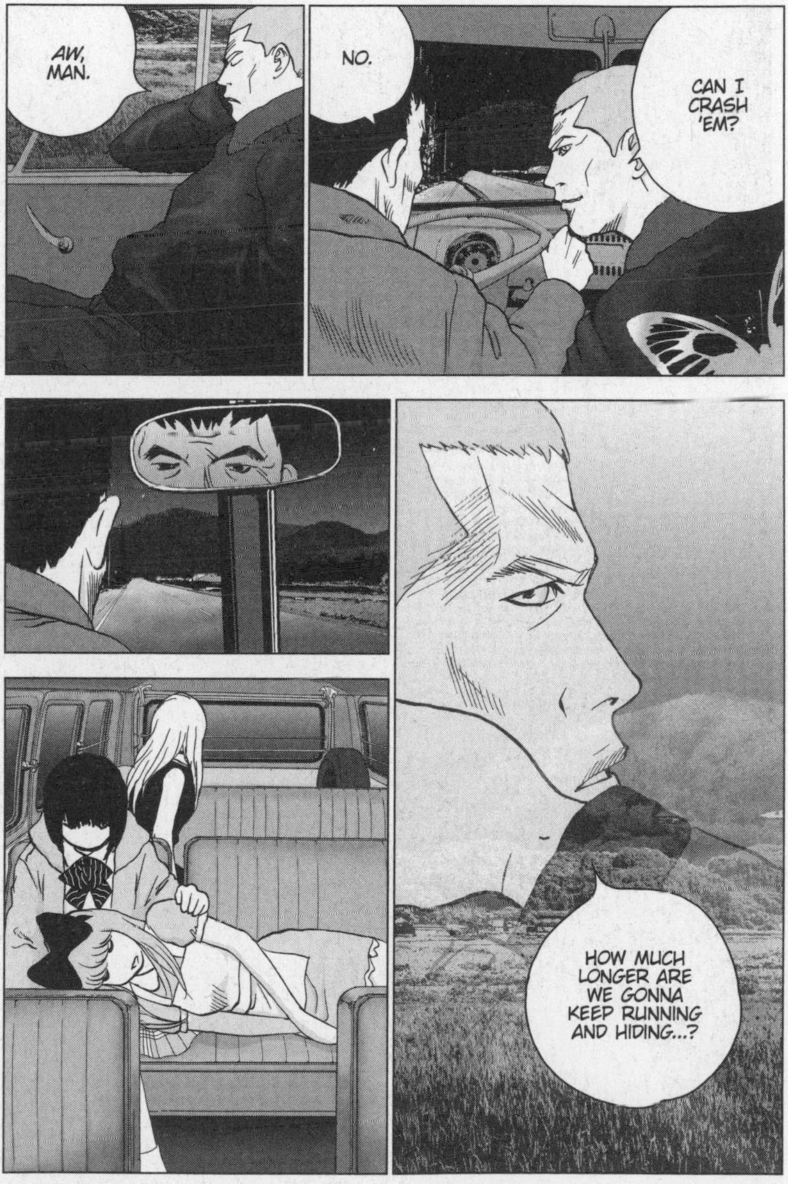
CAN I CRASH 'EM?
NO.
AW, MAN.
HOW MUCH LONGER ARE WE GONNA KEEP RUNNING AND HIDING...?

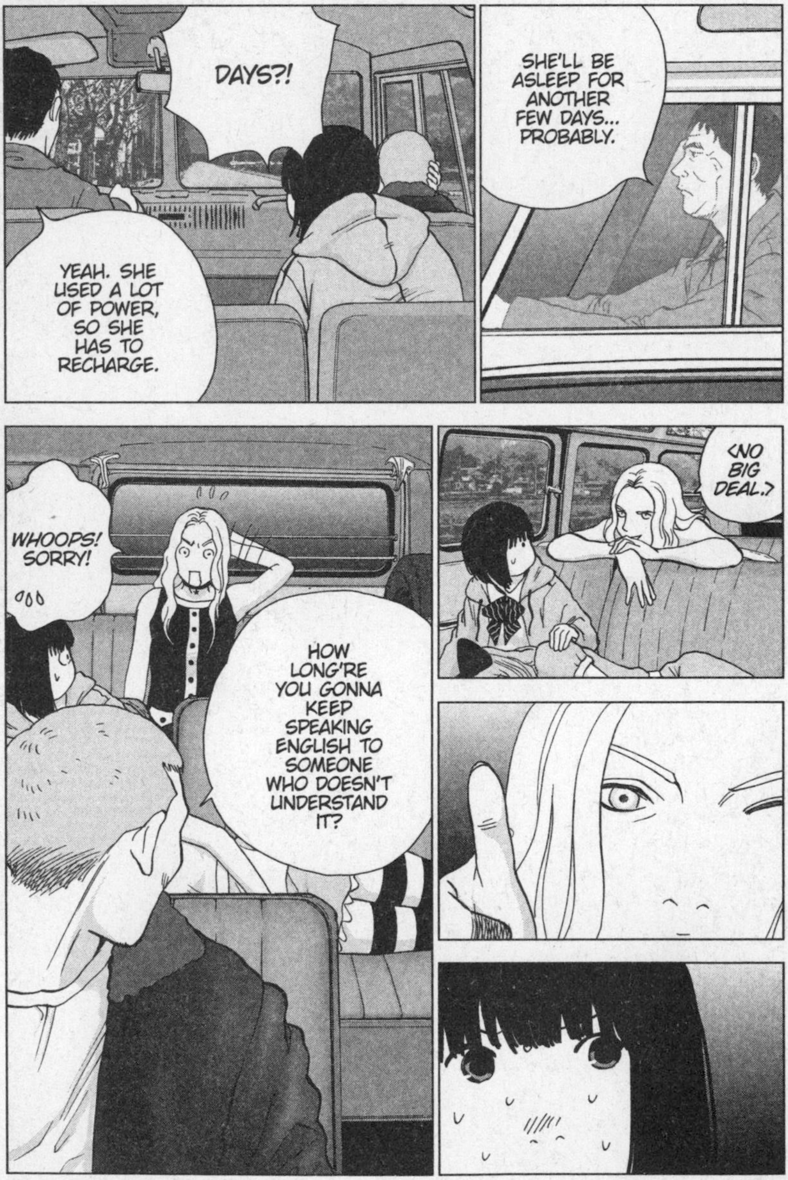
SHE'LL BE ASLEEP FOR ANOTHER FEW DAYS... PROBABLY.
DAYS?!
YEAH. SHE USED A LOT OF POWER, SO SHE HAS TO RECHARGE.
<NO BIG DEAL.>
HOW LONG'RE YOU GONNA KEEP SPEAKING ENGLISH TO SOMEONE WHO DOESN'T UNDERSTAND IT?
WHOOPS! SORRY!

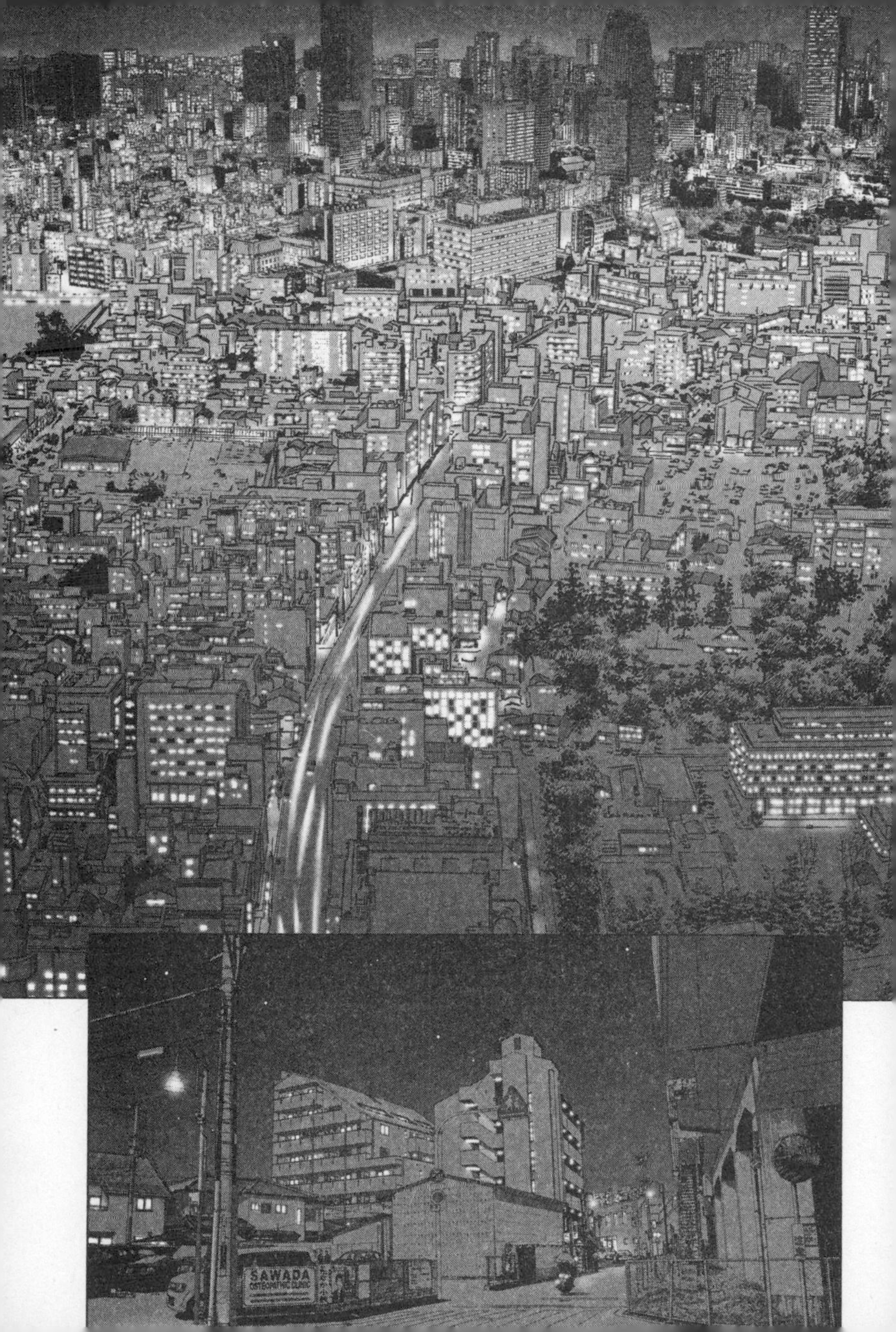
SAWADA

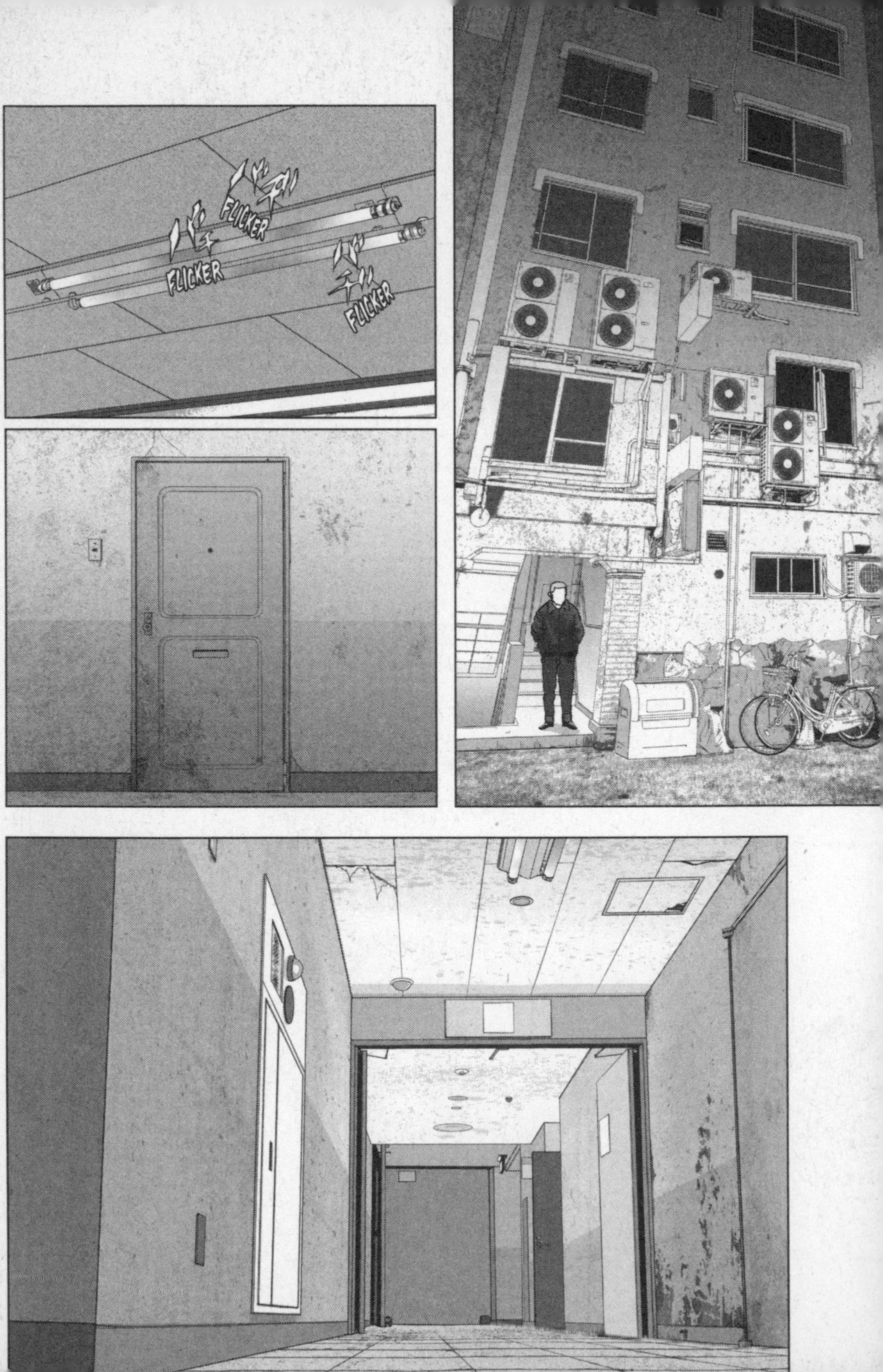
FLICKER
FLICKER
FLICKER

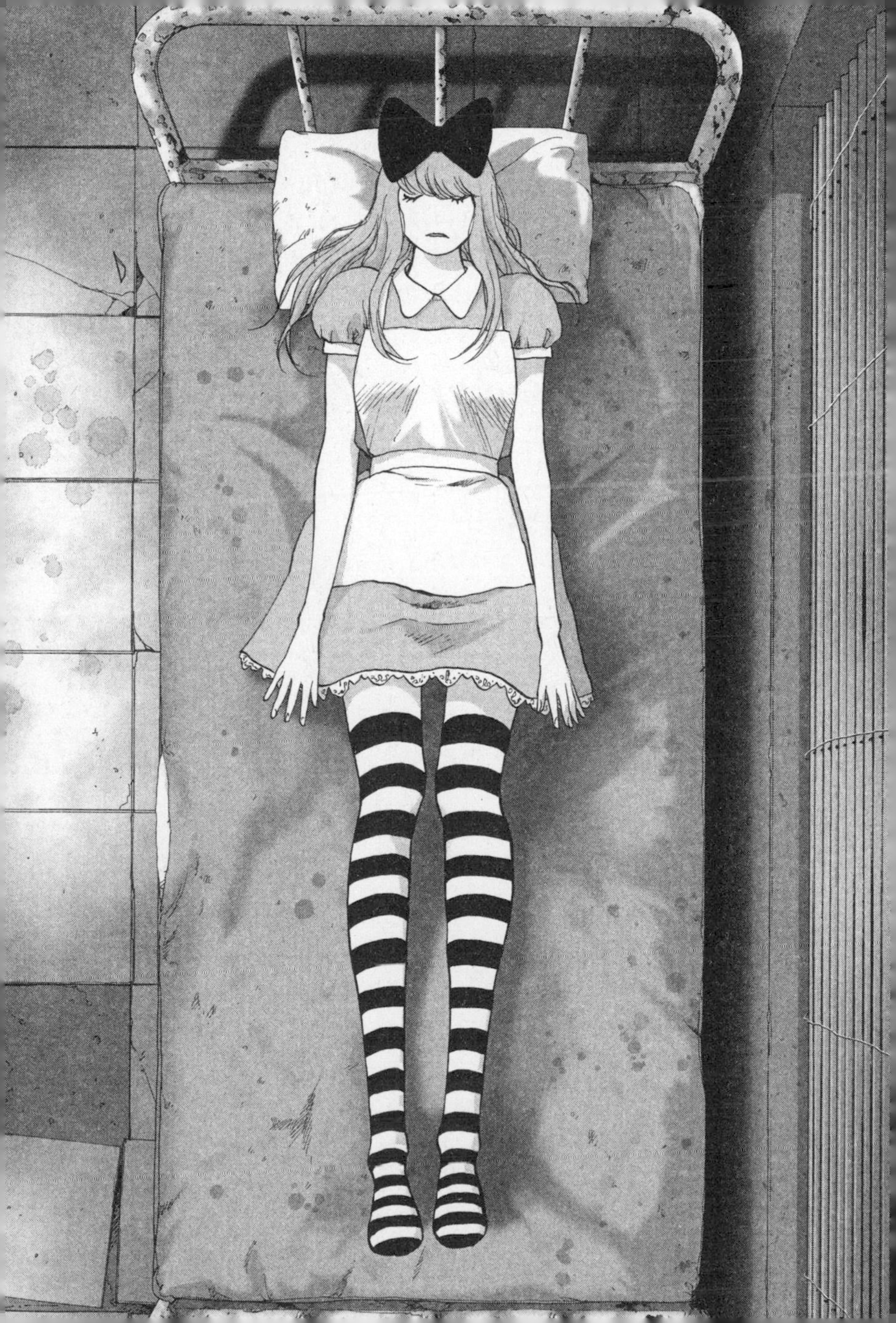

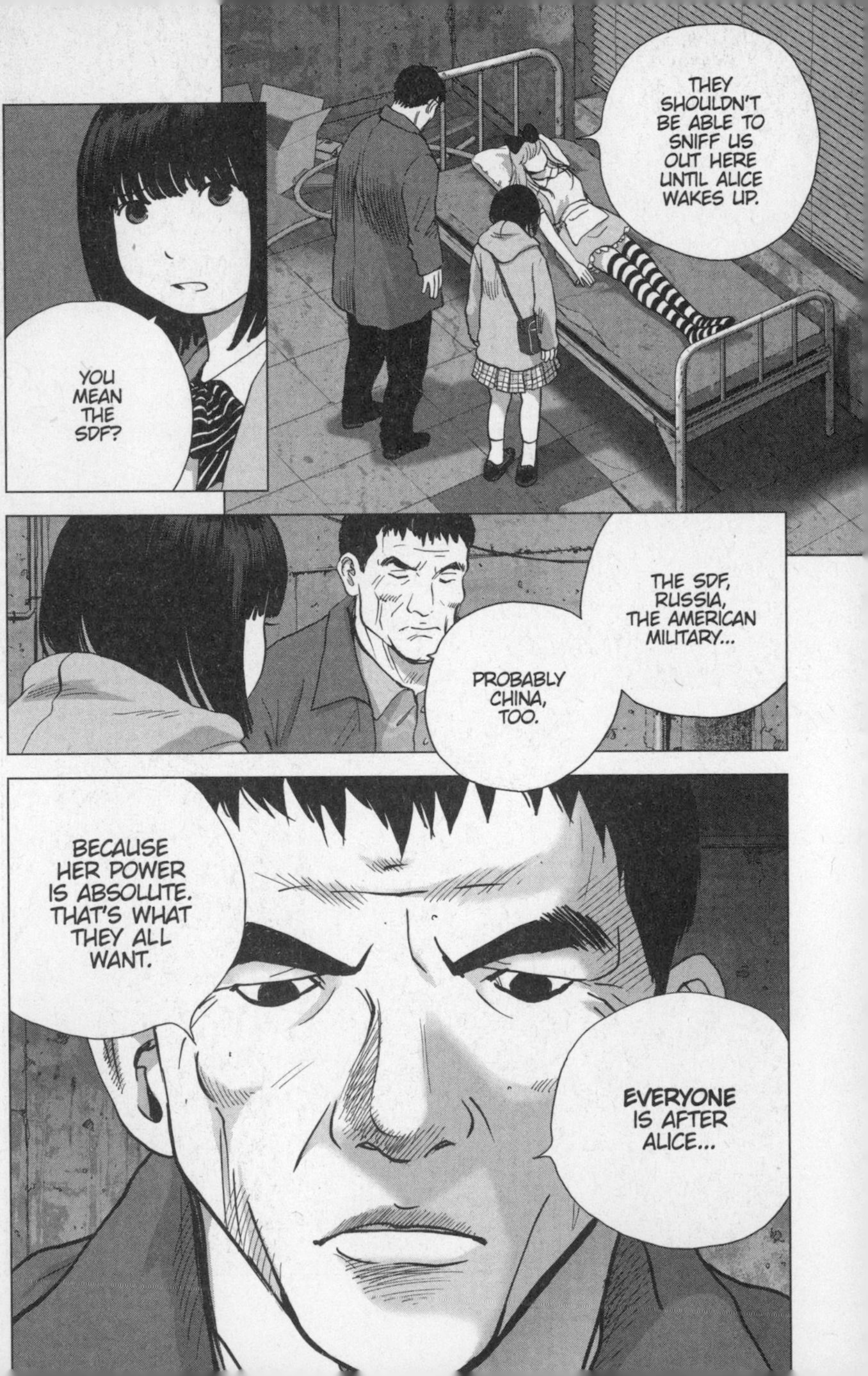
THEY SHOULDN'T BE ABLE TO SNIFF US OUT HERE UNTIL ALICE WAKES UP.
YOU MEAN THE SDF?
THE SDF, RUSSIA, THE AMERICAN MILITARY...
PROBABLY CHINA, TOO.
EVERYONE IS AFTER ALICE...
BECAUSE HER POWER IS ABSOLUTE. THAT'S WHAT THEY ALL WANT.

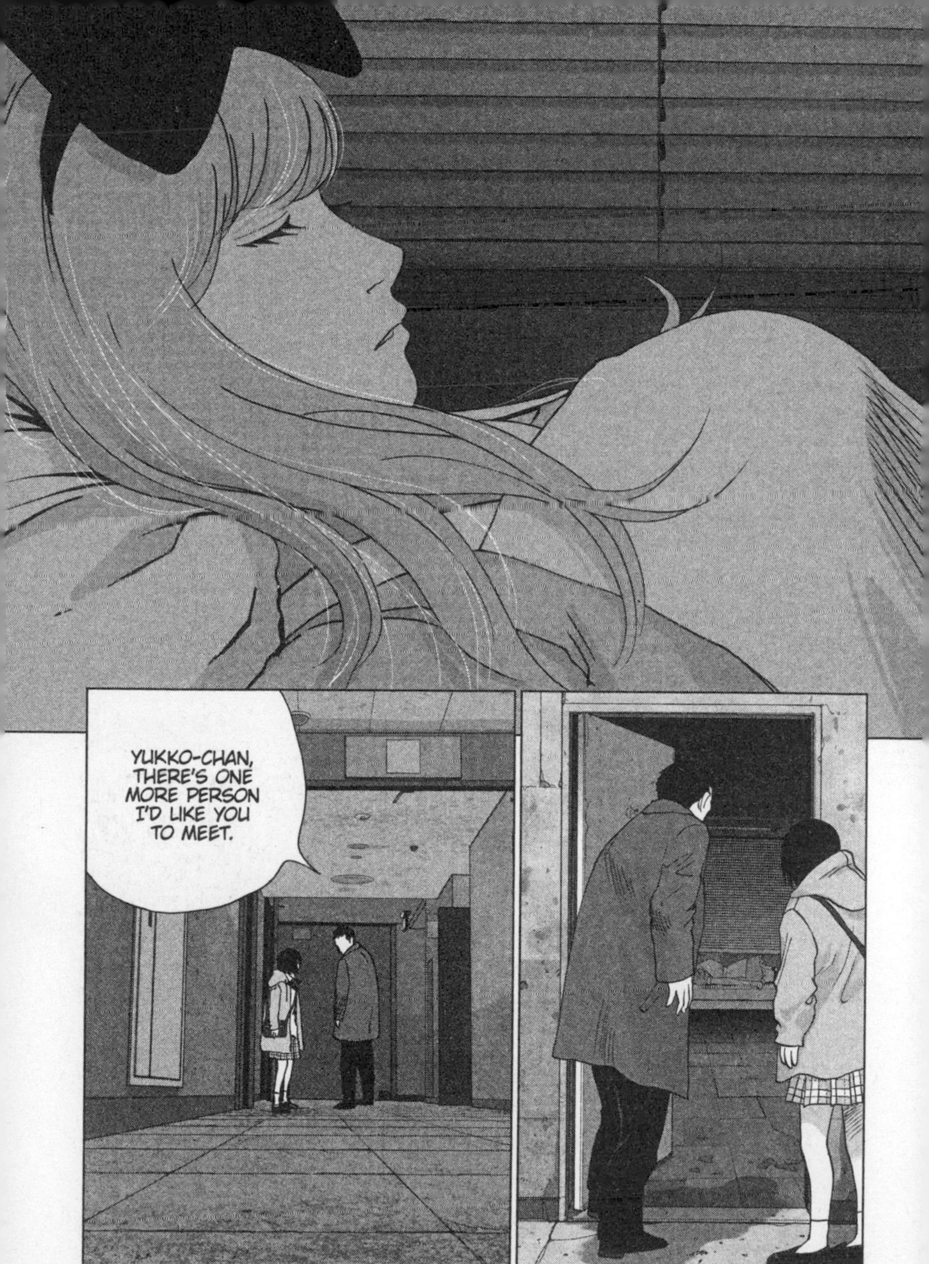
YUKKO-CHAN, THERE'S ONE MORE PERSON I'D LIKE YOU TO MEET.

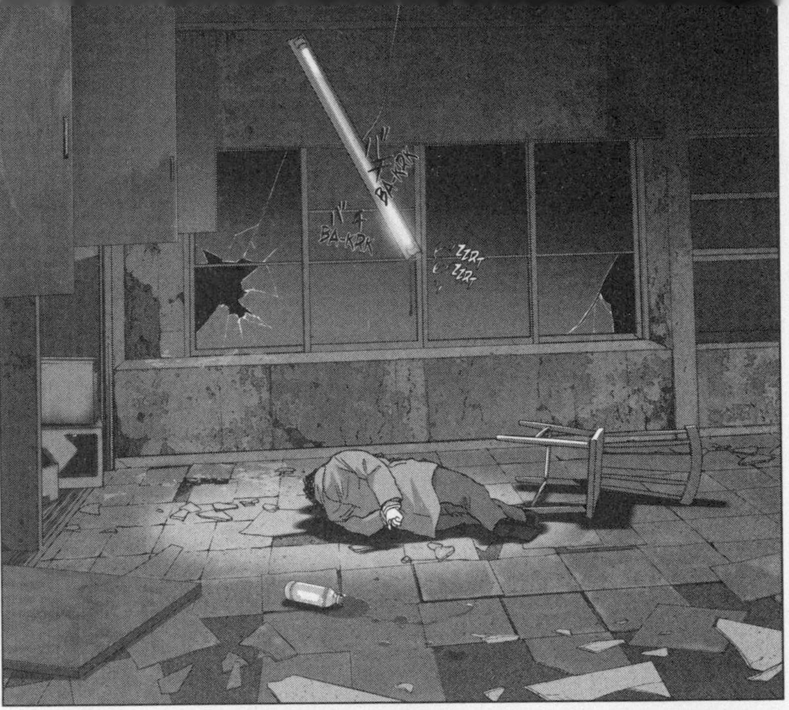
BA-KRK
BA-KRK
ZZRT
ZZRT

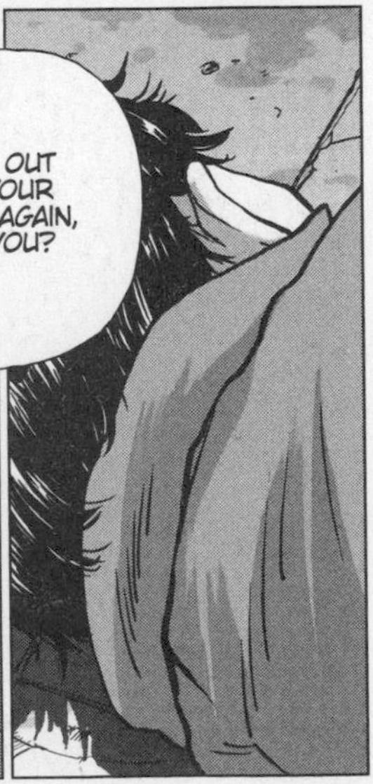

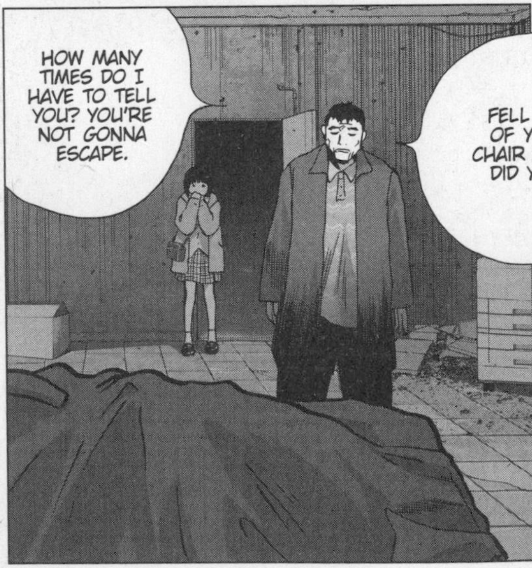
FELL OUT OF YOUR CHAIR AGAIN, DID YOU?
HOW MANY TIMES DO I HAVE TO TELL YOU? YOU'RE NOT GONNA ESCAPE.

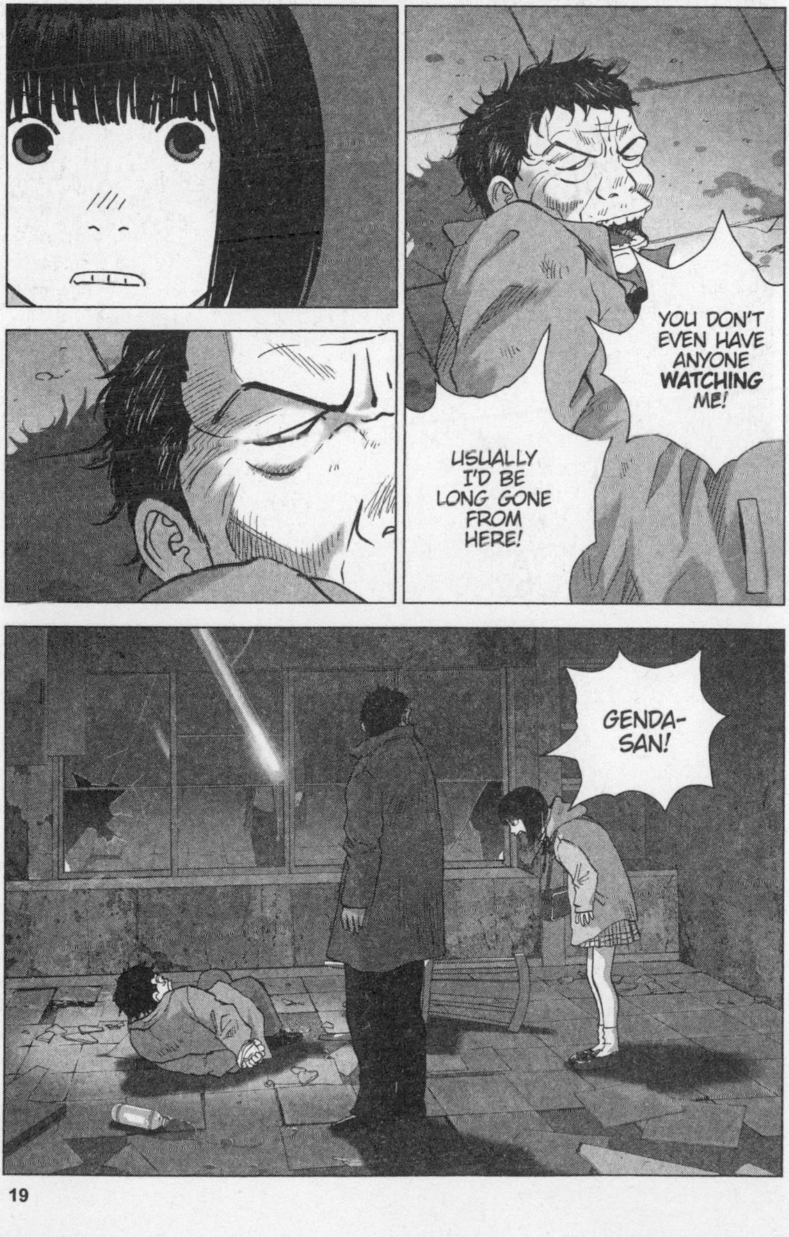
YOU DON'T EVEN HAVE ANYONE WATCHING ME!
USUALLY I'D BE LONG GONE FROM HERE!
GENDA-SAN!

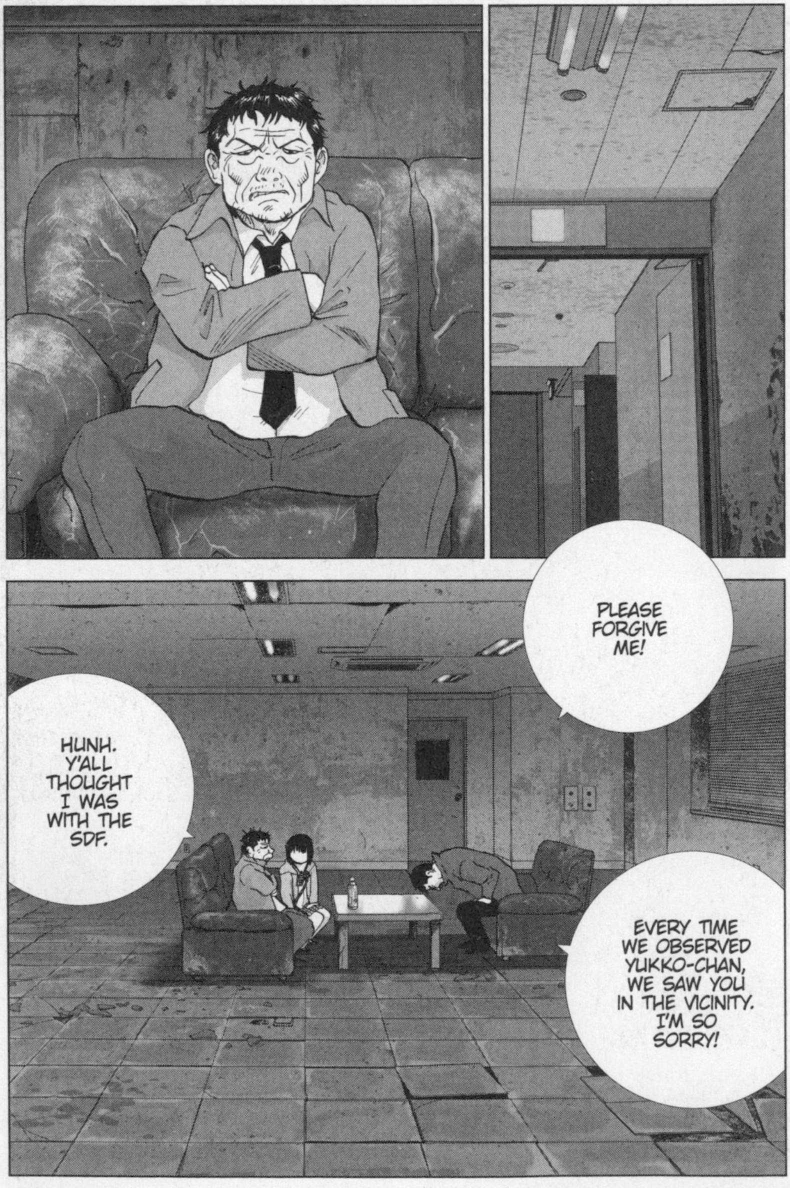
PLEASE FORGIVE ME!
HUNH. Y'ALL THOUGHT I WAS WITH THE SDF.
EVERY TIME WE OBSERVED YUKKO-CHAN, WE SAW YOU IN THE VICINITY. I'M SO SORRY!

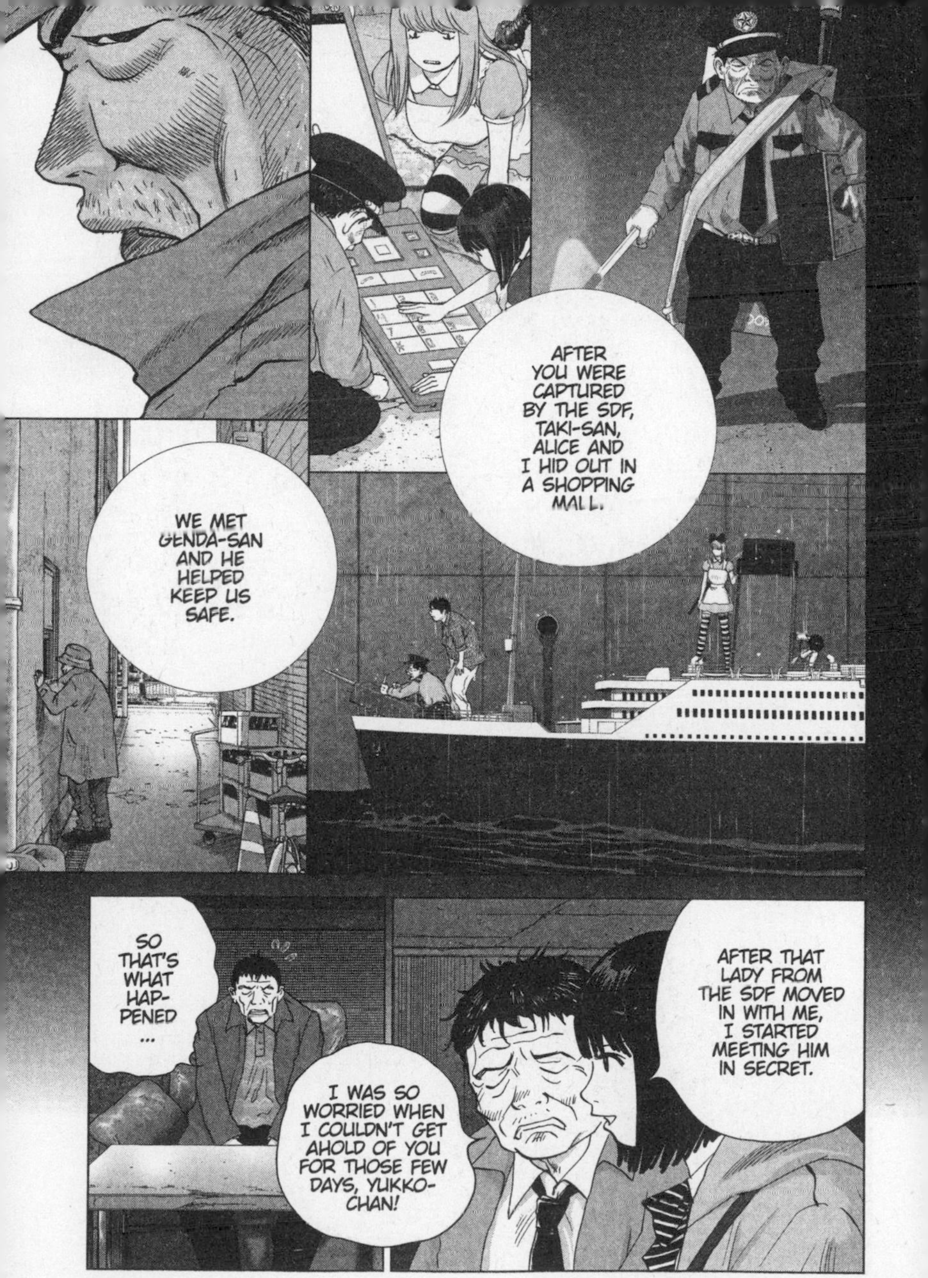
AFTER YOU WERE CAPTURED BY THE SDF, TAKI-SAN, ALICE AND I HID OUT IN A SHOPPING MALL.
WE MET GENDA-SAN AND HE HELPED KEEP US SAFE.
AFTER THAT LADY FROM THE SDF MOVED IN WITH ME, I STARTED MEETING HIM IN SECRET.
I WAS SO WORRIED WHEN I COULDN'T GET AHOLD OF YOU FOR THOSE FEW DAYS, YUKKO-CHAN!
SO THAT'S WHAT HAP-PENED ...

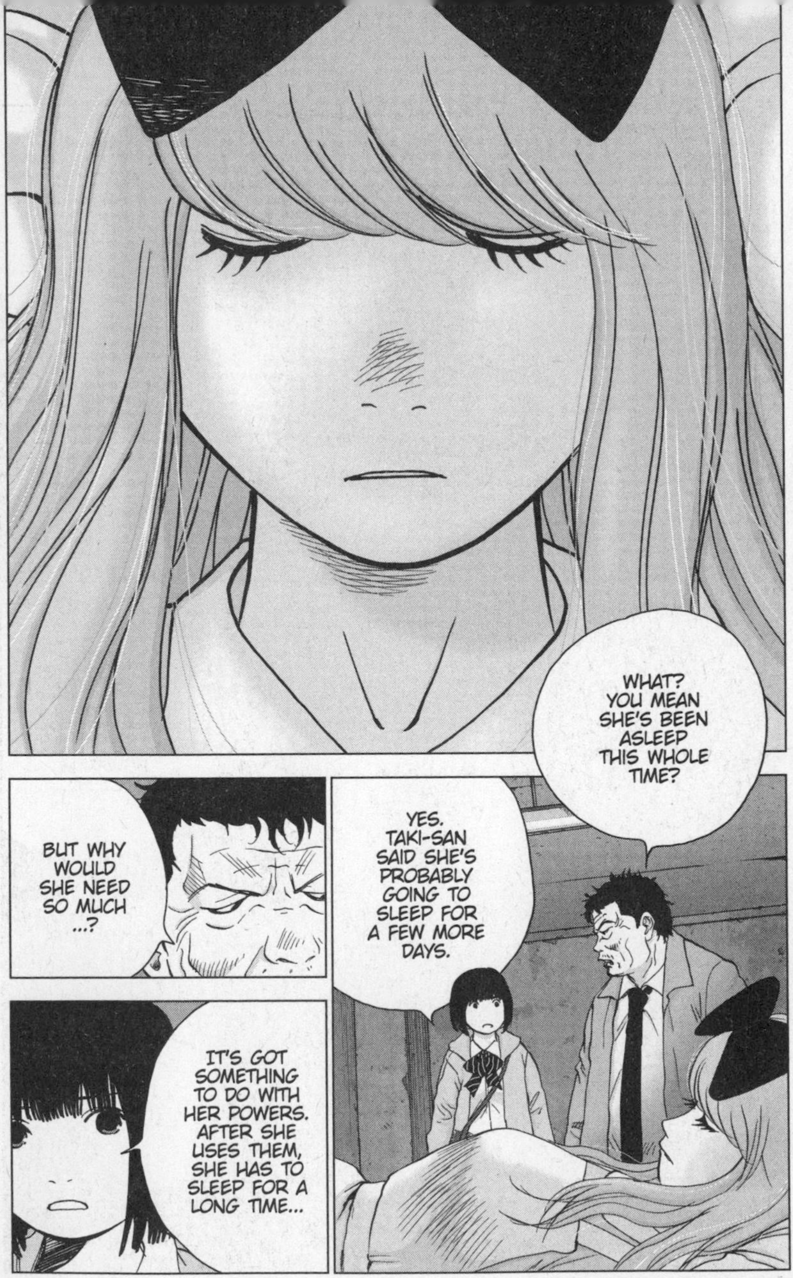
WHAT? YOU MEAN SHE'S BEEN ASLEEP THIS WHOLE TIME?
YES. TAKI-SAN SAID SHE'S PROBABLY GOING TO SLEEP FOR A FEW MORE DAYS.
BUT WHY WOULD SHE NEED SO MUCH ...?
IT'S GOT SOMETHING TO DO WITH HER POWERS. AFTER SHE USES THEM, SHE HAS TO SLEEP FOR A LONG TIME...

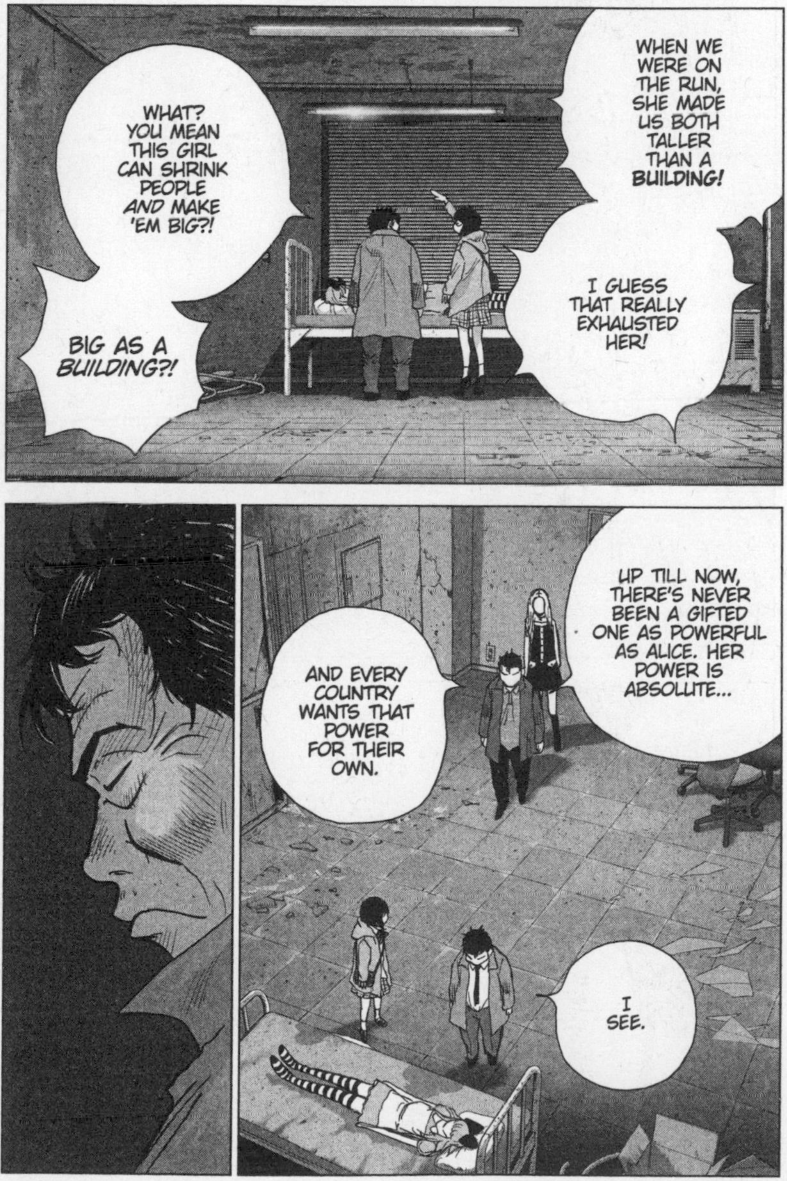
WHEN WE WERE ON THE RUN, SHE MADE US BOTH TALLER THAN A **BUILDING!**
I GUESS THAT REALLY EXHAUSTED HER!
WHAT? YOU MEAN THIS GIRL CAN SHRINK PEOPLE *AND MAKE* 'EM BIG?!
BIG AS A *BUILDING?!*
UP TILL NOW, THERE'S NEVER BEEN A GIFTED ONE AS POWERFUL AS ALICE. HER POWER IS ABSOLUTE...
AND EVERY COUNTRY WANTS THAT POWER FOR THEIR OWN.
I SEE.

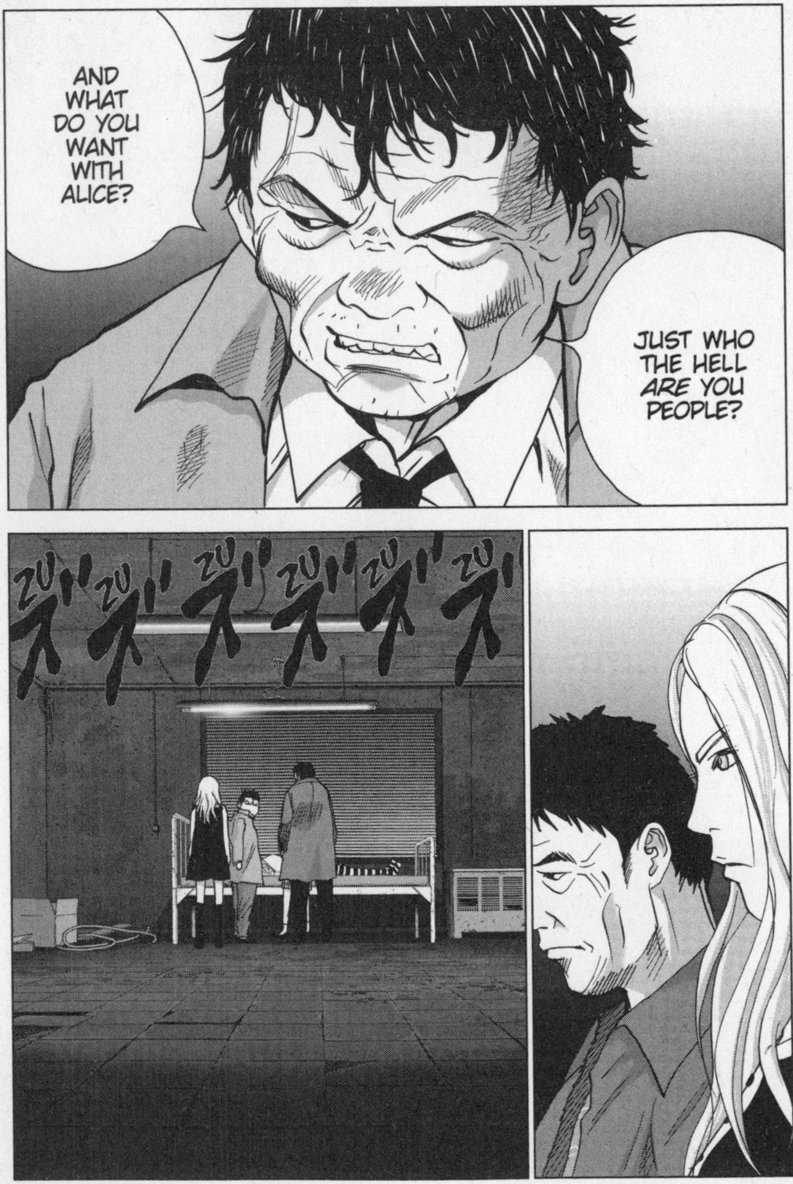
JUST WHO THE HELL ARE YOU PEOPLE?
AND WHAT DO YOU WANT WITH ALICE?
ZU ZU ZU ZU ZU ZU

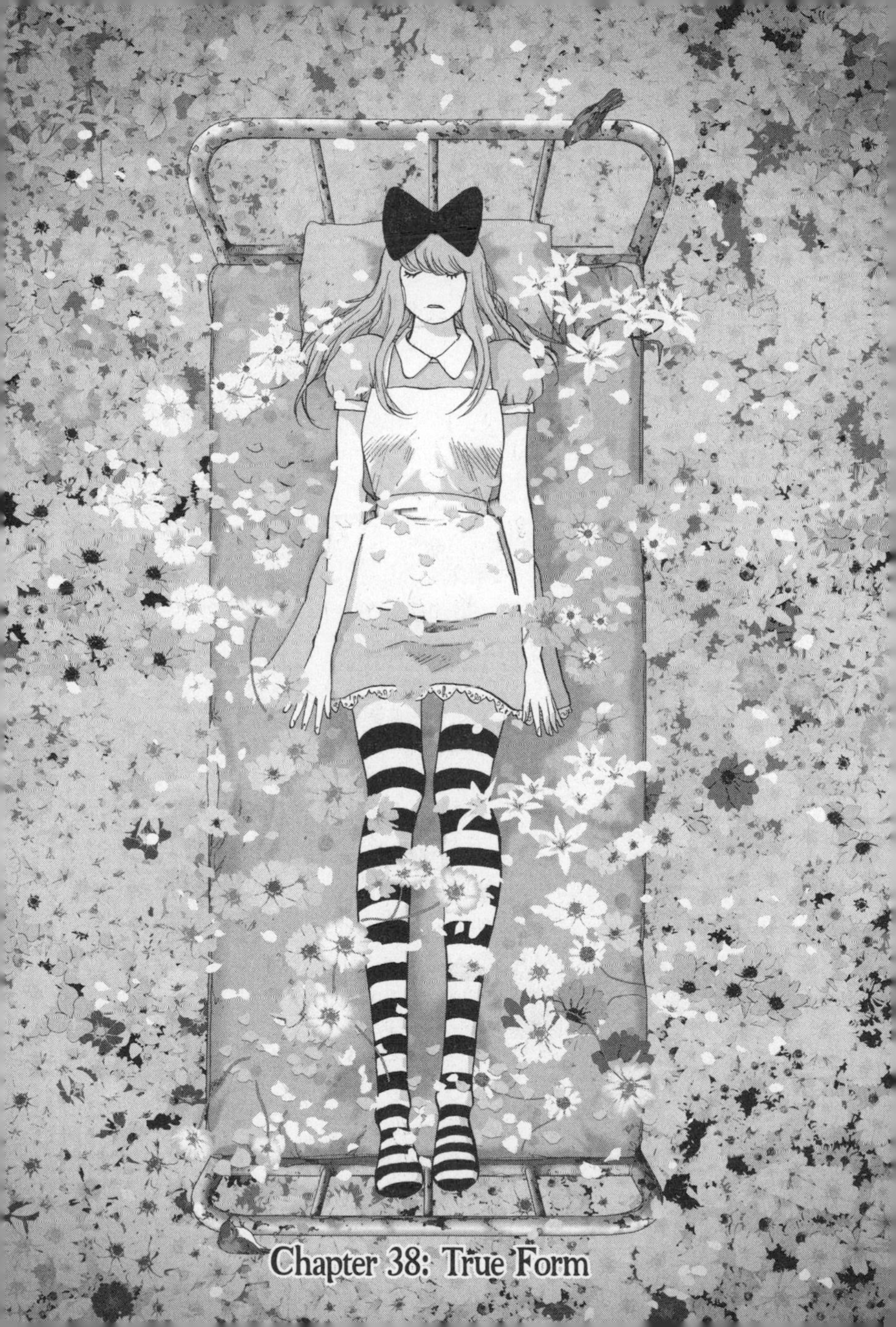

Chapter 38: True Form

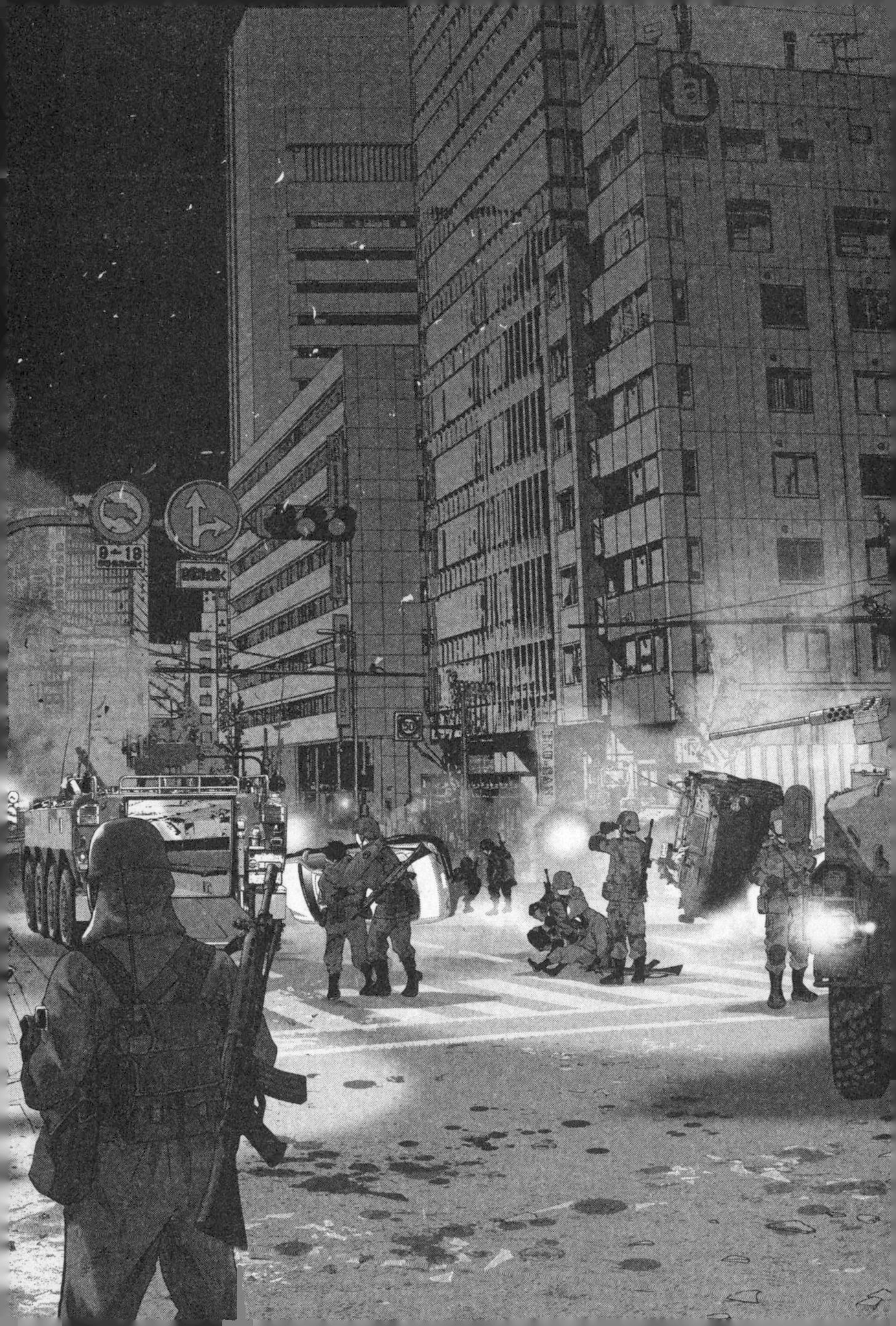
9 – 18
50

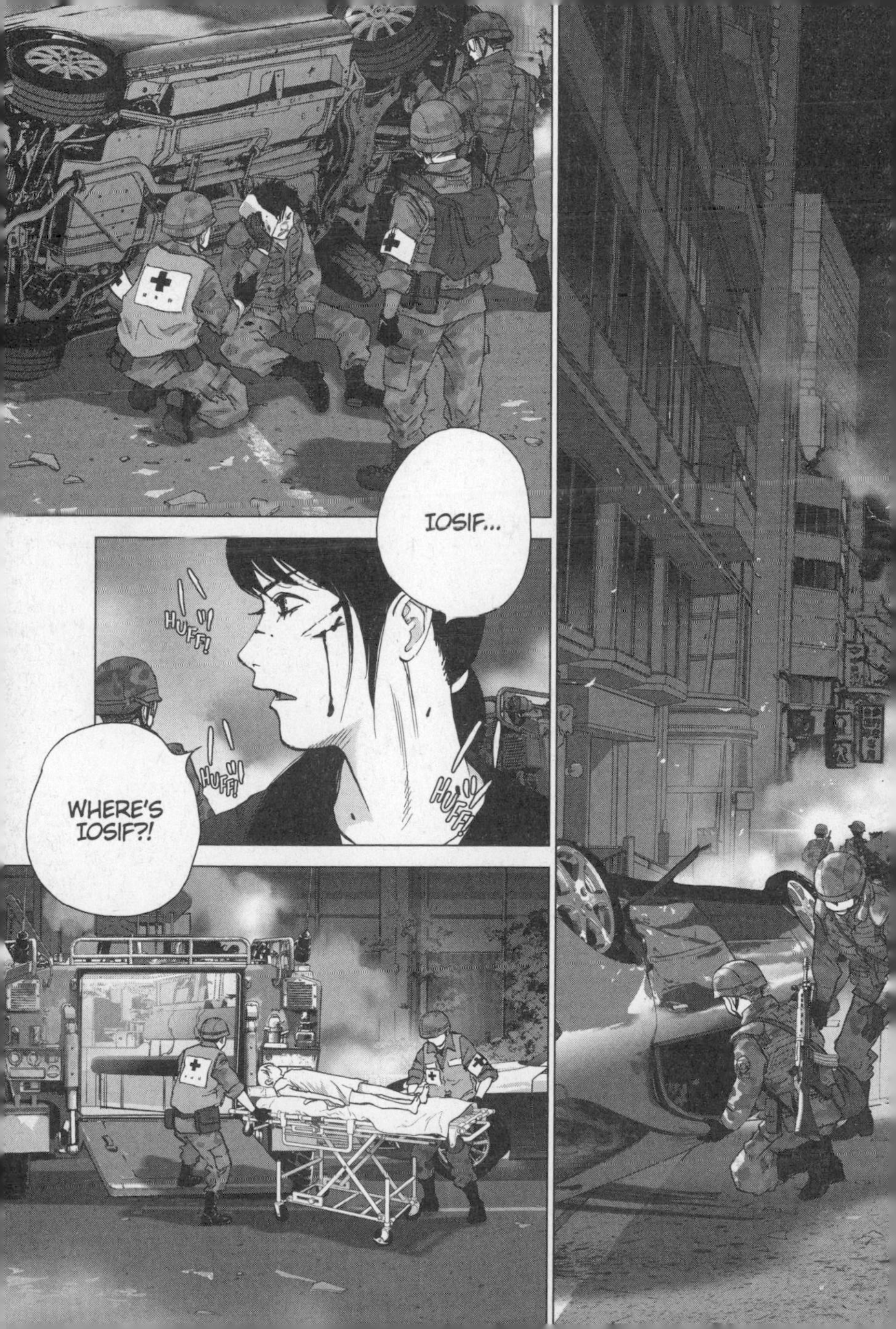
IOSIF...
HUFF!
HUFF!
HUFF!
WHERE'S IOSIF?!

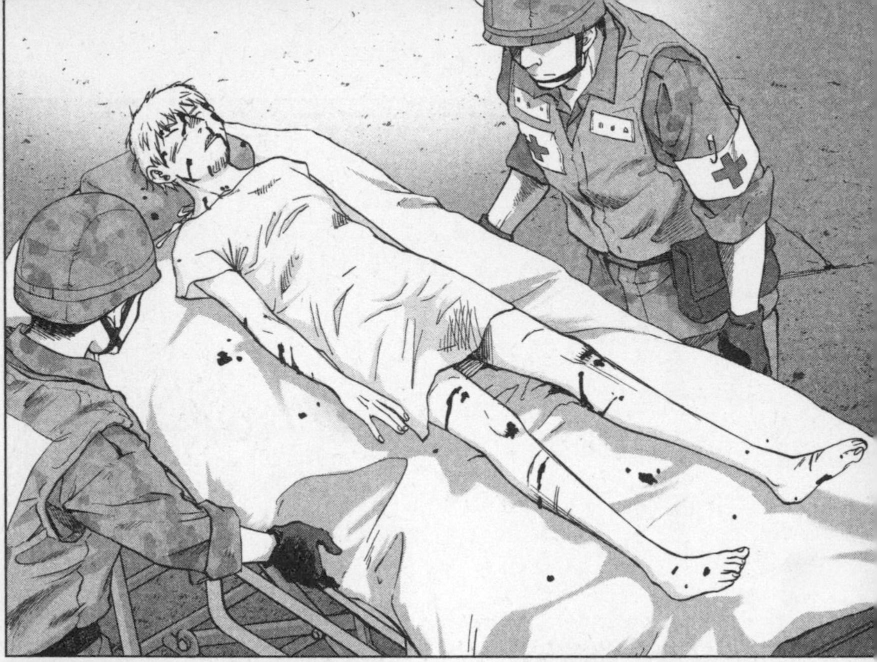
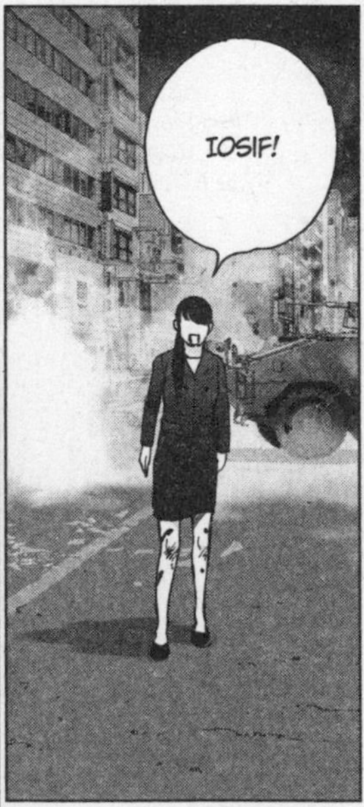
IOSIF!
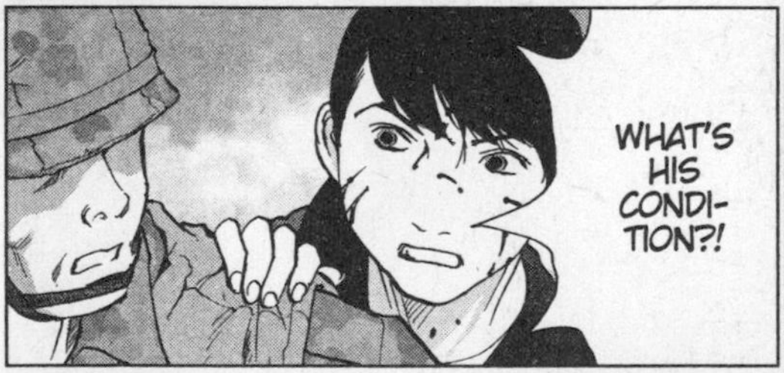
WHAT'S HIS CONDITION?!
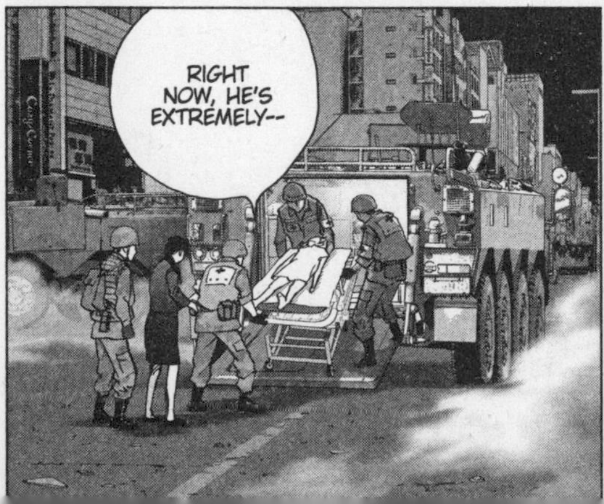
RIGHT NOW, HE'S EXTREMELY--

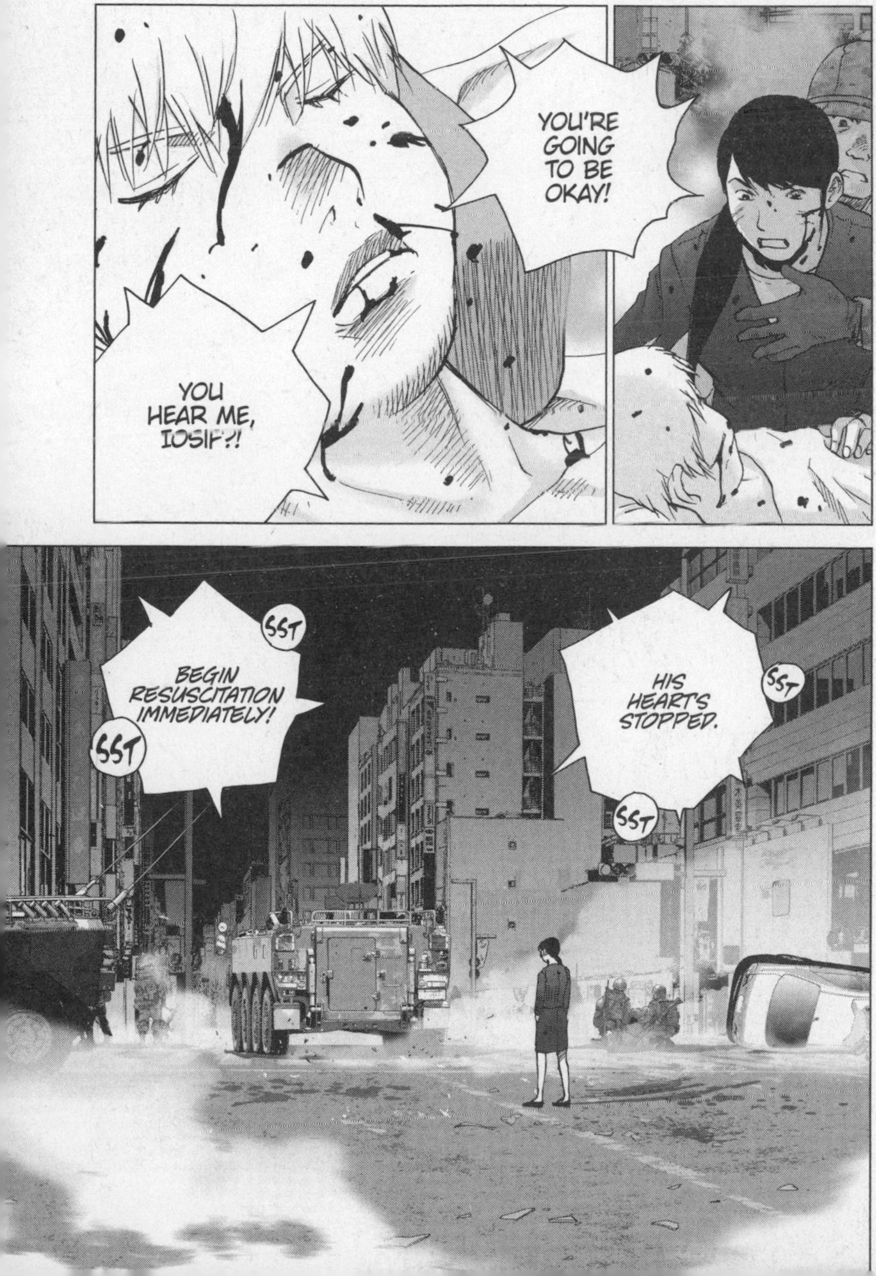
YOU'RE GOING TO BE OKAY!
YOU HEAR ME, IOSIF?!
SST
HIS HEART'S STOPPED.
SST
SST
BEGIN RESUSCITATION IMMEDIATELY!
SST

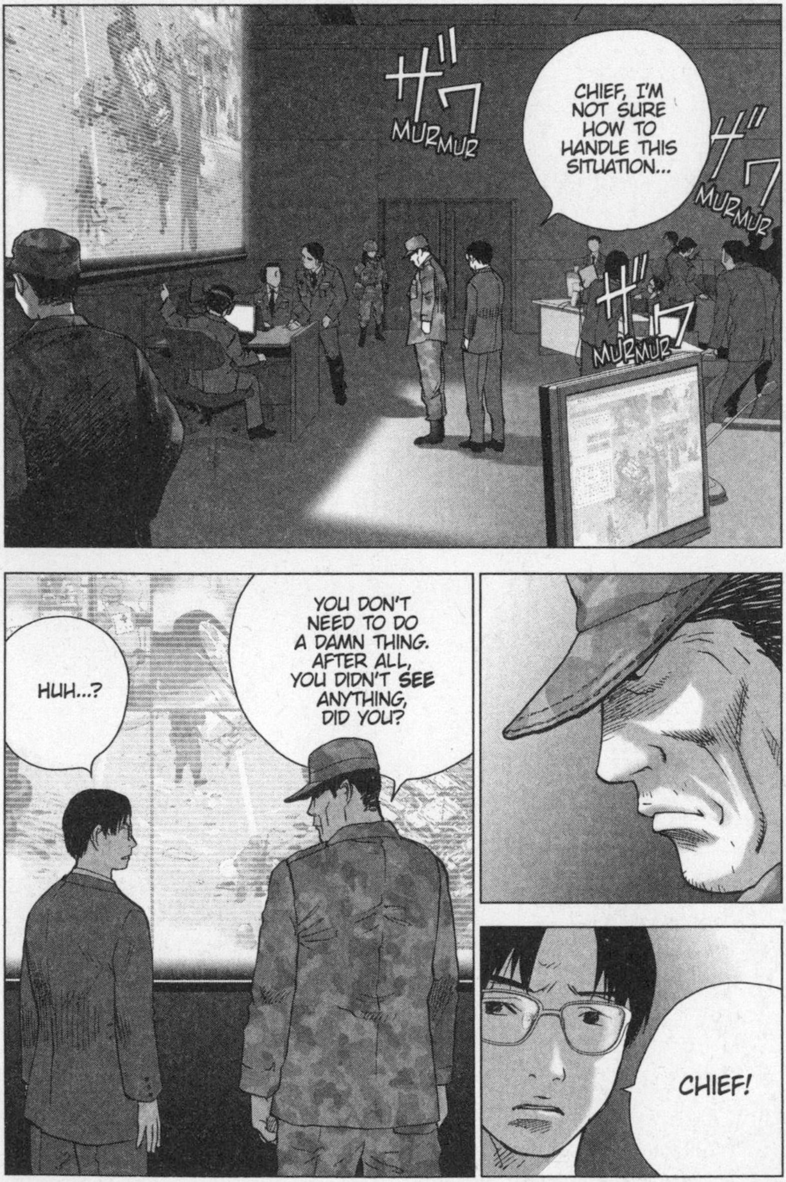
CHIEF, I'M NOT SURE HOW TO HANDLE THIS SITUATION...
ザワ MURMUR
ザワ MURMUR
ザワ MURMUR
CHIEF!
YOU DON'T NEED TO DO A DAMN THING. AFTER ALL, YOU DIDN'T SEE ANYTHING, DID YOU?
HUH...?

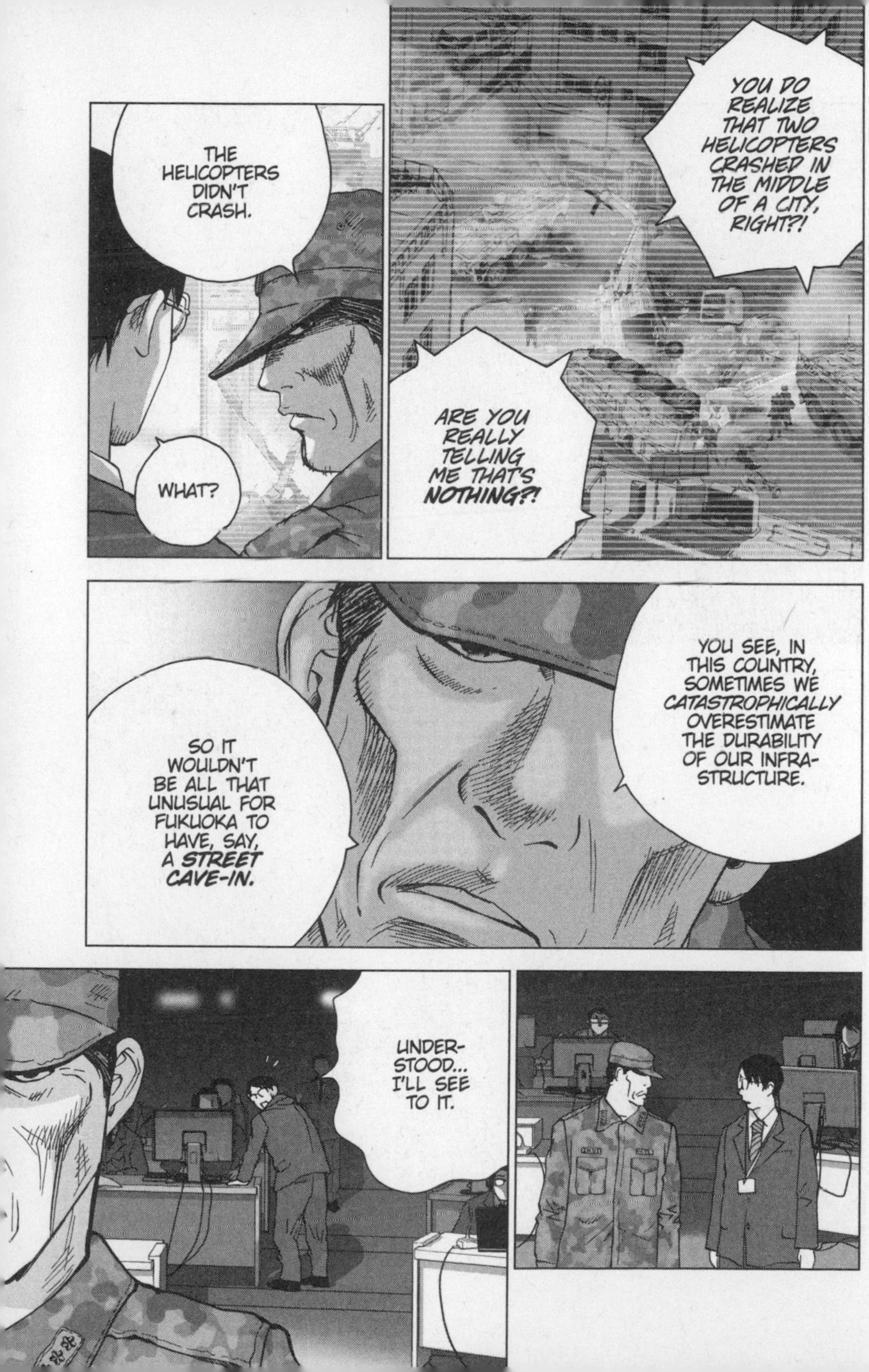
YOU DO REALIZE THAT TWO HELICOPTERS CRASHED IN THE MIDDLE OF A CITY, RIGHT?!
ARE YOU REALLY TELLING ME THAT'S *NOTHING?!*
THE HELICOPTERS DIDN'T CRASH.
WHAT?
YOU SEE, IN THIS COUNTRY, SOMETIMES WE *CATASTROPHICALLY* OVERESTIMATE THE DURABILITY OF OUR INFRA-STRUCTURE.
SO IT WOULDN'T BE ALL THAT UNUSUAL FOR FUKUOKA TO HAVE, SAY, A ***STREET CAVE-IN.***
UNDER-STOOD... I'LL SEE TO IT.

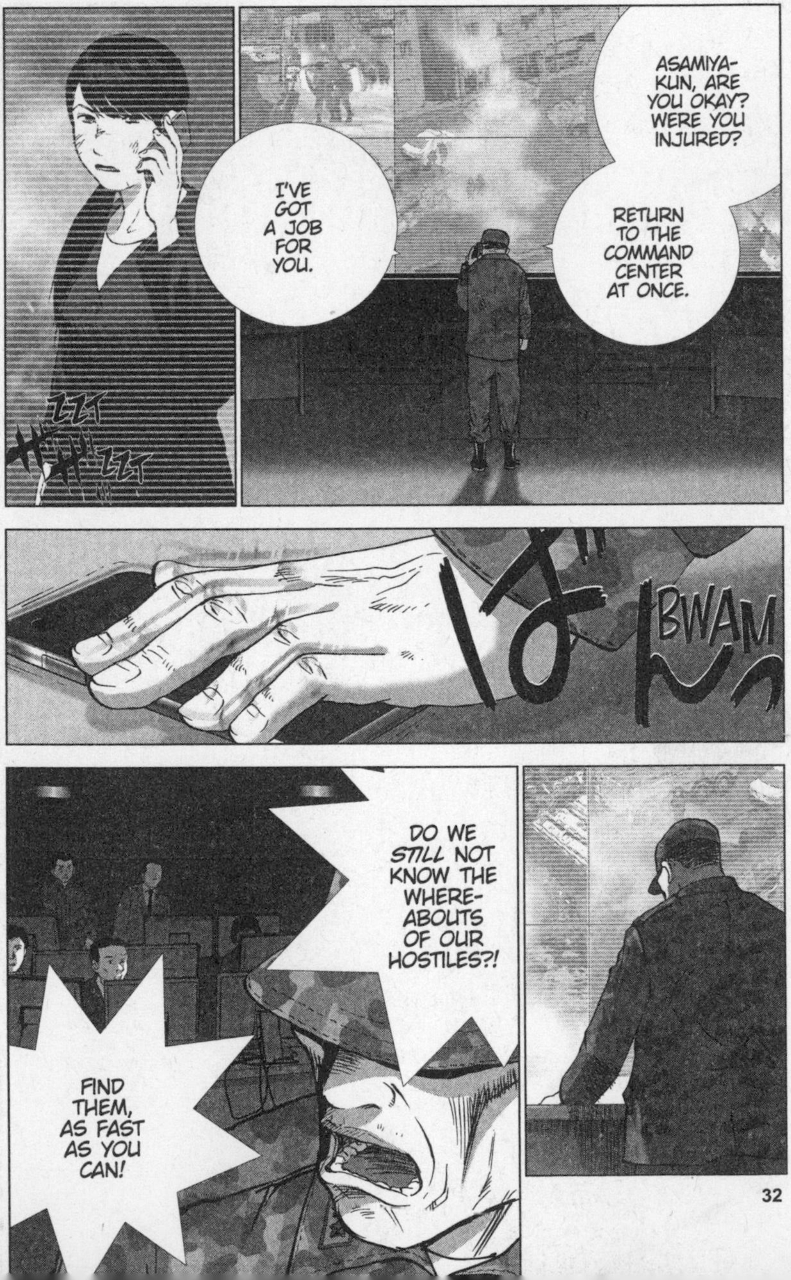

ASAMIYA-KUN, ARE YOU OKAY? WERE YOU INJURED?
RETURN TO THE COMMAND CENTER AT ONCE.
I'VE GOT A JOB FOR YOU.
ZZT
ZZT
BWAM
DO WE *STILL* NOT KNOW THE WHERE-ABOUTS OF OUR HOSTILES?!
FIND THEM, AS FAST AS YOU CAN!

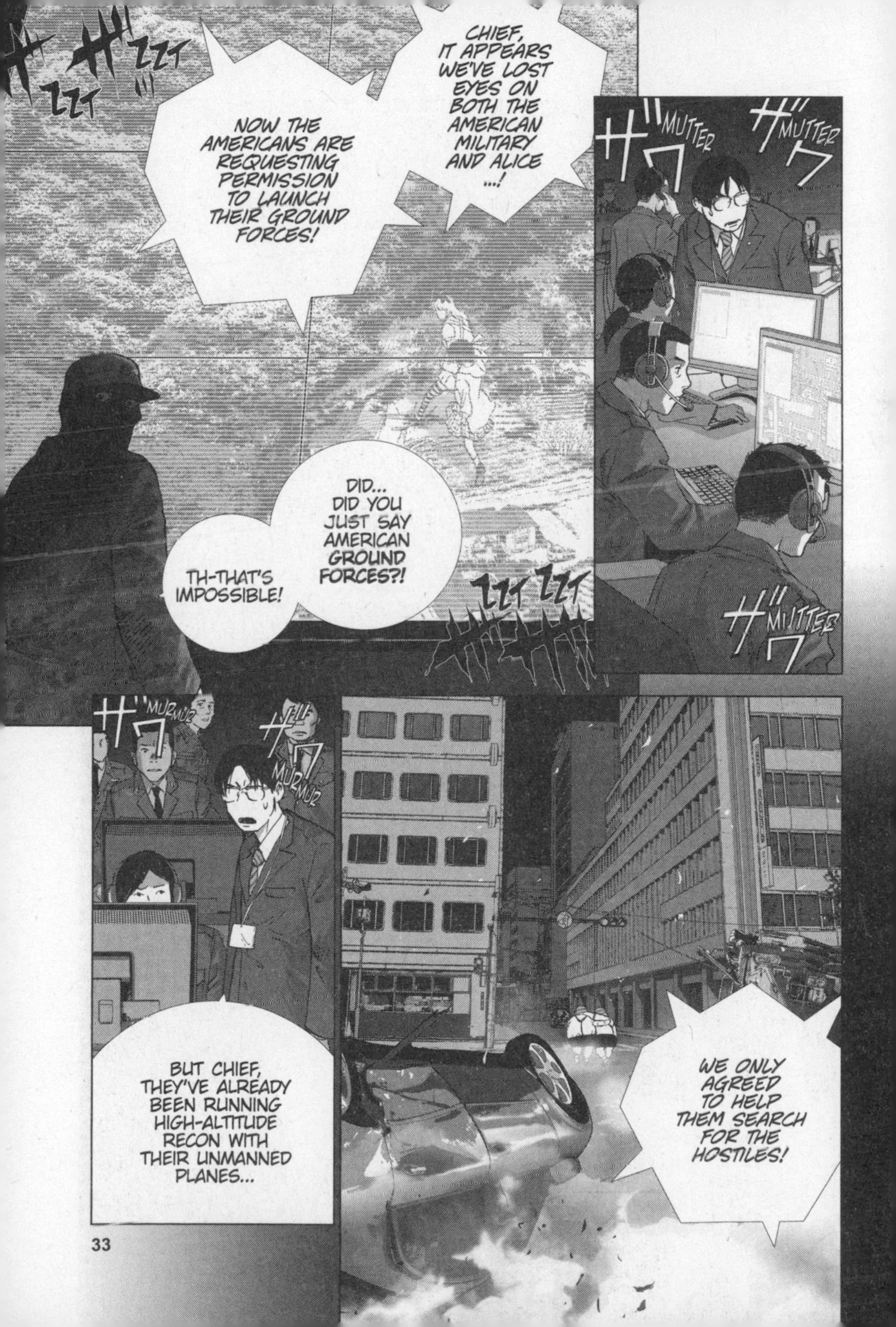
ZZZT ZZZT
CHIEF, IT APPEARS WE'VE LOST EYES ON BOTH THE AMERICAN MILITARY AND ALICE ...!
NOW THE AMERICANS ARE REQUESTING PERMISSION TO LAUNCH THEIR GROUND FORCES!
MUTTER MUTTER
DID... DID YOU JUST SAY AMERICAN GROUND FORCES?!
TH-THAT'S IMPOSSIBLE!
ZZZT ZZZT
MUTTER
WE ONLY AGREED TO HELP THEM SEARCH FOR THE HOSTILES!
MURMUR MURMUR
BUT CHIEF, THEY'VE ALREADY BEEN RUNNING HIGH-ALTITUDE RECON WITH THEIR UNMANNED PLANES...

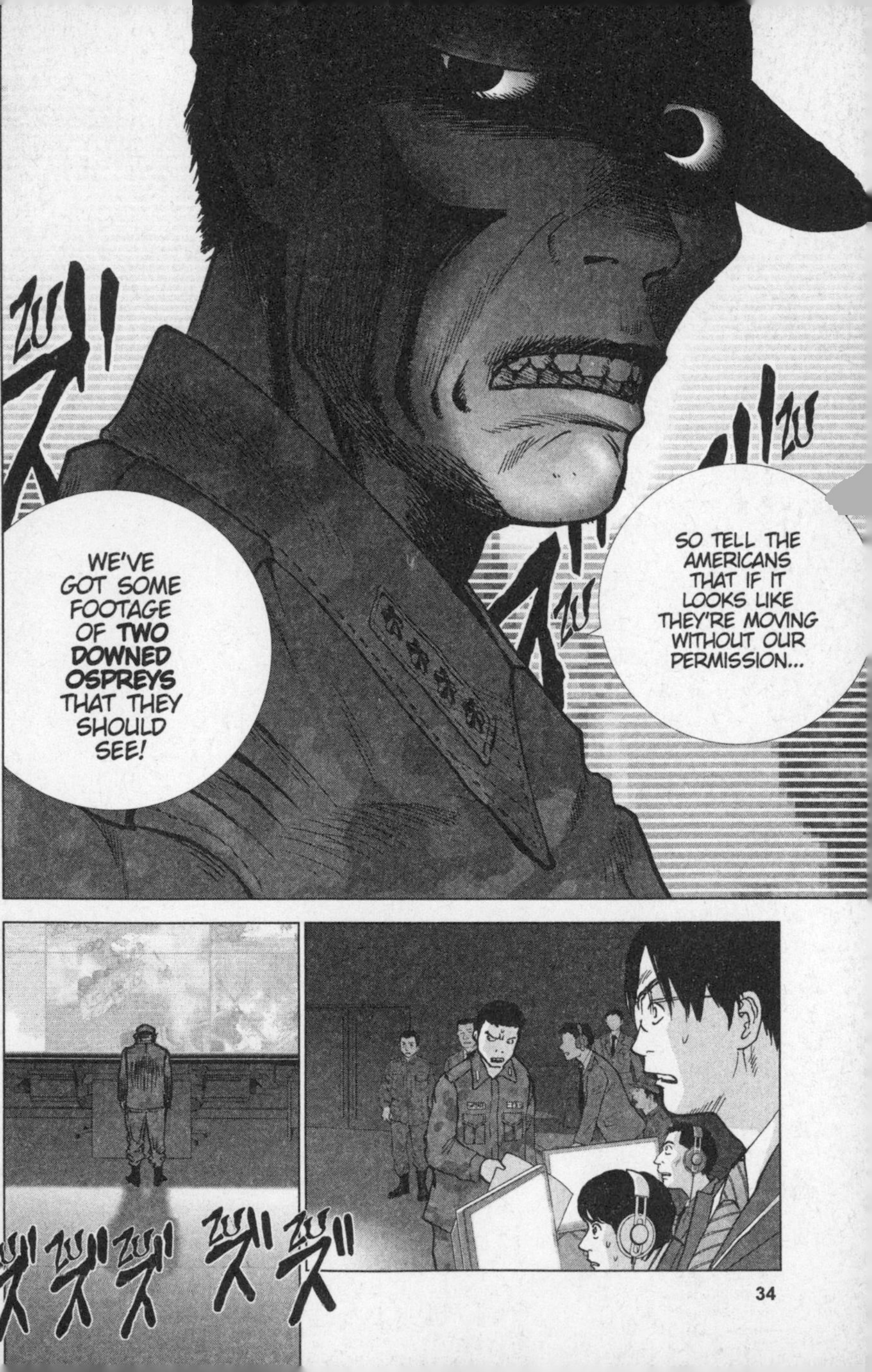
ZU
ZU
ZU
SO TELL THE AMERICANS THAT IF IT LOOKS LIKE THEY'RE MOVING WITHOUT OUR PERMISSION...
WE'VE GOT SOME FOOTAGE OF **TWO DOWNED OSPREYS** THAT THEY SHOULD SEE!
ZU ZU ZU ZU ZU

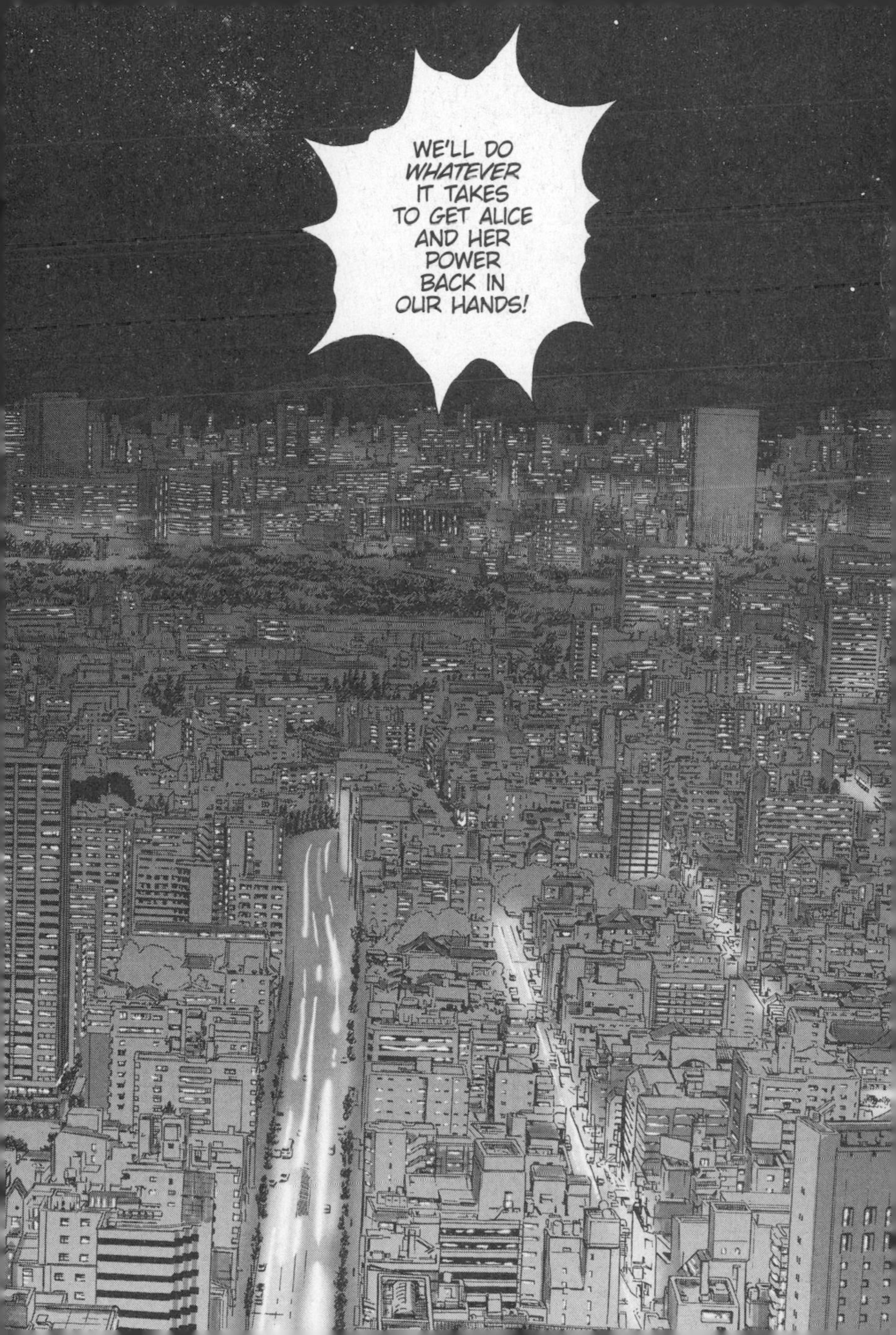
WE'LL DO *WHATEVER* IT TAKES TO GET ALICE AND HER POWER BACK IN OUR HANDS!

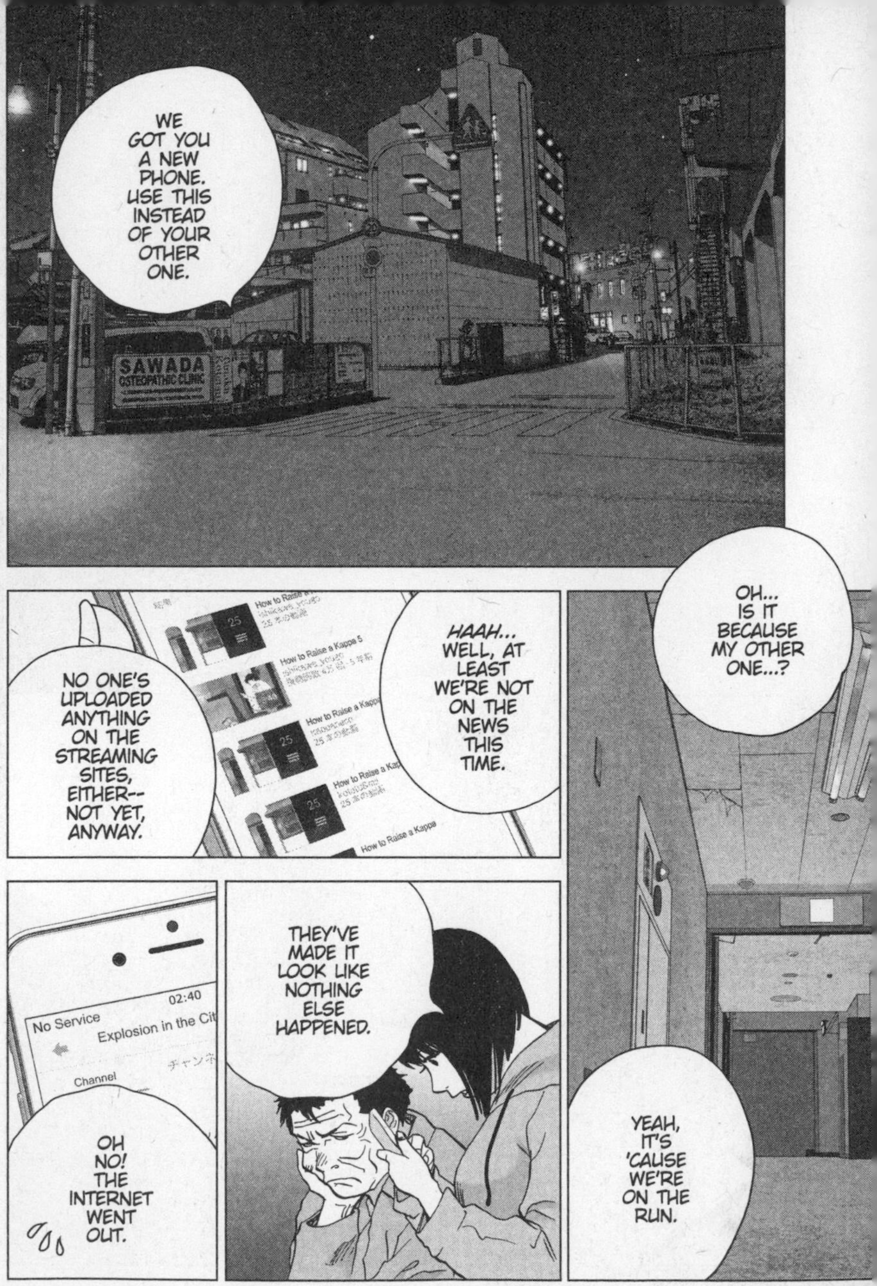
WE GOT YOU A NEW PHONE. USE THIS INSTEAD OF YOUR OTHER ONE.
SAWADA OSTEOPATHIC CLINIC
OH... IS IT BECAUSE MY OTHER ONE...?
YEAH, IT'S 'CAUSE WE'RE ON THE RUN.
HAAH... WELL, AT LEAST WE'RE NOT ON THE NEWS THIS TIME.
NO ONE'S UPLOADED ANYTHING ON THE STREAMING SITES, EITHER-- NOT YET, ANYWAY.
How to Raise a Kappa 5
How to Raise a Kappa
THEY'VE MADE IT LOOK LIKE NOTHING ELSE HAPPENED.
02:40
No Service
Explosion in the Cit
Channel
OH NO! THE INTERNET WENT OUT.

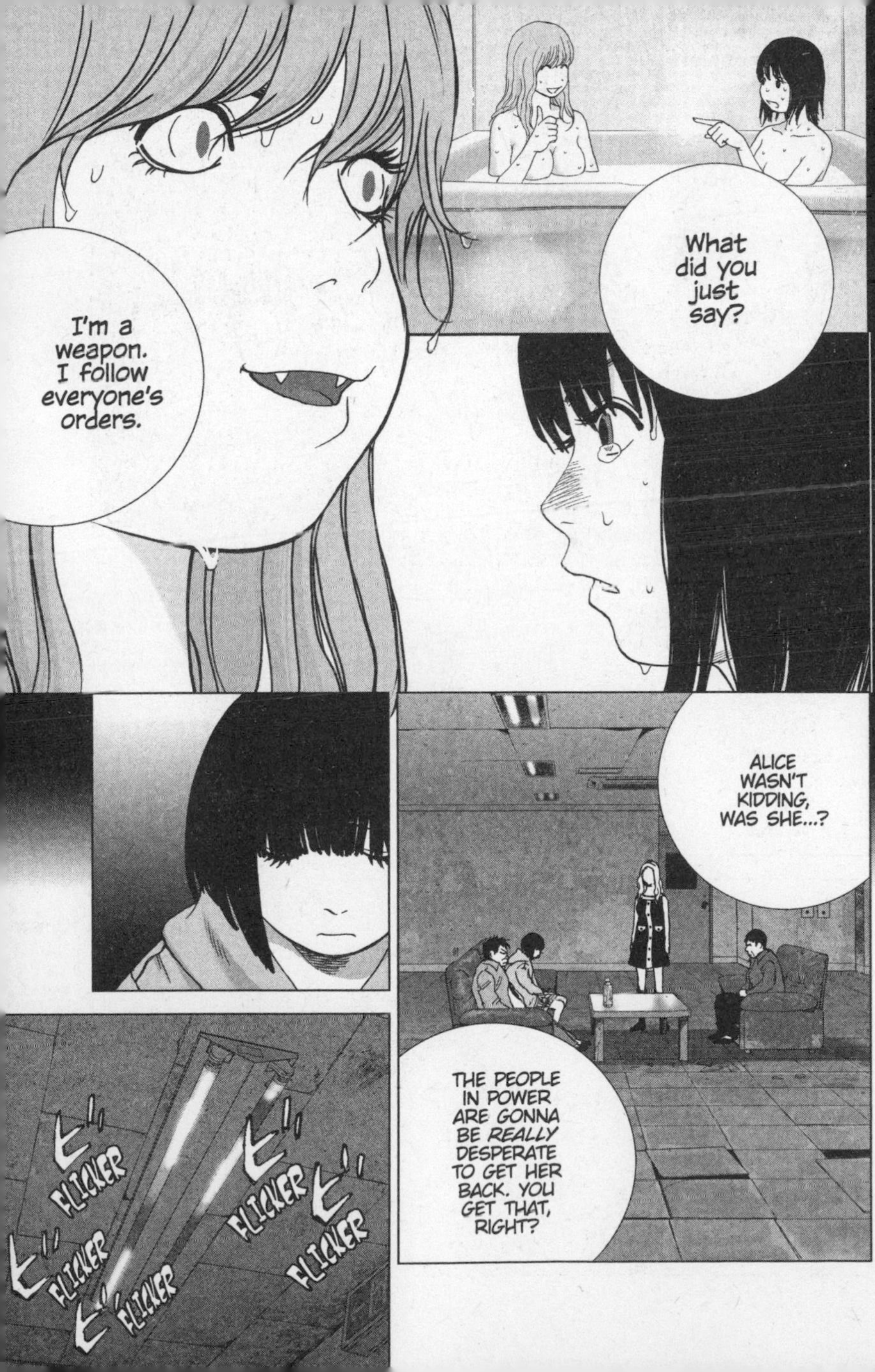

What did you just say?
I'm a weapon. I follow everyone's orders.
ALICE WASN'T KIDDING, WAS SHE...?
THE PEOPLE IN POWER ARE GONNA BE *REALLY* DESPERATE TO GET HER BACK. YOU GET THAT, RIGHT?
FLICKER
FLICKER
FLICKER
FLICKER
FLICKER

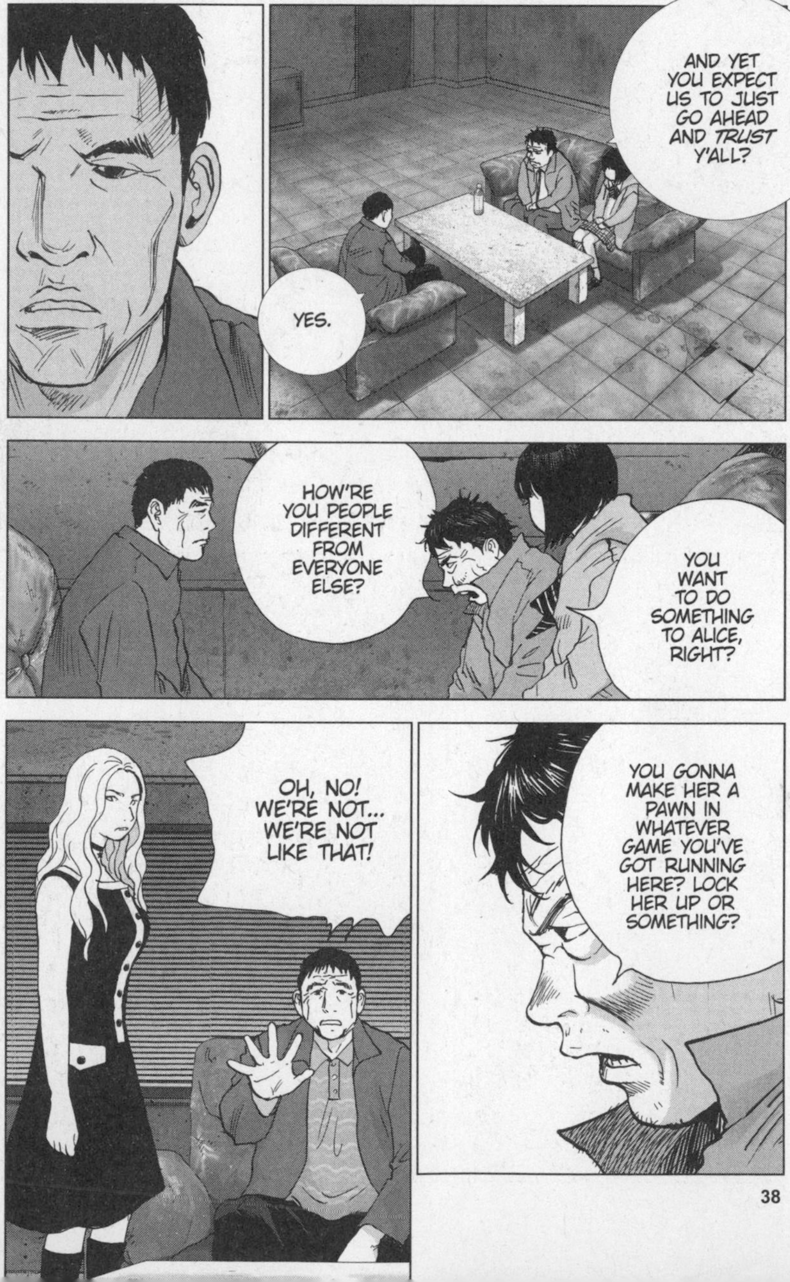
AND YET YOU EXPECT US TO JUST GO AHEAD AND *TRUST* Y'ALL?
YES.
YOU WANT TO DO SOMETHING TO ALICE, RIGHT?
HOW'RE YOU PEOPLE DIFFERENT FROM EVERYONE ELSE?
YOU GONNA MAKE HER A PAWN IN WHATEVER GAME YOU'VE GOT RUNNING HERE? LOCK HER UP OR SOMETHING?
OH, NO! WE'RE NOT... WE'RE NOT LIKE THAT!

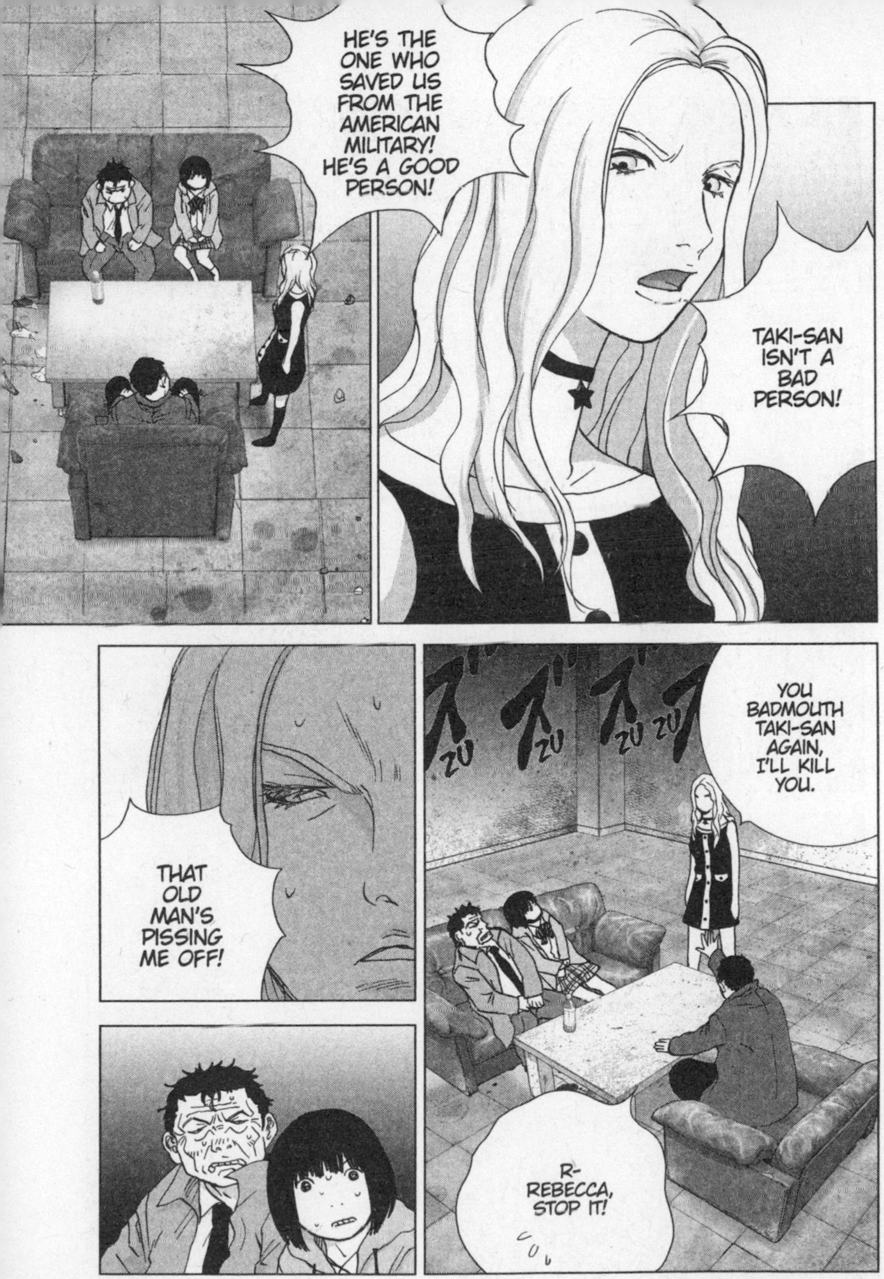
TAKI-SAN ISN'T A BAD PERSON!
HE'S THE ONE WHO SAVED US FROM THE AMERICAN MILITARY! HE'S A GOOD PERSON!
ZU ZU ZU ZU
YOU BADMOUTH TAKI-SAN AGAIN, I'LL KILL YOU.
R-REBECCA, STOP IT!
THAT OLD MAN'S PISSING ME OFF!

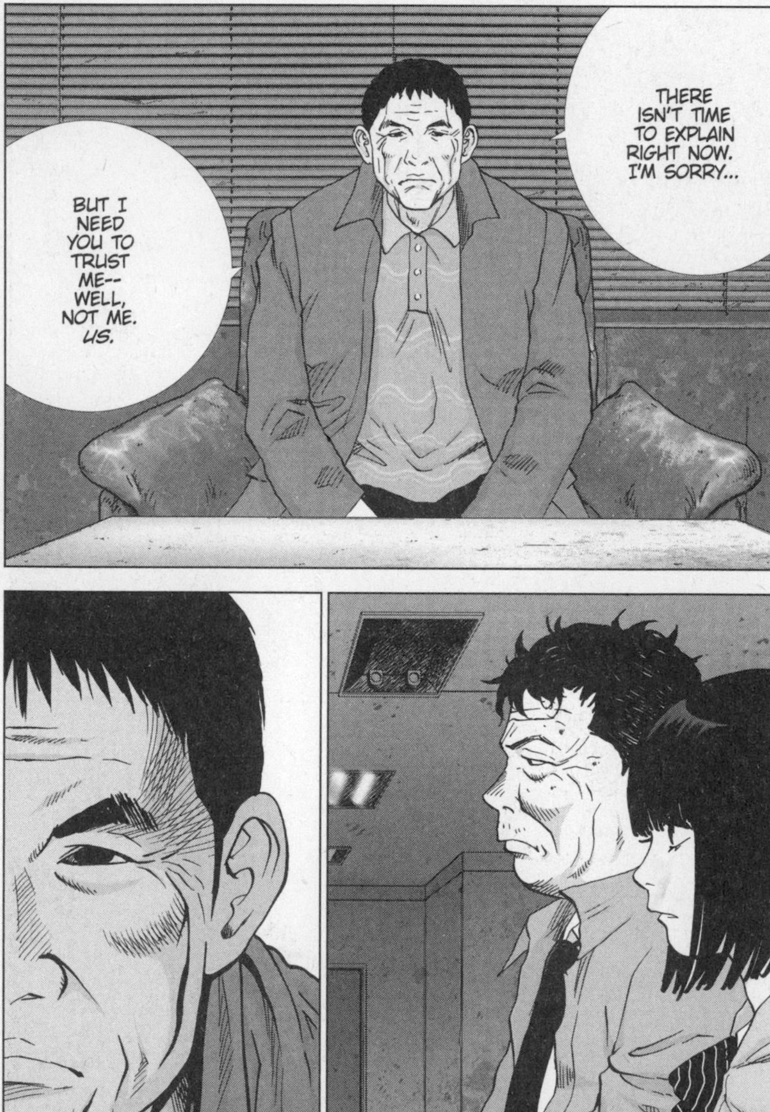
THERE ISN'T TIME TO EXPLAIN RIGHT NOW. I'M SORRY...
BUT I NEED YOU TO TRUST ME-- WELL, NOT ME. US.

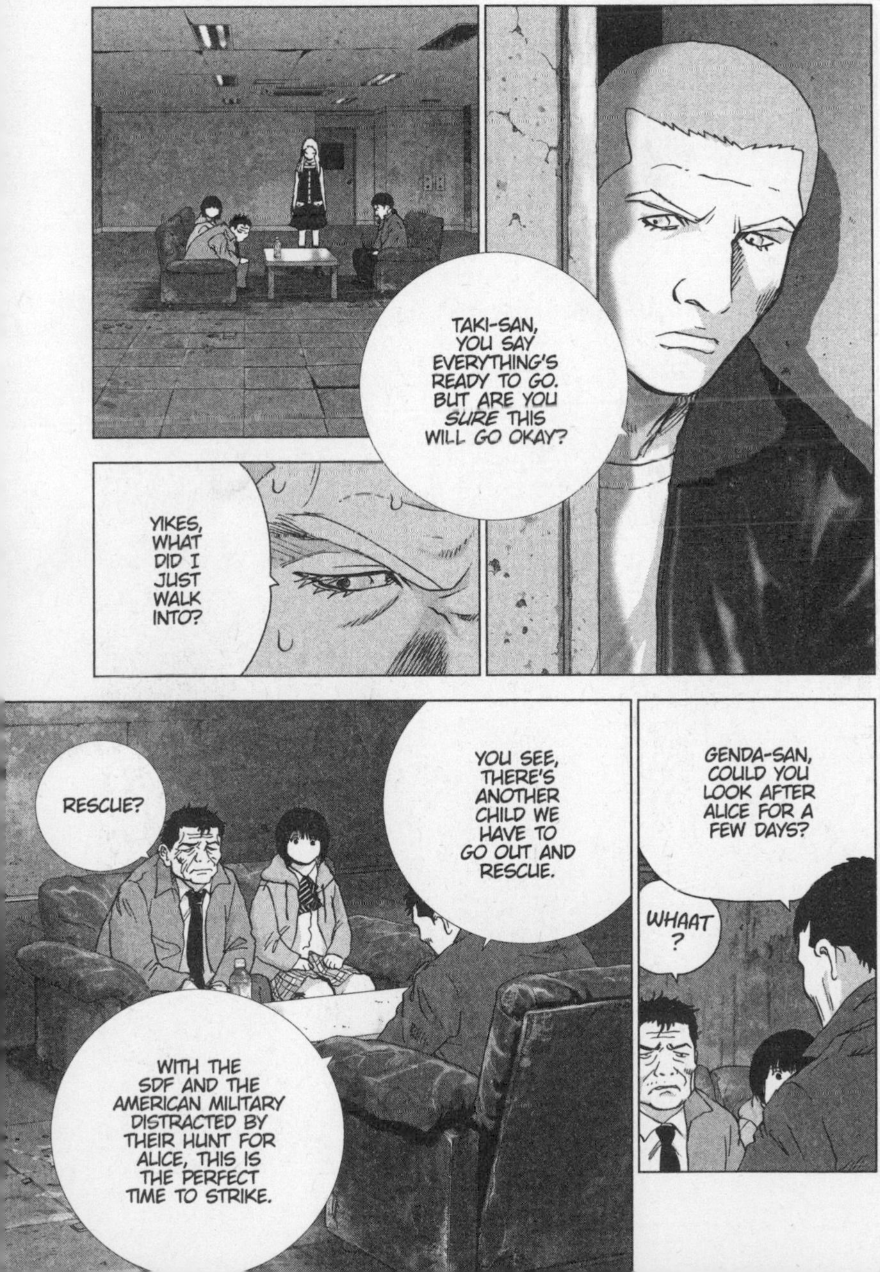
TAKI-SAN, YOU SAY EVERYTHING'S READY TO GO. BUT ARE YOU *SURE* THIS WILL GO OKAY?
YIKES, WHAT DID I JUST WALK INTO?
GENDA-SAN, COULD YOU LOOK AFTER ALICE FOR A FEW DAYS?
WHAAT?
YOU SEE, THERE'S ANOTHER CHILD WE HAVE TO GO OUT AND RESCUE.
RESCUE?
WITH THE SDF AND THE AMERICAN MILITARY DISTRACTED BY THEIR HUNT FOR ALICE, THIS IS THE PERFECT TIME TO STRIKE.

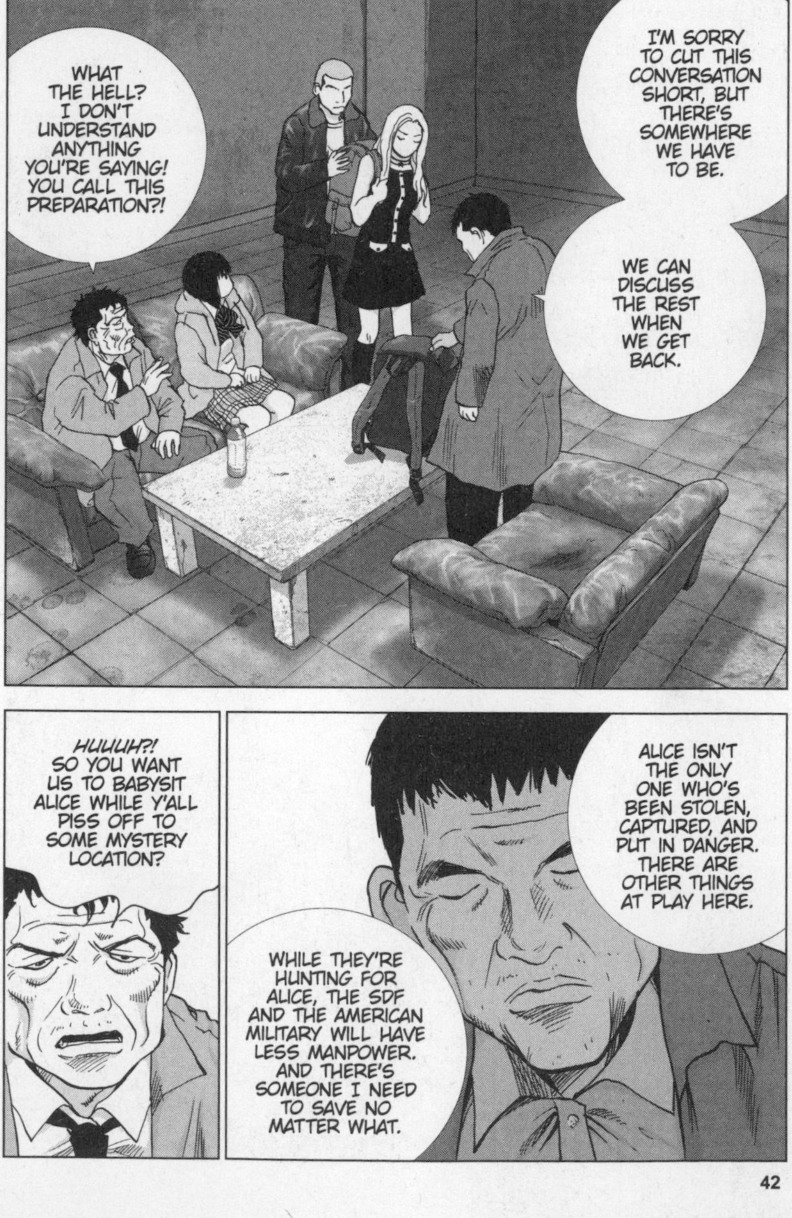
I'M SORRY TO CUT THIS CONVERSATION SHORT, BUT THERE'S SOMEWHERE WE HAVE TO BE.
WE CAN DISCUSS THE REST WHEN WE GET BACK.
WHAT THE HELL? I DON'T UNDERSTAND ANYTHING YOU'RE SAYING! YOU CALL THIS PREPARATION?!
ALICE ISN'T THE ONLY ONE WHO'S BEEN STOLEN, CAPTURED, AND PUT IN DANGER. THERE ARE OTHER THINGS AT PLAY HERE.
WHILE THEY'RE HUNTING FOR ALICE, THE SDF AND THE AMERICAN MILITARY WILL HAVE LESS MANPOWER. AND THERE'S SOMEONE I NEED TO SAVE NO MATTER WHAT.
HUUUH?! SO YOU WANT US TO BABYSIT ALICE WHILE Y'ALL PISS OFF TO SOME MYSTERY LOCATION?

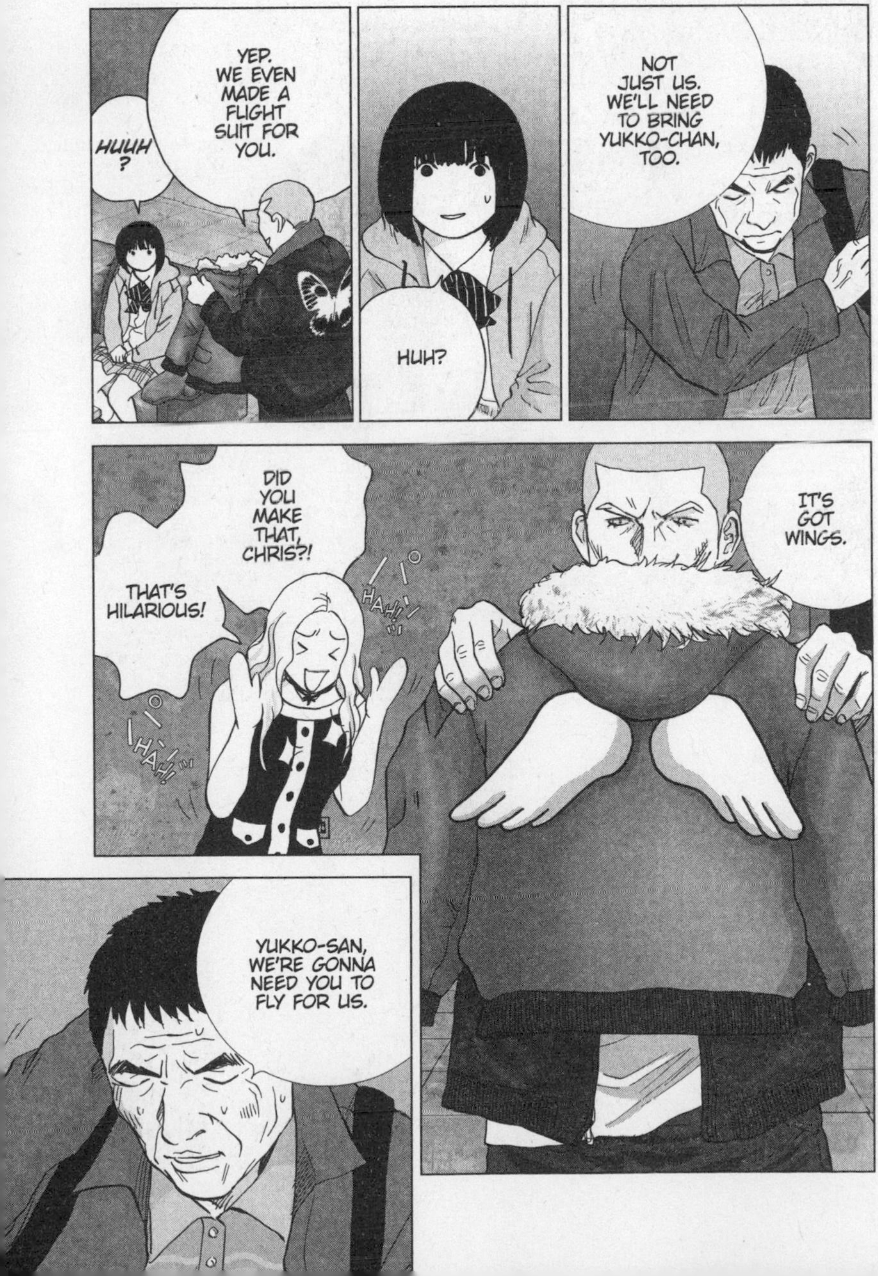
NOT JUST US. WE'LL NEED TO BRING YUKKO-CHAN, TOO.
HUH?
YEP. WE EVEN MADE A FLIGHT SUIT FOR YOU.
HUUH?
IT'S GOT WINGS.
DID YOU MAKE THAT, CHRIS?!
HAH!
THAT'S HILARIOUS!
HAH!
YUKKO-SAN, WE'RE GONNA NEED YOU TO FLY FOR US.

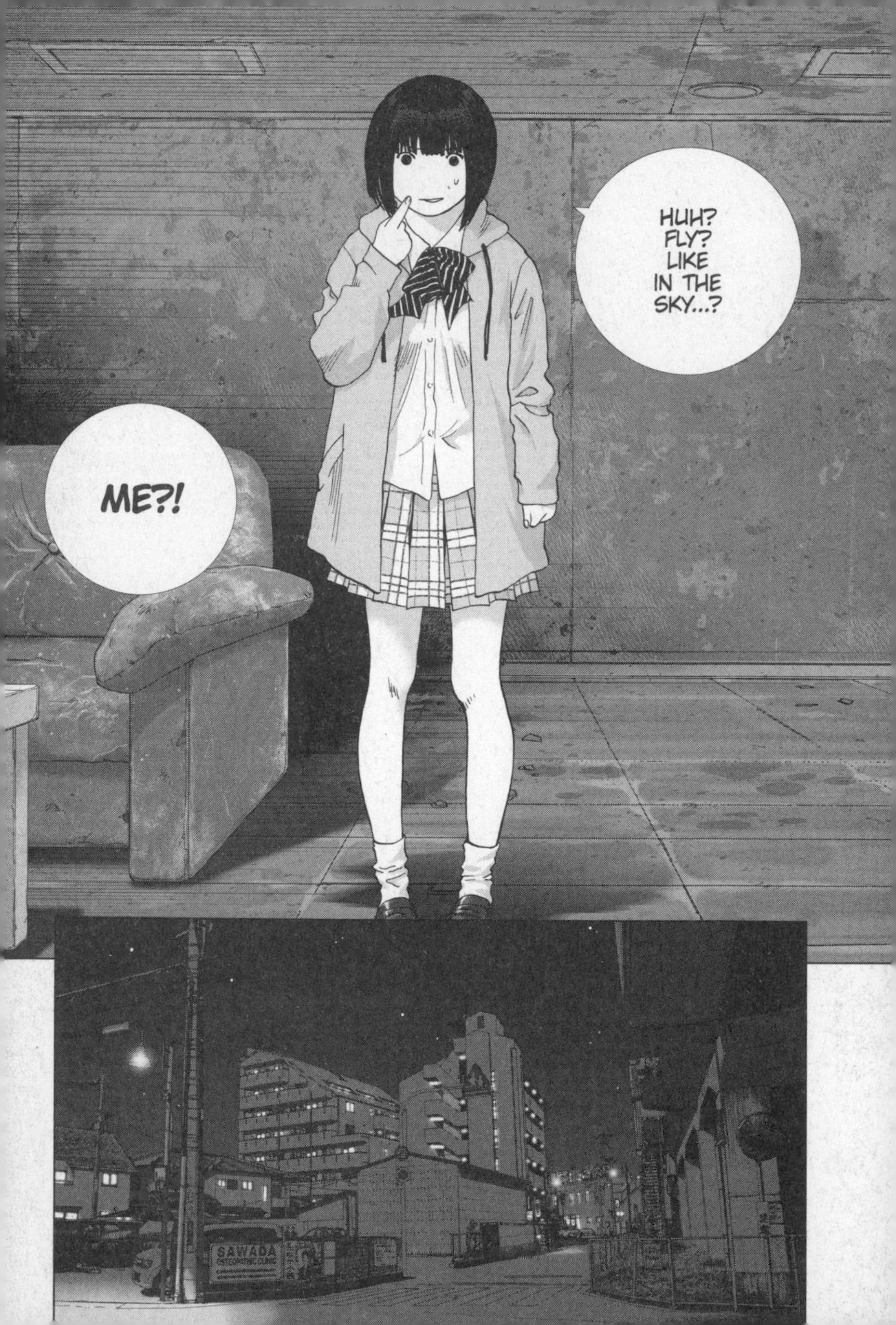
HUH? FLY? LIKE IN THE SKY...?
ME?!
SAWADA

Chapter 39: Genesis

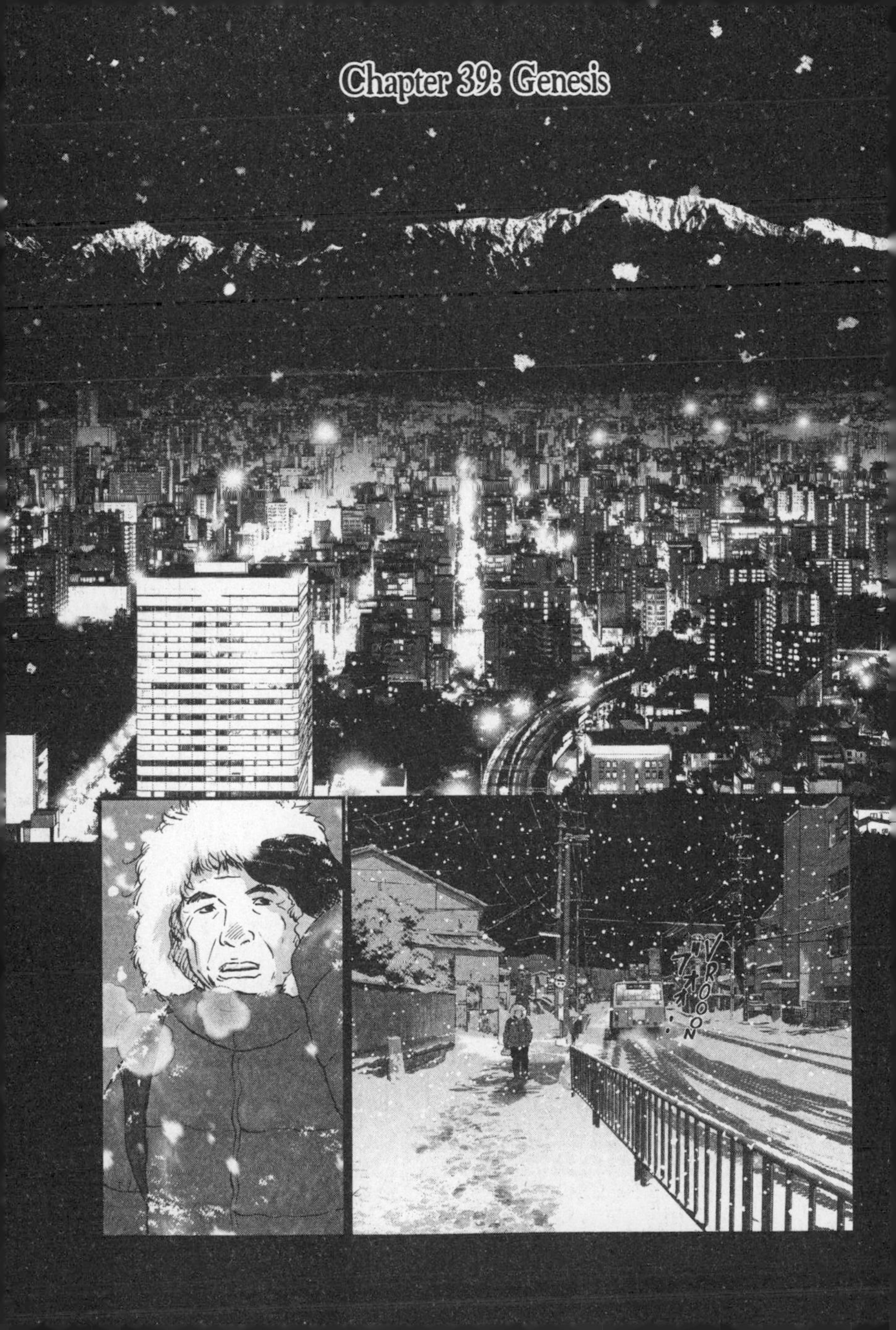
VROOOON

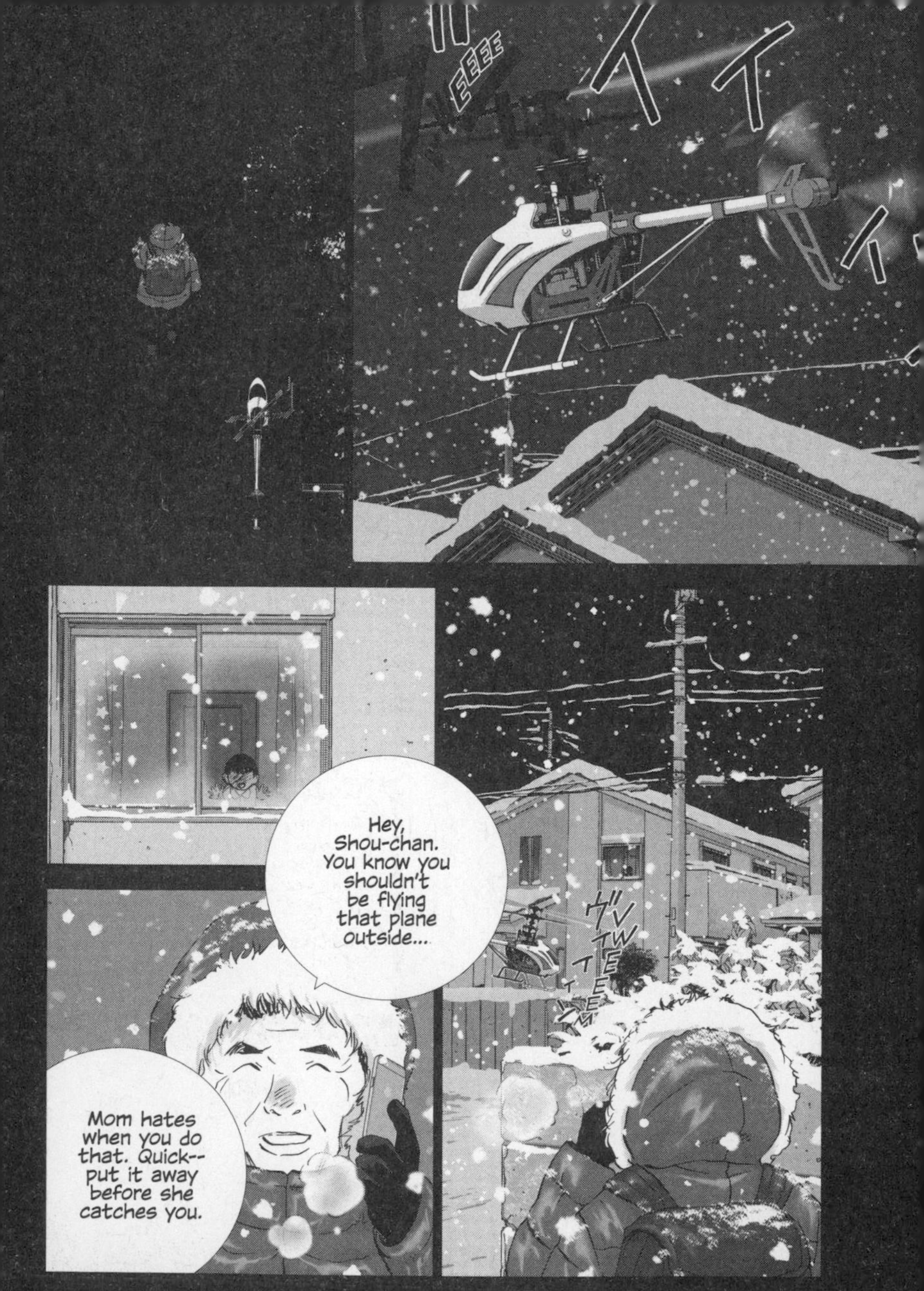
EEEE
VWEEEM
Hey, Shou-chan. You know you shouldn't be flying that plane outside...
Mom hates when you do that. Quick--put it away before she catches you.

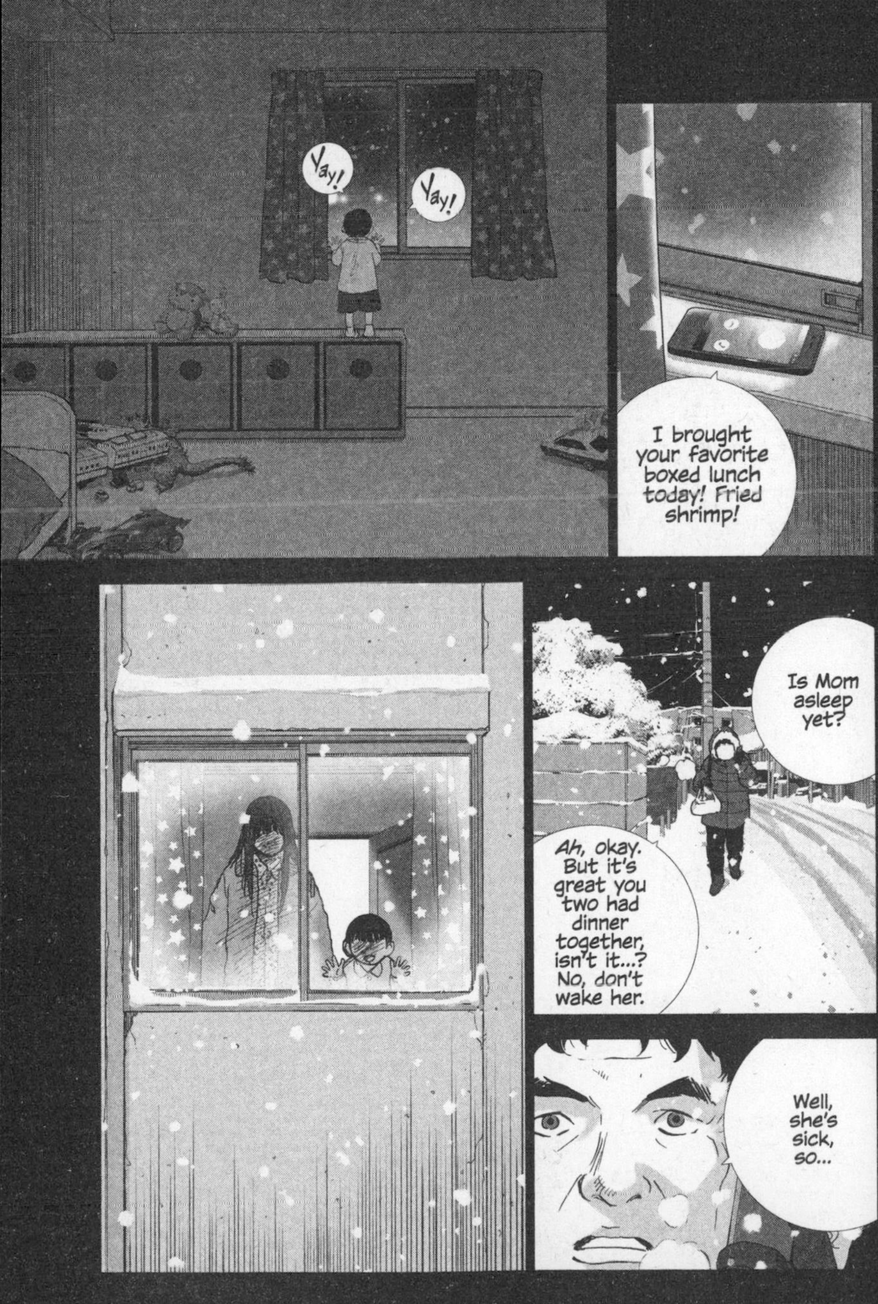
I brought your favorite boxed lunch today! Fried shrimp!
Yay!
Yay!
Is Mom asleep yet?
Ah, okay. But it's great you two had dinner together, isn't it...? No, don't wake her.
Well, she's sick, so...

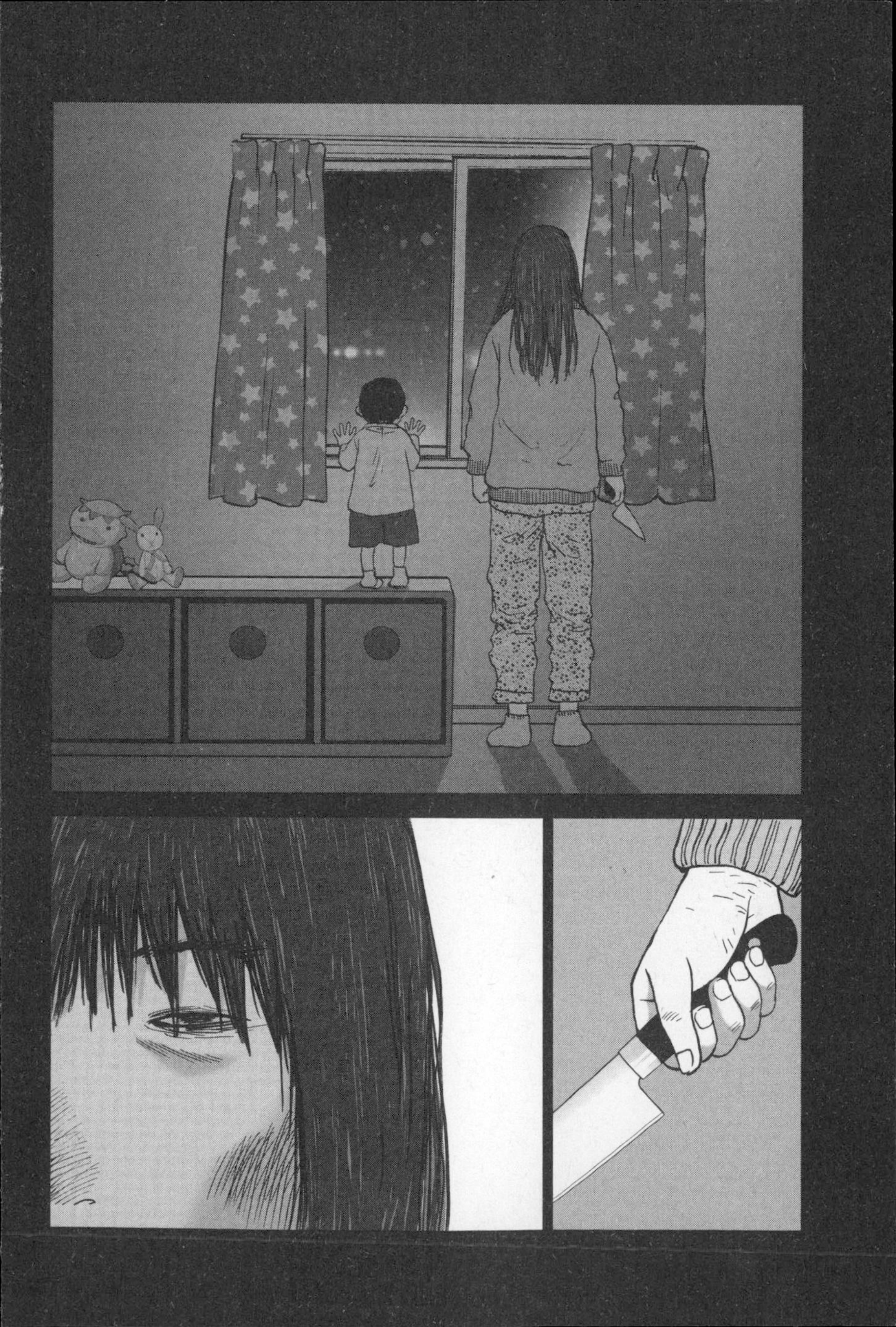

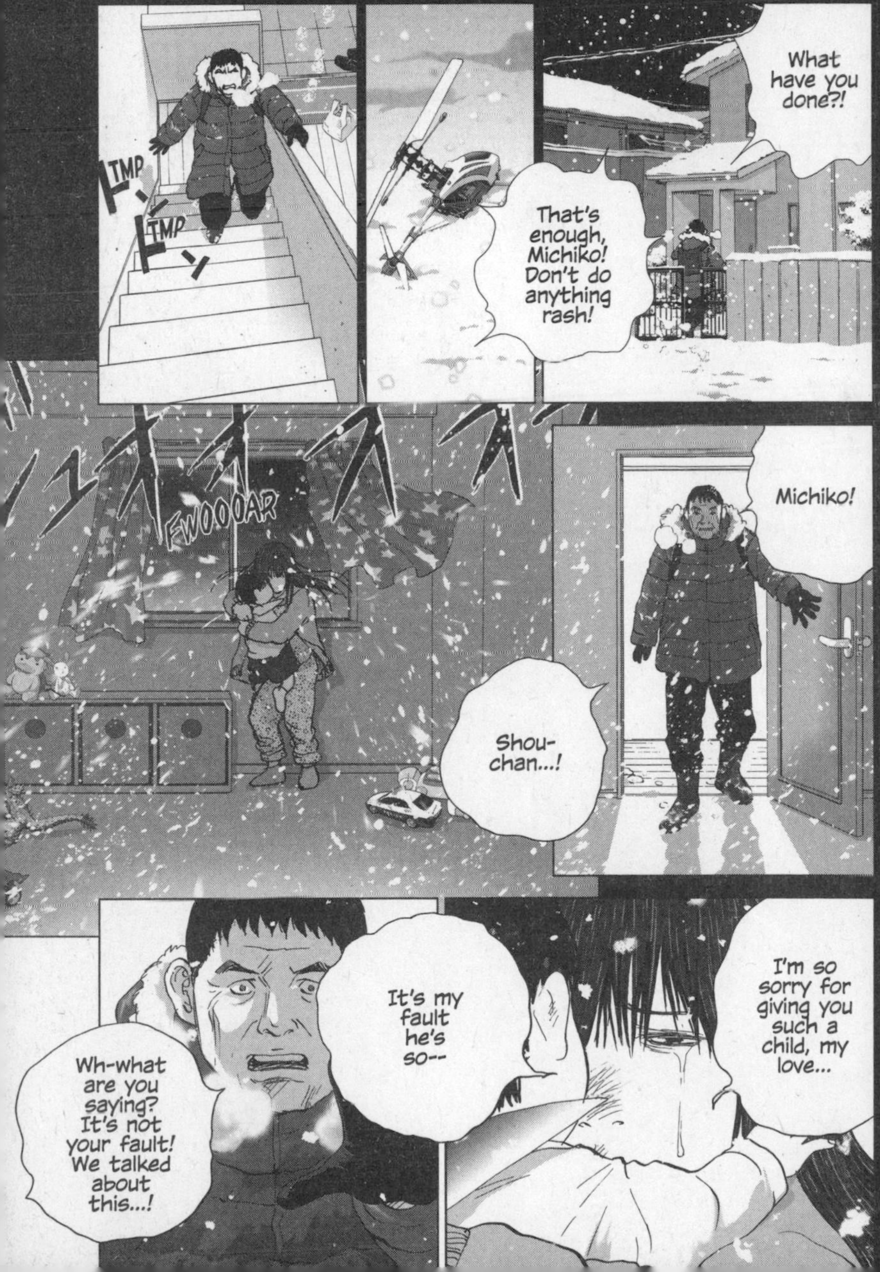

What have you done?!
That's enough, Michiko! Don't do anything rash!
LIMP
LIMP
Michiko!
FWOOOAR
Shou-chan...!
I'm so sorry for giving you such a child, my love...
It's my fault he's so--
Wh-what are you saying? It's not your fault! We talked about this...!

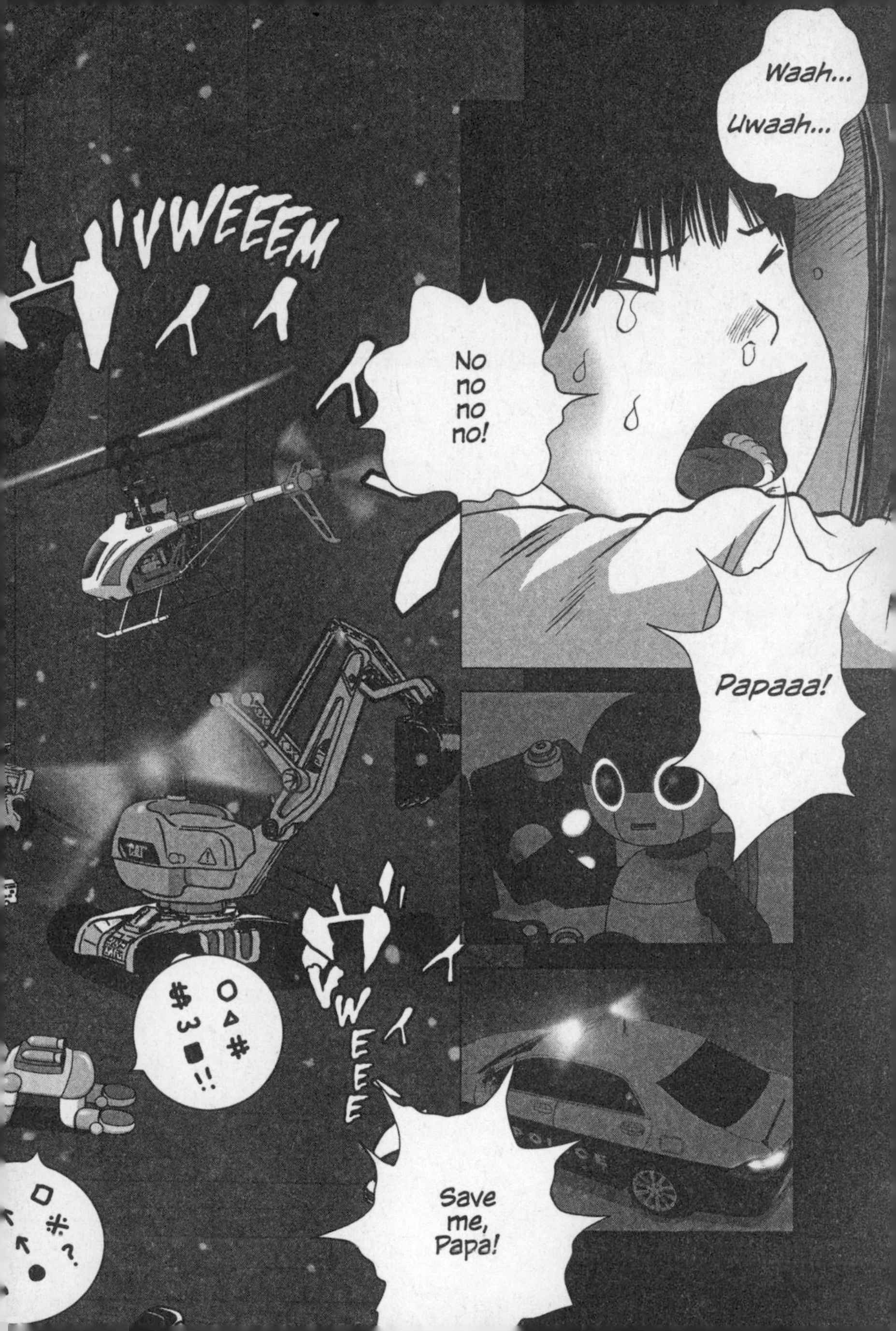
Waah...
Uwaah...
No no no no!
Papaaa!
Save me, Papa!
VWEEEM
VWEEE

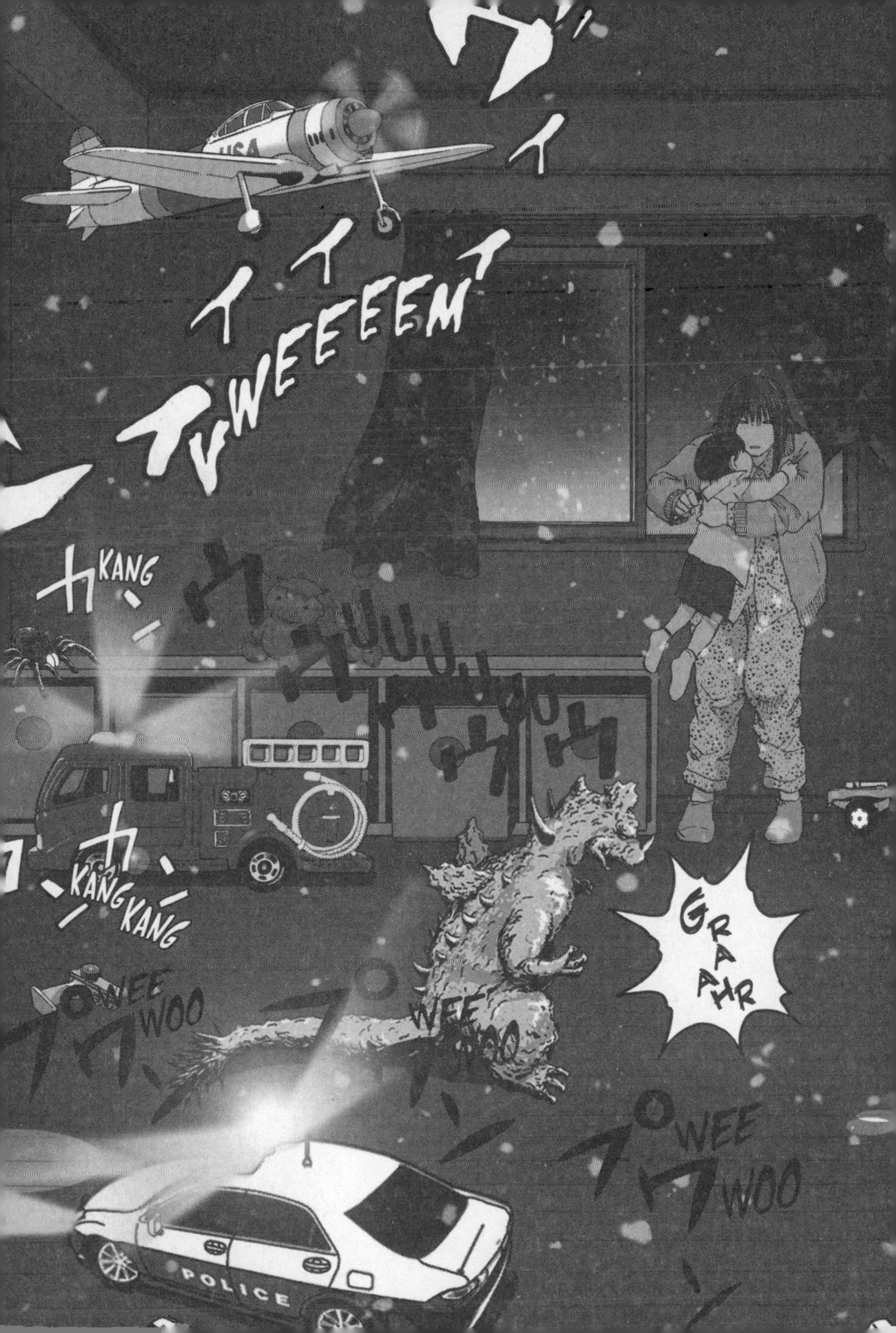

VWEEEEM
KANG
KANG KANG
KANG
GRAAHR
WEE WOO
WEE WOO
WEE WOO
POLICE
USA

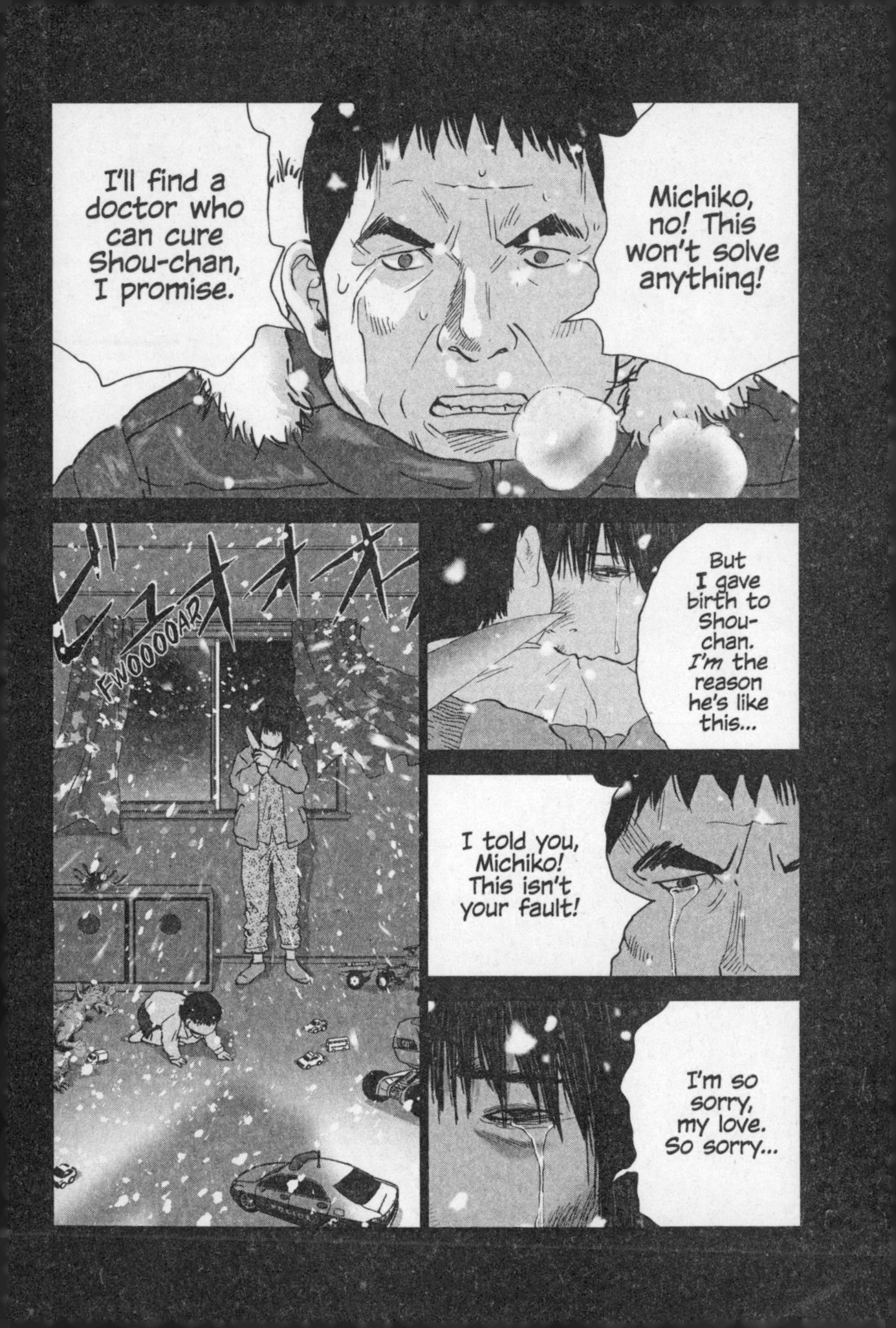
Michiko, no! This won't solve anything!
I'll find a doctor who can cure Shou-chan, I promise.
But I gave birth to Shou-chan. *I'm* the reason he's like this...
I told you, Michiko! This isn't your fault!
I'm so sorry, my love. So sorry...
FWOOOOAR

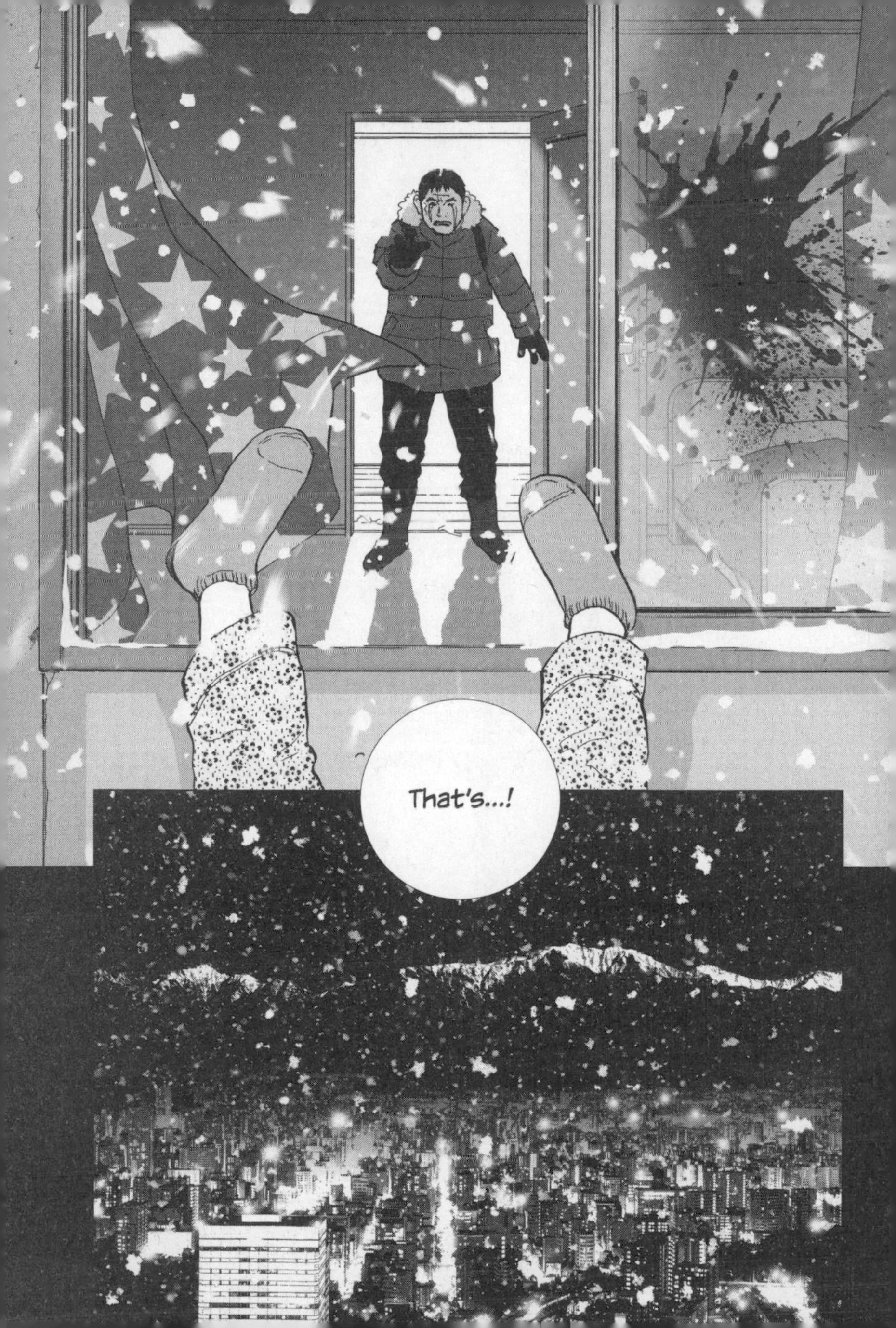
That's...!

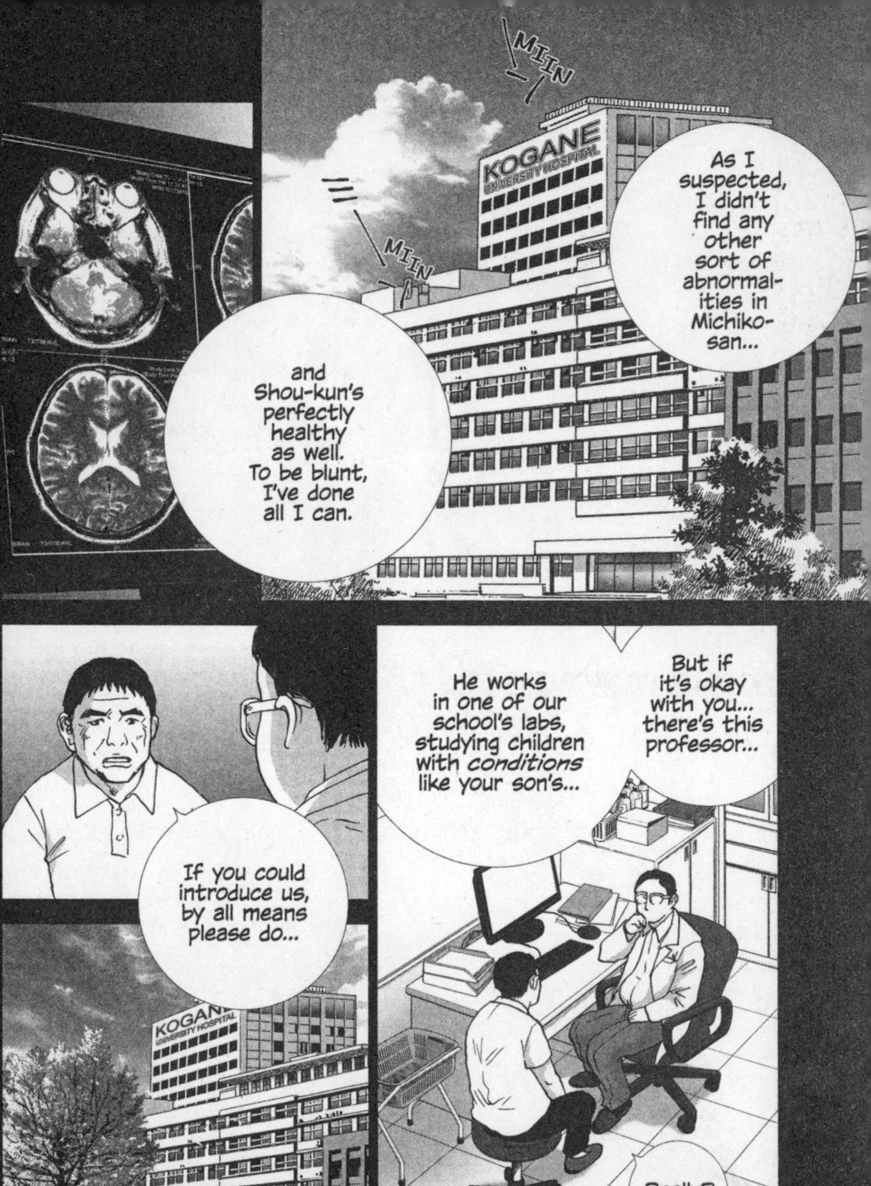
MIIN
MIIN
As I suspected, I didn't find any other sort of abnormalities in Michiko-san...
and Shou-kun's perfectly healthy as well. To be blunt, I've done all I can.
But if it's okay with you... there's this professor...
He works in one of our school's labs, studying children with *conditions* like your son's...
Really?
If you could introduce us, by all means please do...
KOGANE UNIVERSITY HOSPITAL

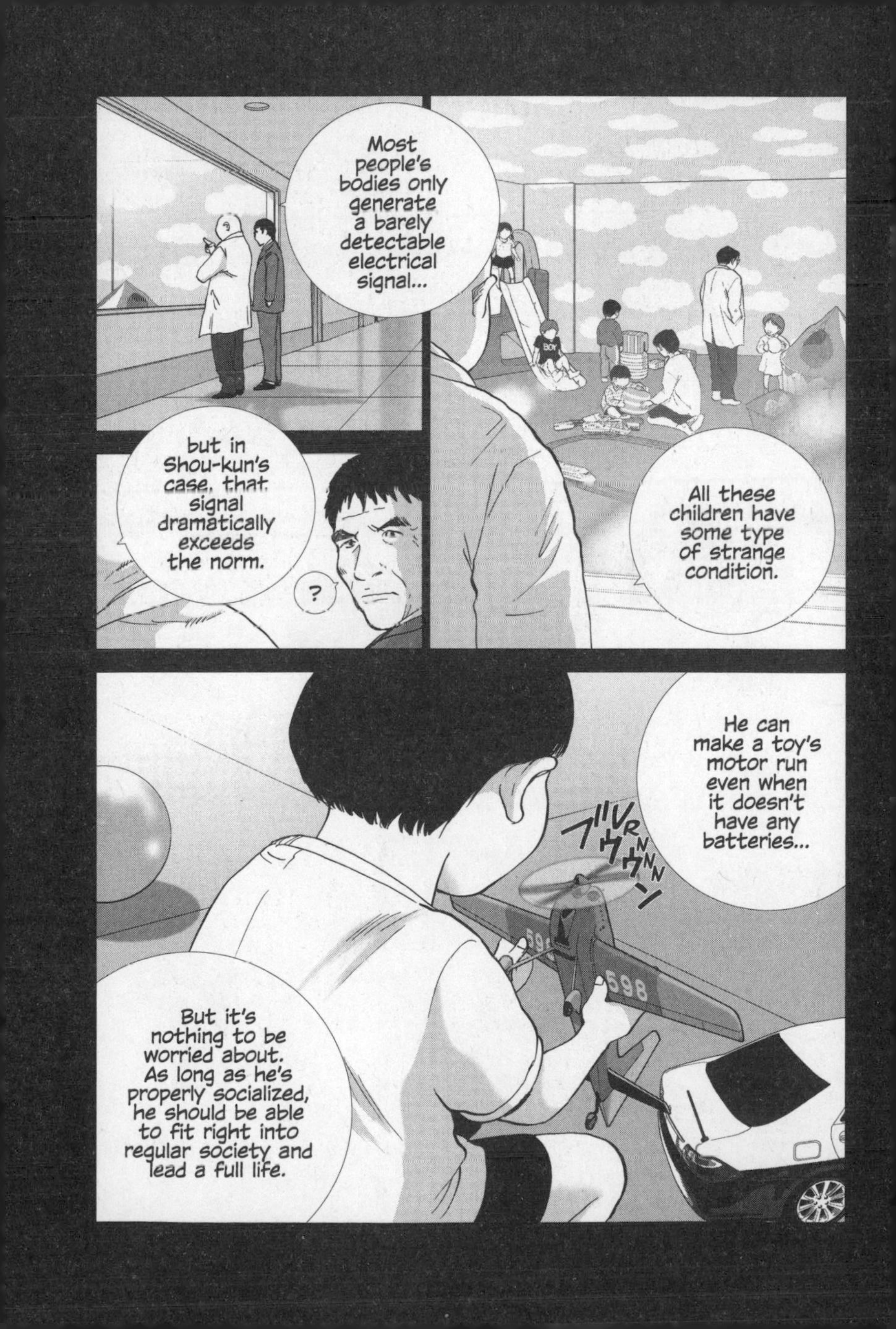
All these children have some type of strange condition.
Most people's bodies only generate a barely detectable electrical signal...
but in Shou-kun's case, that signal dramatically exceeds the norm.
?
He can make a toy's motor run even when it doesn't have any batteries...
VRNNN
598
But it's nothing to be worried about. As long as he's properly socialized, he should be able to fit right into regular society and lead a full life.

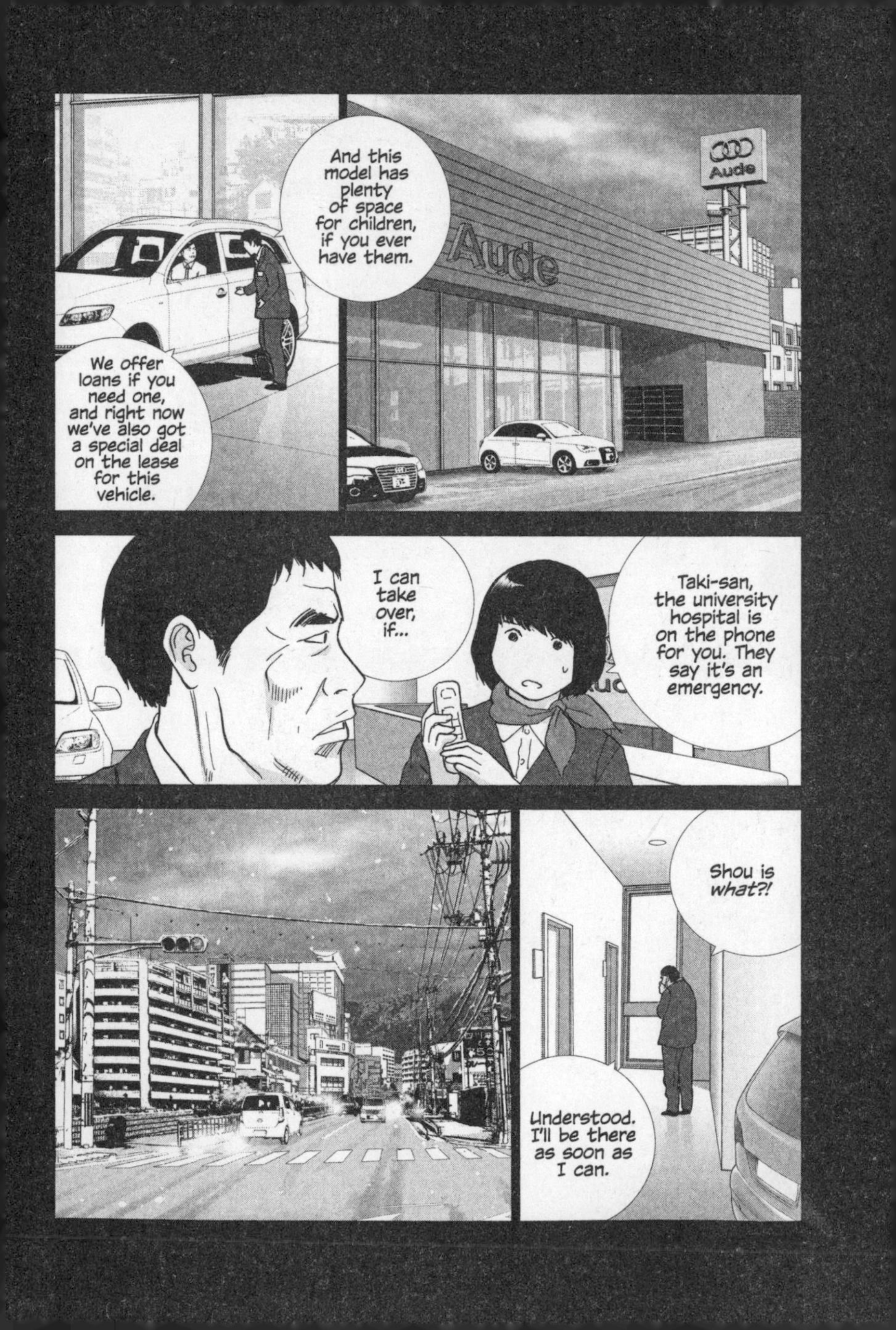

And this model has plenty of space for children, if you ever have them.
We offer loans if you need one, and right now we've also got a special deal on the lease for this vehicle.
Aude
Taki-san, the university hospital is on the phone for you. They say it's an emergency.
I can take over, if...
Shou is *what?!*
Understood. I'll be there as soon as I can.

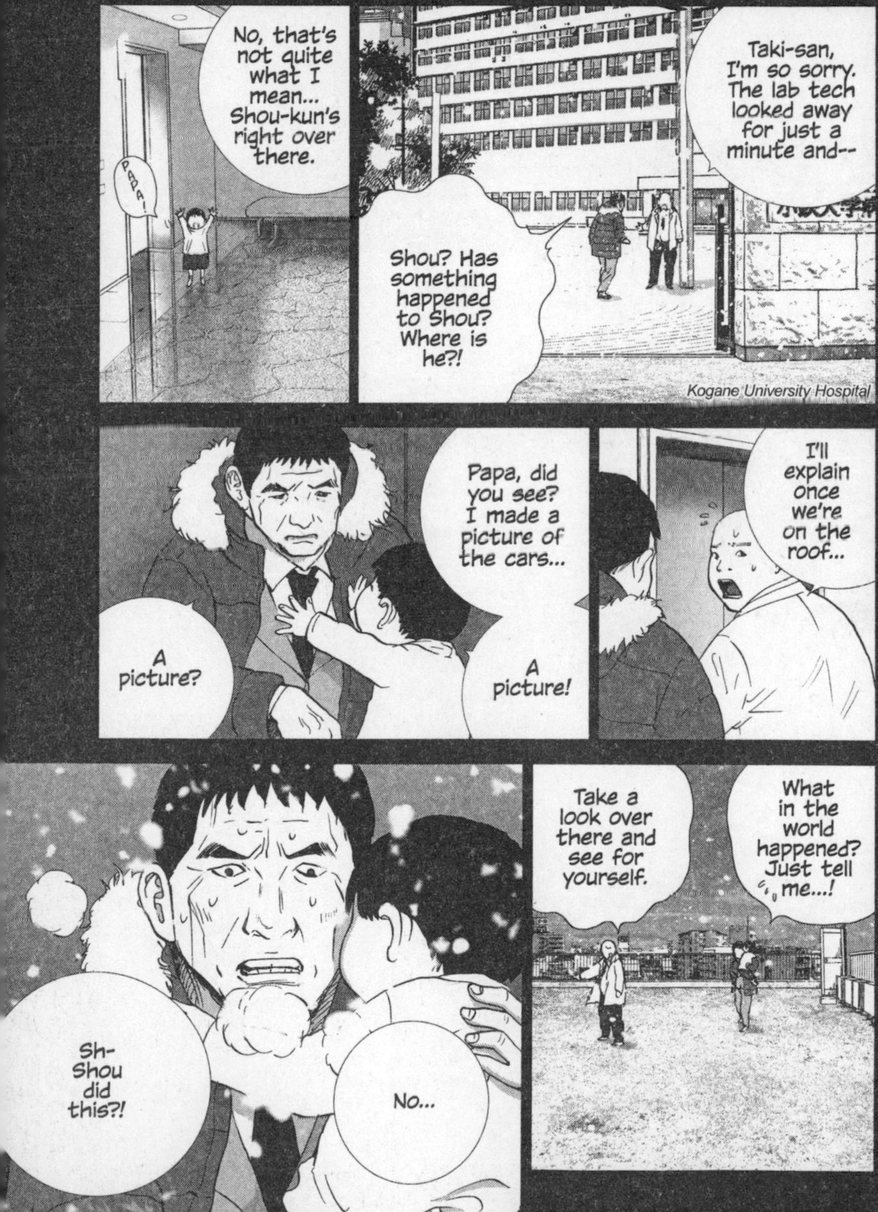
Taki-san, I'm so sorry. The lab tech looked away for just a minute and--
Shou? Has something happened to Shou? Where is he?!
Kogane University Hospital
No, that's not quite what I mean... Shou-kun's right over there.
PAPA!
I'll explain once we're on the roof...
Papa, did you see? I made a picture of the cars...
A picture!
A picture?
What in the world happened? Just tell me...!
Take a look over there and see for yourself.
No...
Sh- Shou did this?!

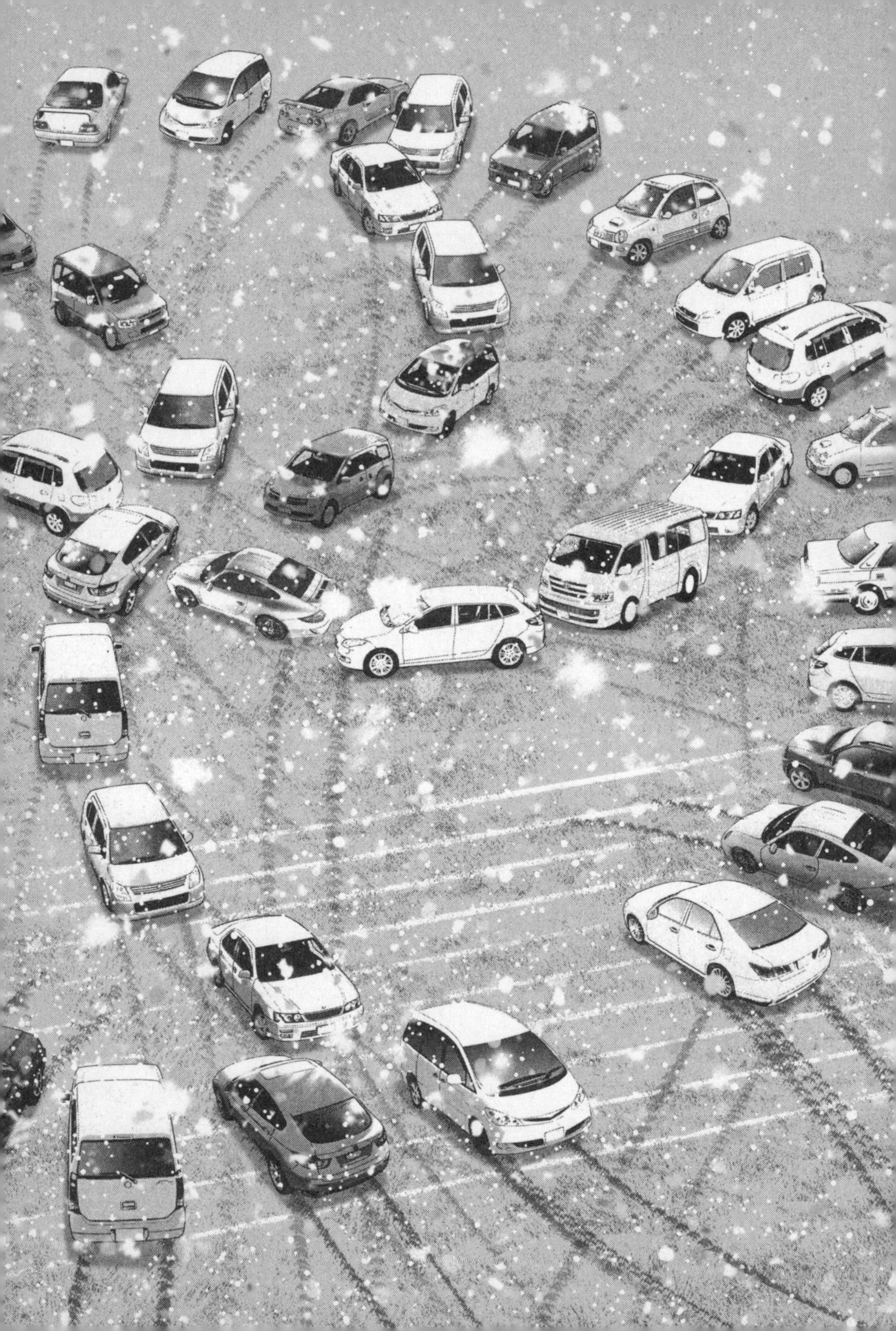

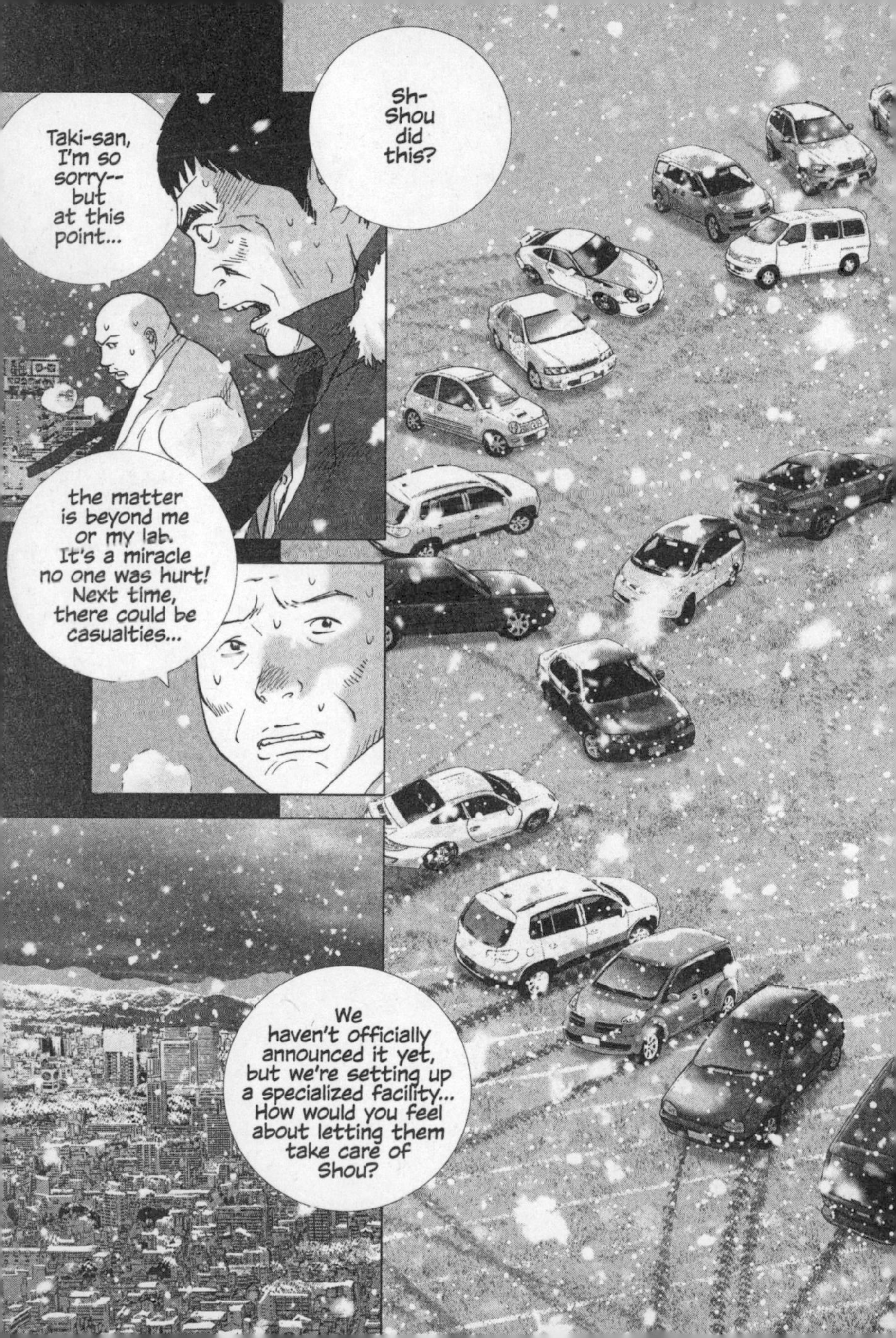
Sh-Shou did this?
Taki-san, I'm so sorry-- but at this point...
the matter is beyond me or my lab. It's a miracle no one was hurt! Next time, there could be casualties...
We haven't officially announced it yet, but we're setting up a specialized facility... How would you feel about letting them take care of Shou?

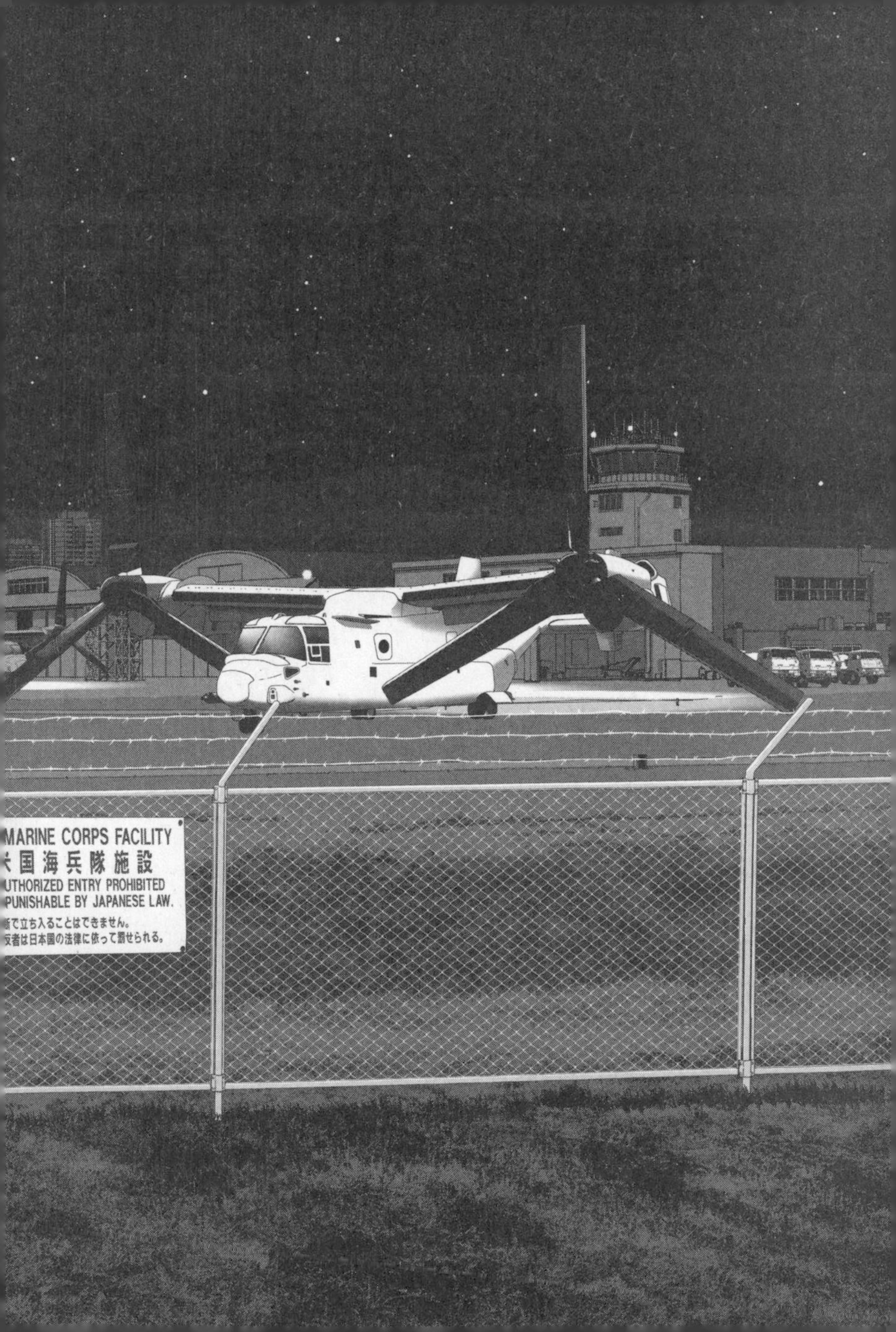
MARINE CORPS FACILITY
国海兵隊施設
UTHORIZED ENTRY PROHIBITED
PUNISHABLE BY JAPANESE LAW.
で立ち入ることはできません。
者は日本国の法律に依って罰せられる。

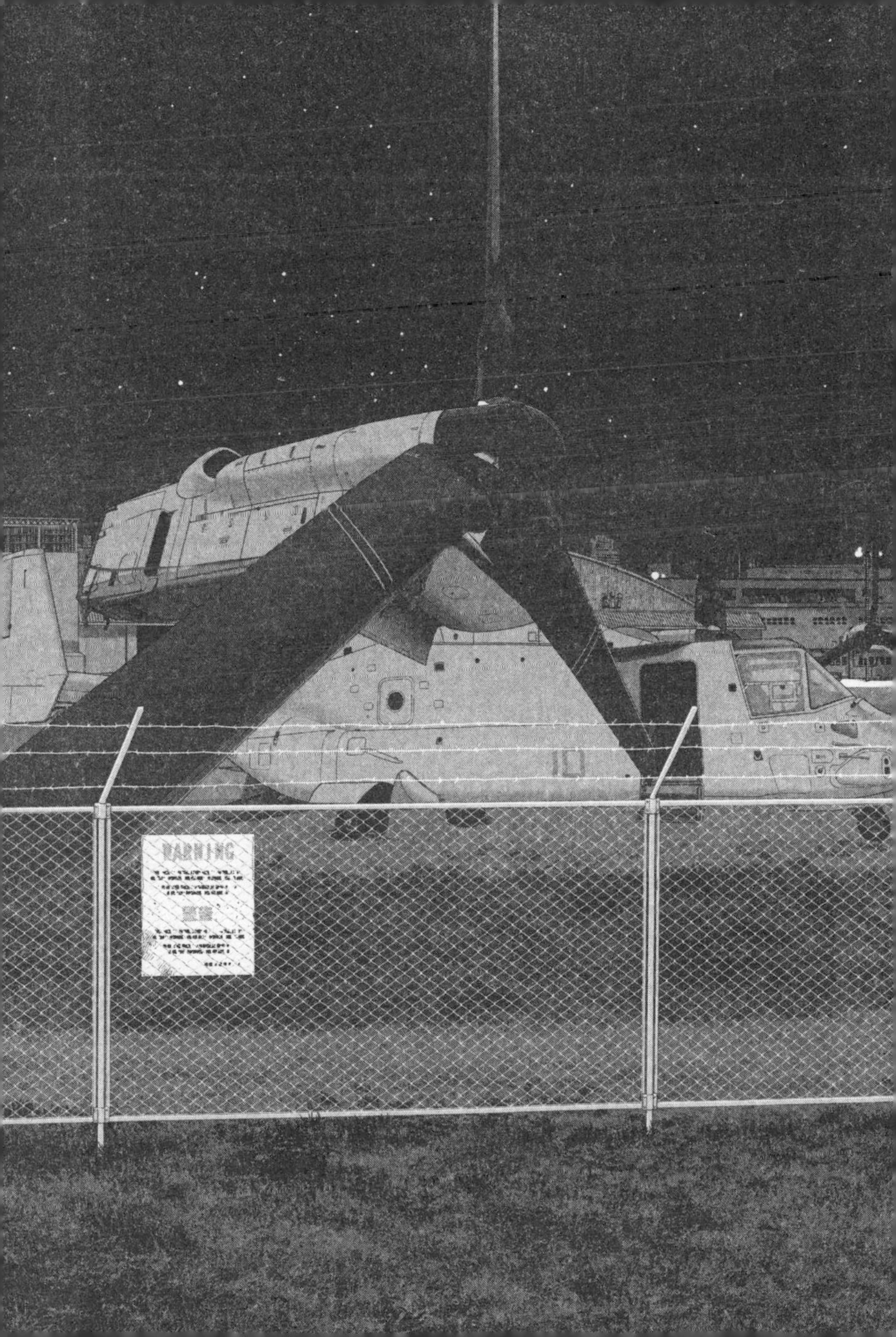
WARNING

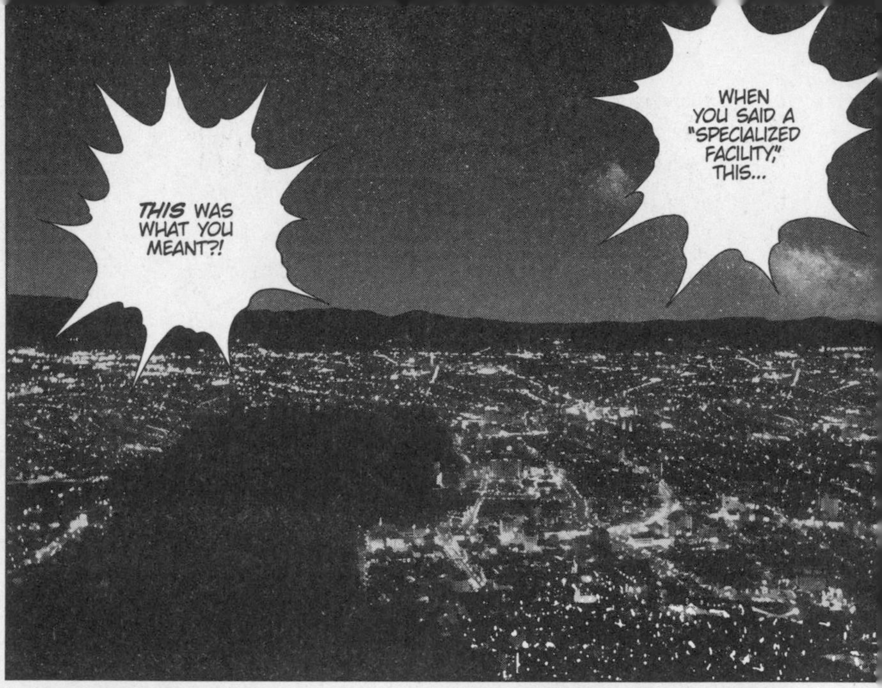
WHEN YOU SAID A "SPECIALIZED FACILITY," THIS...
THIS WAS WHAT YOU MEANT?!

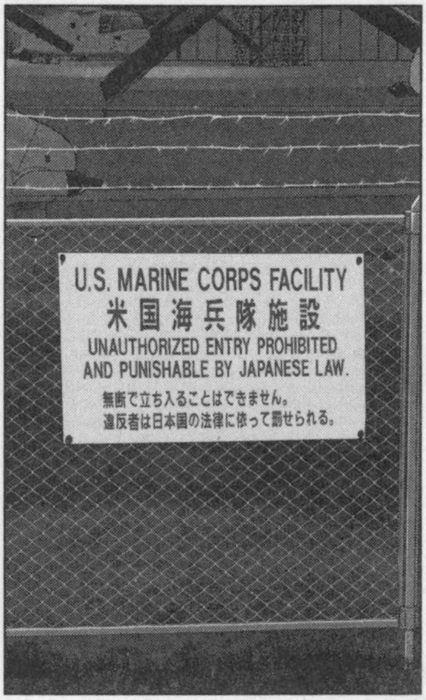
U.S. MARINE CORPS FACILITY
米国海兵隊施設
UNAUTHORIZED ENTRY PROHIBITED AND PUNISHABLE BY JAPANESE LAW.
無断で立ち入ることはできません。
違反者は日本国の法律に依って罰せられる。

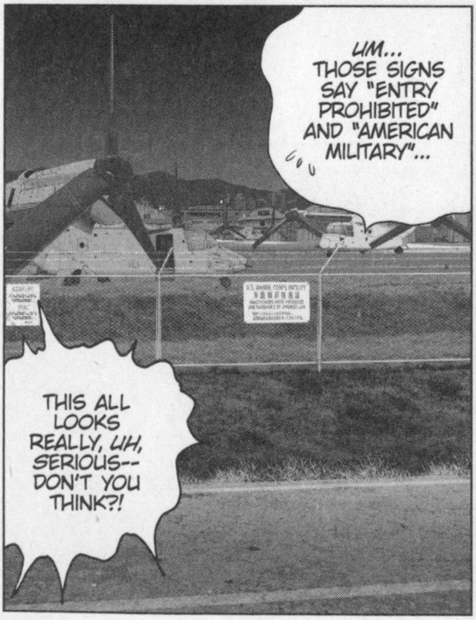
UM... THOSE SIGNS SAY "ENTRY PROHIBITED" AND "AMERICAN MILITARY"...
THIS ALL LOOKS REALLY, UH, SERIOUS-- DON'T YOU THINK?!

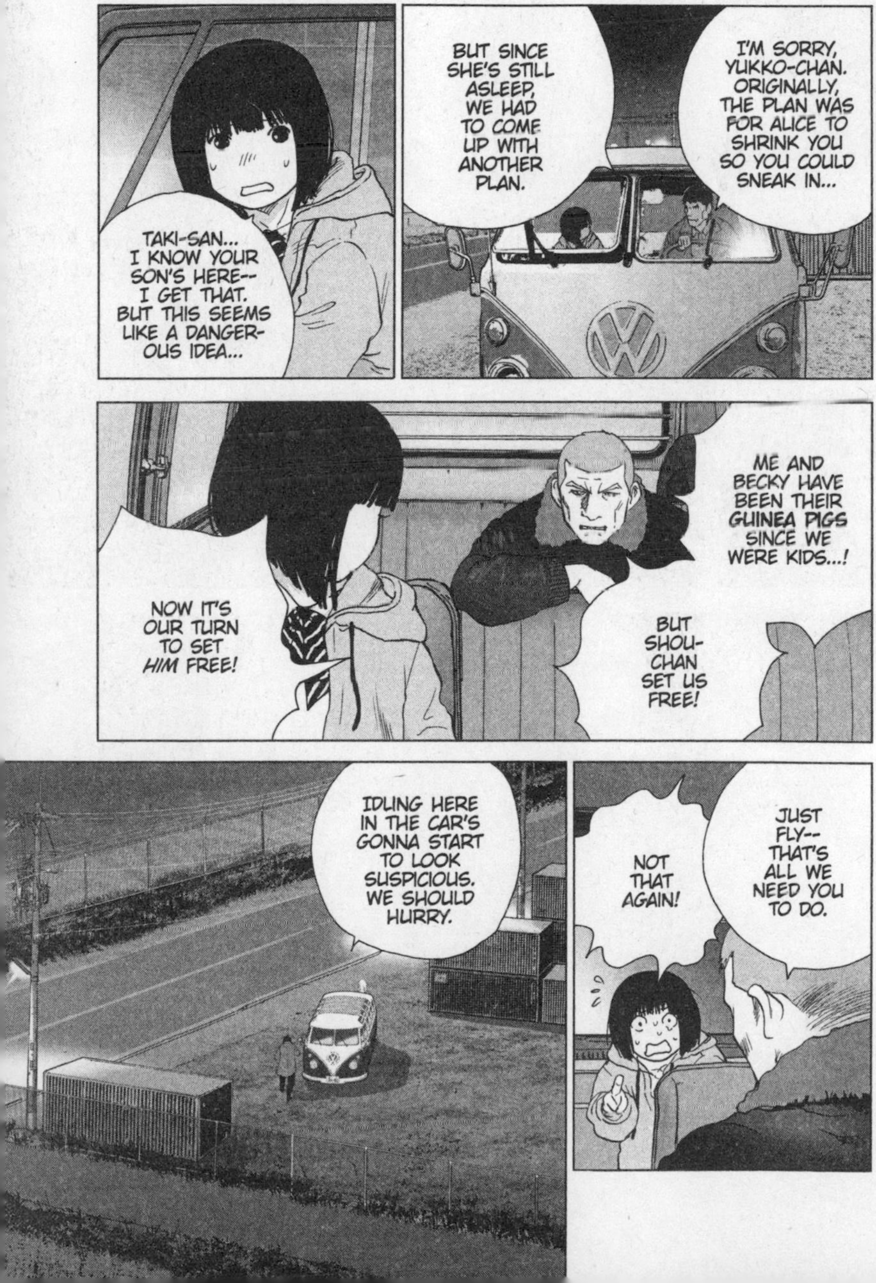
I'M SORRY, YUKKO-CHAN. ORIGINALLY, THE PLAN WAS FOR ALICE TO SHRINK YOU SO YOU COULD SNEAK IN...
BUT SINCE SHE'S STILL ASLEEP, WE HAD TO COME UP WITH ANOTHER PLAN.
TAKI-SAN... I KNOW YOUR SON'S HERE-- I GET THAT. BUT THIS SEEMS LIKE A DANGER-OUS IDEA...
ME AND BECKY HAVE BEEN THEIR GUINEA PIGS SINCE WE WERE KIDS...!
BUT SHOU-CHAN SET US FREE!
NOW IT'S OUR TURN TO SET *HIM* FREE!
JUST FLY-- THAT'S ALL WE NEED YOU TO DO.
NOT THAT AGAIN!
IDLING HERE IN THE CAR'S GONNA START TO LOOK SUSPICIOUS. WE SHOULD HURRY.

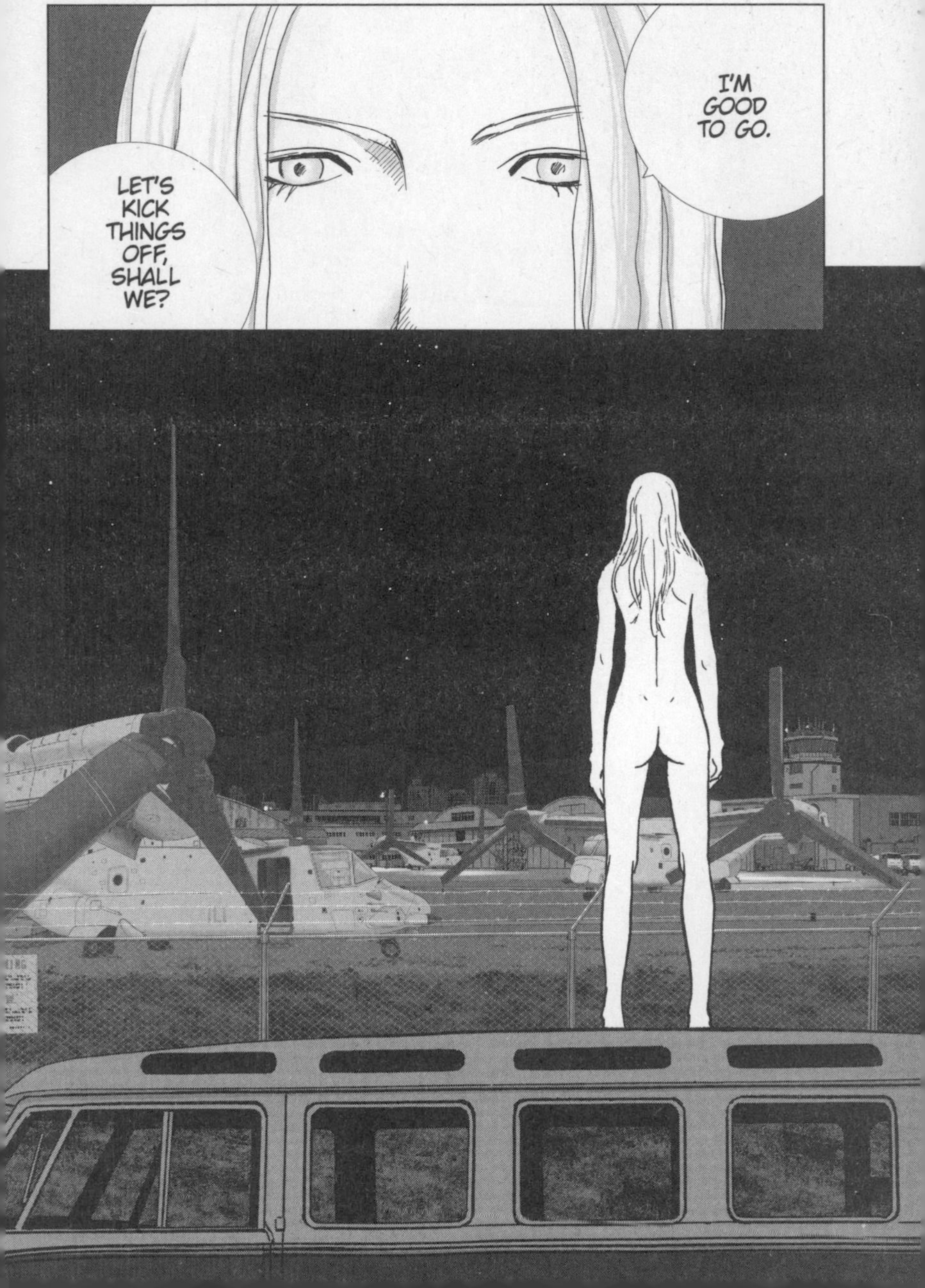
I'M GOOD TO GO.
LET'S KICK THINGS OFF, SHALL WE?

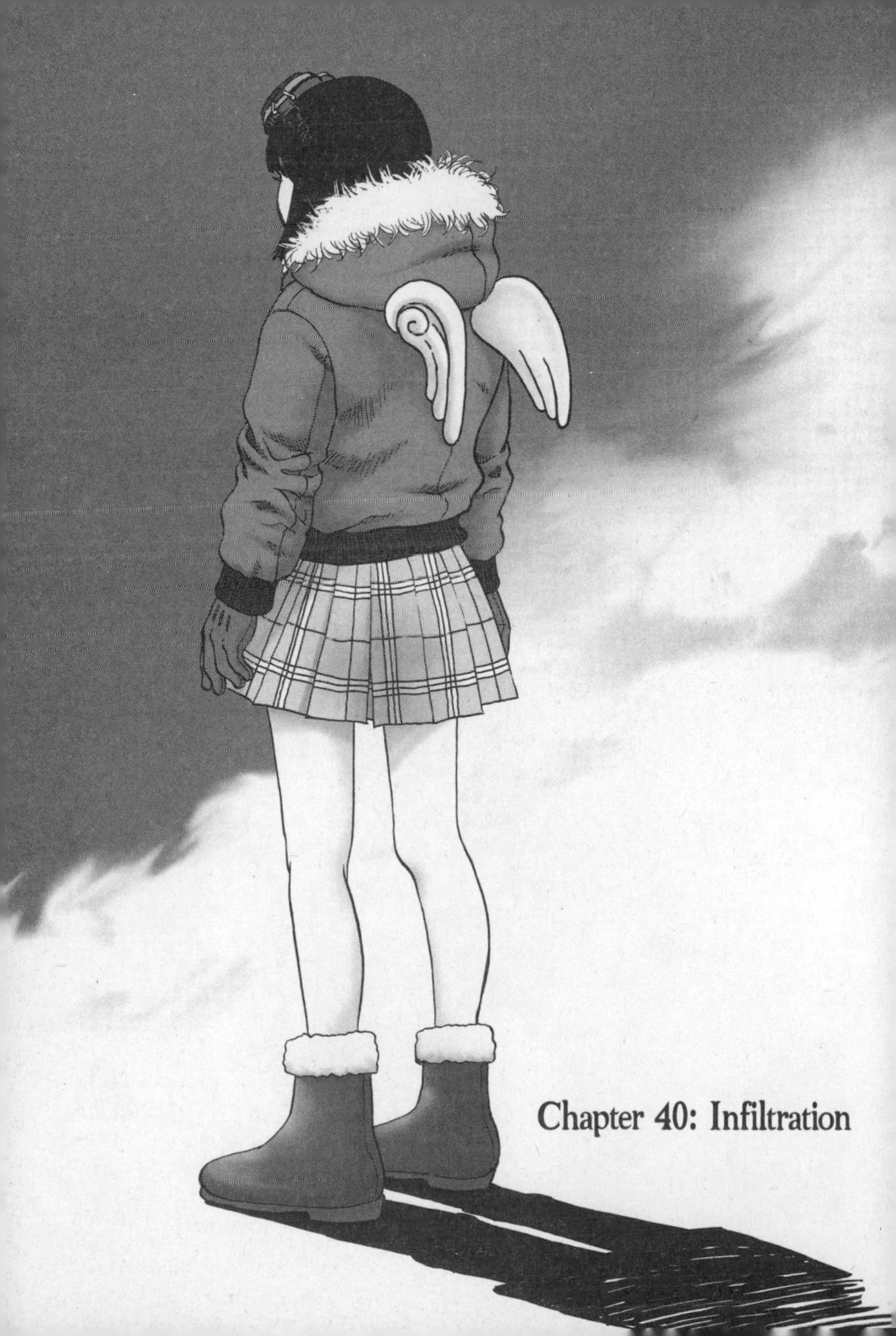

Chapter 40: Infiltration

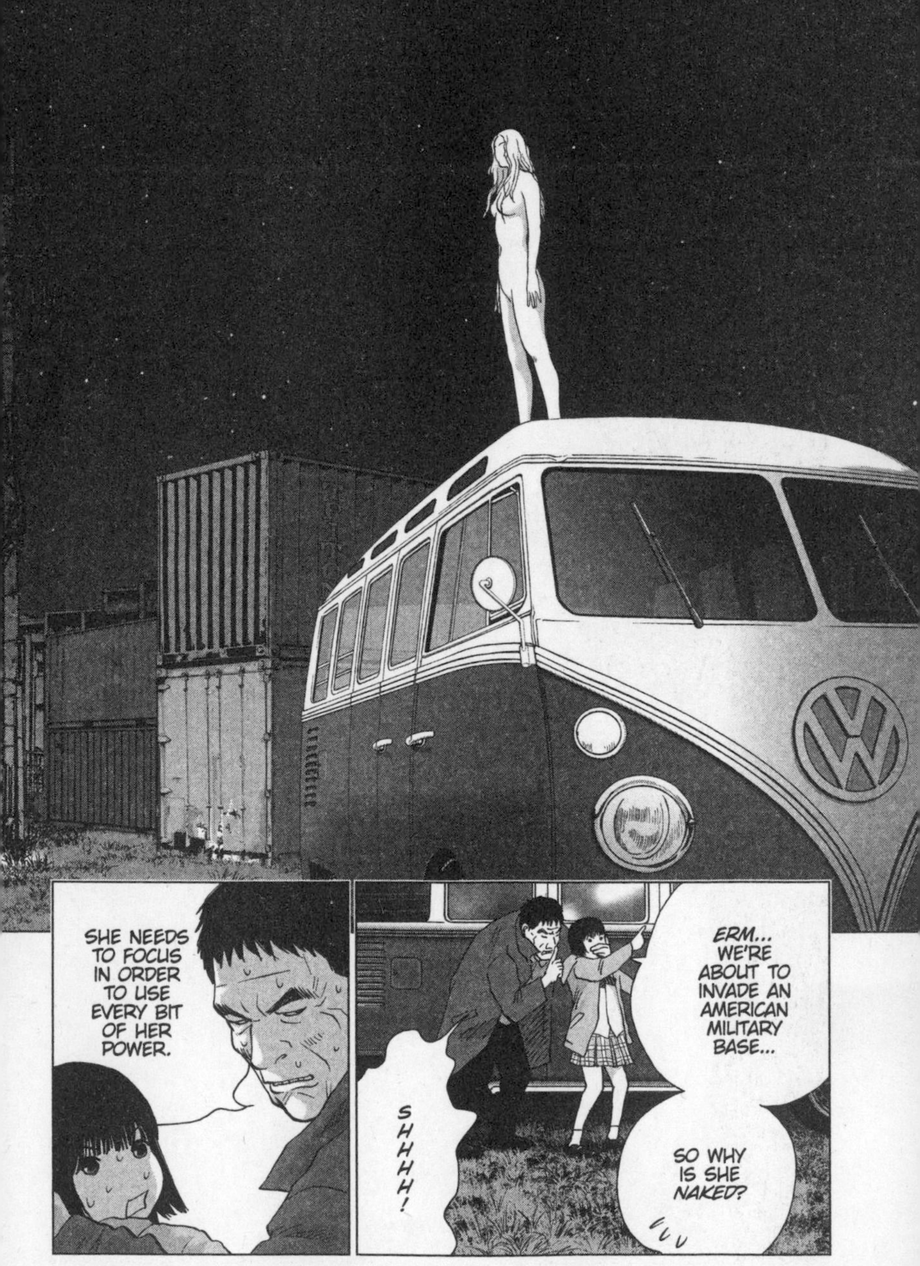
ERM... WE'RE ABOUT TO INVADE AN AMERICAN MILITARY BASE...
SO WHY IS SHE NAKED?
SHHHH!
SHE NEEDS TO FOCUS IN ORDER TO USE EVERY BIT OF HER POWER.

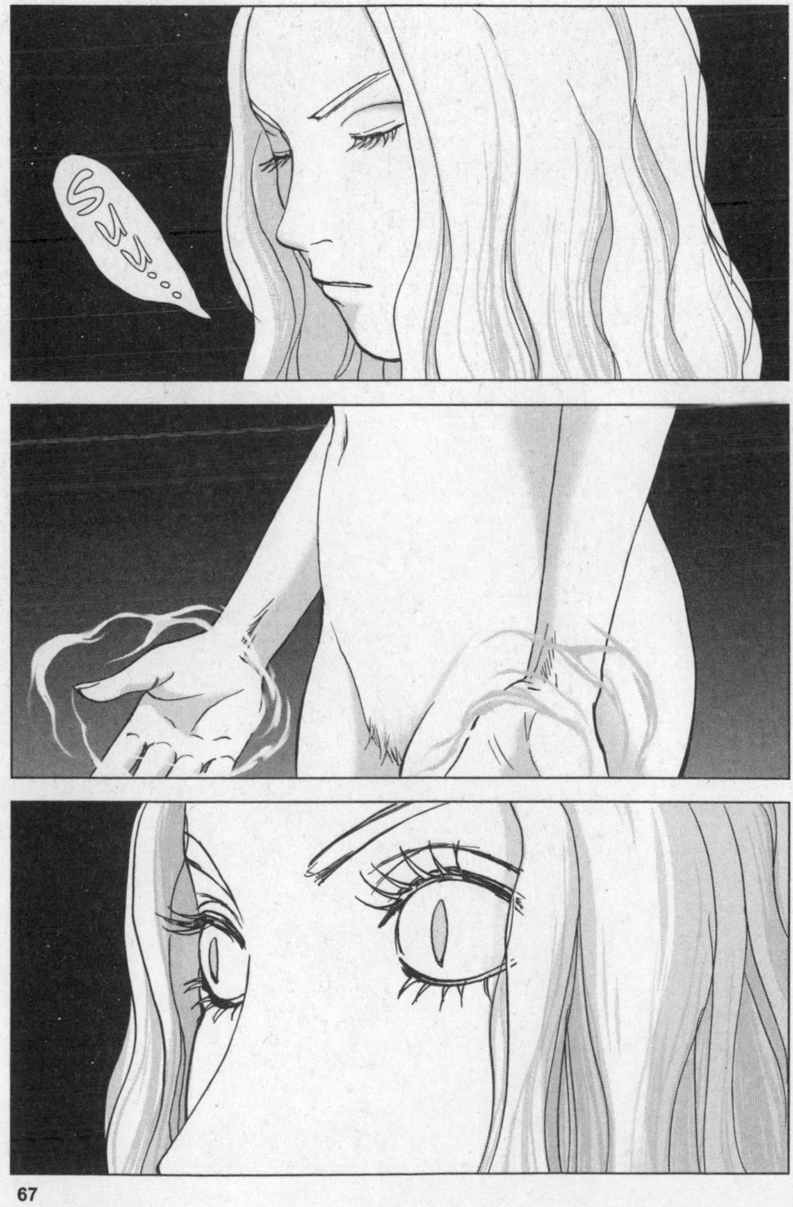
Suu...

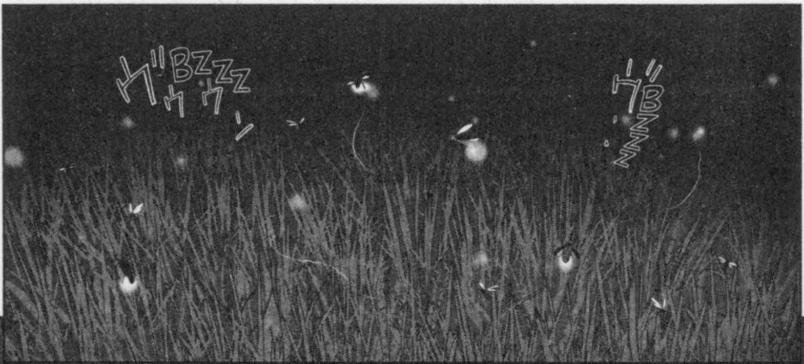
BZZZZ
BZZZZ
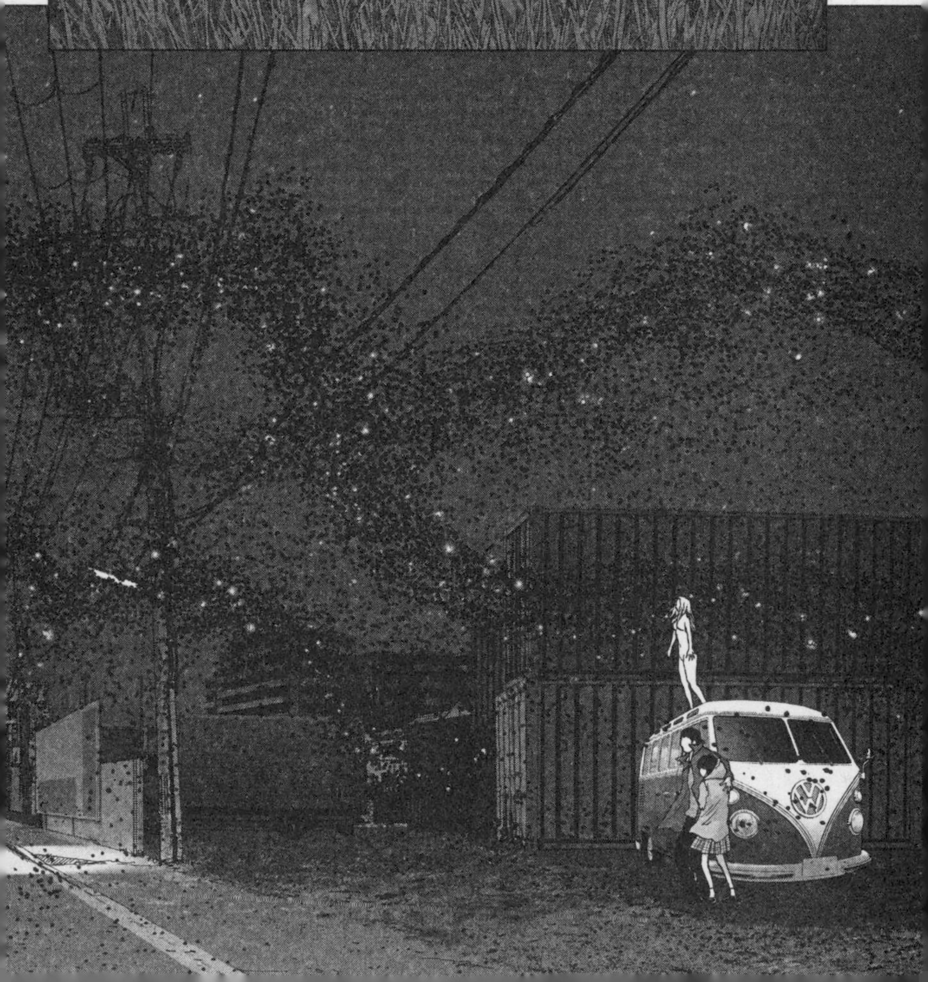

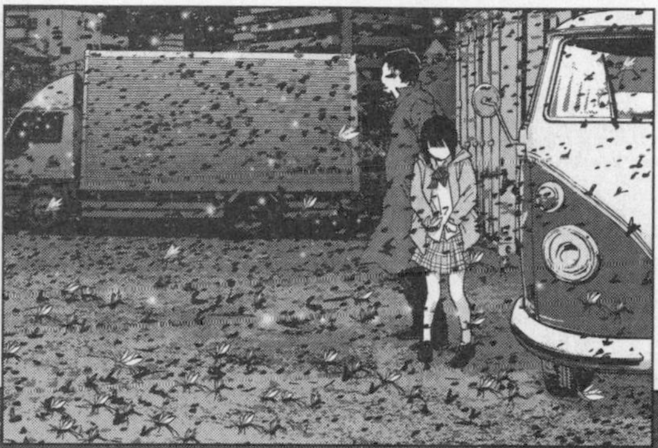
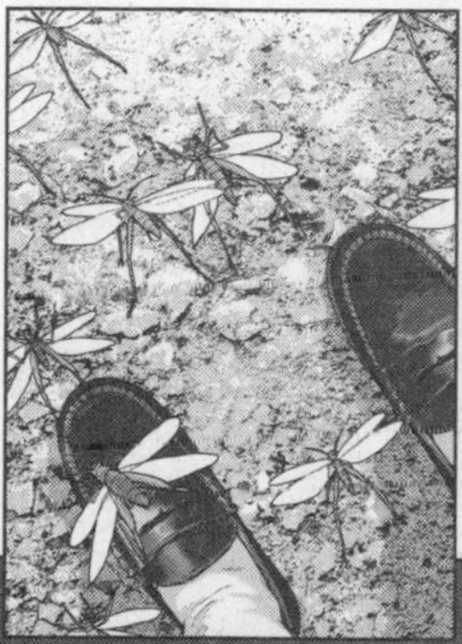
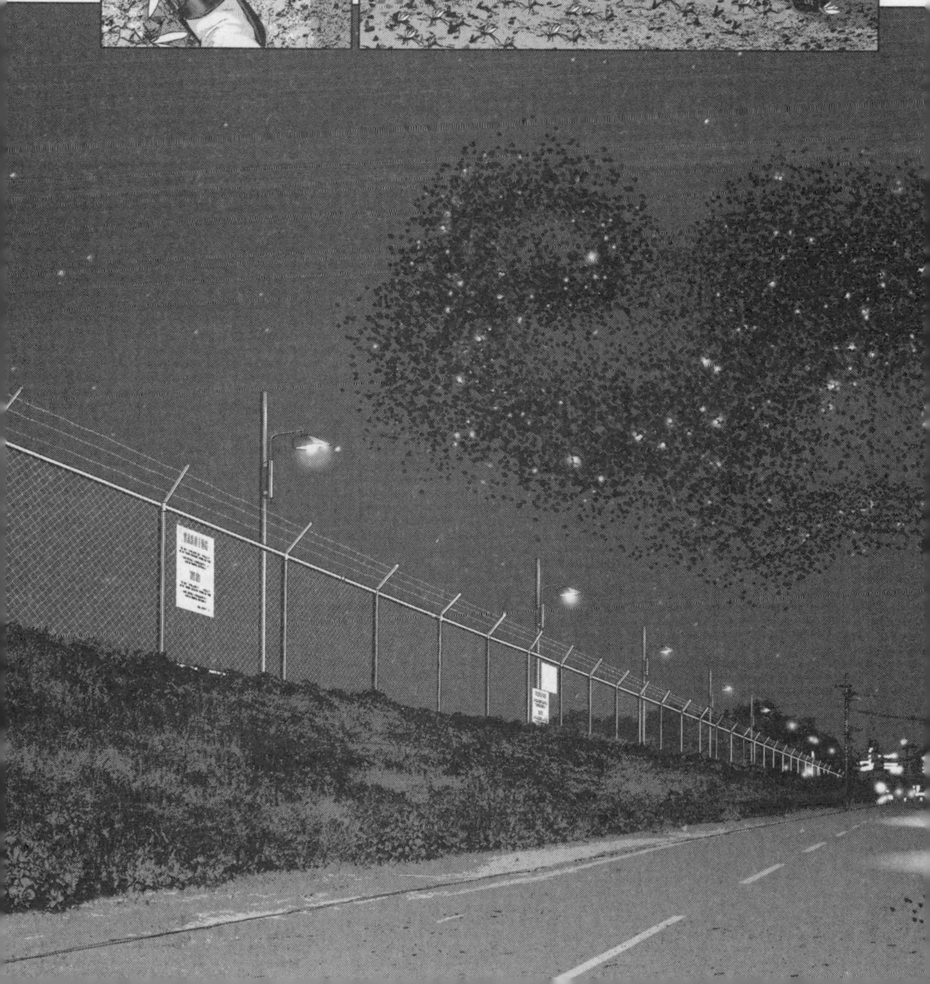

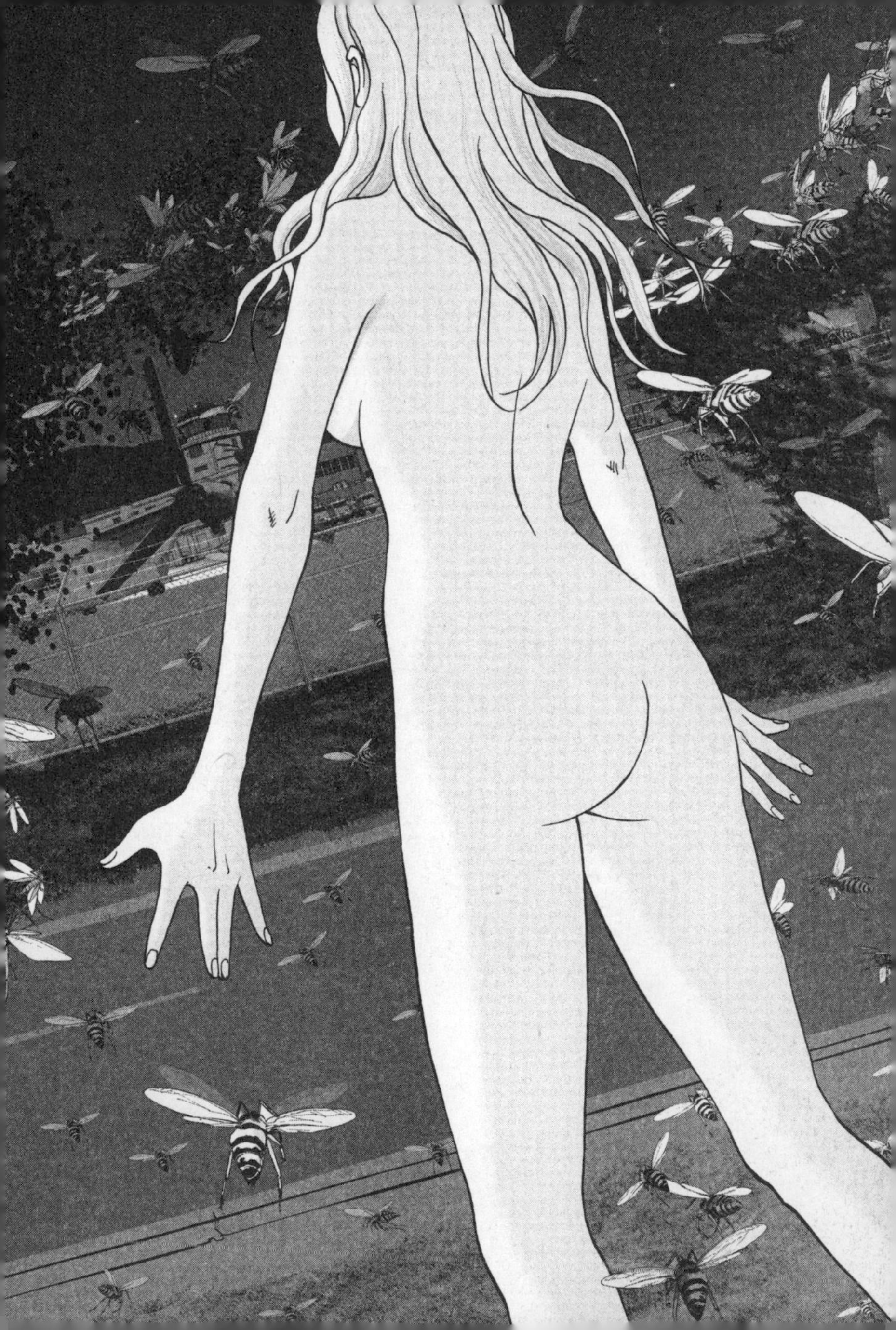

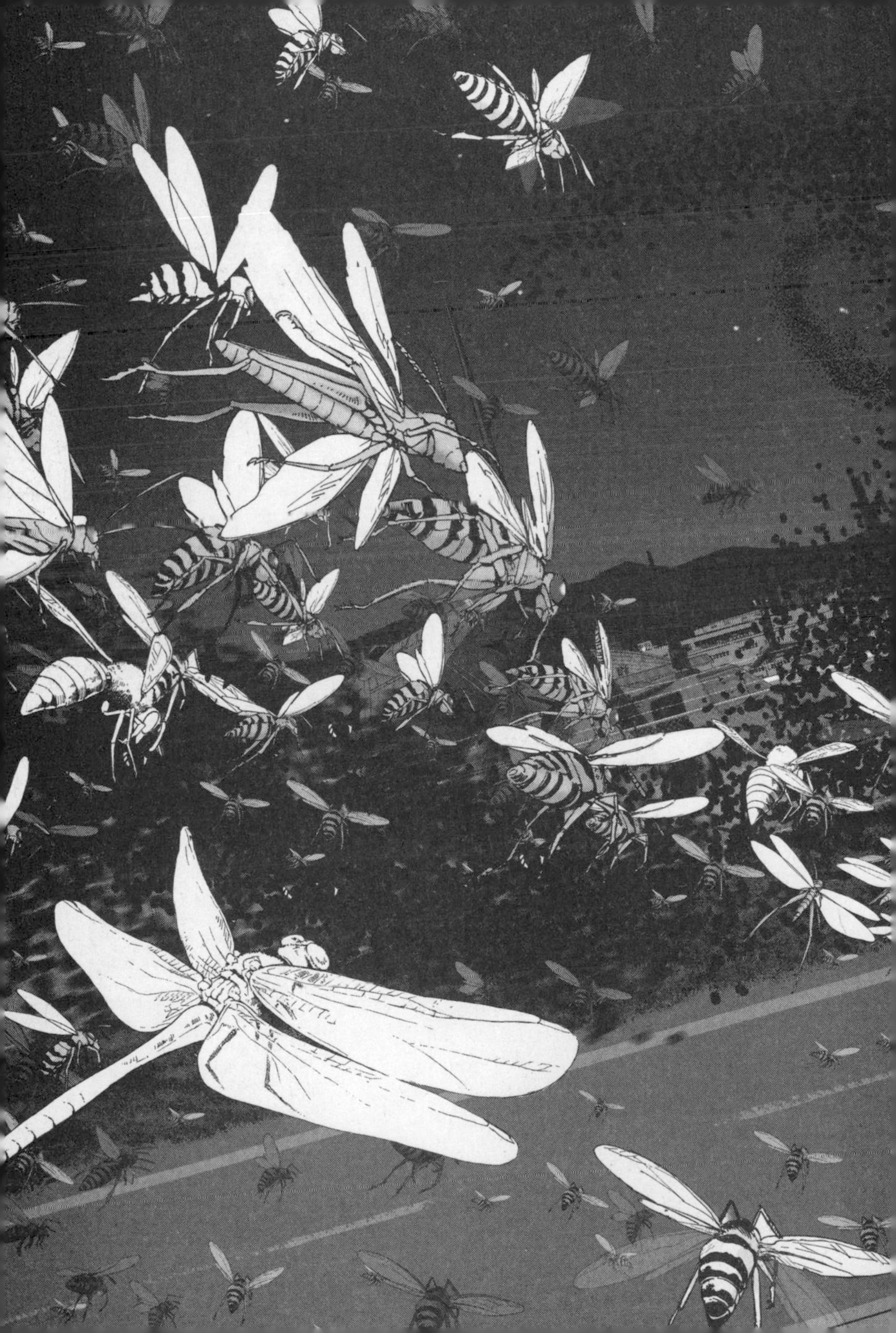

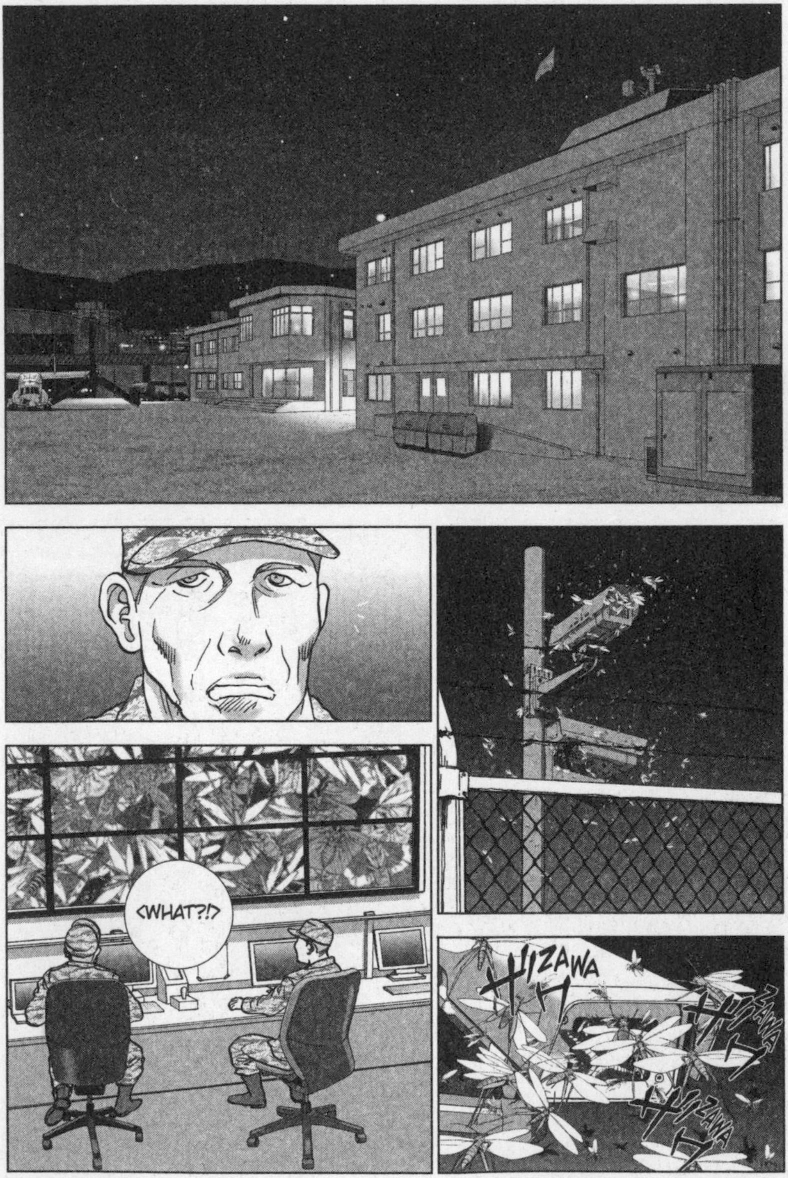
ZAWA
ZAWA
ZAWA
<WHAT?!>

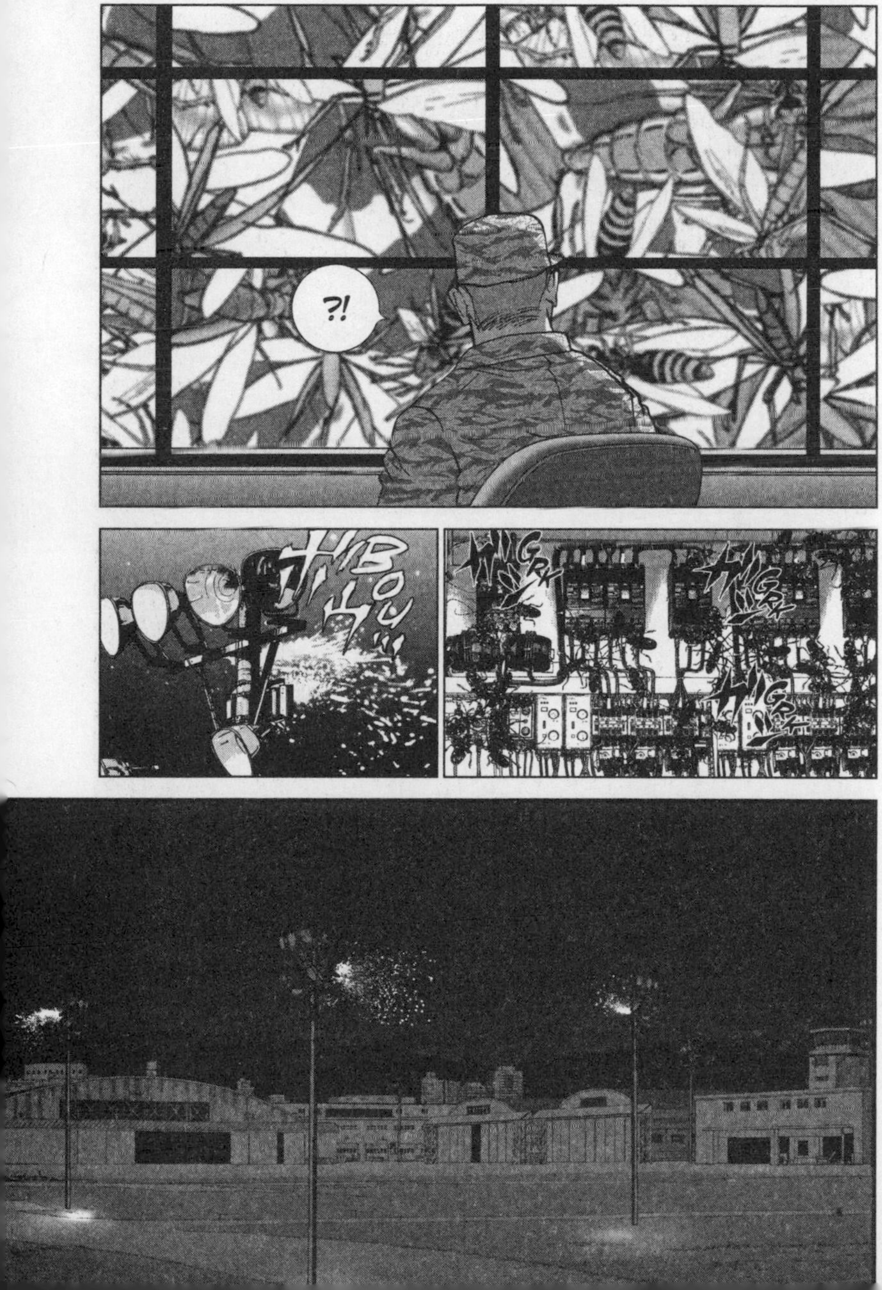
?!
GRK
GRK
GRK
BOUM...

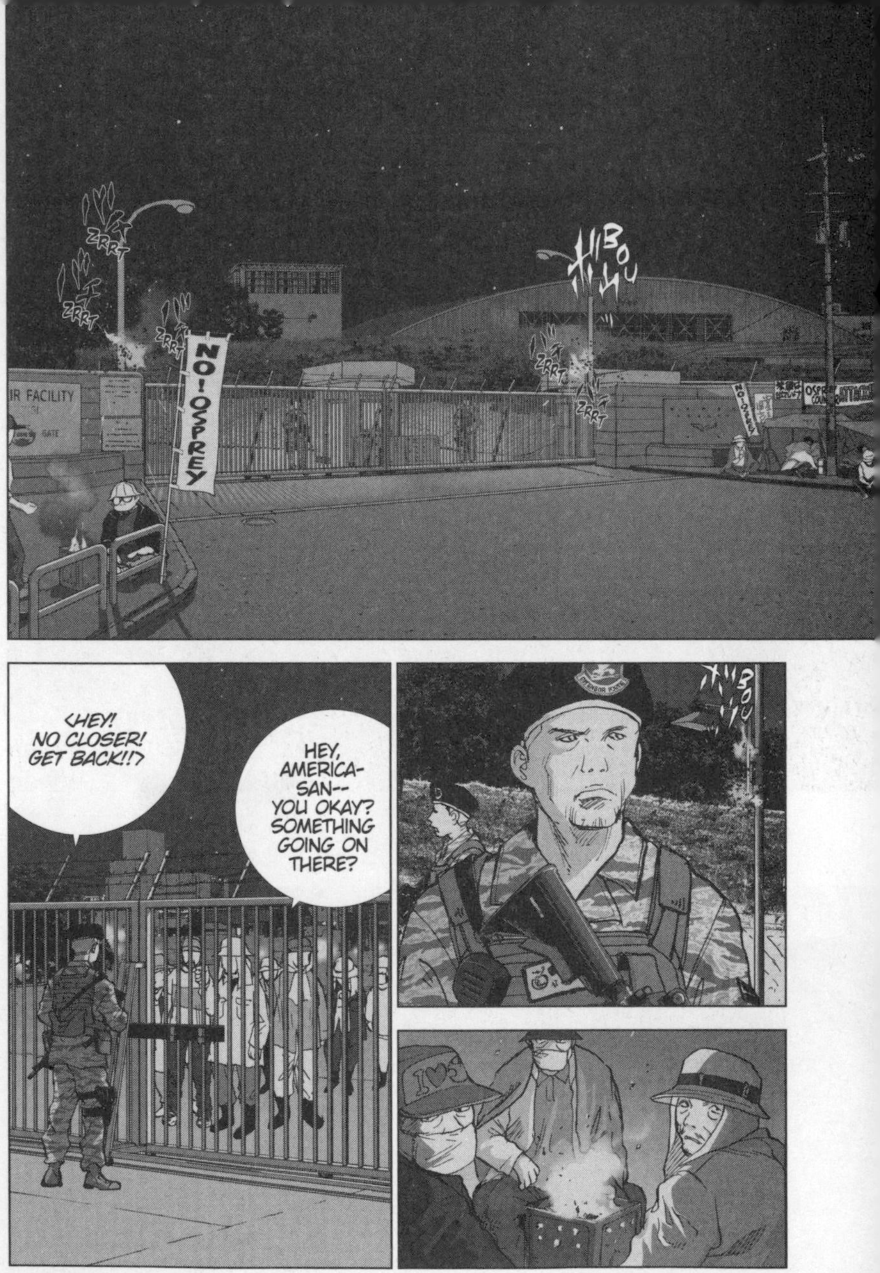
ZRRT
ZRRT
ZRRT
BOU
ZRRT
ZRRT
NO! OSPREY
IR FACILITY
GATE
NO! OSPREY
BOU
HEY, AMERICA-SAN-- YOU OKAY? SOMETHING GOING ON THERE?
<HEY! NO CLOSER! GET BACK!!>

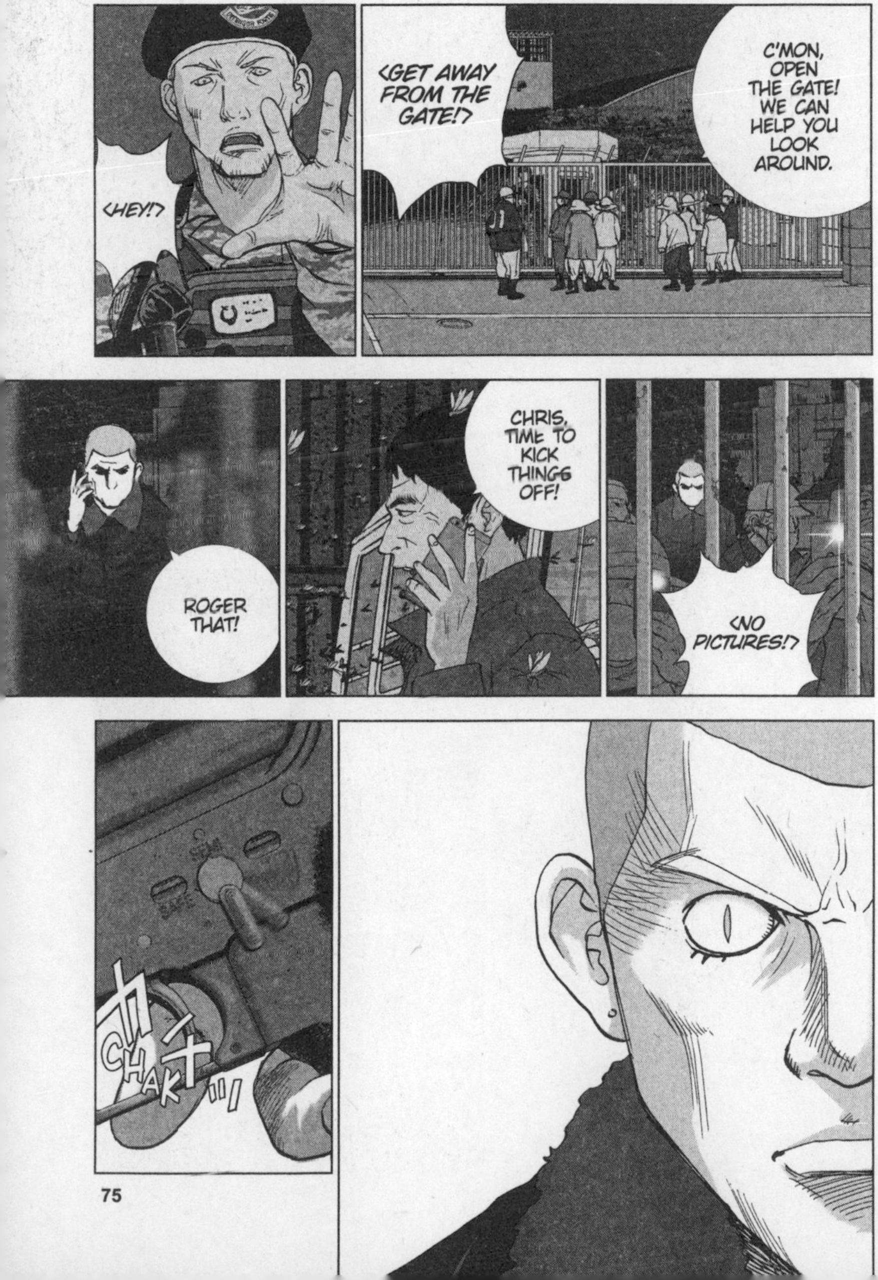
C'MON, OPEN THE GATE! WE CAN HELP YOU LOOK AROUND.
<GET AWAY FROM THE GATE!>
<HEY!>
<NO PICTURES!>
CHRIS, TIME TO KICK THINGS OFF!
ROGER THAT!
CHAK

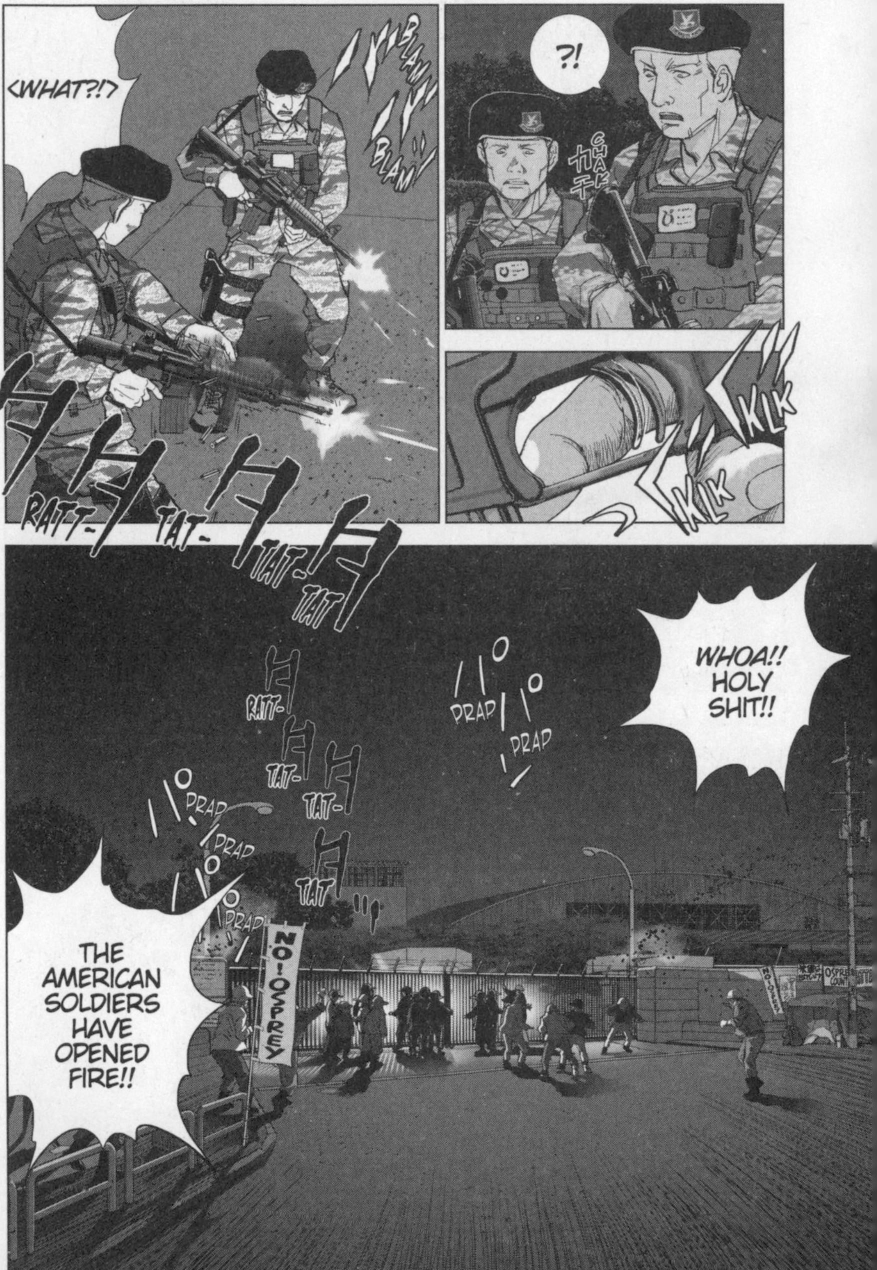
?!
CHAK
KLK
KLK
<WHAT?!?>
BLAM
BLAM!!
RATT- TAT- TAT- TAT
WHOA!! HOLY SHIT!!
PRAP PRAP
RATT- TAT- TAT- TAT
PRAP PRAP PRAP
THE AMERICAN SOLDIERS HAVE OPENED FIRE!!
NO! OSPREY

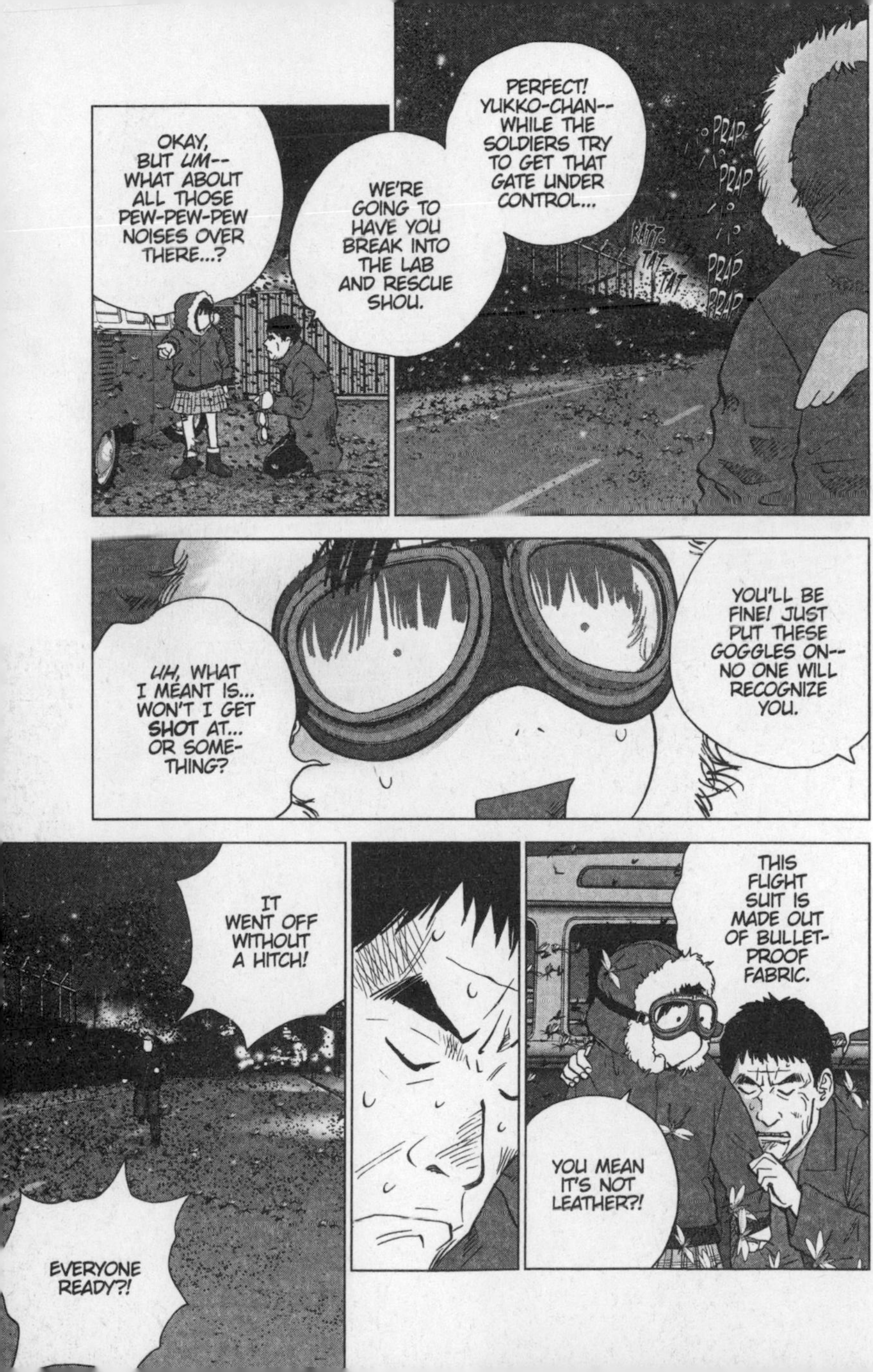
PERFECT! YUKKO-CHAN-- WHILE THE SOLDIERS TRY TO GET THAT GATE UNDER CONTROL...
PRAP PRAP PRAP PRAP
RATT-TAT-TAT
WE'RE GOING TO HAVE YOU BREAK INTO THE LAB AND RESCUE SHOU.
OKAY, BUT *UM*-- WHAT ABOUT ALL THOSE PEW-PEW-PEW NOISES OVER THERE...?
YOU'LL BE FINE! JUST PUT THESE GOGGLES ON-- NO ONE WILL RECOGNIZE YOU.
UH, WHAT I MEANT IS... WON'T I GET SHOT AT... OR SOME-THING?
THIS FLIGHT SUIT IS MADE OUT OF BULLET-PROOF FABRIC.
YOU MEAN IT'S NOT LEATHER?!
IT WENT OFF WITHOUT A HITCH!
EVERYONE READY?!

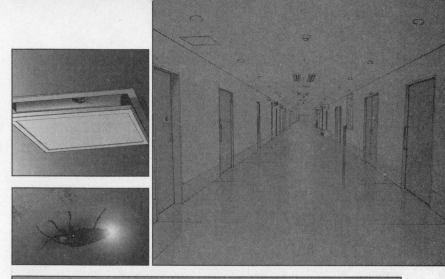

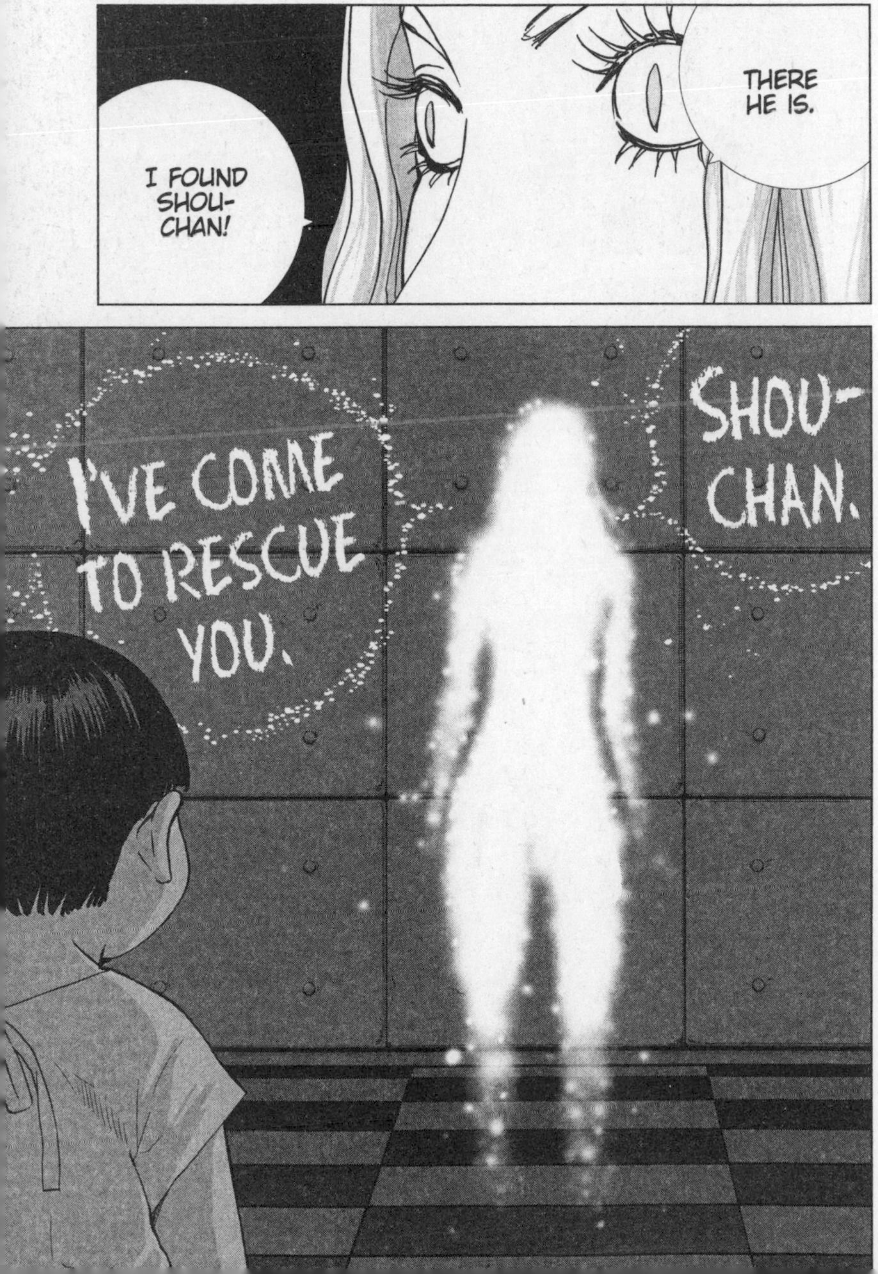
THERE HE IS.
I FOUND SHOU-CHAN!
SHOU-CHAN.
I'VE COME TO RESCUE YOU.

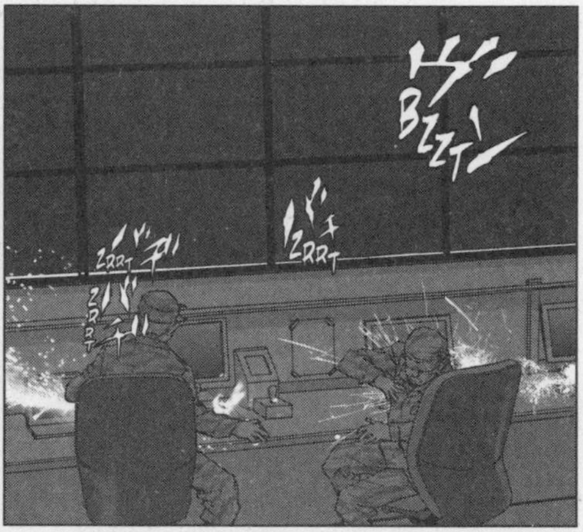
BZZT
ZRRT
ZRRT
ZRRT
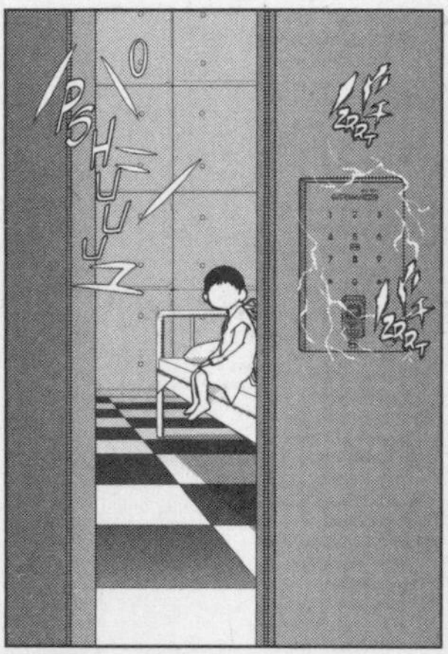
PSHUUU
ZRRT
ZRRT
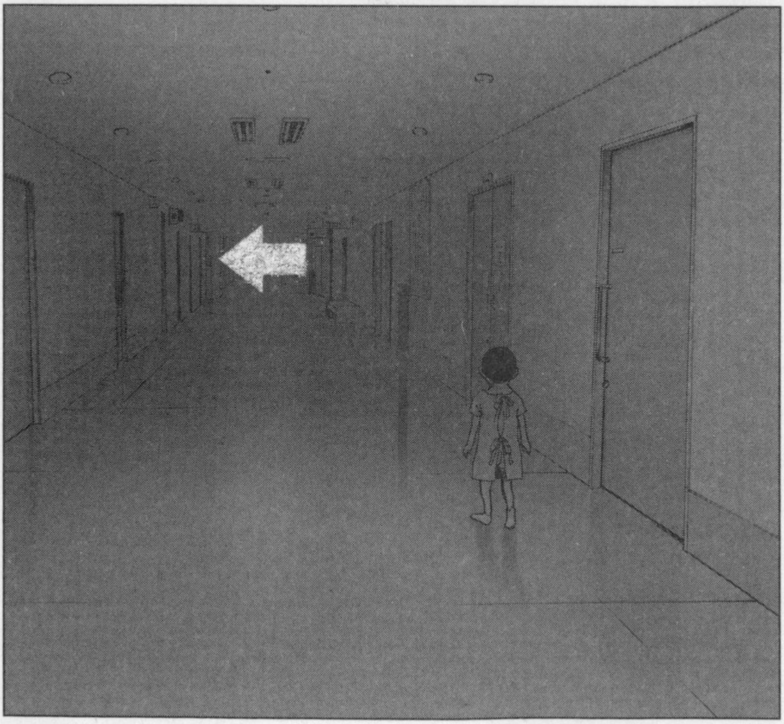

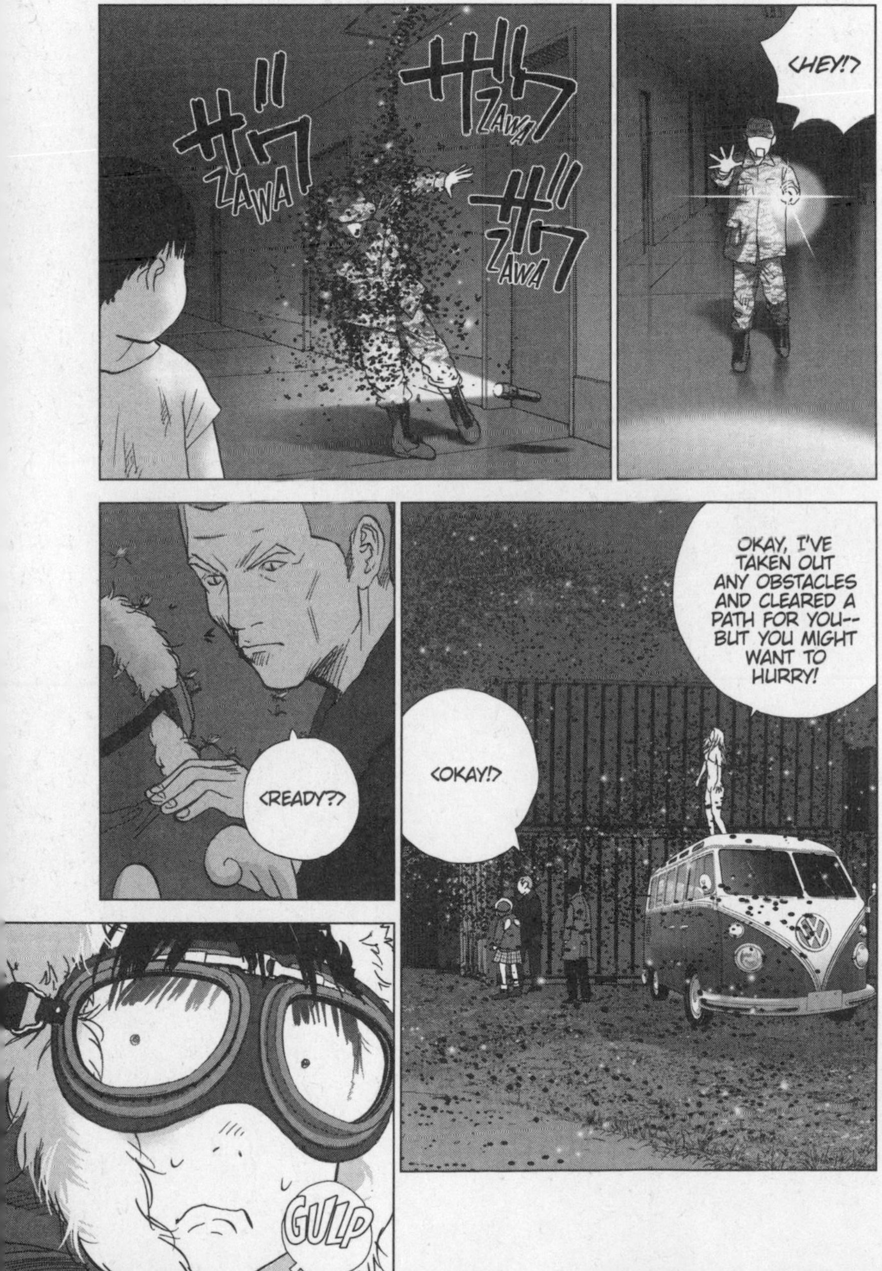
<HEY!>
ザワ ZAWA
ザワ ZAWA
ザワ ZAWA
OKAY, I'VE TAKEN OUT ANY OBSTACLES AND CLEARED A PATH FOR YOU-- BUT YOU MIGHT WANT TO HURRY!
<OKAY!>
<READY?>
GULP

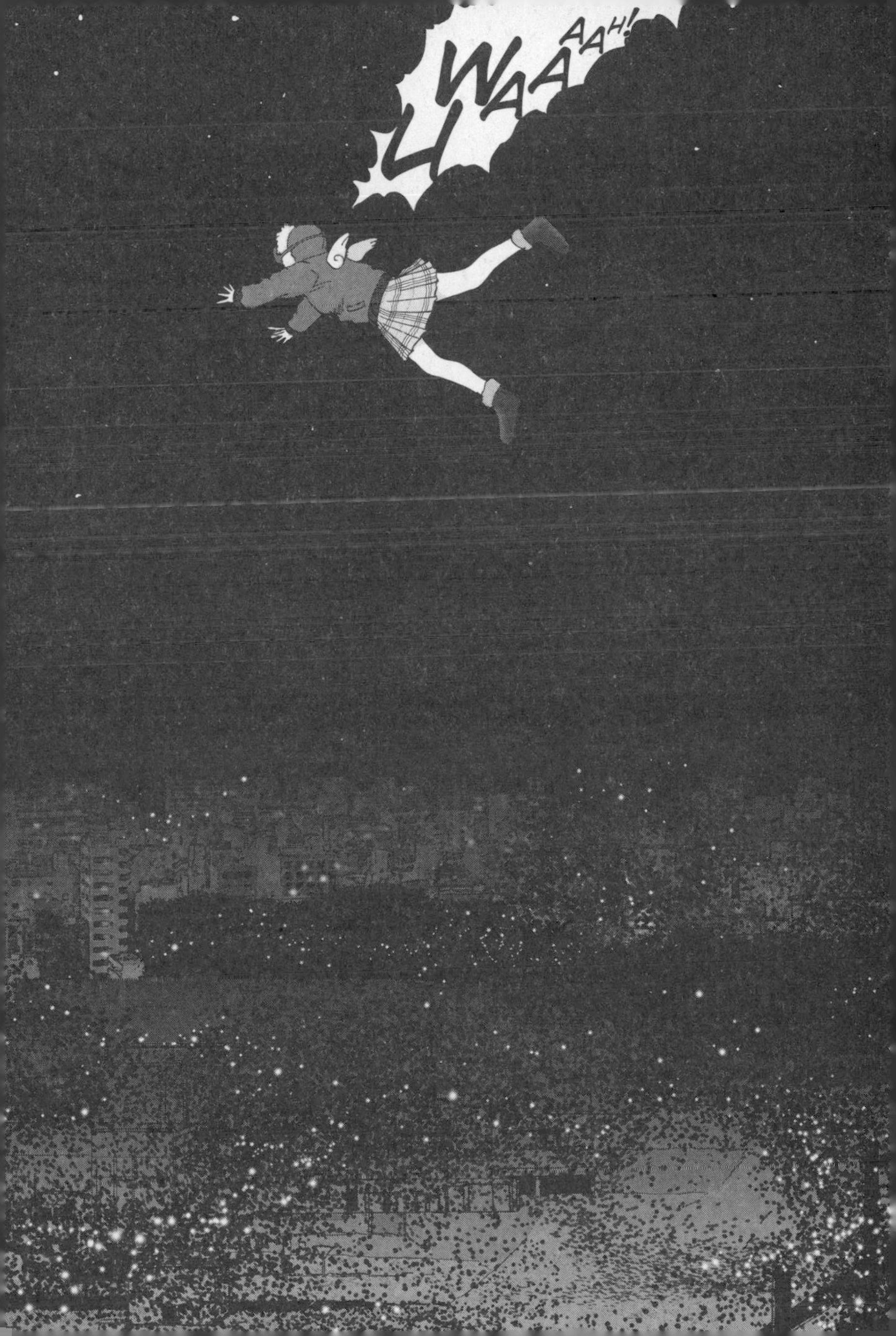
UWAAAAH!

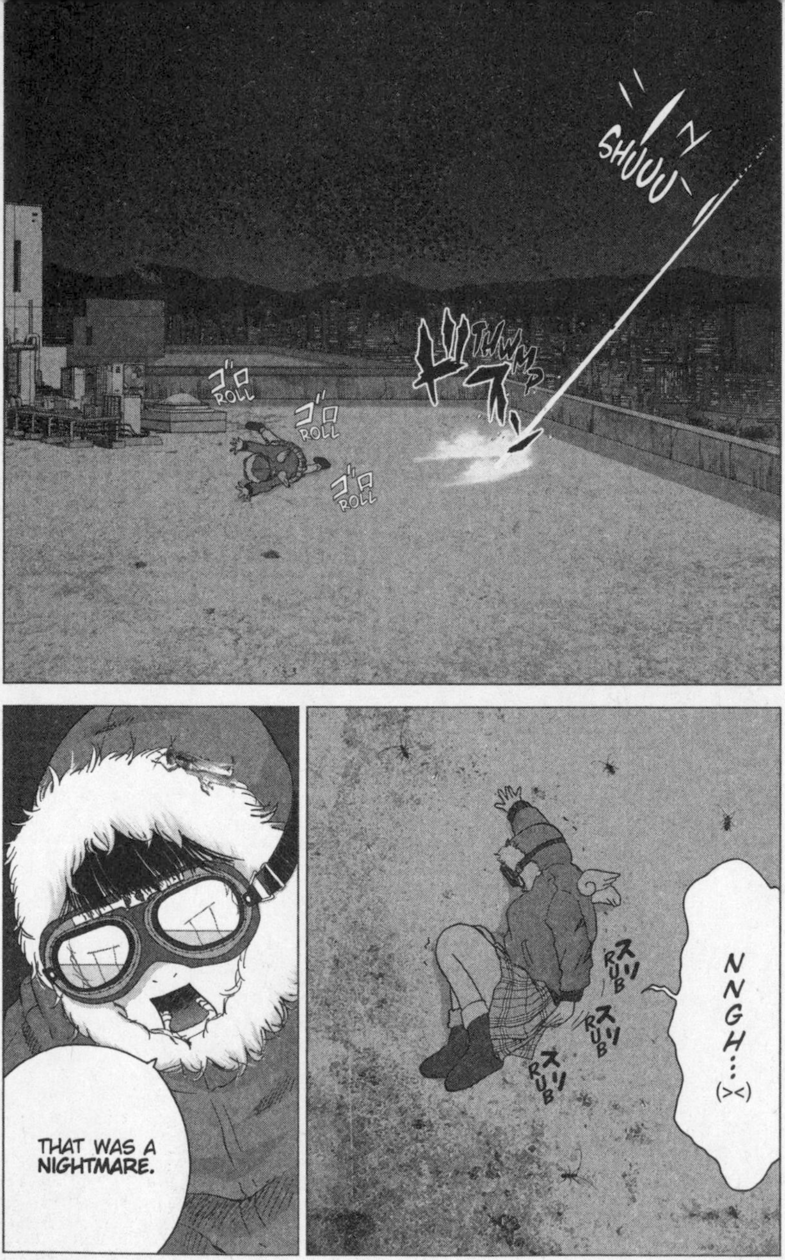
SHUUU
THWMP
ゴロ ROLL
ゴロ ROLL
ゴロ ROLL
NNGH... (><)
スリ RUB
スリ RUB
スリ RUB
THAT WAS A NIGHTMARE.

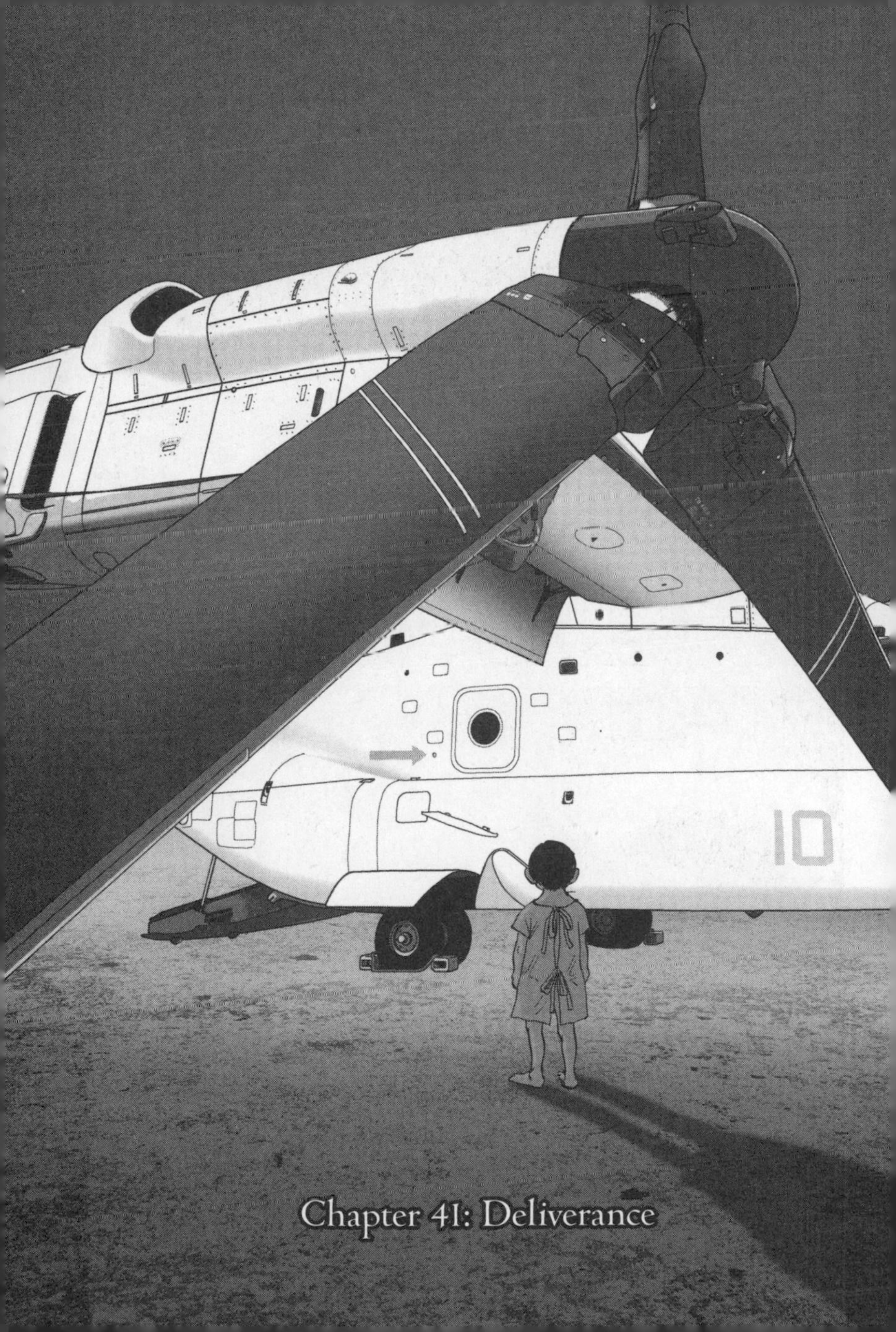
10

Chapter 41: Deliverance

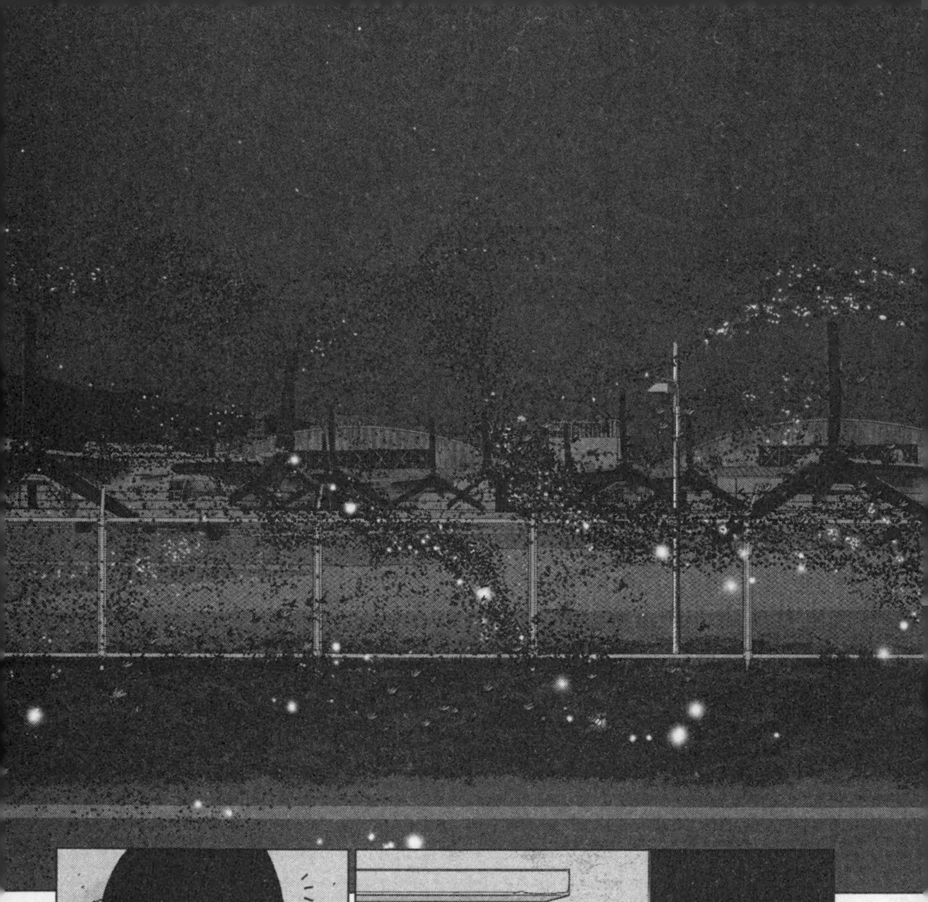

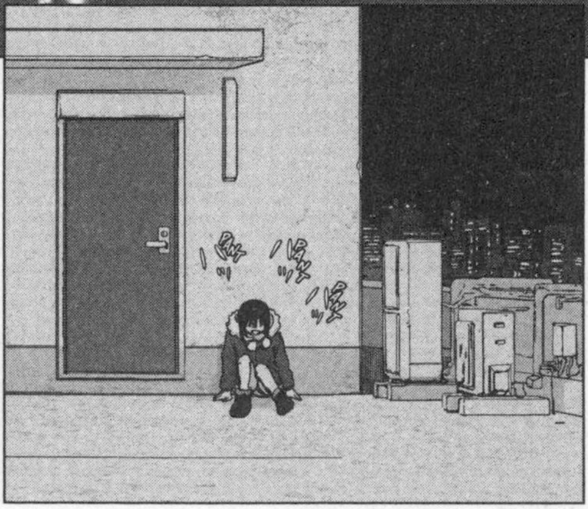
PANT
PANT
PANT

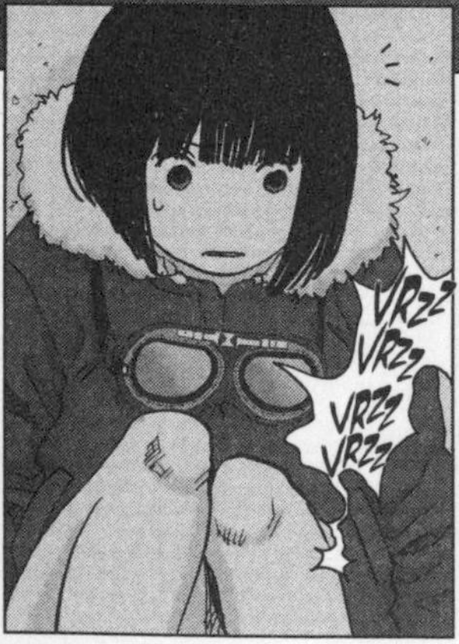
VRZZ
VRZZ
VRZZ
VRZZ

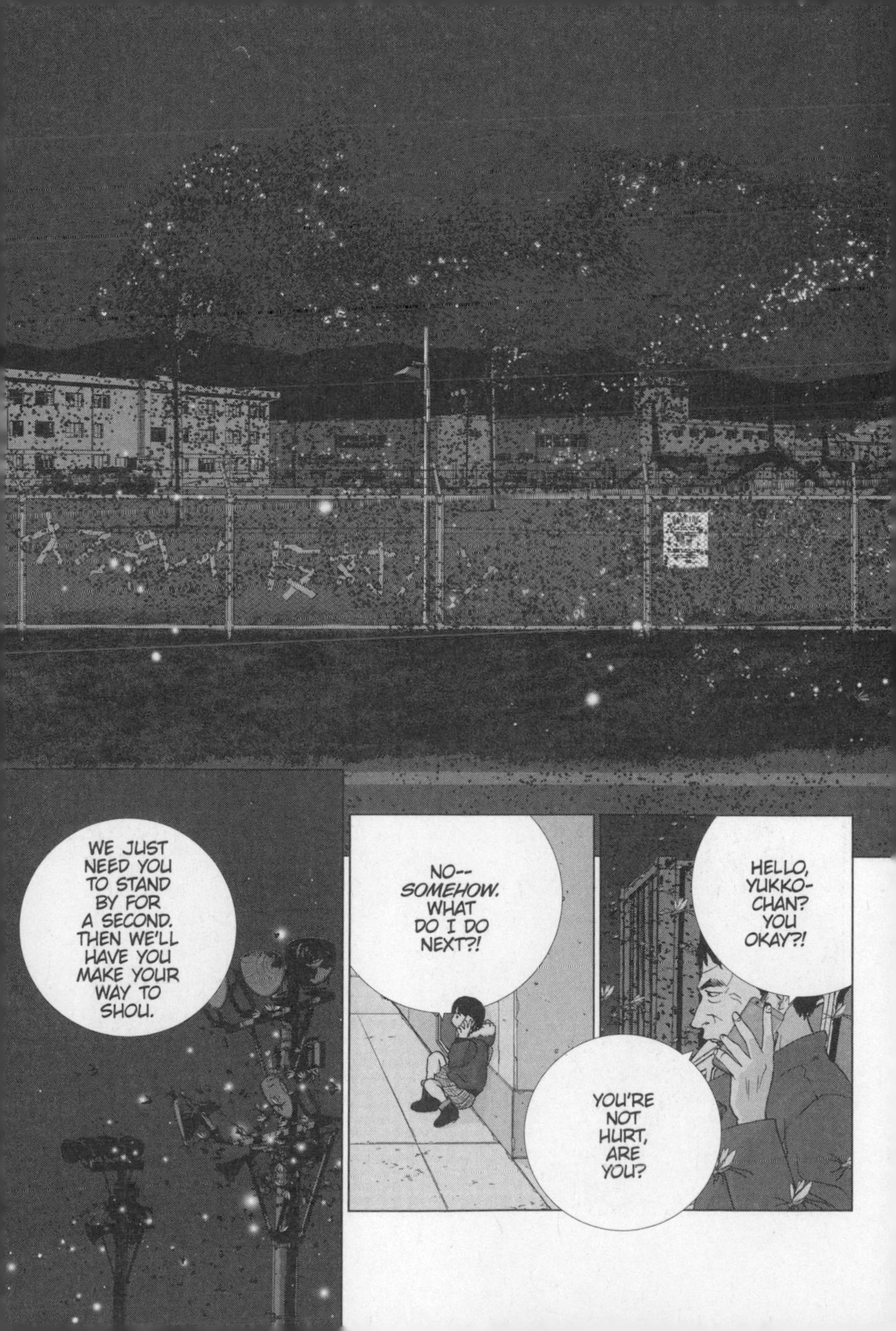
HELLO, YUKKO-CHAN? YOU OKAY?!
YOU'RE NOT HURT, ARE YOU?
NO-- *SOMEHOW.* WHAT DO I DO NEXT?!
WE JUST NEED YOU TO STAND BY FOR A SECOND. THEN WE'LL HAVE YOU MAKE YOUR WAY TO SHOU.

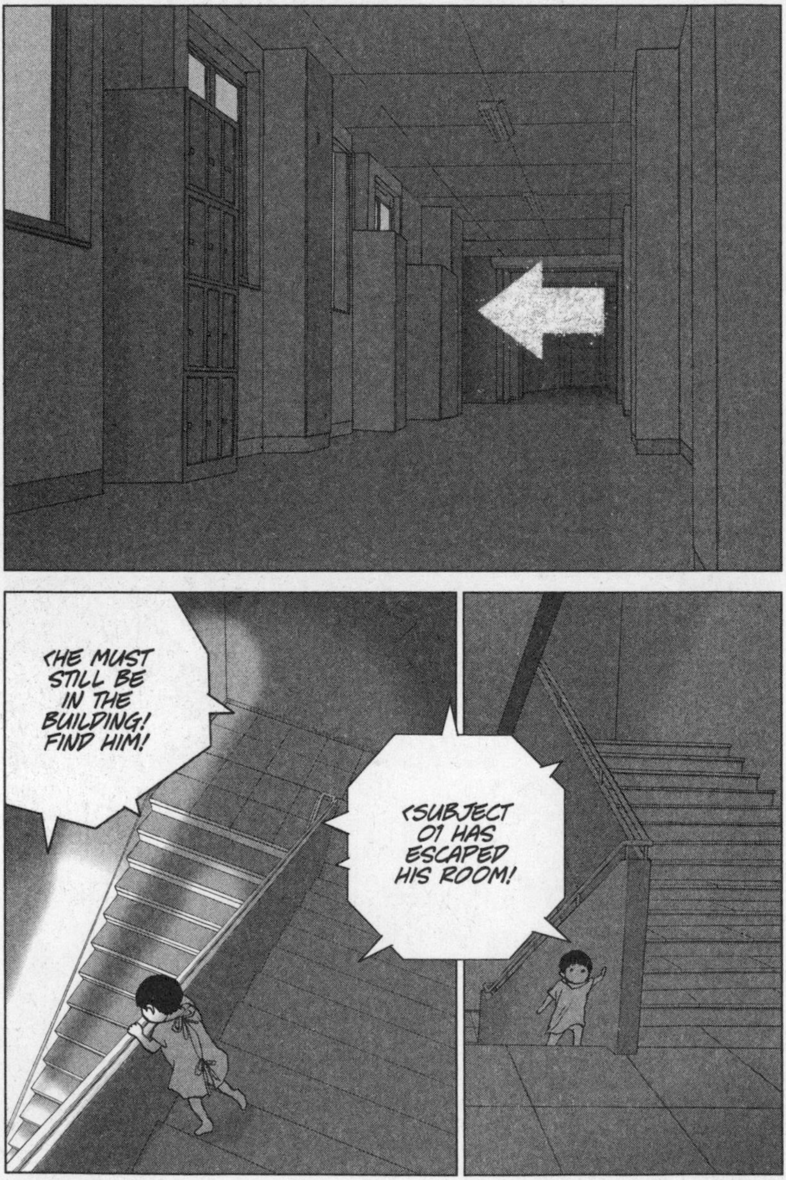
<SUBJECT 01 HAS ESCAPED HIS ROOM!
<HE MUST STILL BE IN THE BUILDING! FIND HIM!

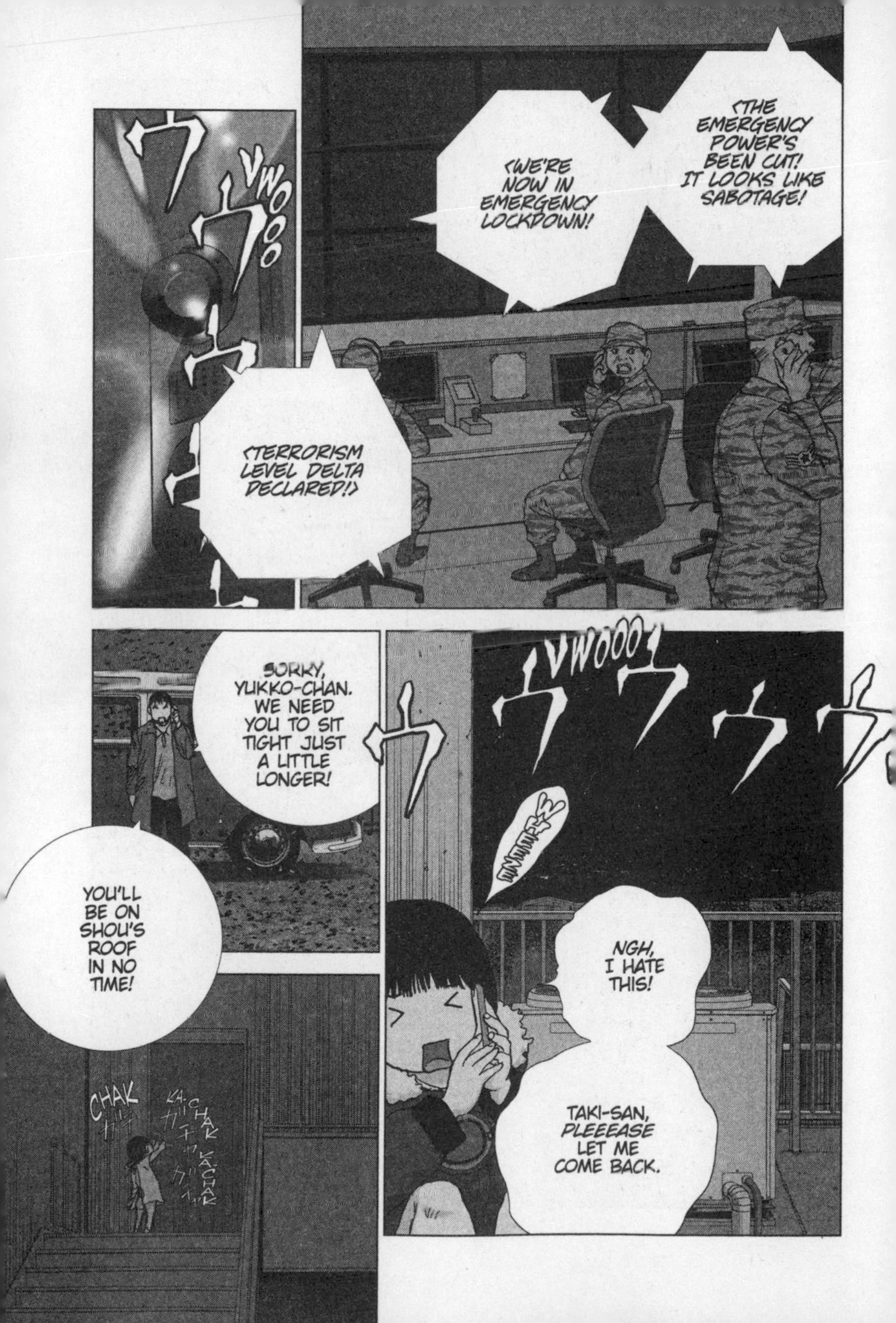

<THE EMERGENCY POWER'S BEEN CUT! IT LOOKS LIKE SABOTAGE!
<WE'RE NOW IN EMERGENCY LOCKDOWN!
<TERRORISM LEVEL DELTA DECLARED!>
VWOOO
VWOOO
NGH, I HATE THIS!
TAKI-SAN, PLEEEASE LET ME COME BACK.
SORRY, YUKKO-CHAN. WE NEED YOU TO SIT TIGHT JUST A LITTLE LONGER!
YOU'LL BE ON SHOU'S ROOF IN NO TIME!
CHAK
KA-CHAK KA-CHAK

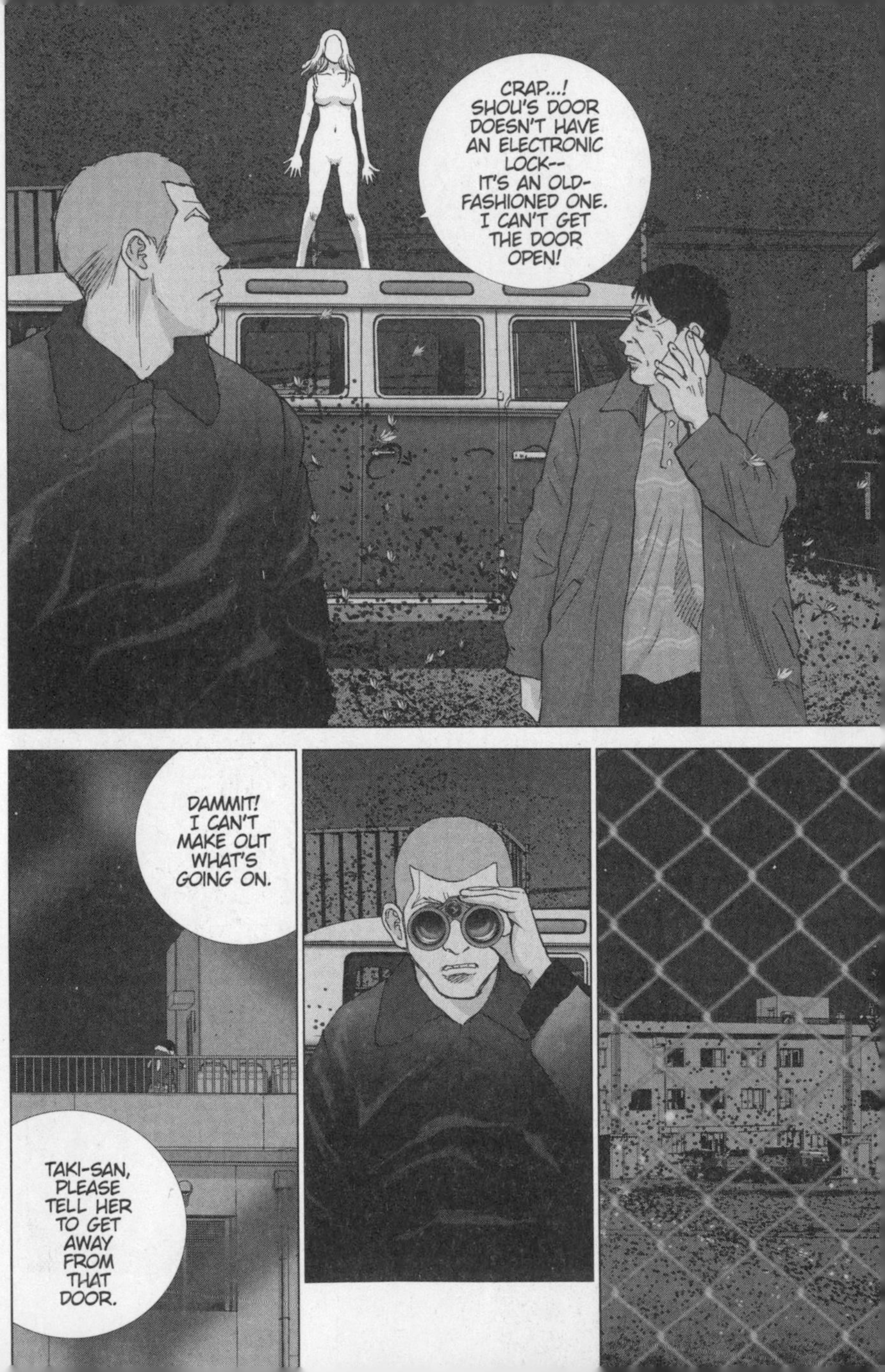
CRAP...! SHOU'S DOOR DOESN'T HAVE AN ELECTRONIC LOCK-- IT'S AN OLD-FASHIONED ONE. I CAN'T GET THE DOOR OPEN!
DAMMIT! I CAN'T MAKE OUT WHAT'S GOING ON.
TAKI-SAN, PLEASE TELL HER TO GET AWAY FROM THAT DOOR.

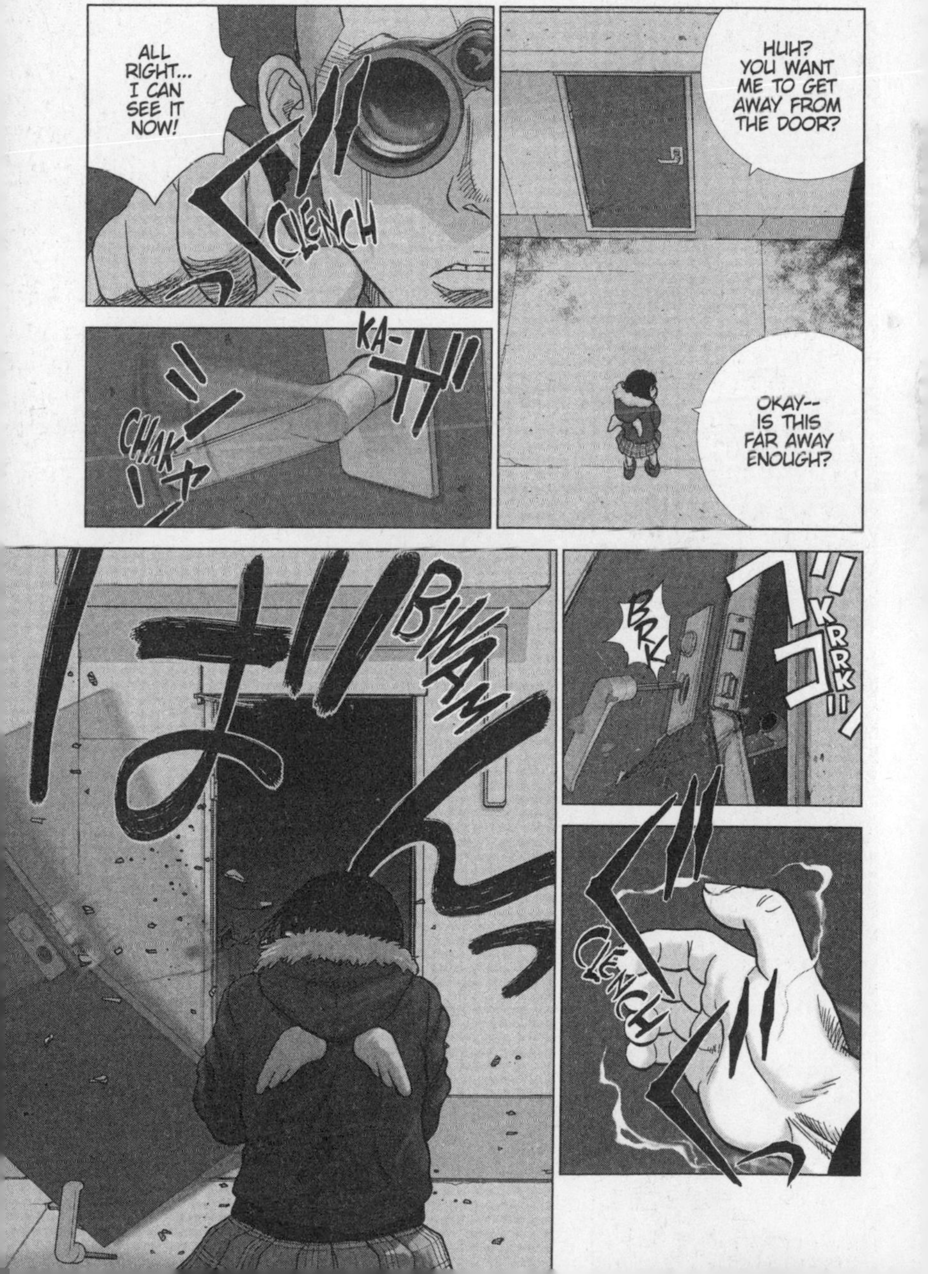
HUH? YOU WANT ME TO GET AWAY FROM THE DOOR?
OKAY-- IS THIS FAR AWAY ENOUGH?
ALL RIGHT... I CAN SEE IT NOW!
CLENCH
KA-
CHAK
KRRK
BRK
CLENCH
BWAM

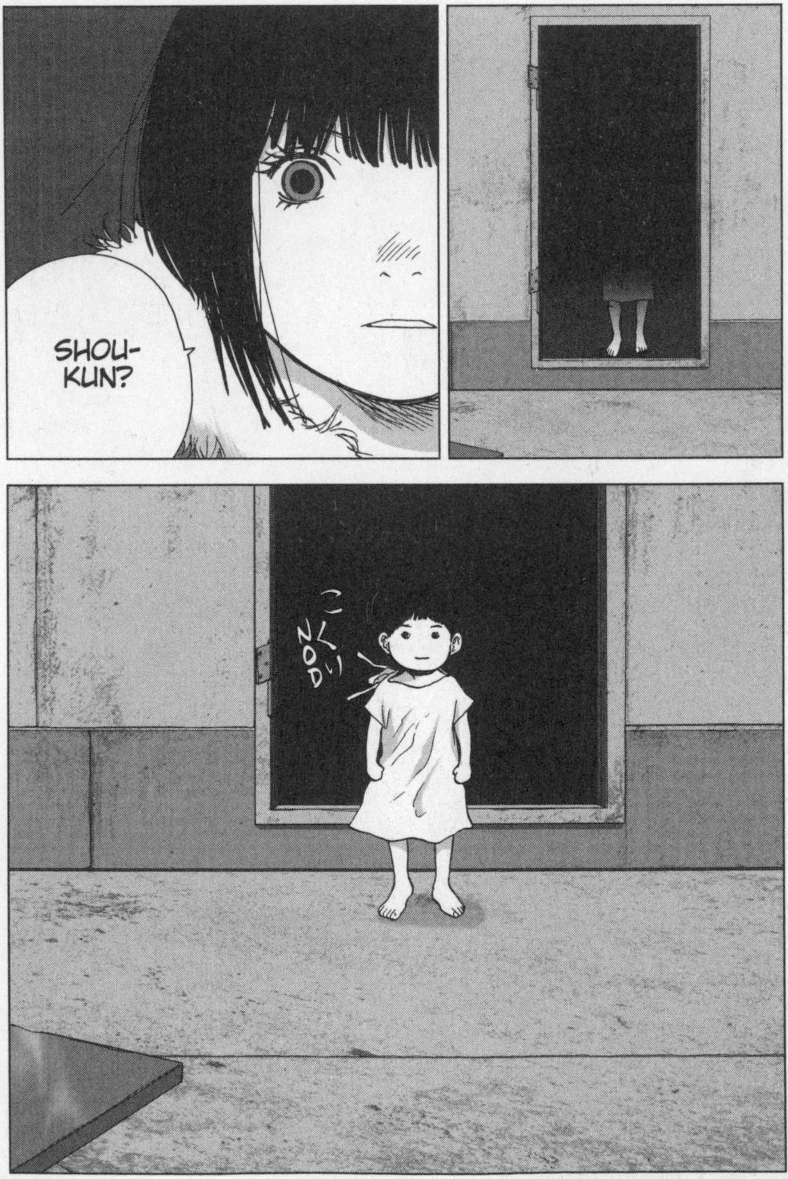
SHOU-KUN?
NOD

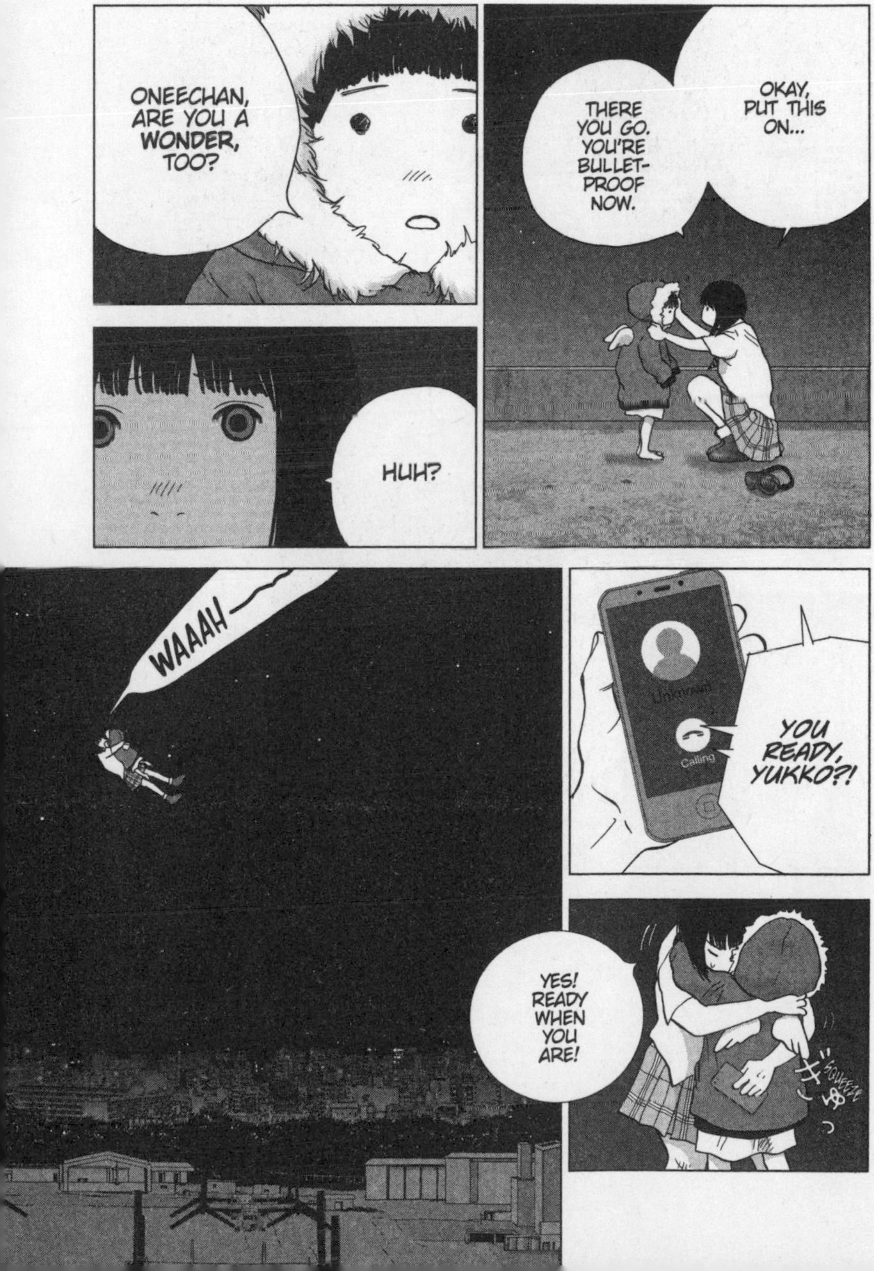
OKAY, PUT THIS ON...
THERE YOU GO. YOU'RE BULLET-PROOF NOW.
ONEECHAN, ARE YOU A WONDER, TOO?
HUH?
YOU READY, YUKKO?!
Calling
YES! READY WHEN YOU ARE!
SQUEEZE
WAAAH

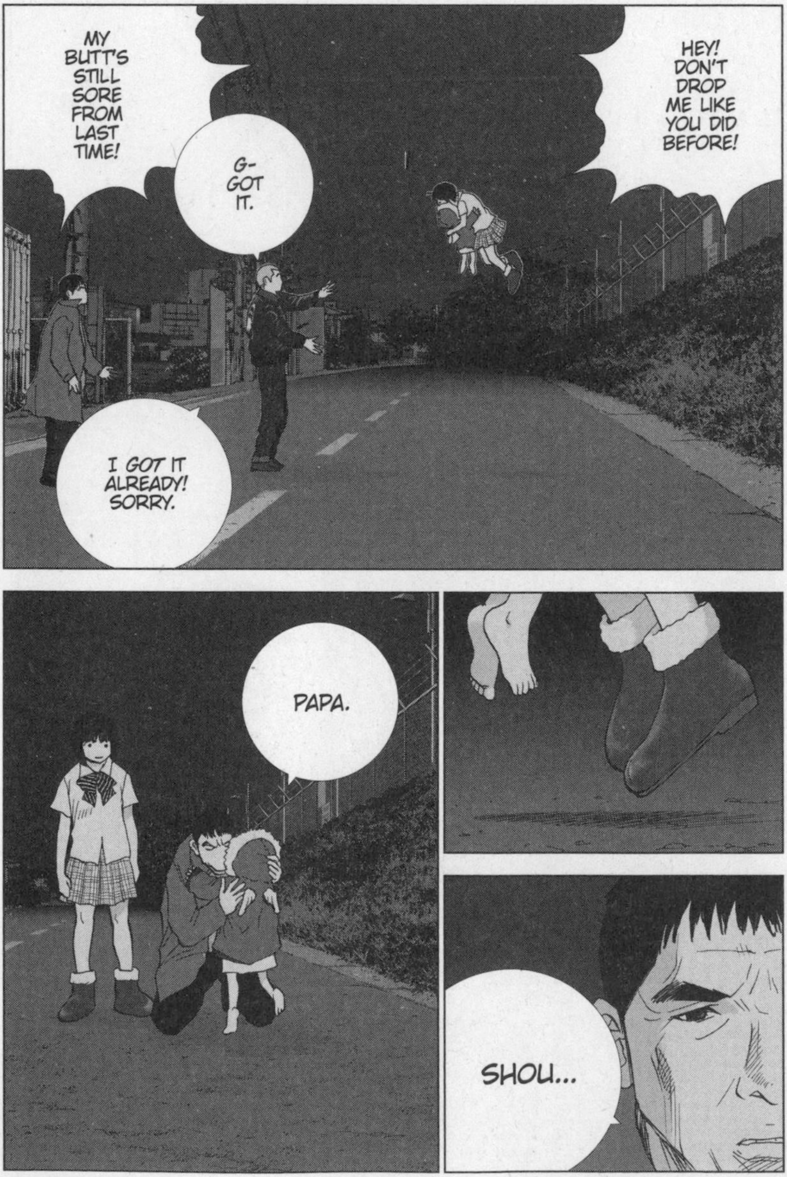
HEY! DON'T DROP ME LIKE YOU DID BEFORE!
MY BUTT'S STILL SORE FROM LAST TIME!
G-GOT IT.
I GOT IT ALREADY! SORRY.
SHOU...
PAPA.

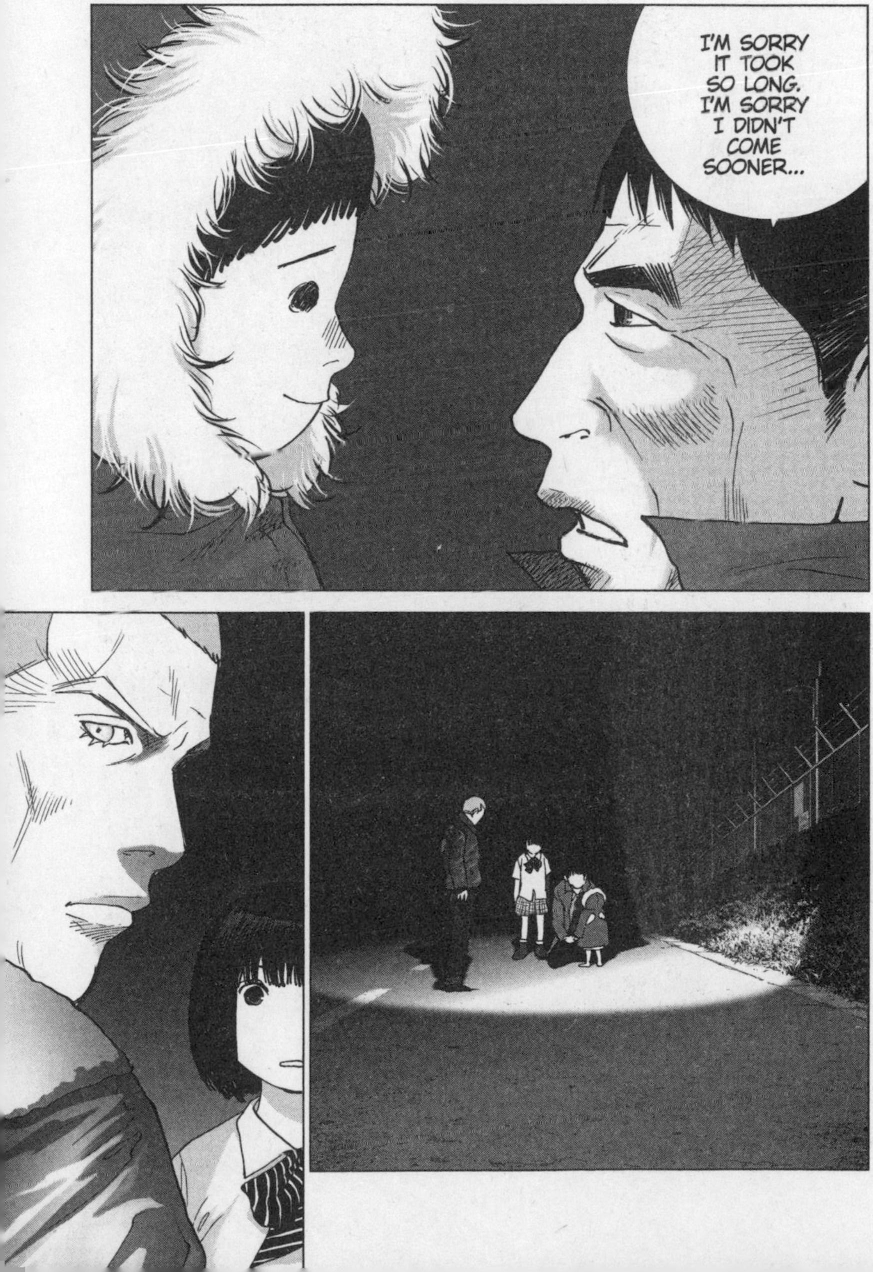
I'M SORRY IT TOOK SO LONG. I'M SORRY I DIDN'T COME SOONER...

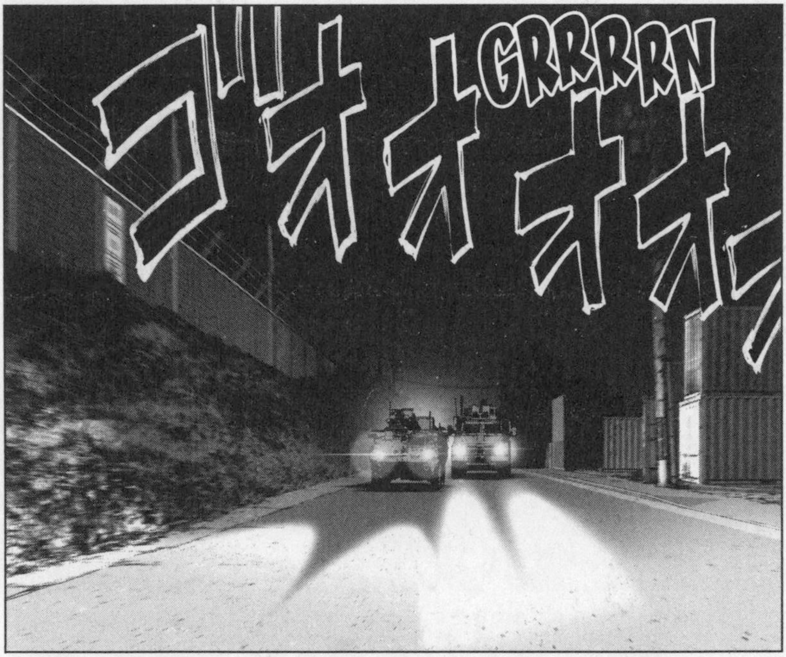
ゴオオオオッ
GRRRRN
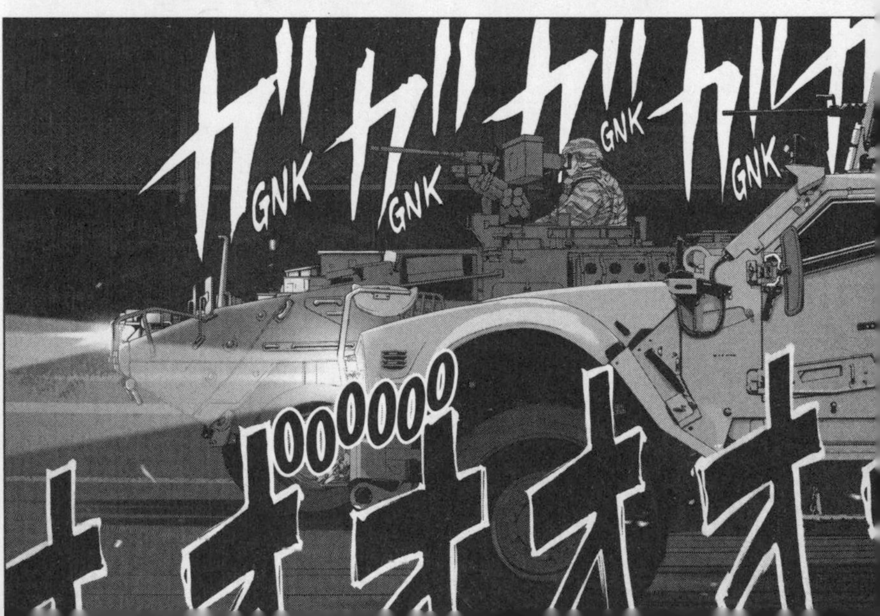
GNK
GNK
GNK
GNK
OOOOOO

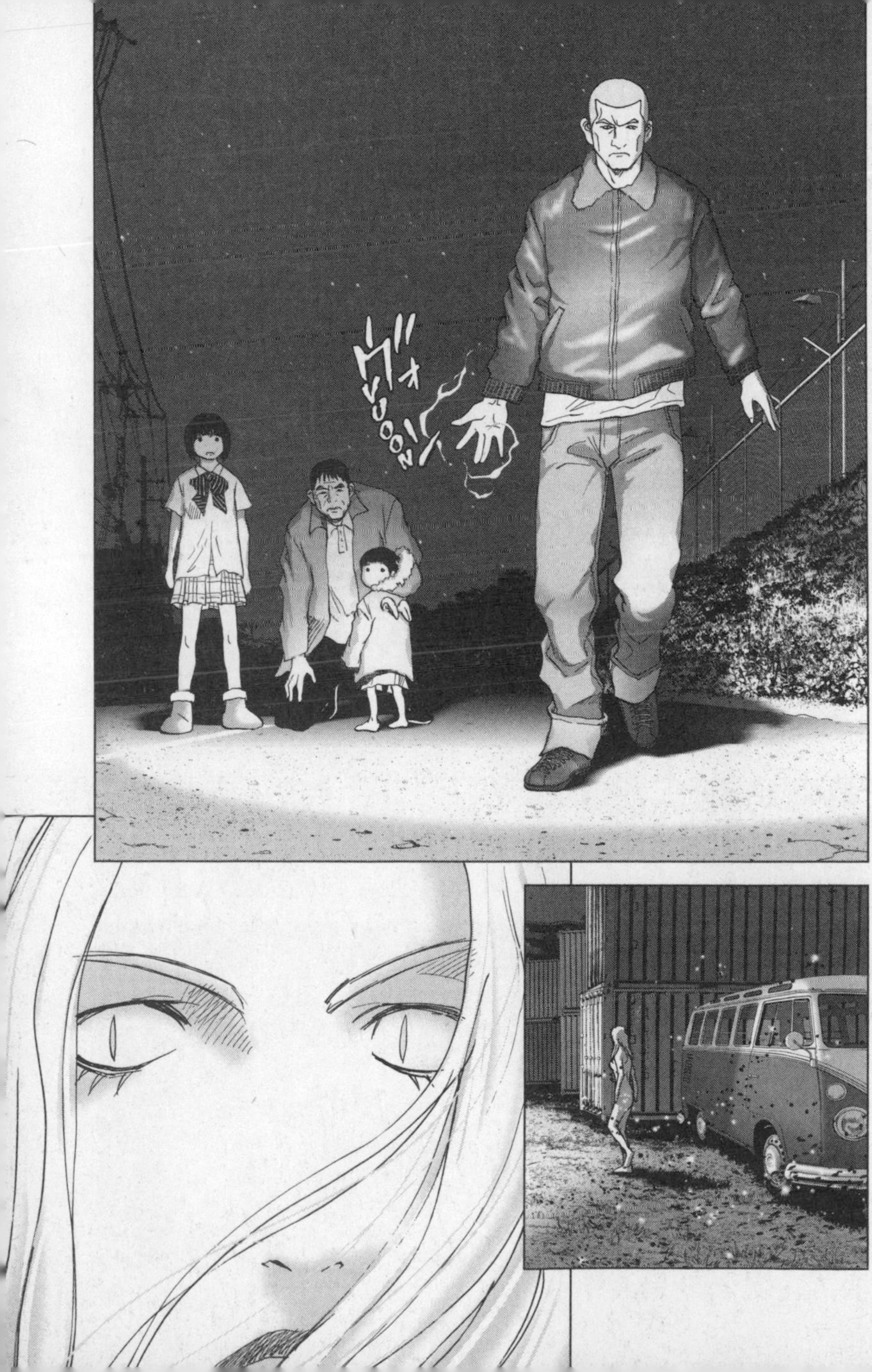
ヴォン
VUOON

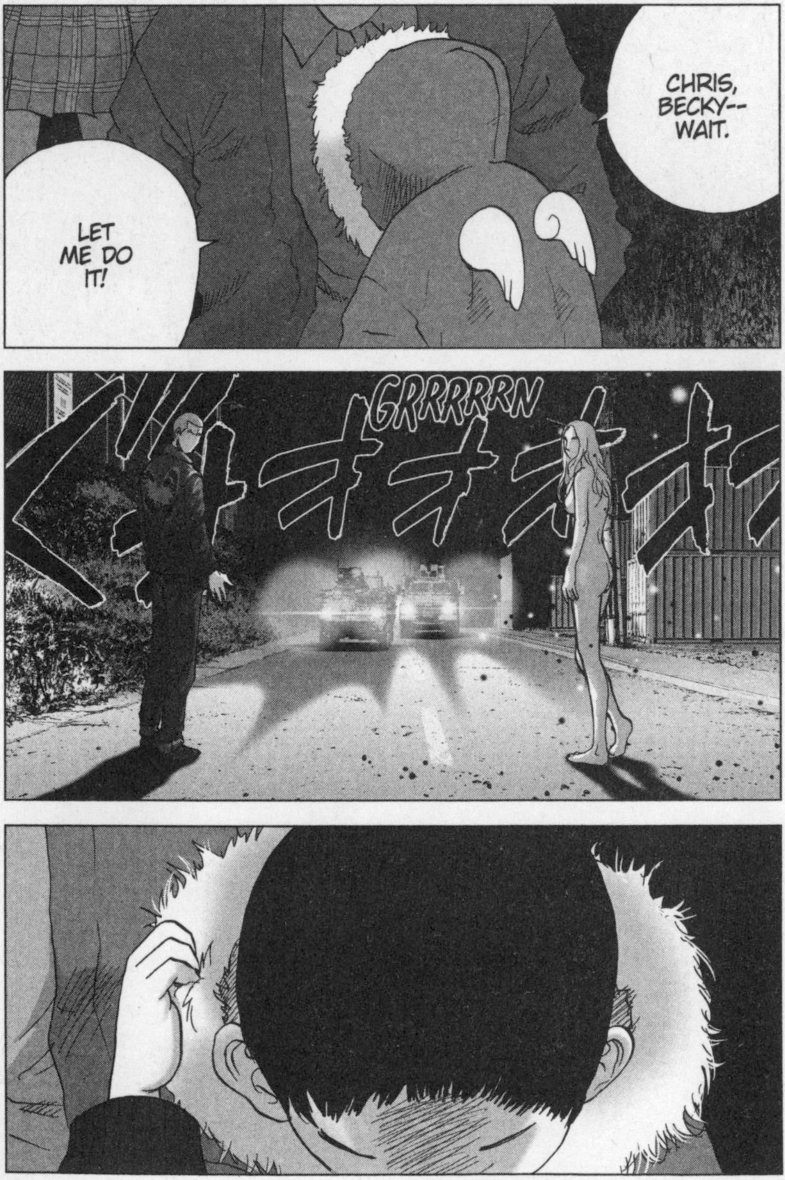
CHRIS, BECKY-- WAIT.
LET ME DO IT!
GRRRRRN

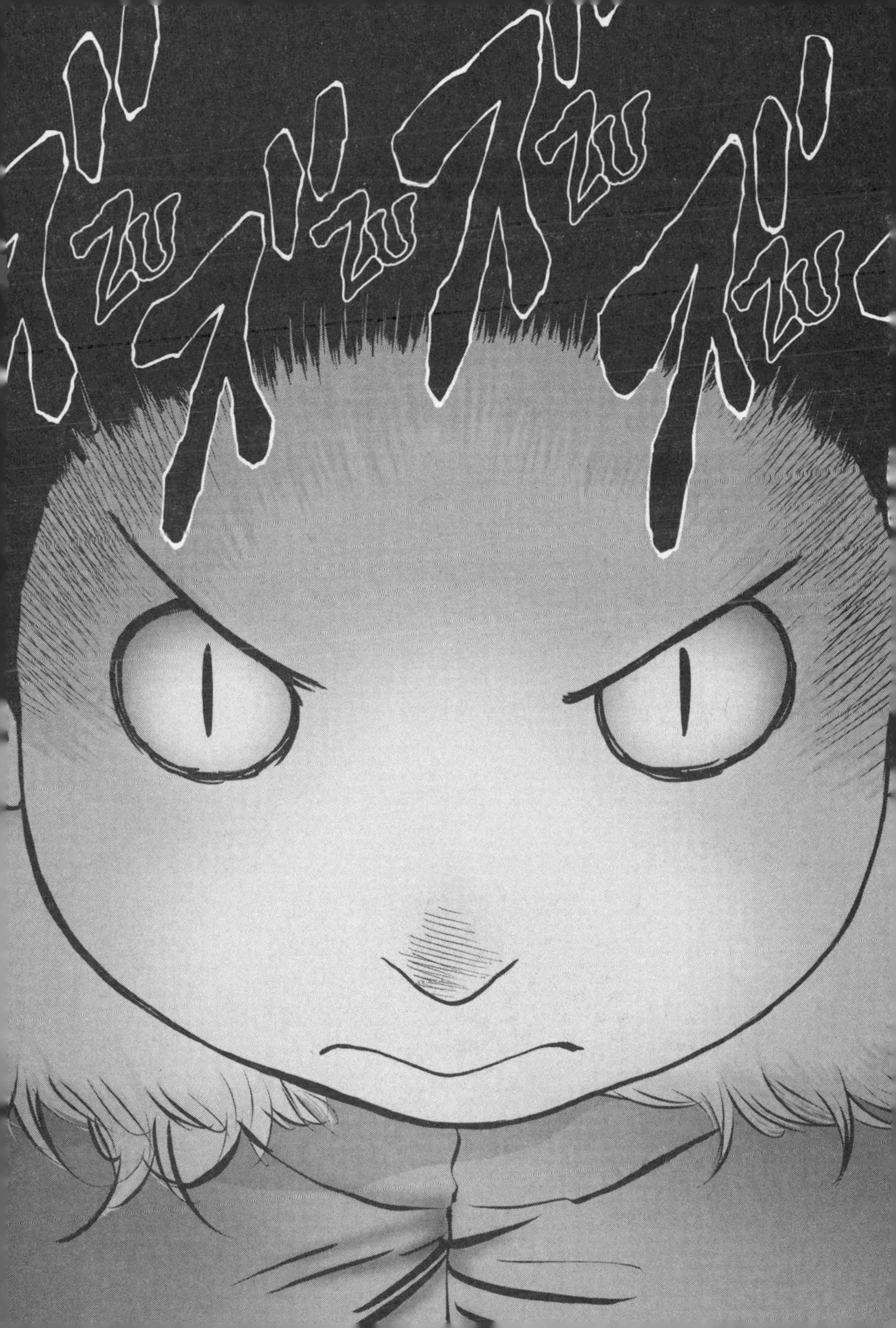
ズズズズ
ZU ZU ZU ZU

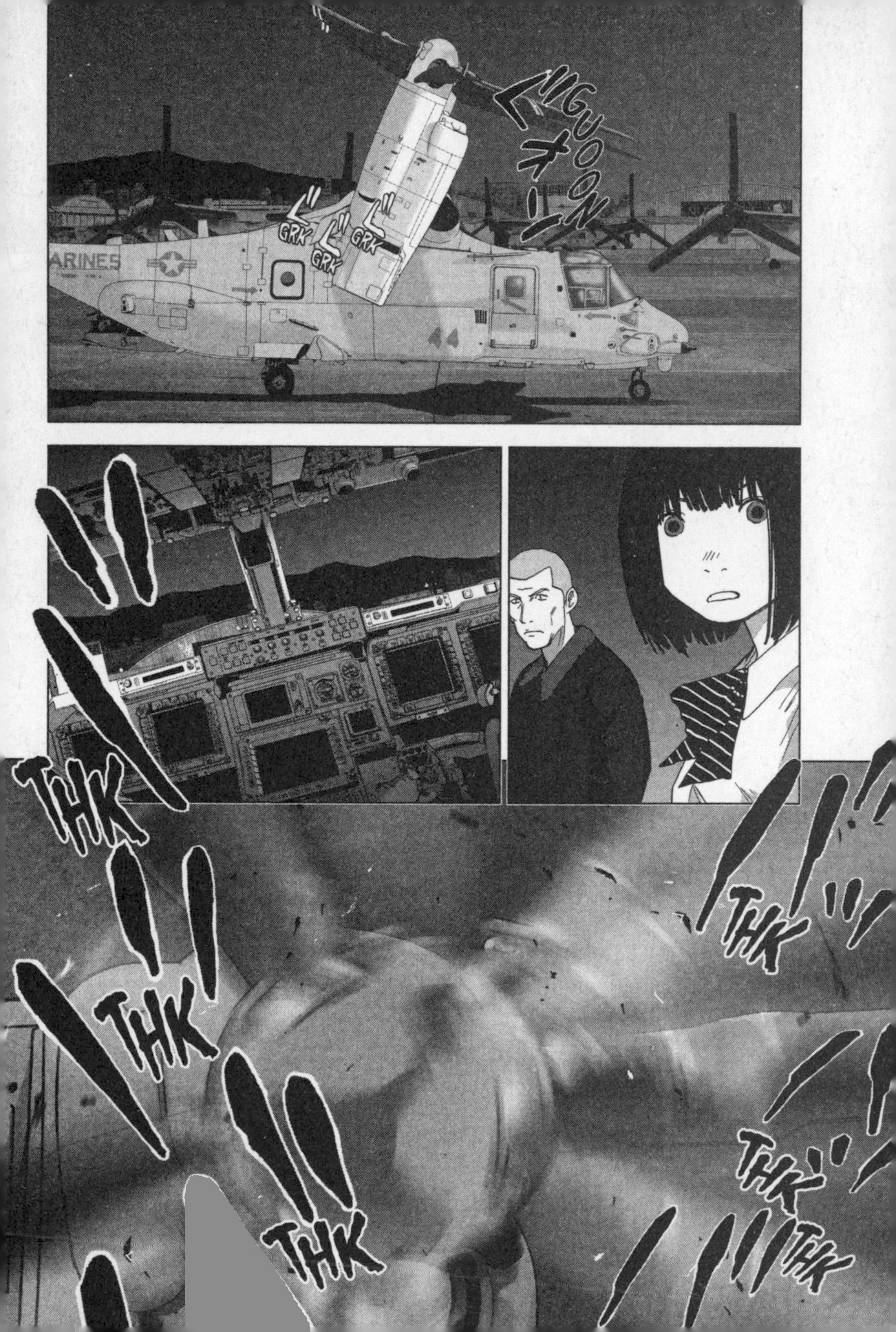
GUOOON
GRK
GRK
GRK
THK
THK
THK
THK
THK
THK

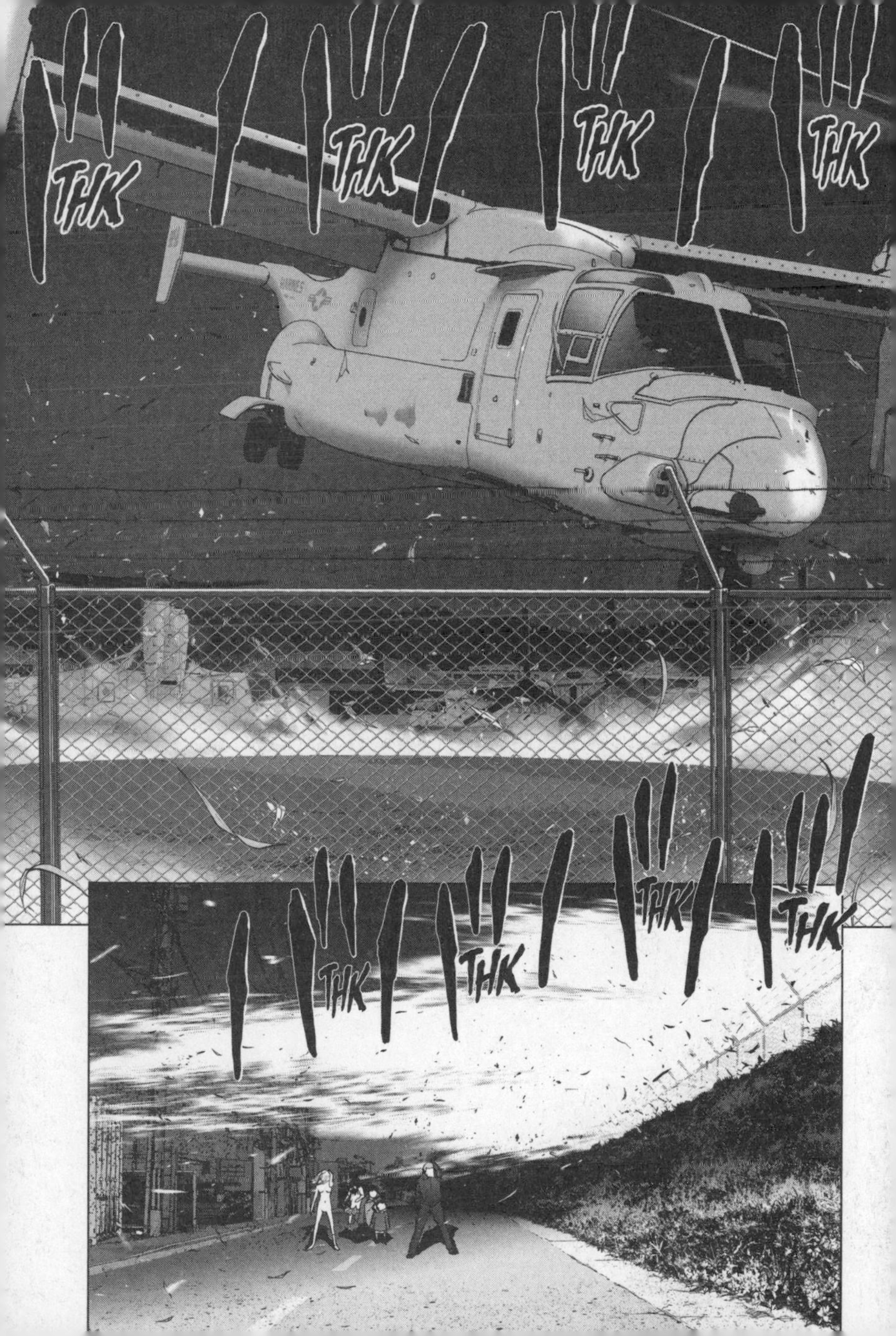
THK
THK
THK
THK
THK
THK
THK
THK

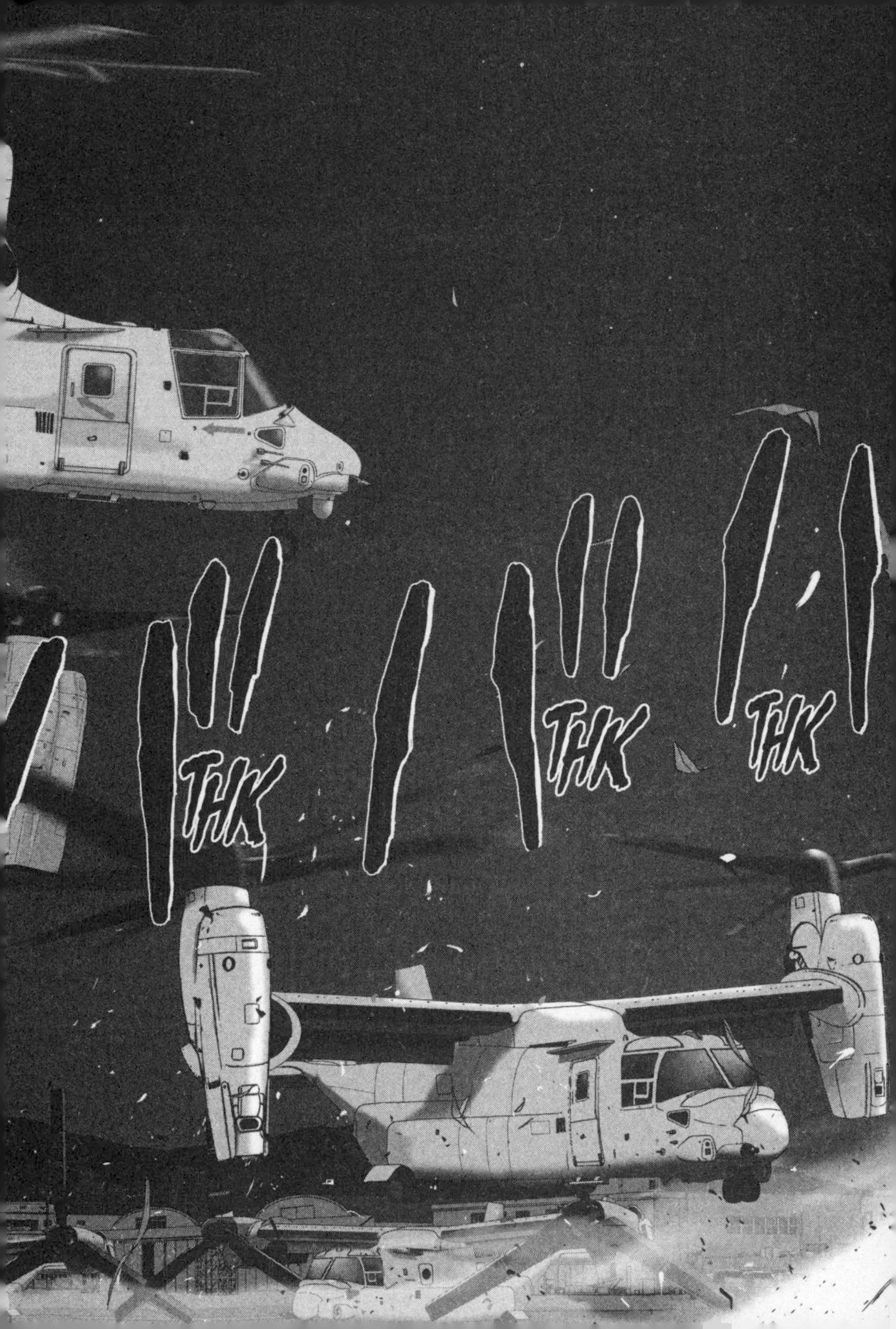
THK
THK
THK

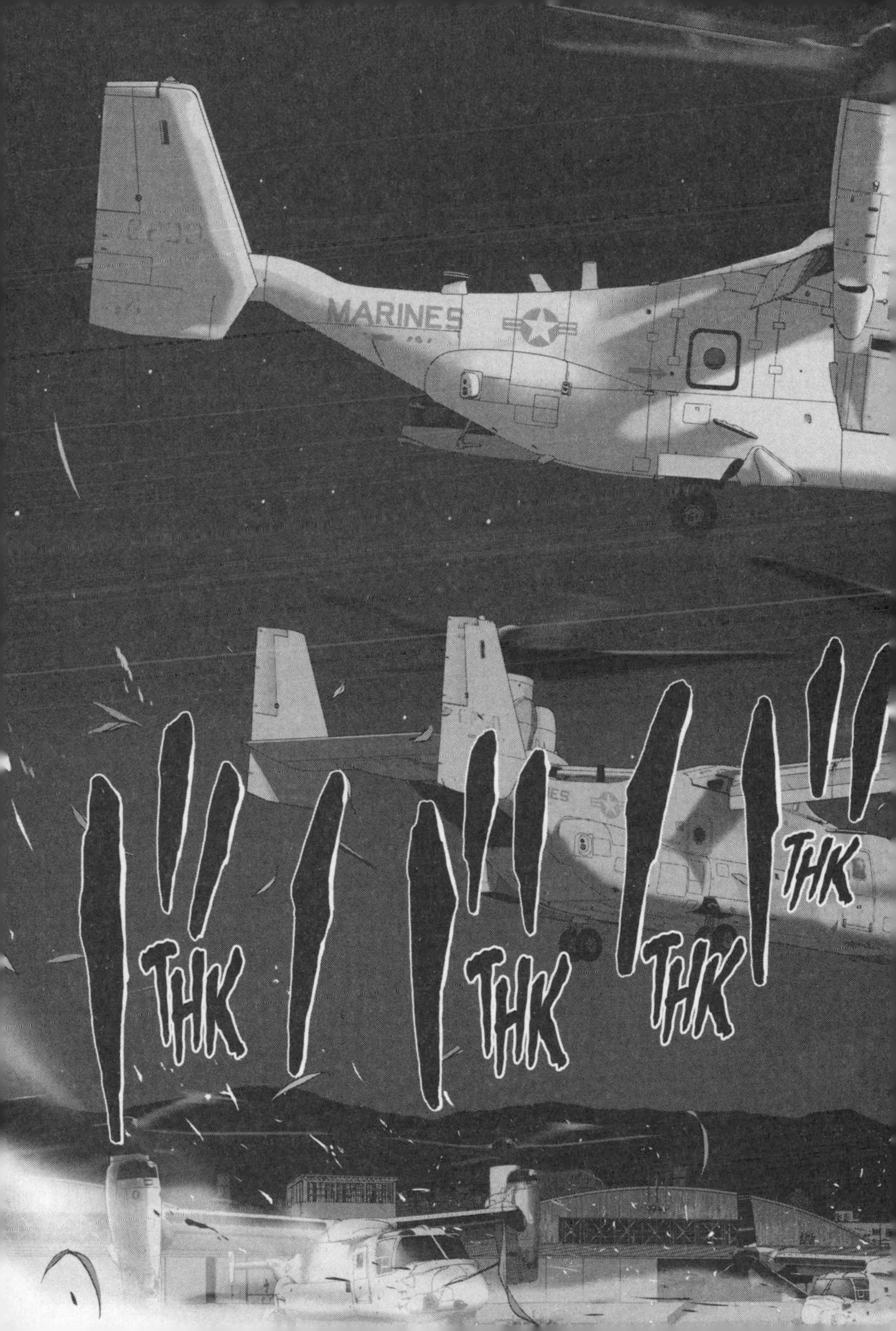
MARINES
THK
THK
THK
THK

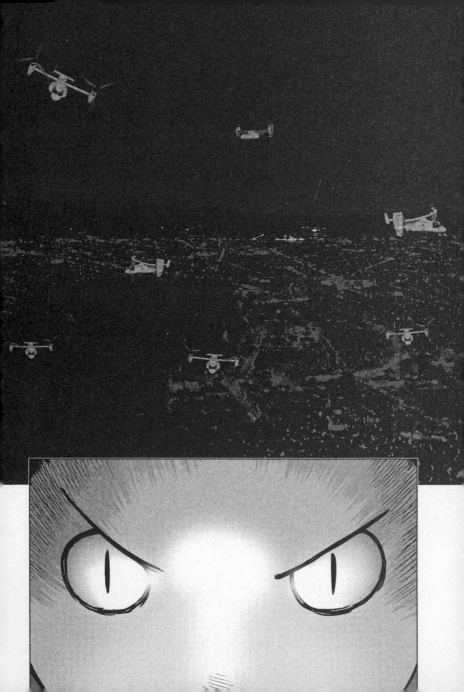

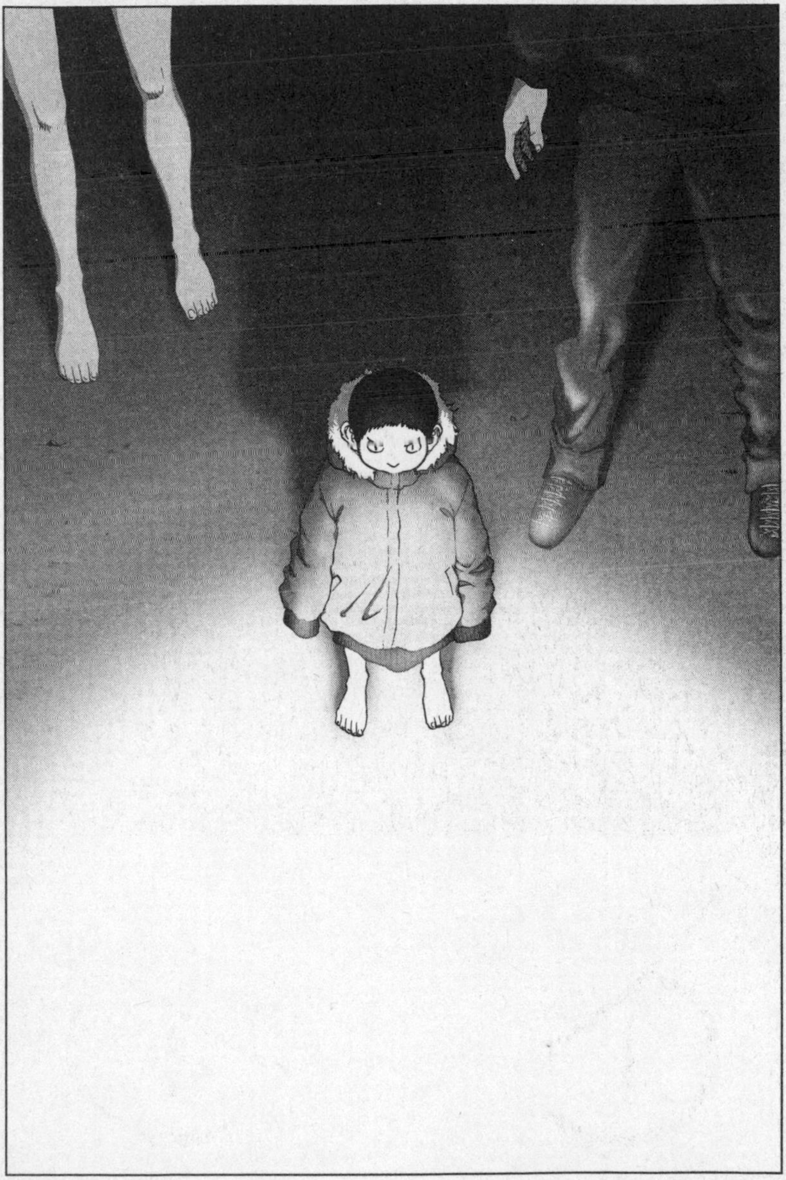

Chapter 42: Wonder

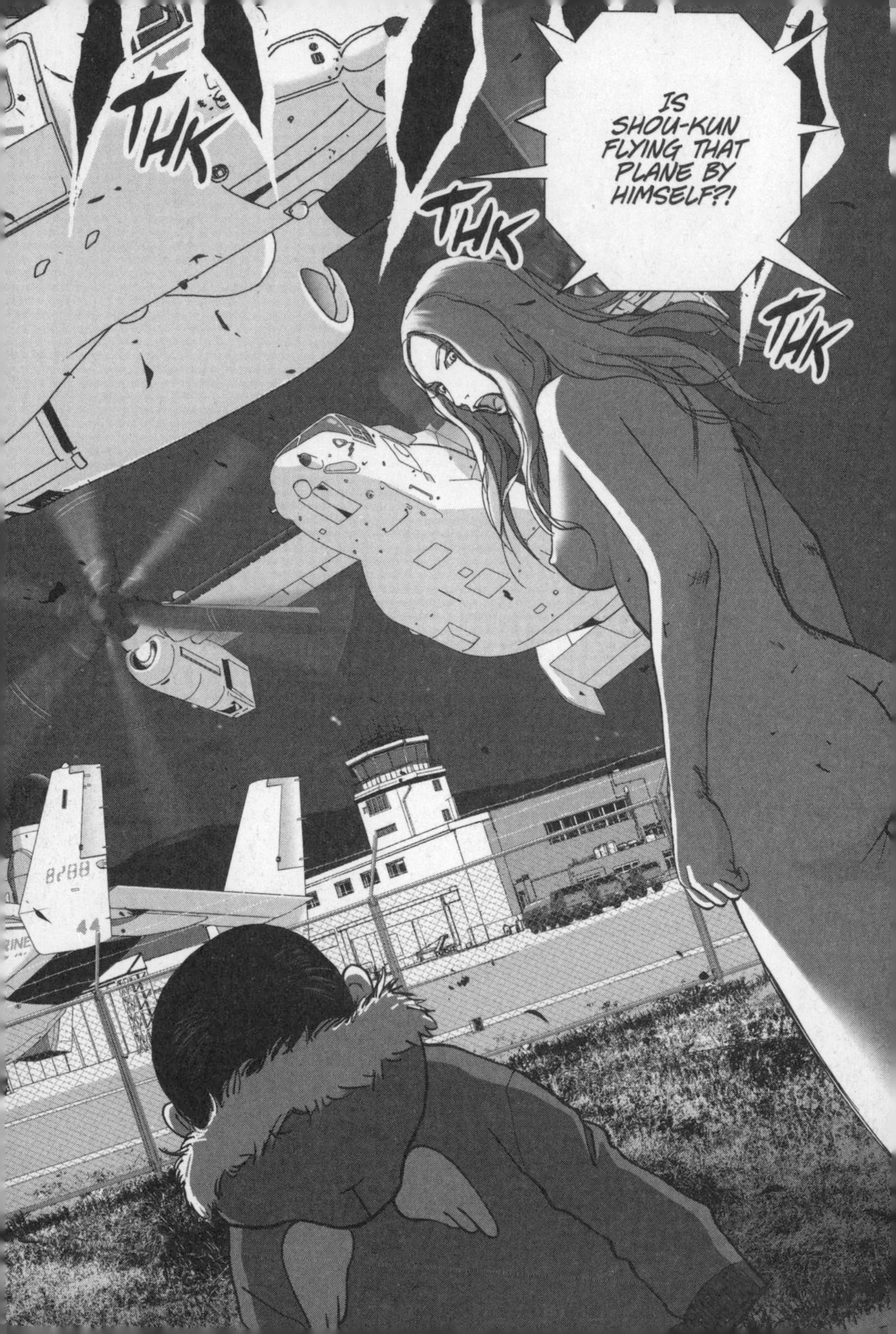
THK
IS SHOU-KUN FLYING THAT PLANE BY HIMSELF?!
THK
THK

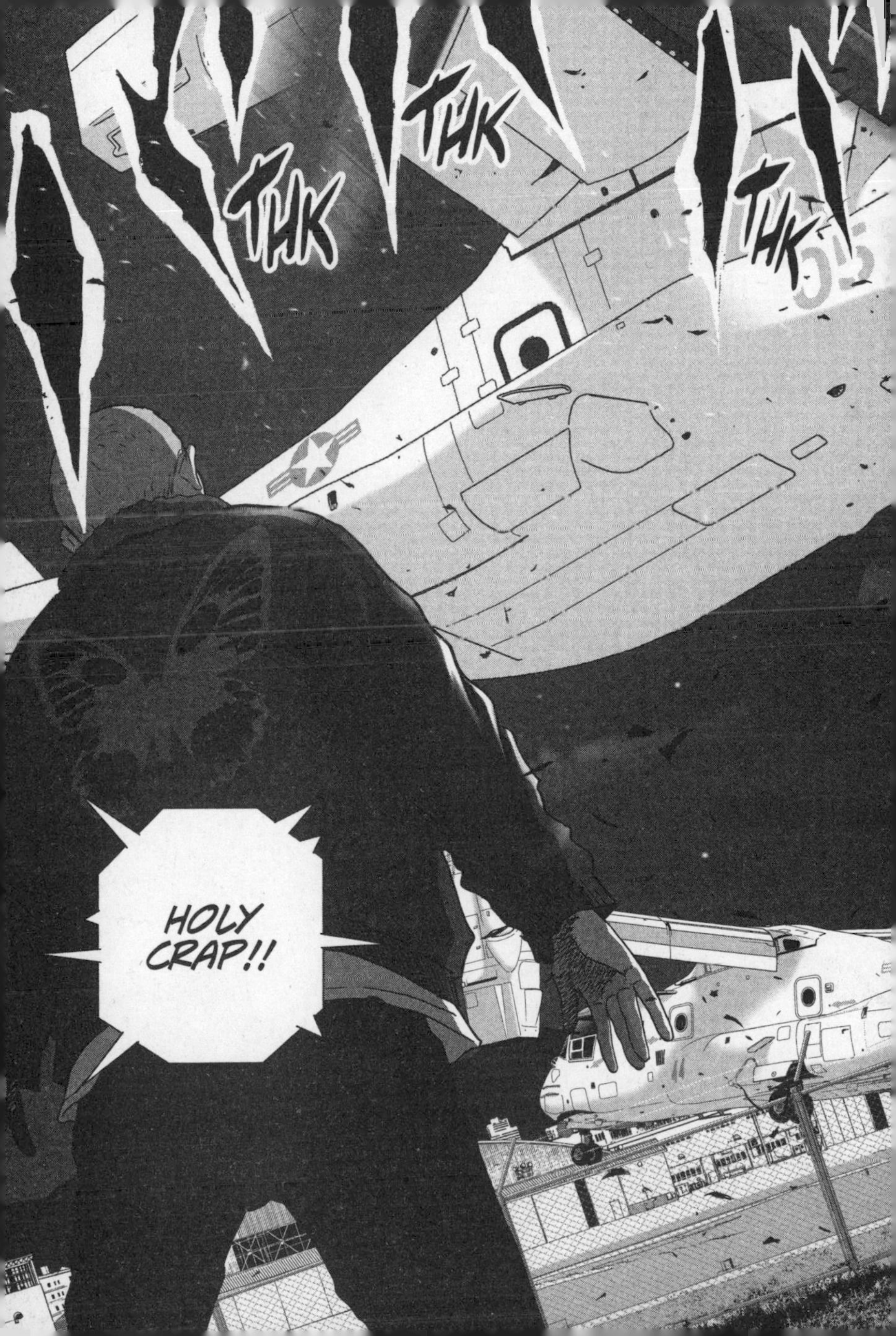
THK
THK
THK
HOLY CRAP!!

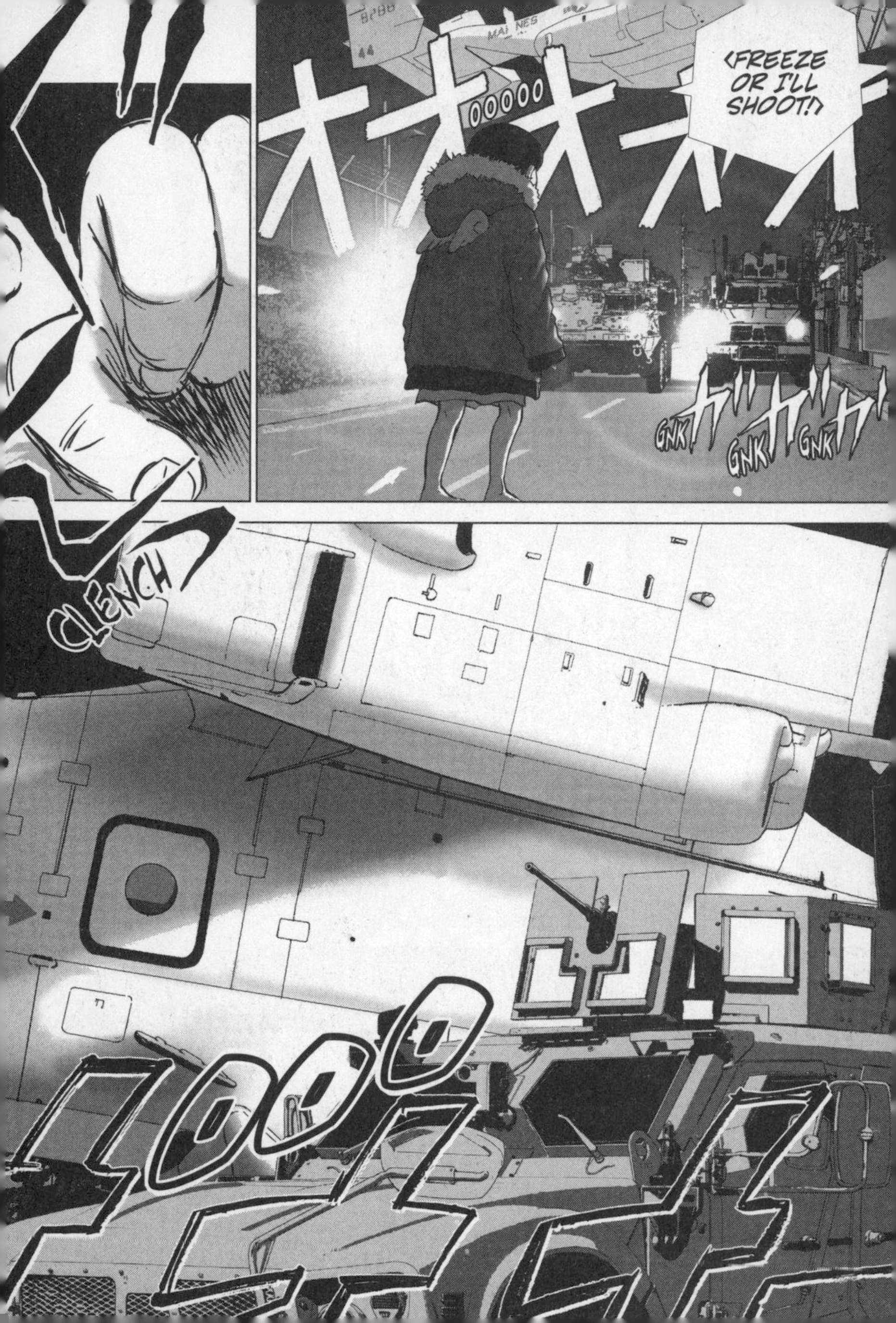
‹FREEZE OR I'LL SHOOT!›
GNK GNK GNK
CLENCH

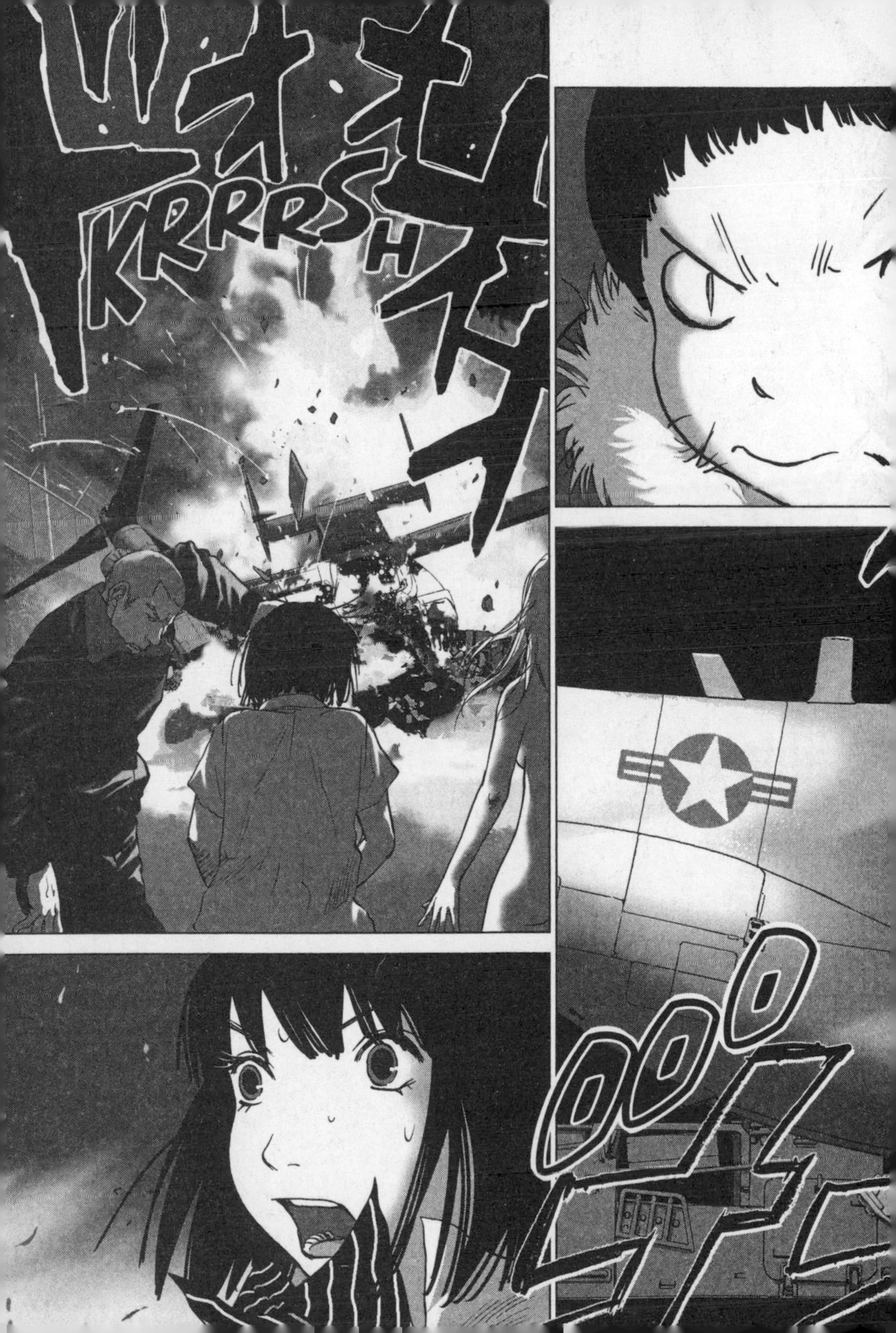
OOO
KRRRSH

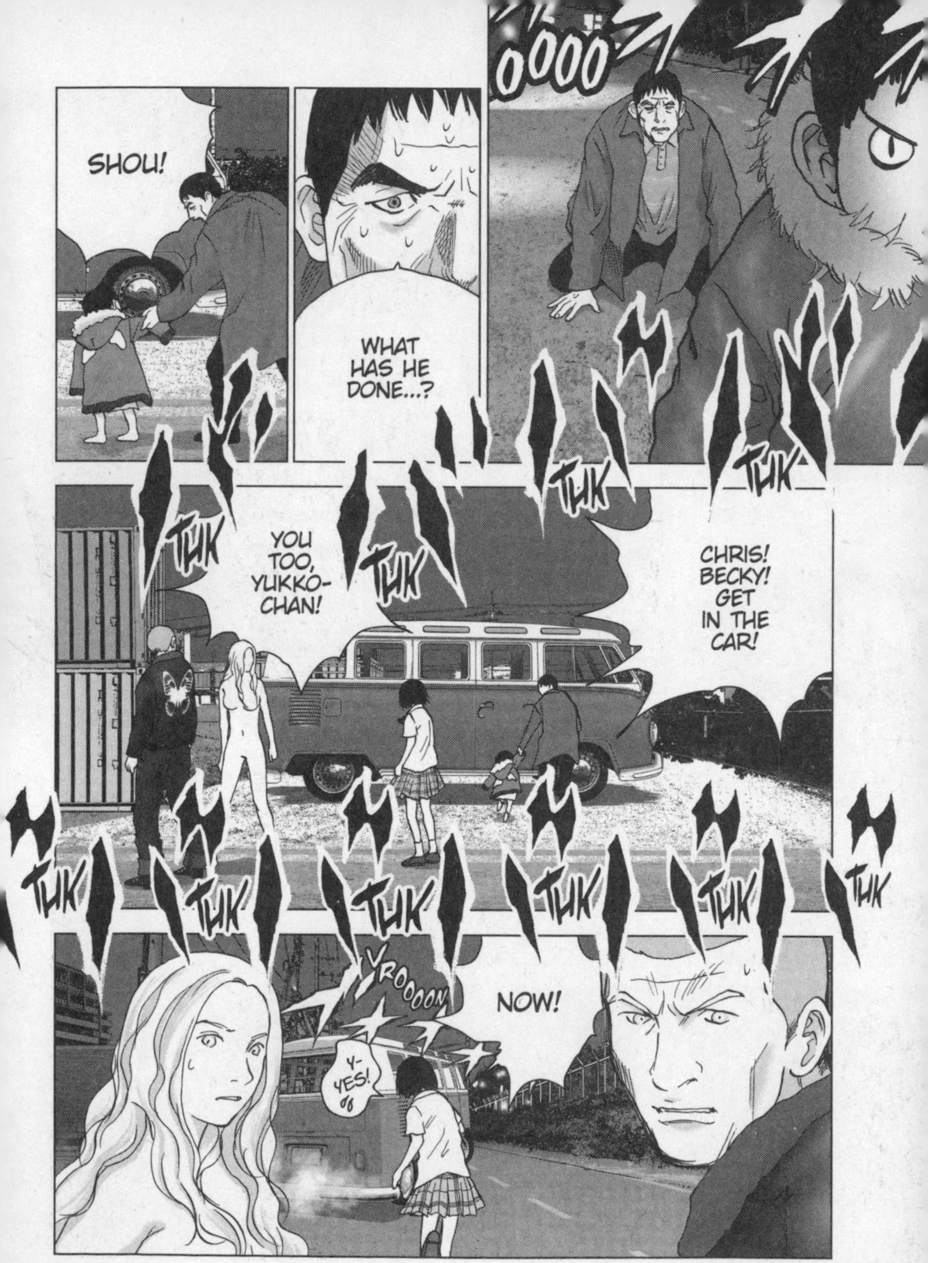
OOOO
WHAT HAS HE DONE...?
SHOU!
TUK
TUK
TUK
TUK
CHRIS! BECKY! GET IN THE CAR!
YOU TOO, YUKKO-CHAN!
TUK
TUK
TUK
TUK
TUK
TUK
NOW!
VROOOOON
Y-YES!

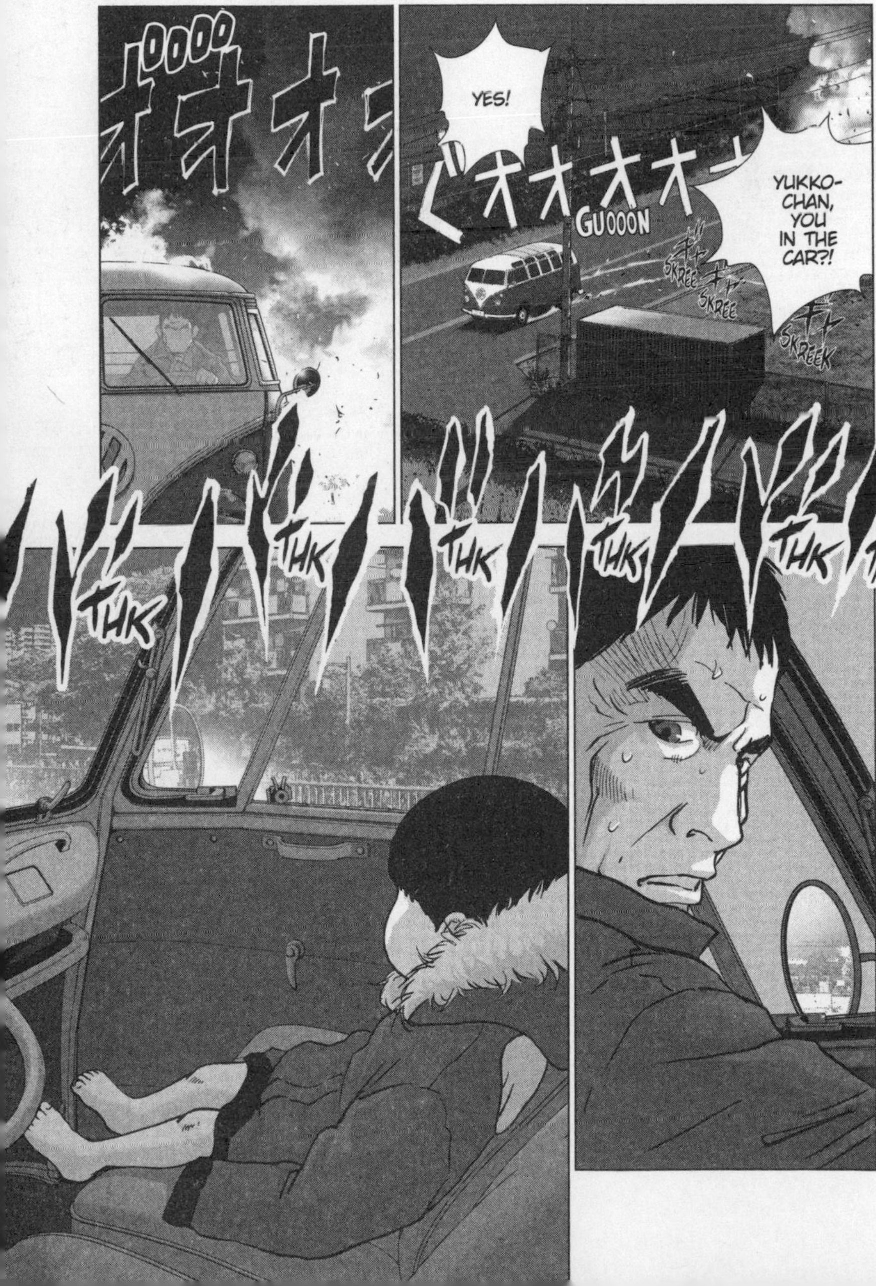
YUKKO-CHAN, YOU IN THE CAR?!
YES!
GUOOON
SKREE
SKREE
SKREEK
OOOO
THK
THK
THK
THK
THK
THK

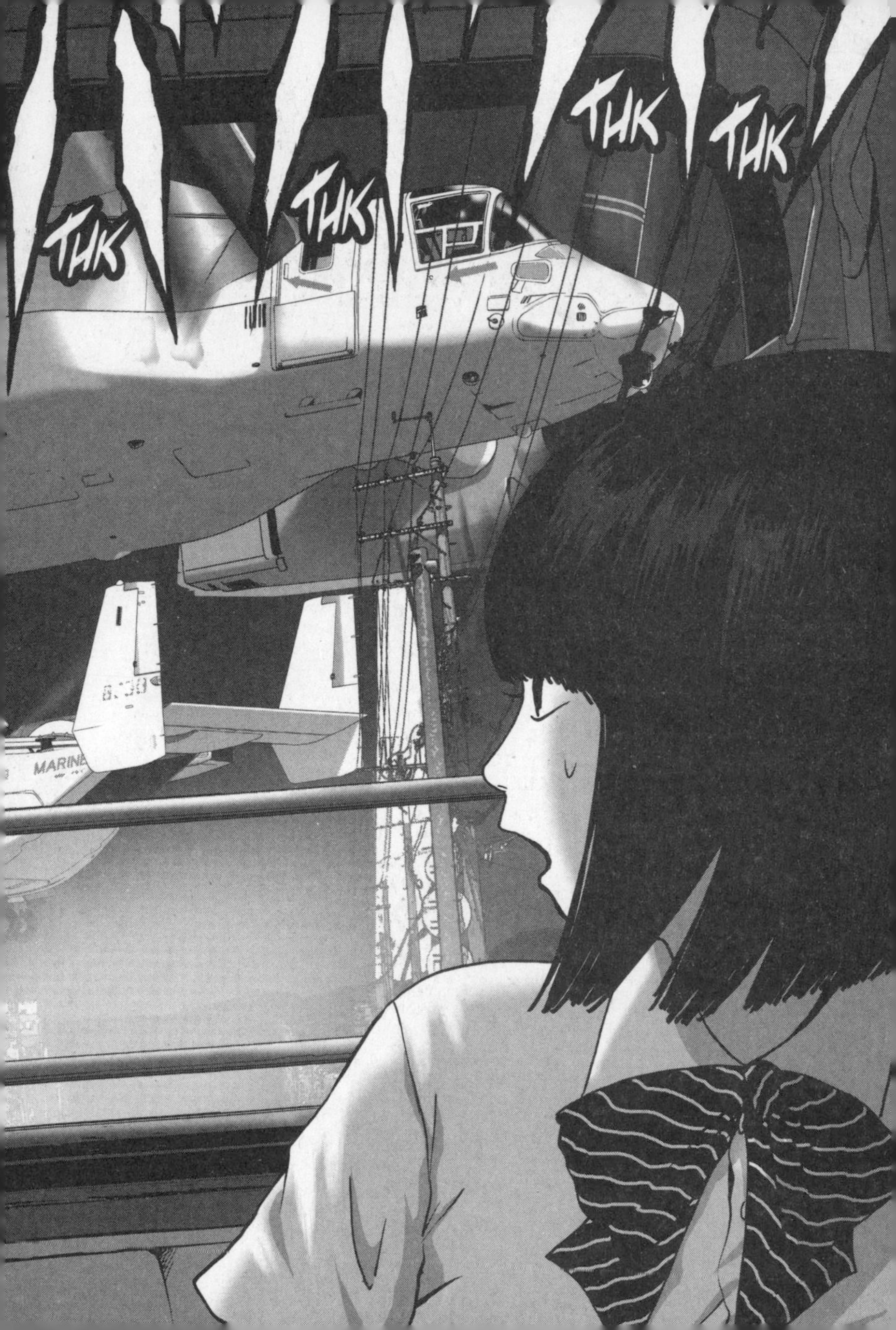
THK
THK
THK
THK
MARINE

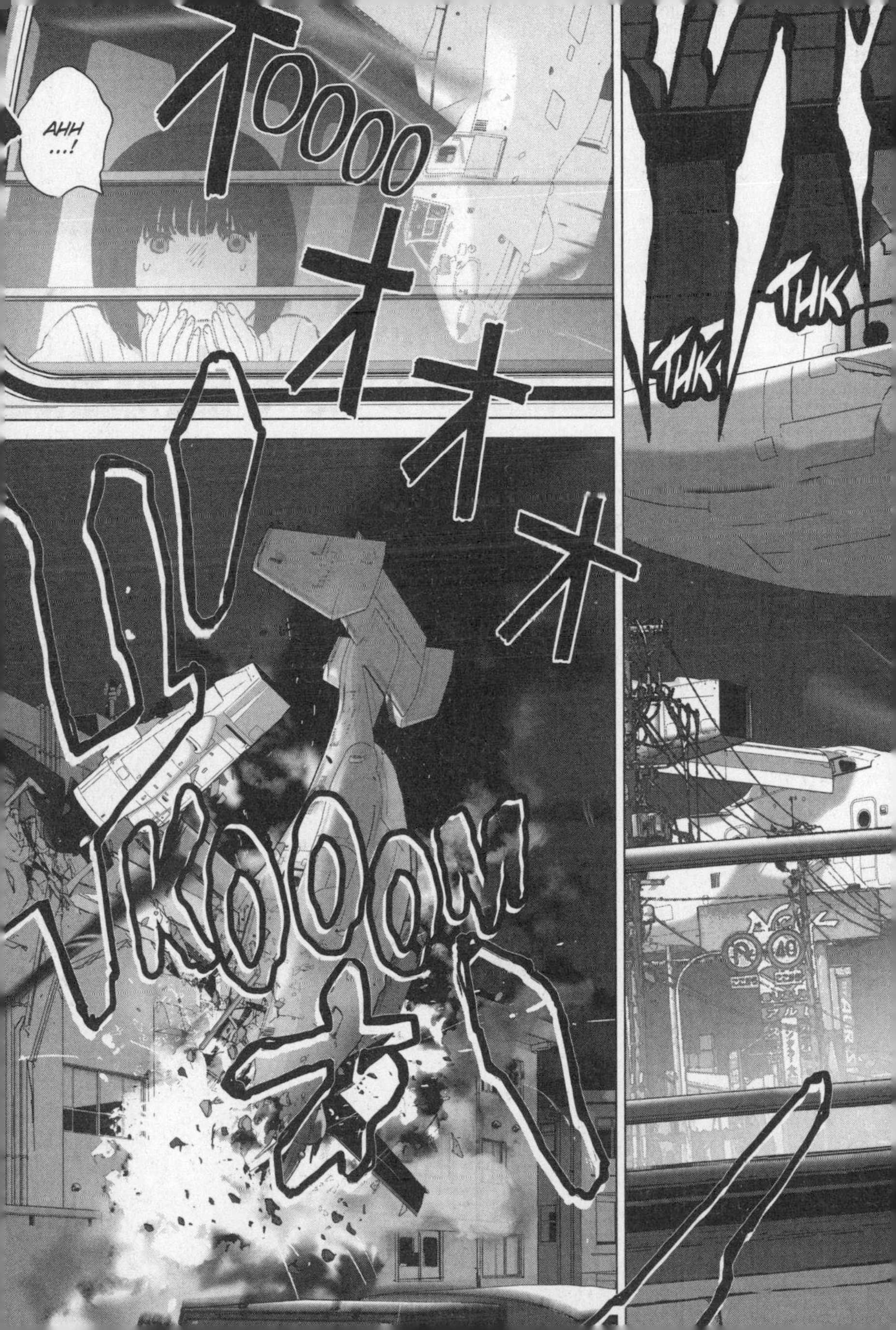
THK
THK
AHH ...!
TOOOOO
オオオオ
VROOOM

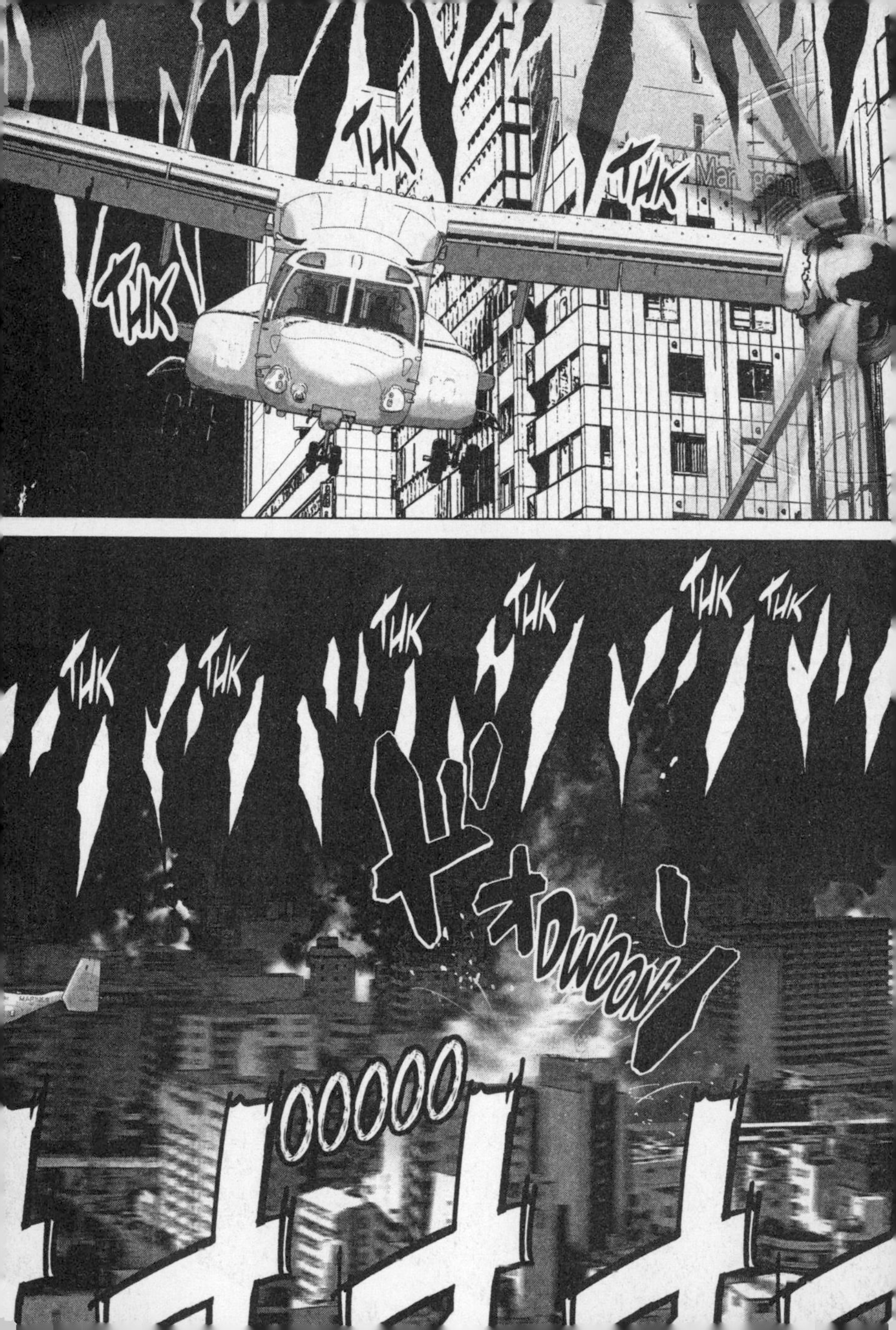
THK
THK
THK
THK
THK
THK
THK
THK
THK
DWOON
OOOOO

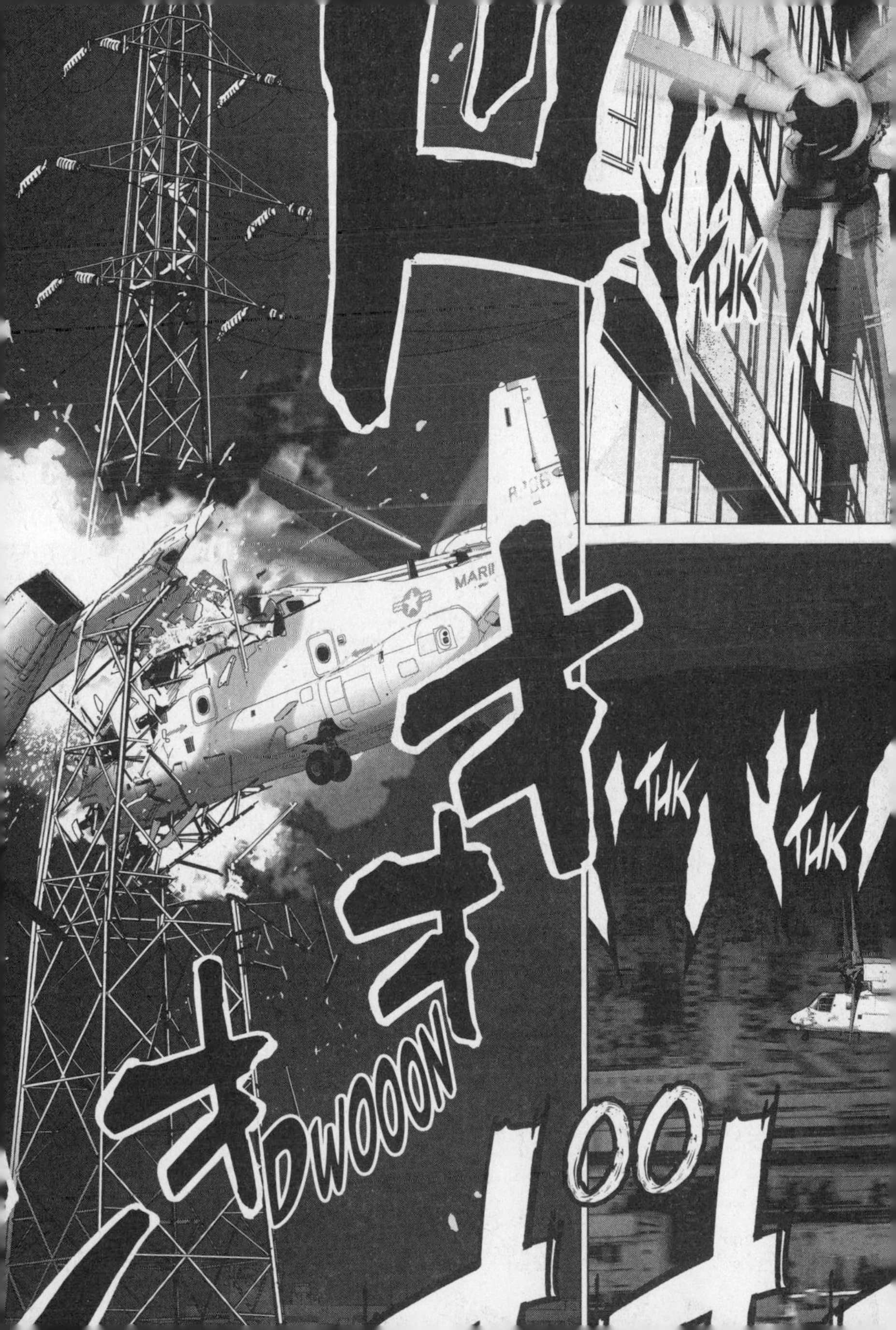
THK
THK
THK
OO
DWOOON

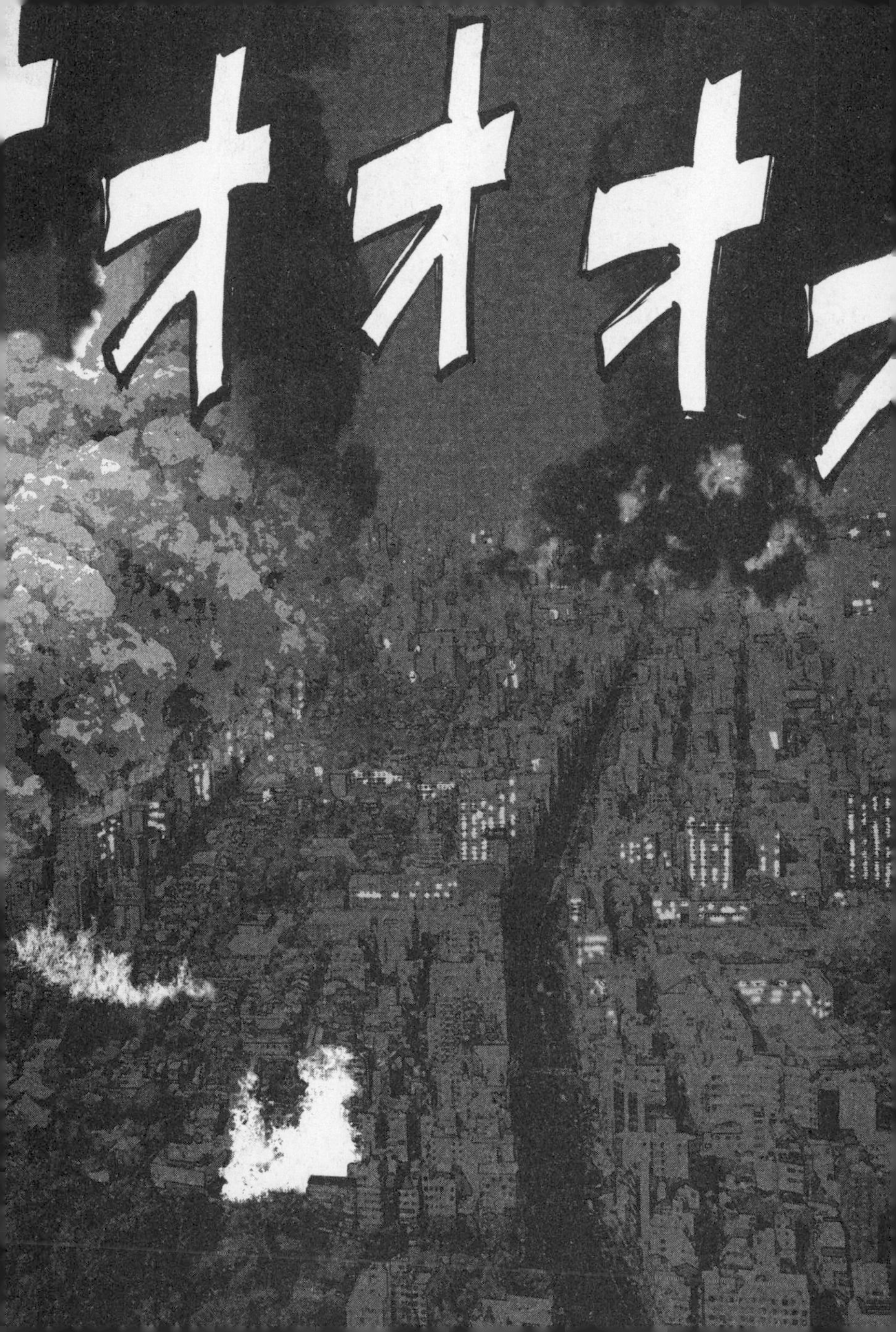
オオオオ

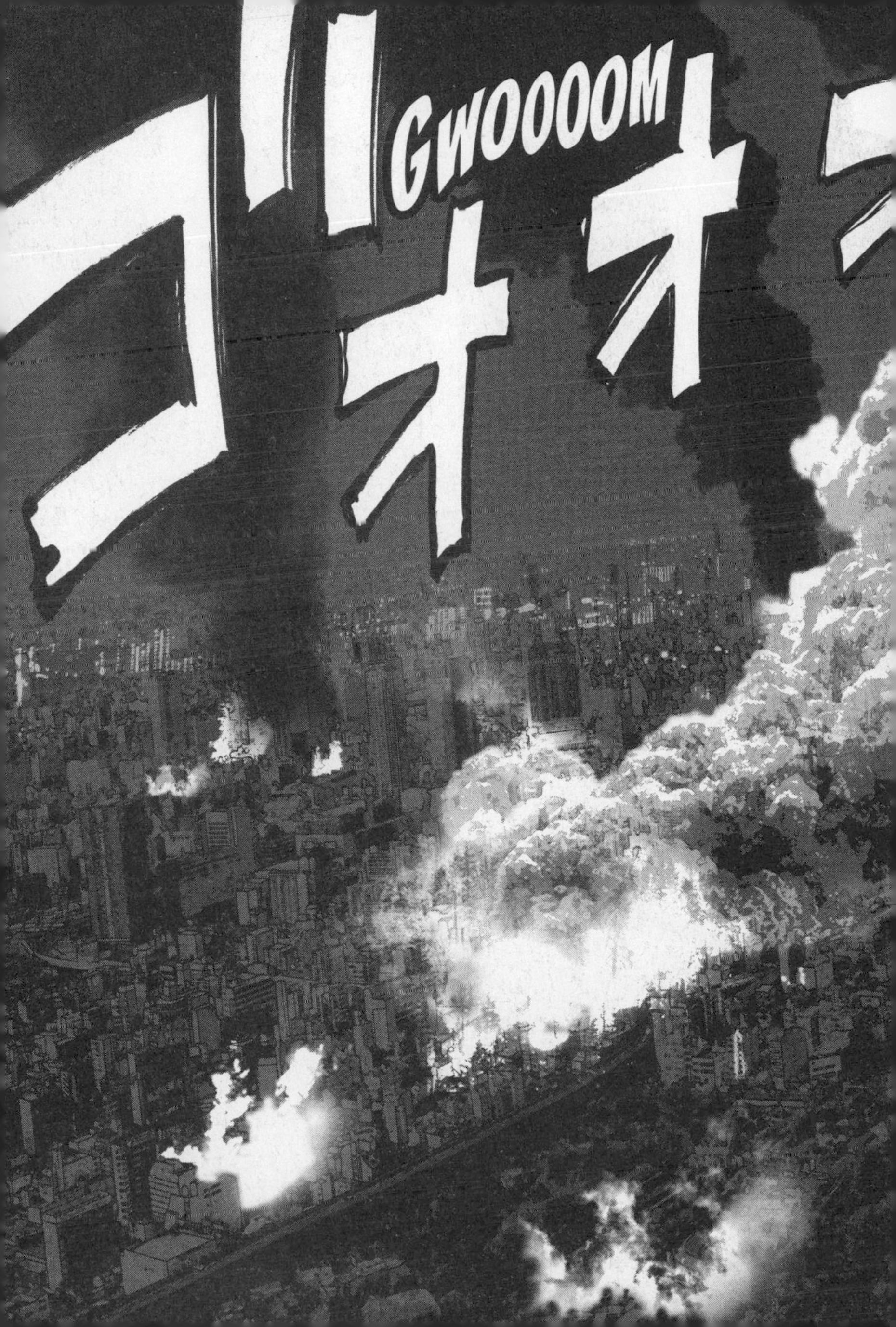
GWOOOOM
ゴオオ

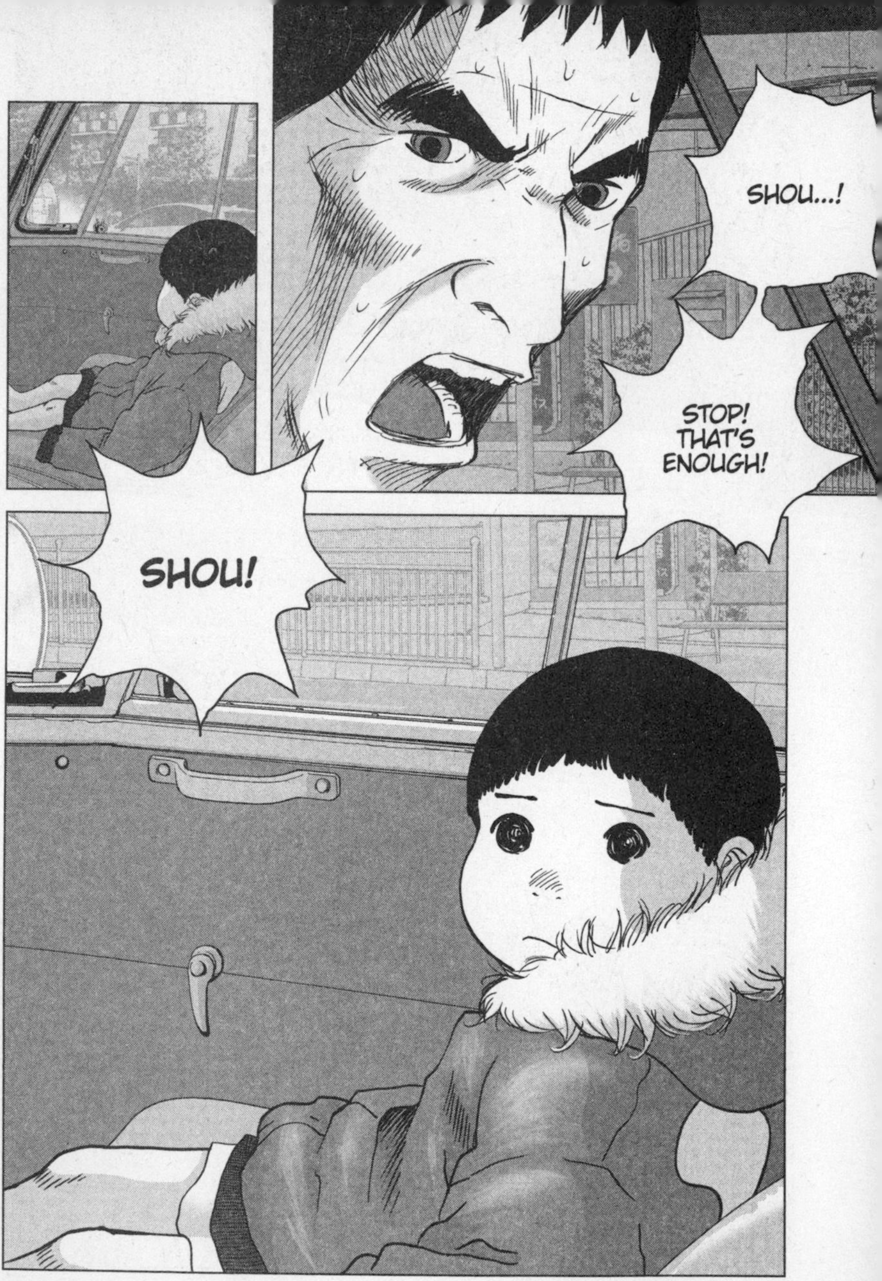
SHOU...!
STOP! THAT'S ENOUGH!
SHOU!

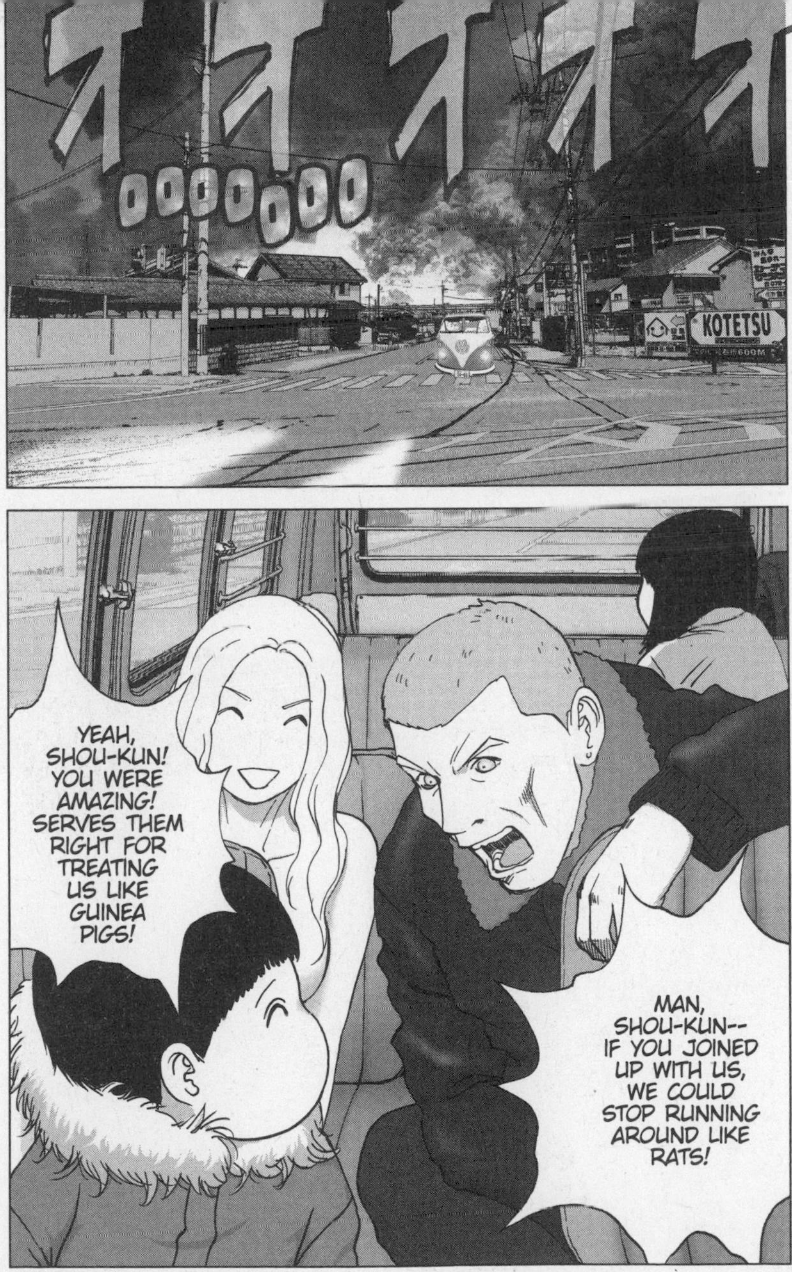
OOOOOOOO
KOTETSU
MAN, SHOU-KUN-- IF YOU JOINED UP WITH US, WE COULD STOP RUNNING AROUND LIKE RATS!
YEAH, SHOU-KUN! YOU WERE AMAZING! SERVES THEM RIGHT FOR TREATING US LIKE GUINEA PIGS!

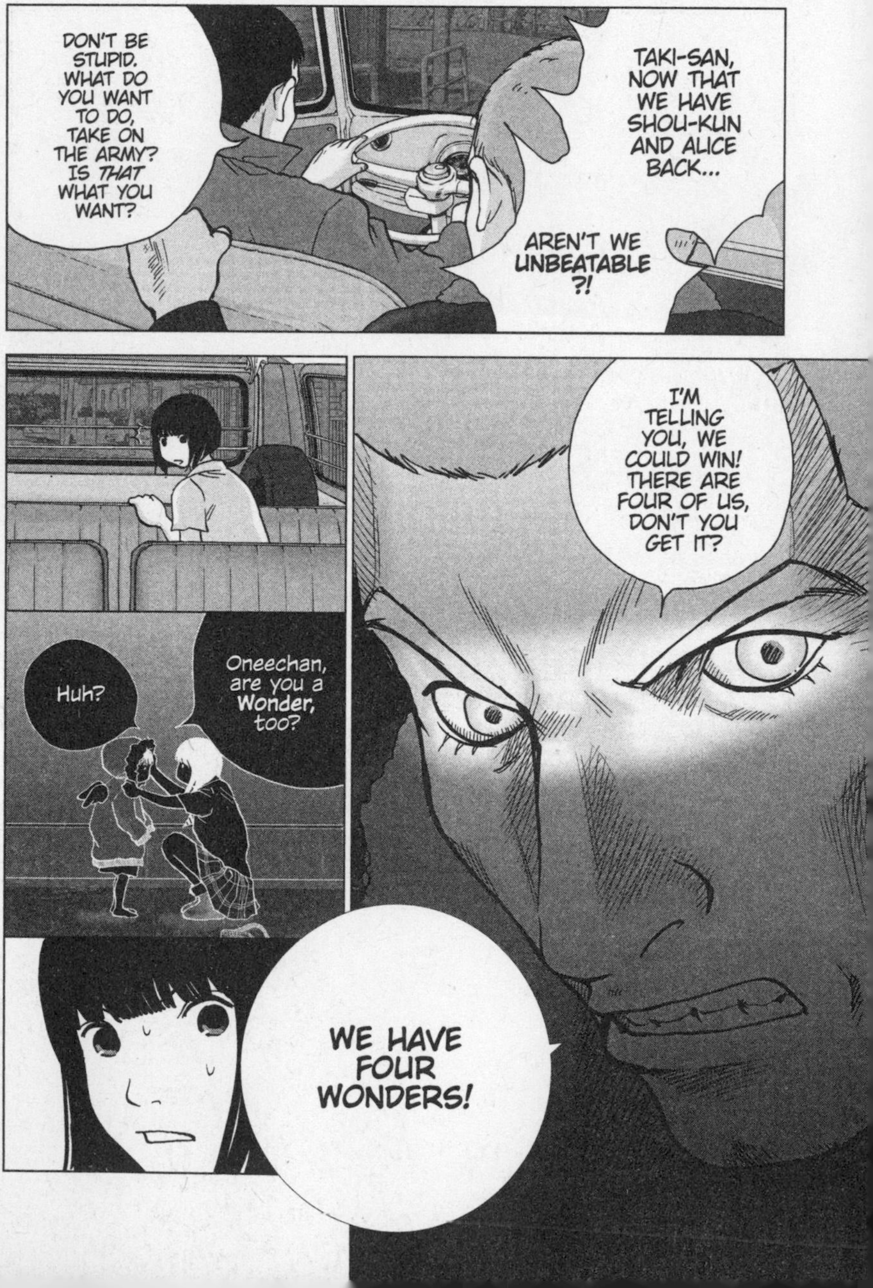
TAKI-SAN, NOW THAT WE HAVE SHOU-KUN AND ALICE BACK...
AREN'T WE UNBEATABLE ?!
DON'T BE STUPID. WHAT DO YOU WANT TO DO, TAKE ON THE ARMY? IS *THAT* WHAT YOU WANT?
I'M TELLING YOU, WE COULD WIN! THERE ARE FOUR OF US, DON'T YOU GET IT?
WE HAVE FOUR WONDERS!
Oneechan, are you a **Wonder,** too?
Huh?

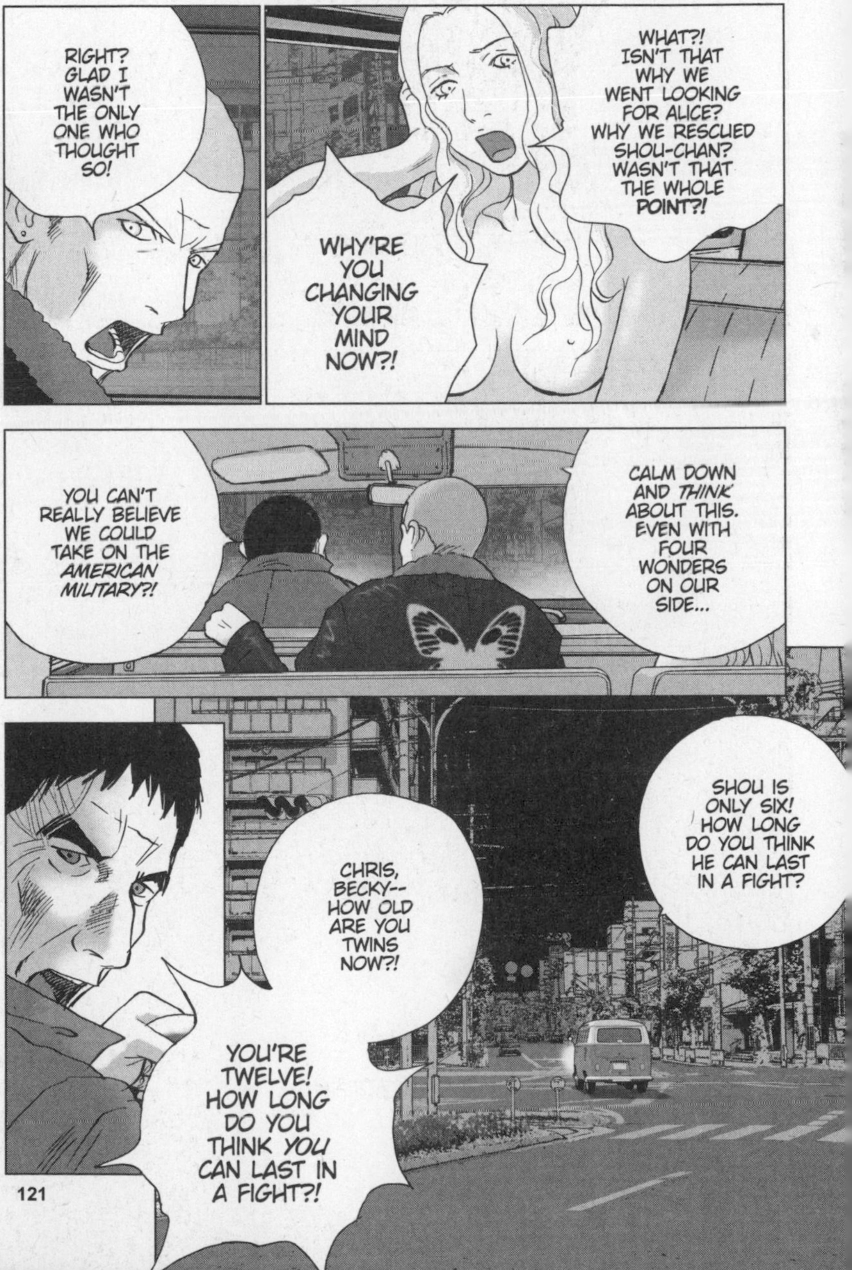
WHAT?! ISN'T THAT WHY WE WENT LOOKING FOR ALICE? WHY WE RESCUED SHOU-CHAN? WASN'T THAT THE WHOLE POINT?!
WHY'RE YOU CHANGING YOUR MIND NOW?!
RIGHT? GLAD I WASN'T THE ONLY ONE WHO THOUGHT SO!
CALM DOWN AND *THINK* ABOUT THIS. EVEN WITH FOUR WONDERS ON OUR SIDE...
YOU CAN'T REALLY BELIEVE WE COULD TAKE ON THE *AMERICAN MILITARY*?!
SHOU IS ONLY SIX! HOW LONG DO YOU THINK HE CAN LAST IN A FIGHT?
CHRIS, BECKY-- HOW OLD ARE YOU TWINS NOW?!
YOU'RE TWELVE! HOW LONG DO YOU THINK *YOU* CAN LAST IN A FIGHT?!

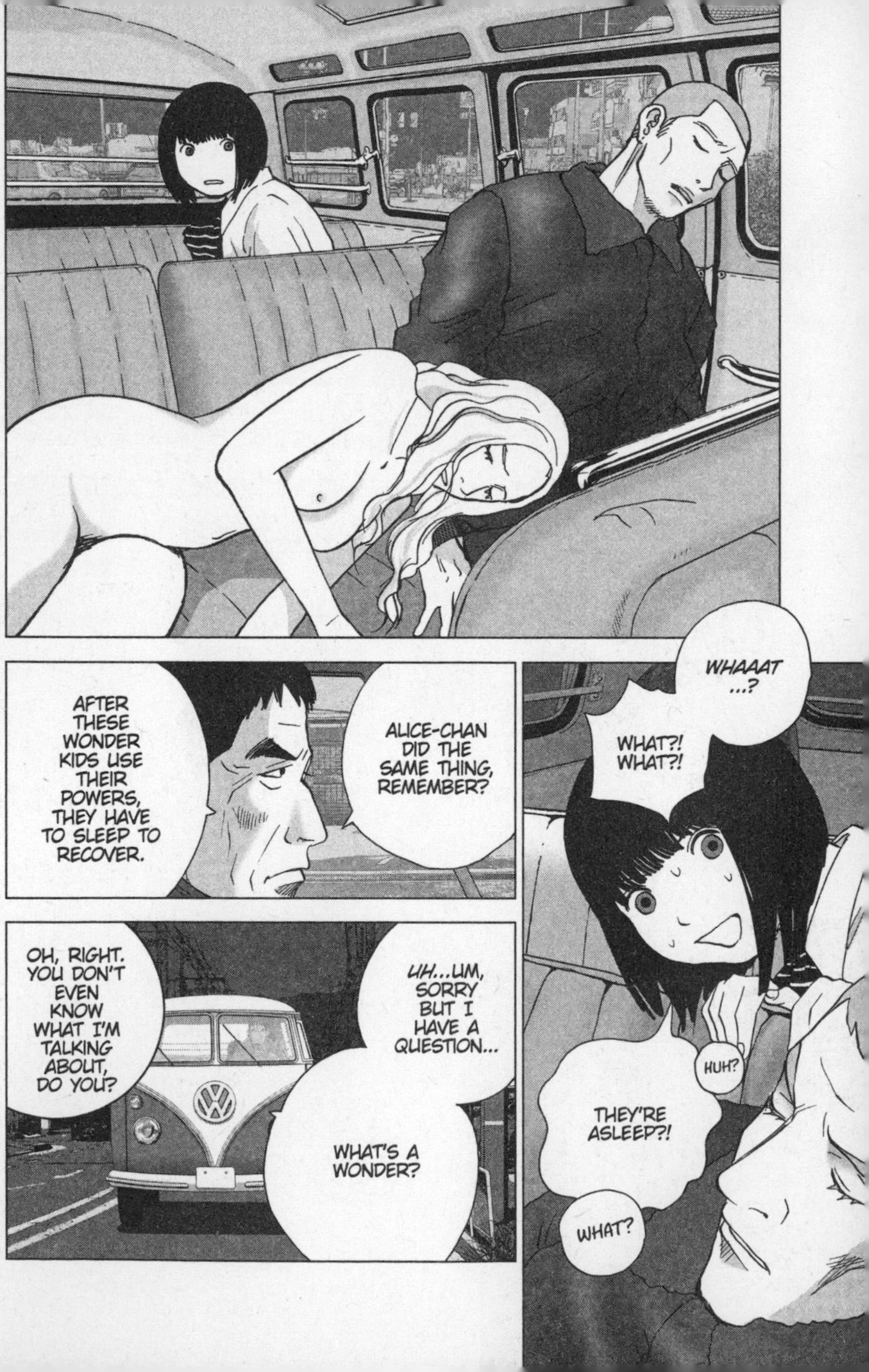
WHAAAT ...?
WHAT?! WHAT?!
HUH?
THEY'RE ASLEEP?!
WHAT?
ALICE-CHAN DID THE SAME THING, REMEMBER?
AFTER THESE WONDER KIDS USE THEIR POWERS, THEY HAVE TO SLEEP TO RECOVER.
UH...UM, SORRY BUT I HAVE A QUESTION...
OH, RIGHT. YOU DON'T EVEN KNOW WHAT I'M TALKING ABOUT, DO YOU?
WHAT'S A WONDER?

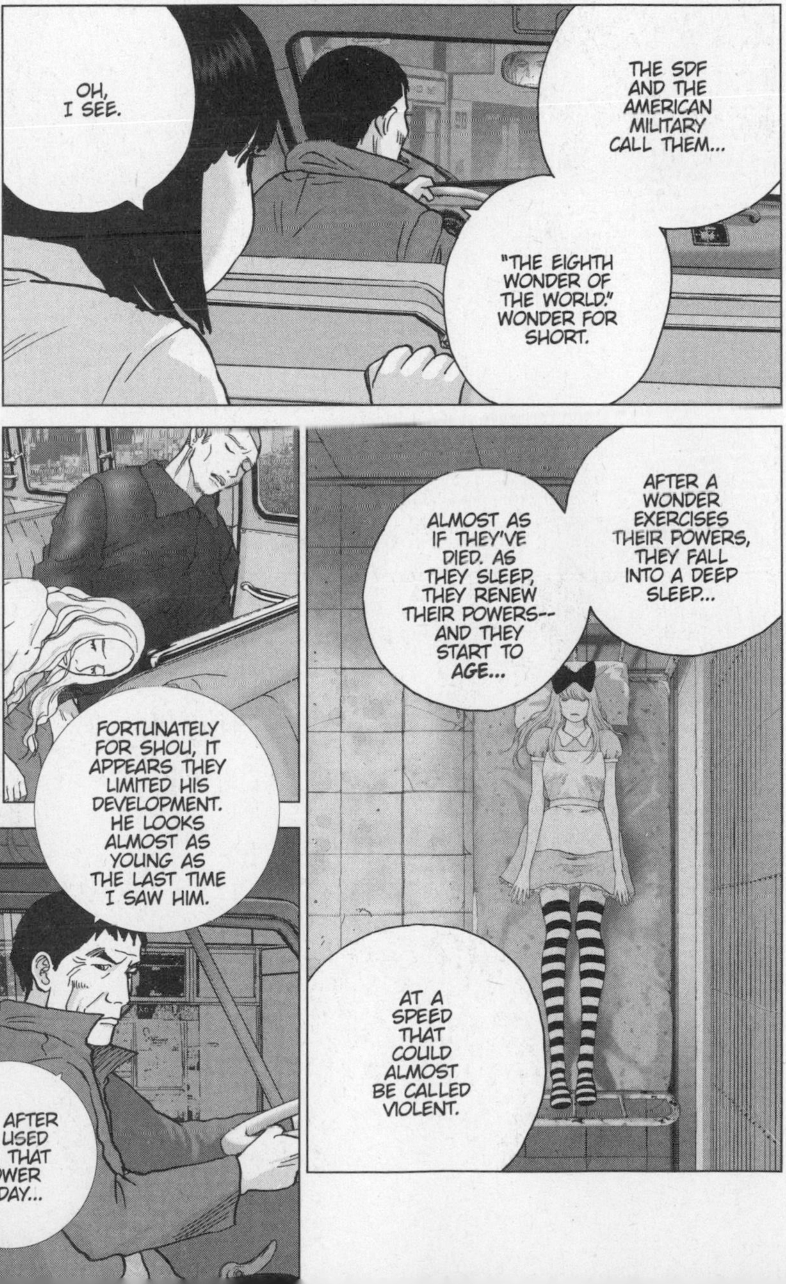
THE SDF AND THE AMERICAN MILITARY CALL THEM...
"THE EIGHTH WONDER OF THE WORLD." WONDER FOR SHORT.
OH, I SEE.
AFTER A WONDER EXERCISES THEIR POWERS, THEY FALL INTO A DEEP SLEEP...
ALMOST AS IF THEY'VE DIED. AS THEY SLEEP, THEY RENEW THEIR POWERS-- AND THEY START TO AGE...
AT A SPEED THAT COULD ALMOST BE CALLED VIOLENT.
FORTUNATELY FOR SHOU, IT APPEARS THEY LIMITED HIS DEVELOPMENT. HE LOOKS ALMOST AS YOUNG AS THE LAST TIME I SAW HIM.
BUT AFTER HE USED ALL THAT POWER TODAY...

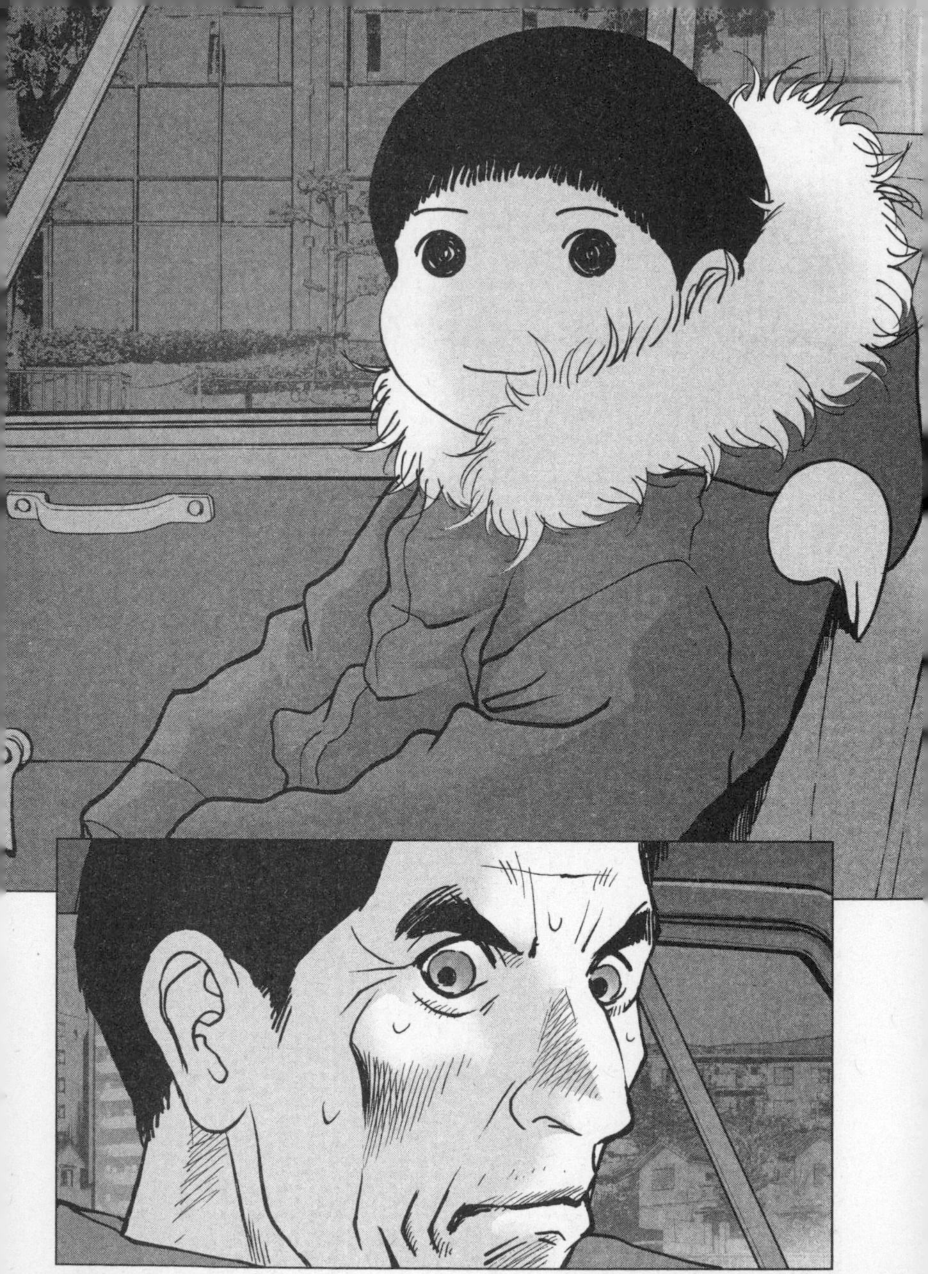

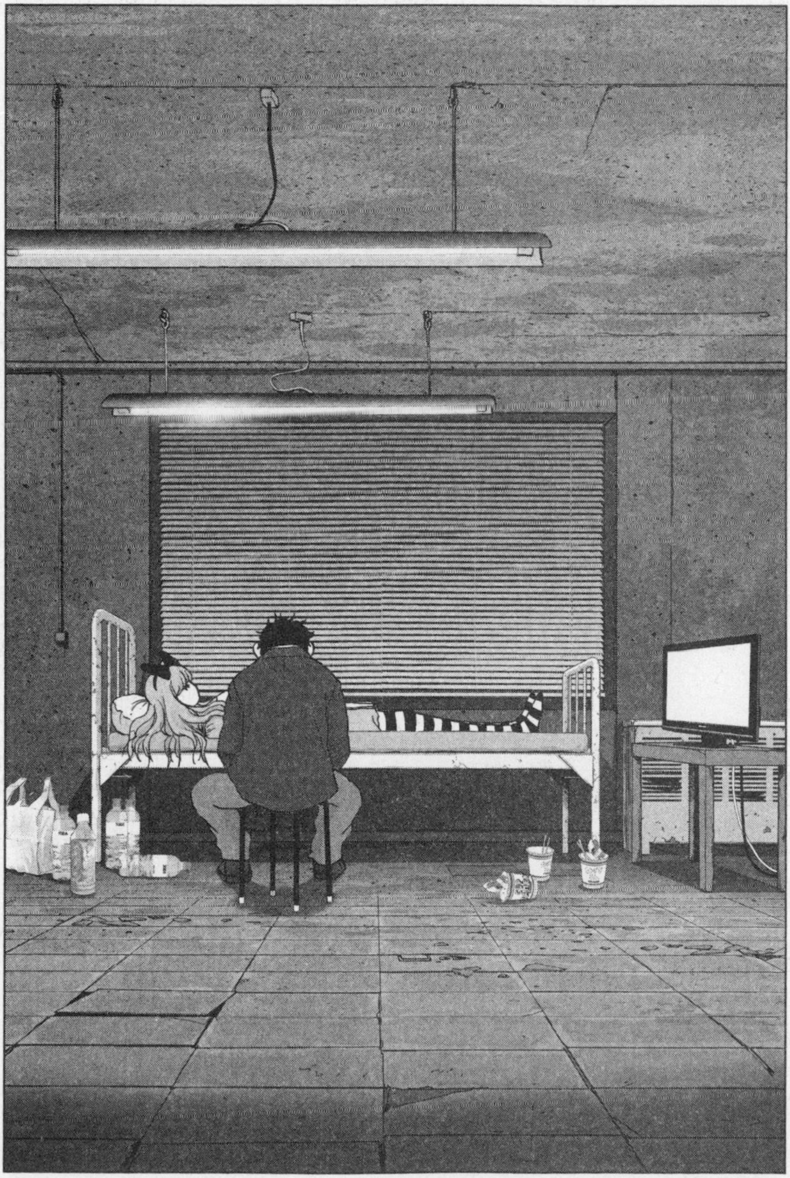

Chapter 43: Reparations

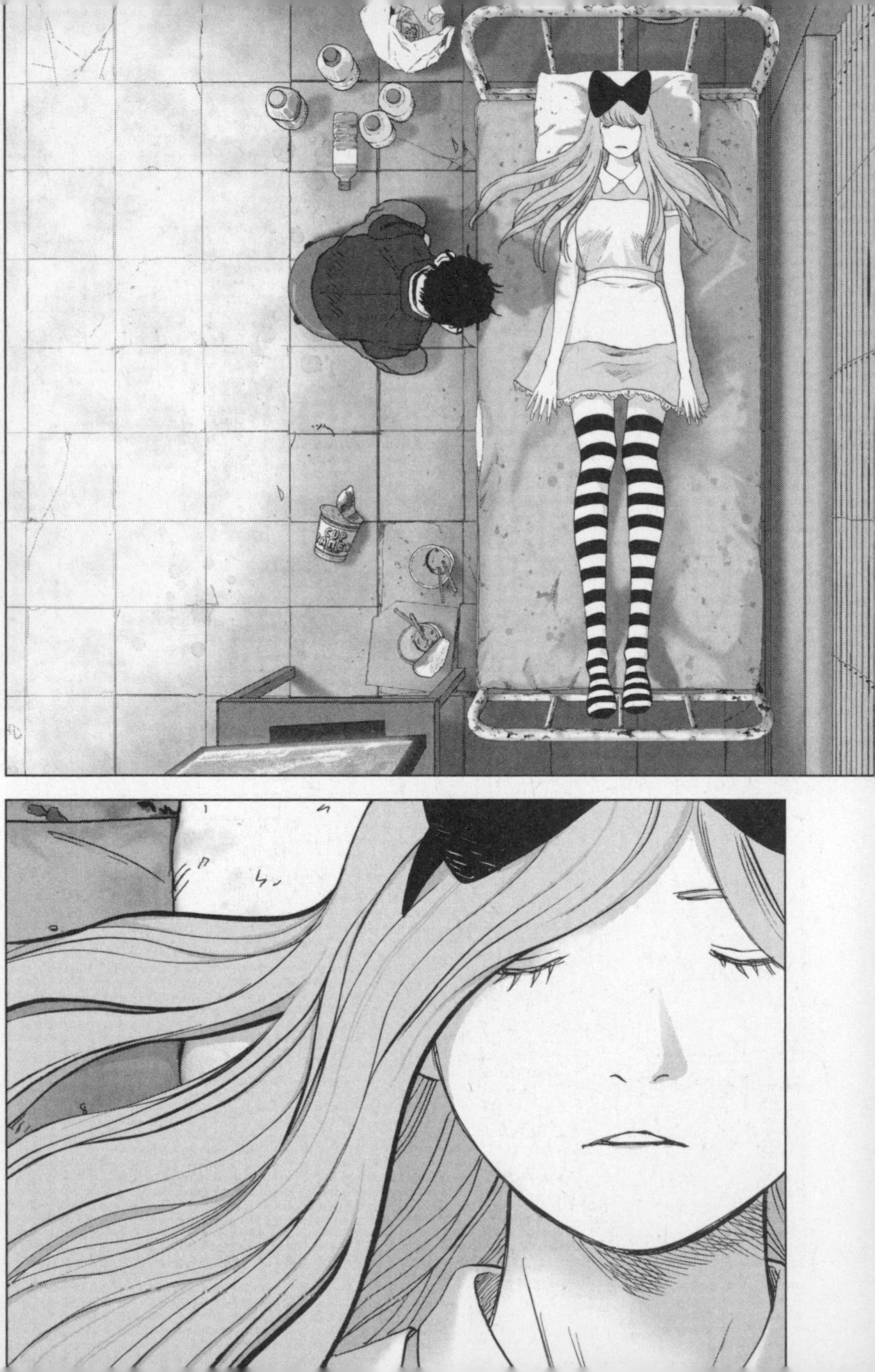

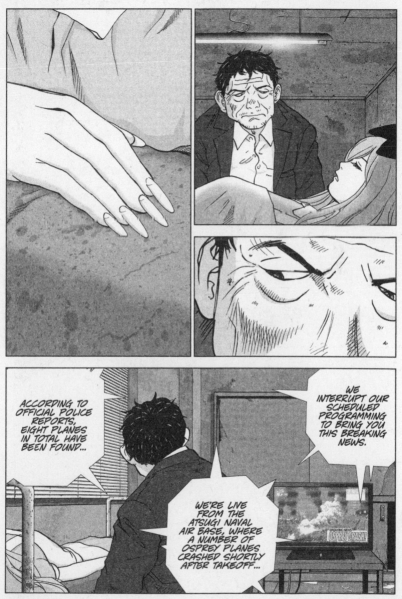

WE INTERRUPT OUR SCHEDULED PROGRAMMING TO BRING YOU THIS BREAKING NEWS.
WE'RE LIVE FROM THE ATSUGI NAVAL AIR BASE, WHERE A NUMBER OF OSPREY PLANES CRASHED SHORTLY AFTER TAKEOFF...
BREAKING NEWS
OSPREY CRASH!
ACCORDING TO OFFICIAL POLICE REPORTS, EIGHT PLANES IN TOTAL HAVE BEEN FOUND...

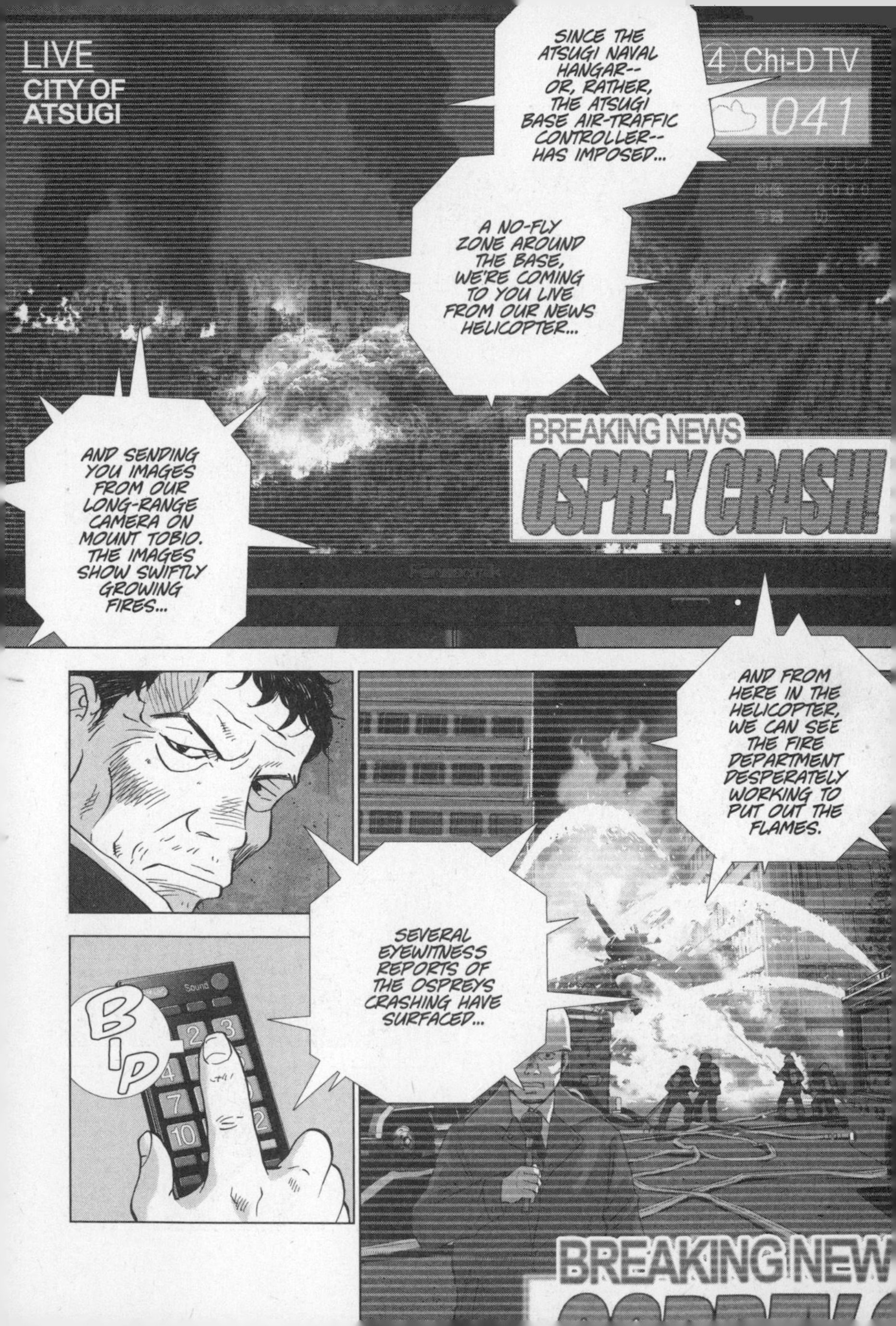
4 Chi-D TV 041
SINCE THE ATSUGI NAVAL HANGAR-- OR, RATHER, THE ATSUGI BASE AIR-TRAFFIC CONTROLLER-- HAS IMPOSED...
LIVE
CITY OF ATSUGI
A NO-FLY ZONE AROUND THE BASE, WE'RE COMING TO YOU LIVE FROM OUR NEWS HELICOPTER...
BREAKING NEWS
OSPREY CRASH!
AND SENDING YOU IMAGES FROM OUR LONG-RANGE CAMERA ON MOUNT TOBIO. THE IMAGES SHOW SWIFTLY GROWING FIRES...
AND FROM HERE IN THE HELICOPTER, WE CAN SEE THE FIRE DEPARTMENT DESPERATELY WORKING TO PUT OUT THE FLAMES.
SEVERAL EYEWITNESS REPORTS OF THE OSPREYS CRASHING HAVE SURFACED...
BREAKING NEW
Sound
BIP

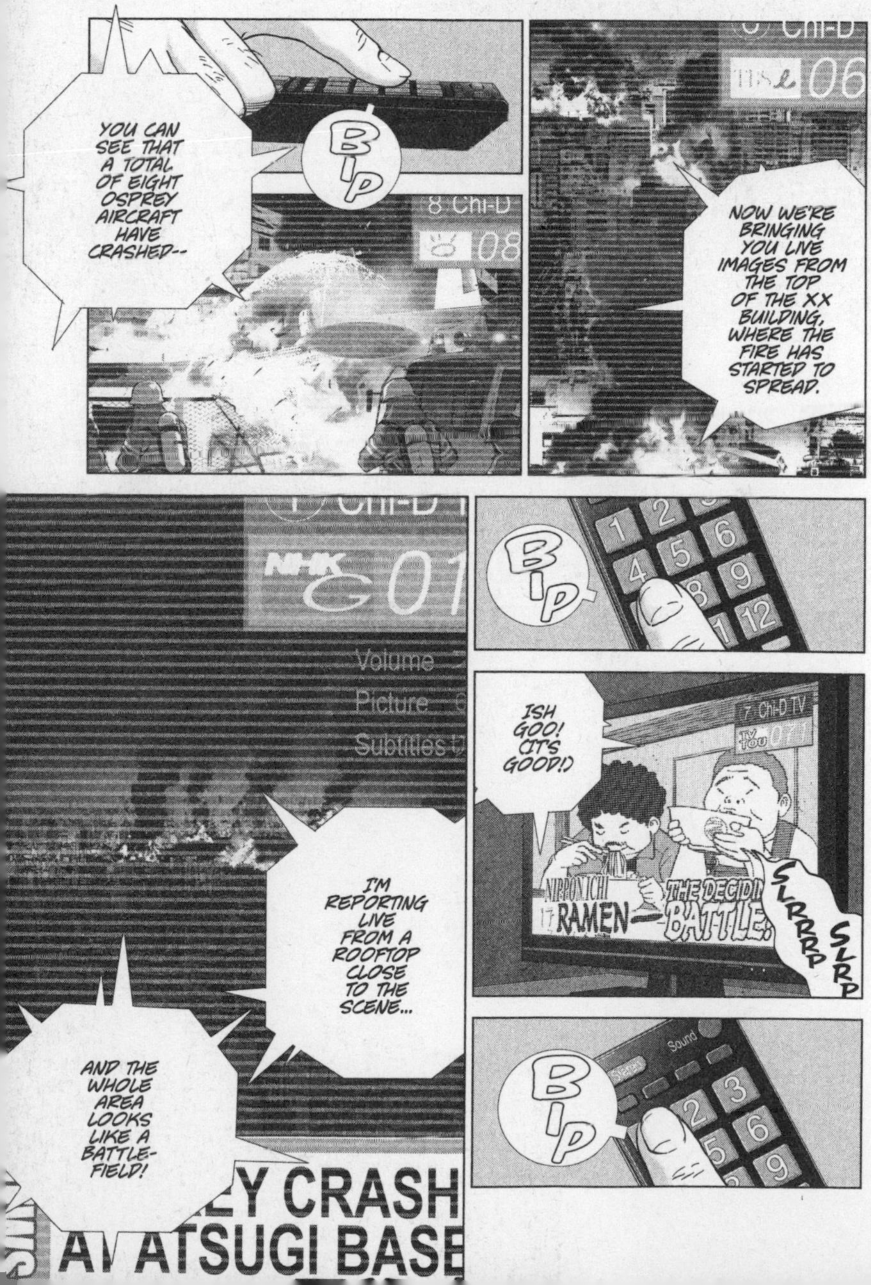

NOW WE'RE BRINGING YOU LIVE IMAGES FROM THE TOP OF THE XX BUILDING, WHERE THE FIRE HAS STARTED TO SPREAD.
BIP
8 Chi-D
YOU CAN SEE THAT A TOTAL OF EIGHT OSPREY AIRCRAFT HAVE CRASHED--
BIP
7 Chi-D TV
ISH GOO! (IT'S GOOD!)
NIPPON ICHI RAMEN
SLRRRP SLRP
BIP
Sound
Volume
Picture
Subtitles
I'M REPORTING LIVE FROM A ROOFTOP CLOSE TO THE SCENE...
AND THE WHOLE AREA LOOKS LIKE A BATTLE-FIELD!
EY CRASH
ATSUGI BASE

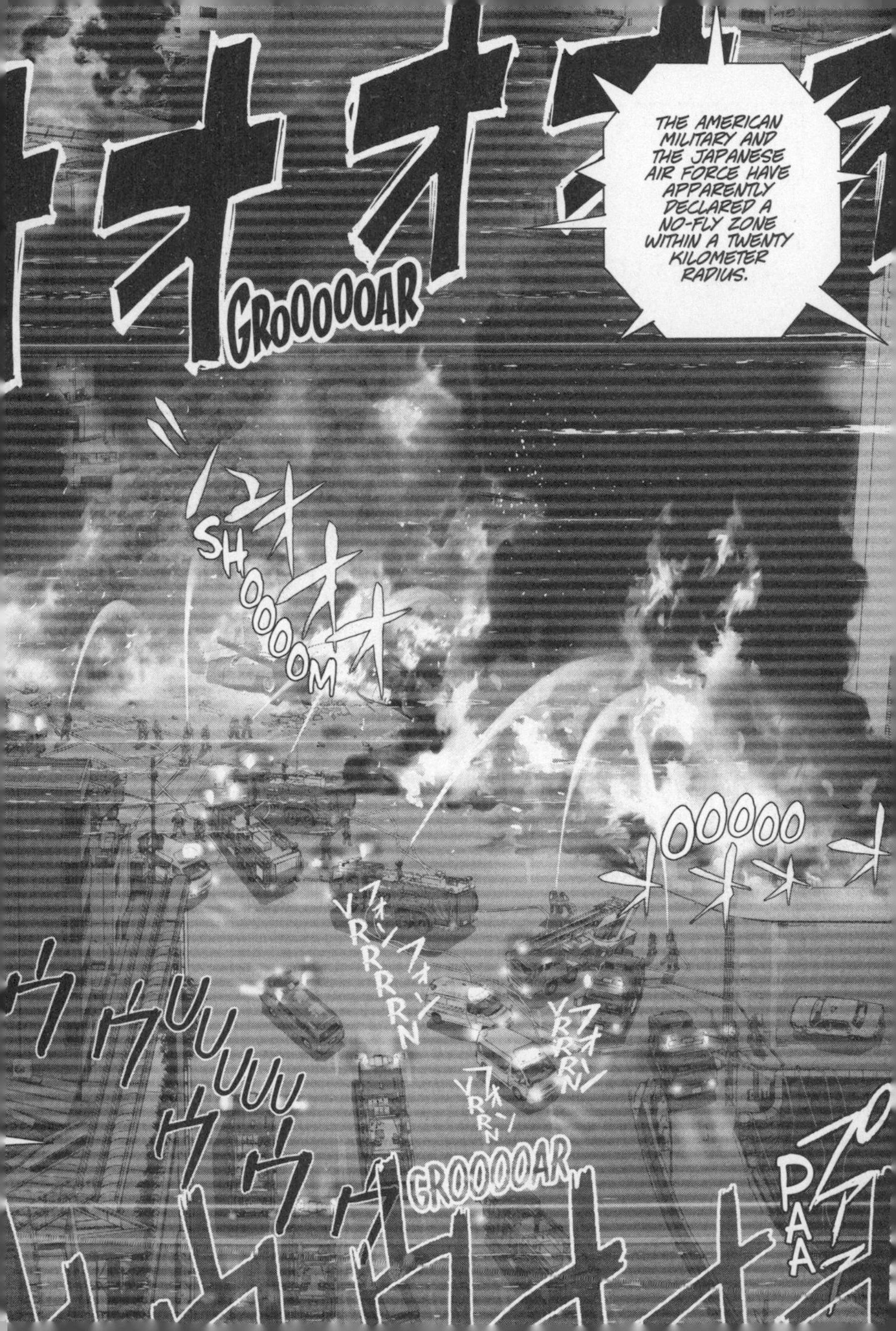
THE AMERICAN MILITARY AND THE JAPANESE AIR FORCE HAVE APPARENTLY DECLARED A NO-FLY ZONE WITHIN A TWENTY KILOMETER RADIUS.
GROOOOOAR
SHOOOOOM
OOOOO
VRRN
VRRRN
VRRRRRN
PAA
GROOOOAR
UUUUUU

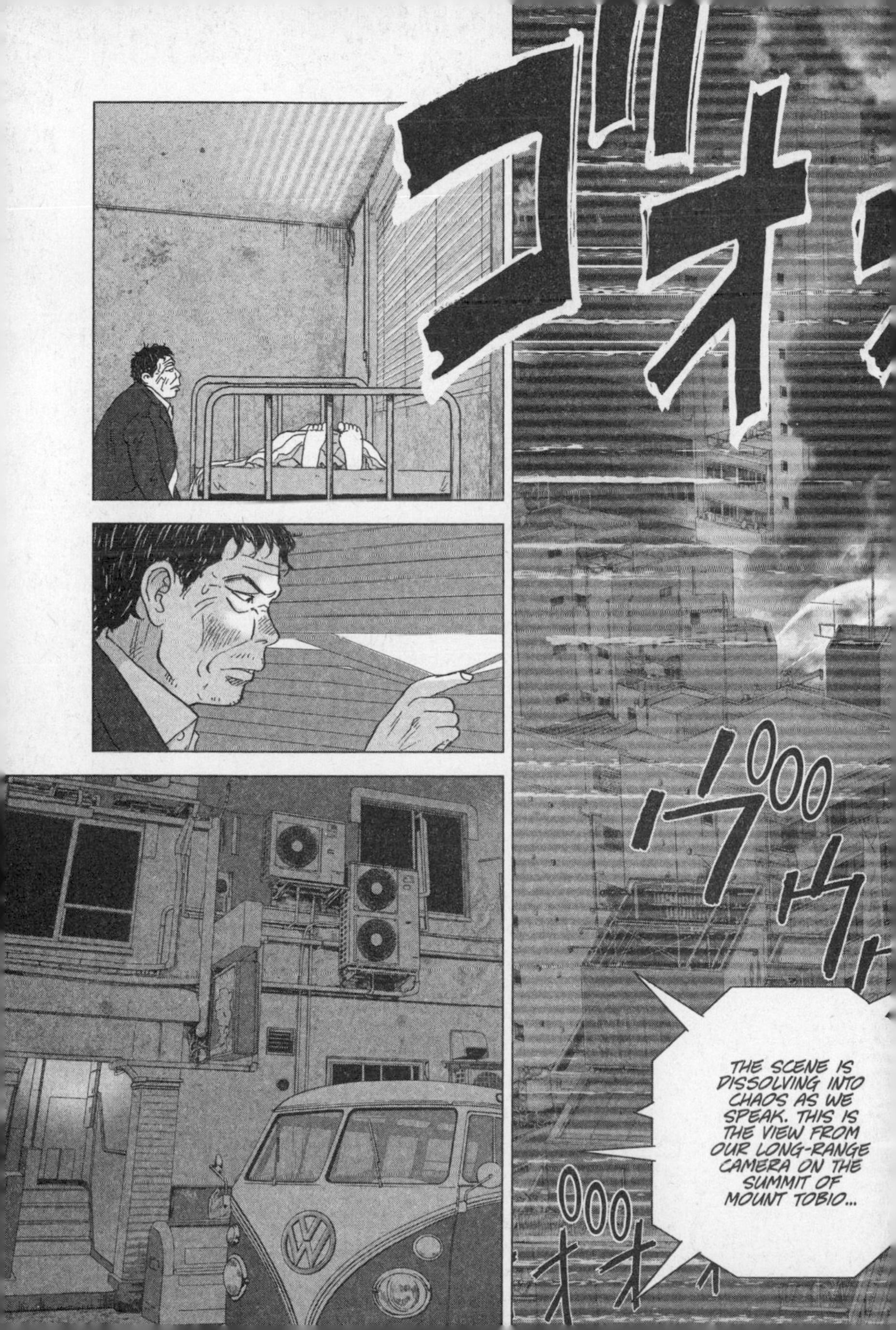
THE SCENE IS DISSOLVING INTO CHAOS AS WE SPEAK. THIS IS THE VIEW FROM OUR LONG-RANGE CAMERA ON THE SUMMIT OF MOUNT TOBIO...

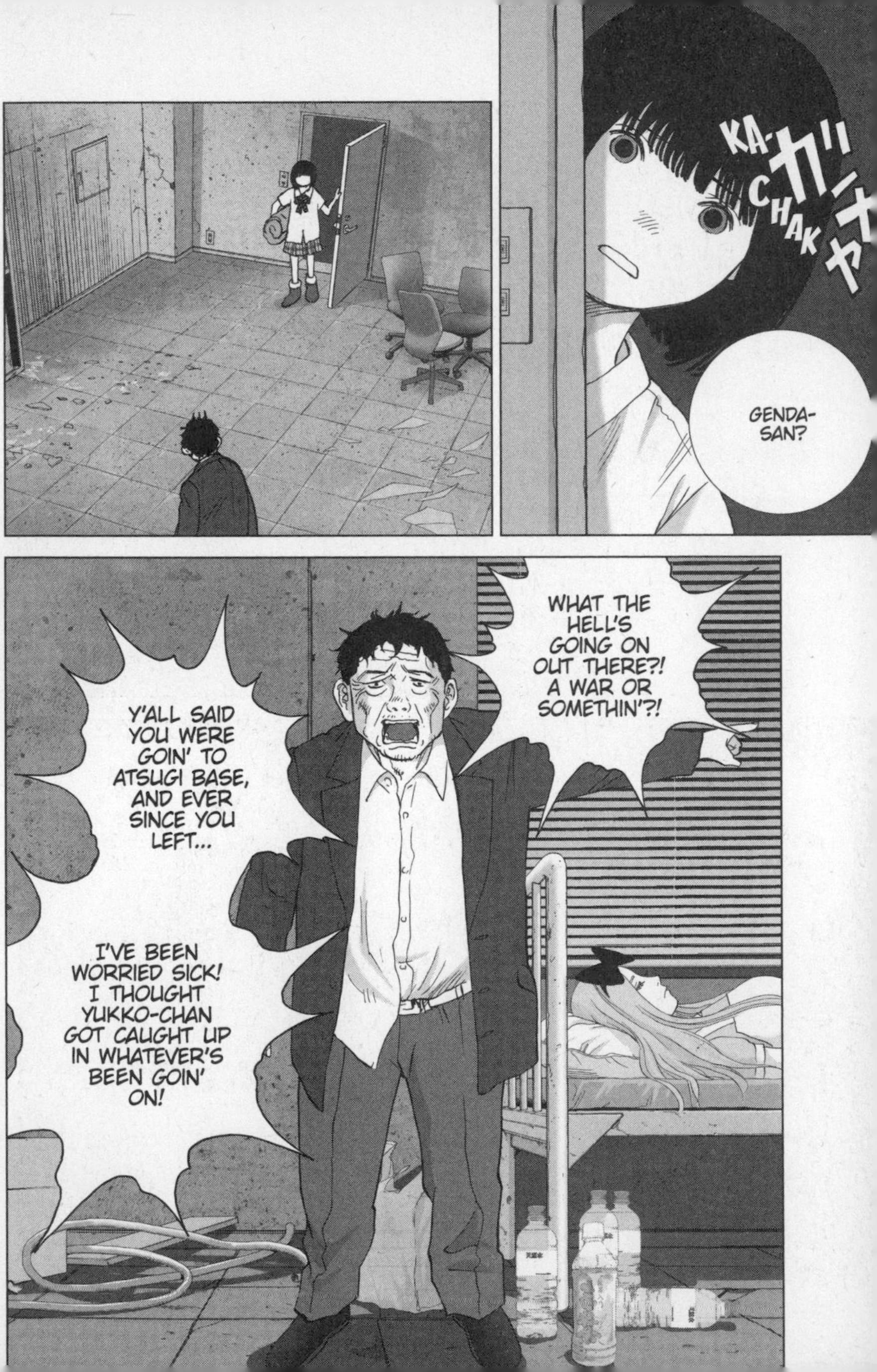
KA-CHAK
GENDA-SAN?
WHAT THE HELL'S GOING ON OUT THERE?! A WAR OR SOMETHIN'?!
Y'ALL SAID YOU WERE GOIN' TO ATSUGI BASE, AND EVER SINCE YOU LEFT...
I'VE BEEN WORRIED SICK! I THOUGHT YUKKO-CHAN GOT CAUGHT UP IN WHATEVER'S BEEN GOIN' ON!

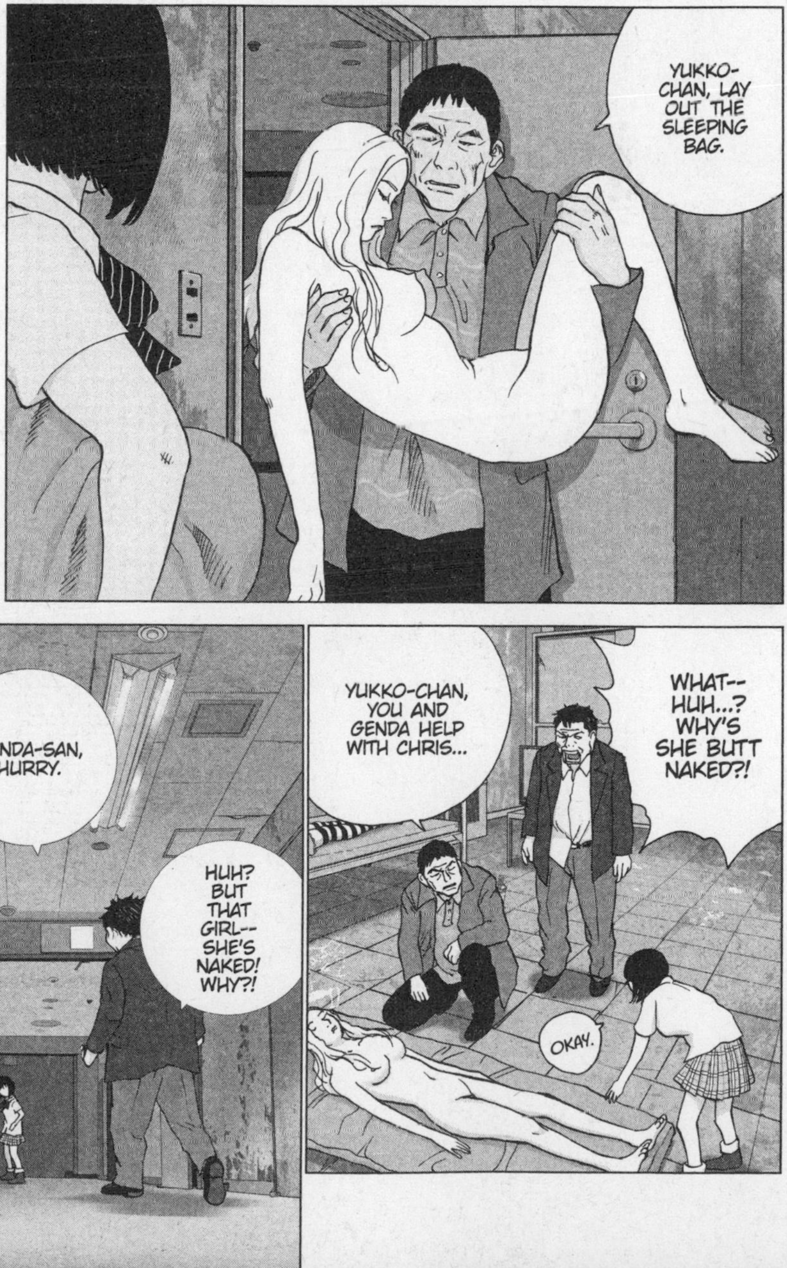
YUKKO-CHAN, LAY OUT THE SLEEPING BAG.
WHAT-- HUH...? WHY'S SHE BUTT NAKED?!
YUKKO-CHAN, YOU AND GENDA HELP WITH CHRIS...
OKAY.
GENDA-SAN, HURRY.
HUH? BUT THAT GIRL--SHE'S NAKED! WHY?!

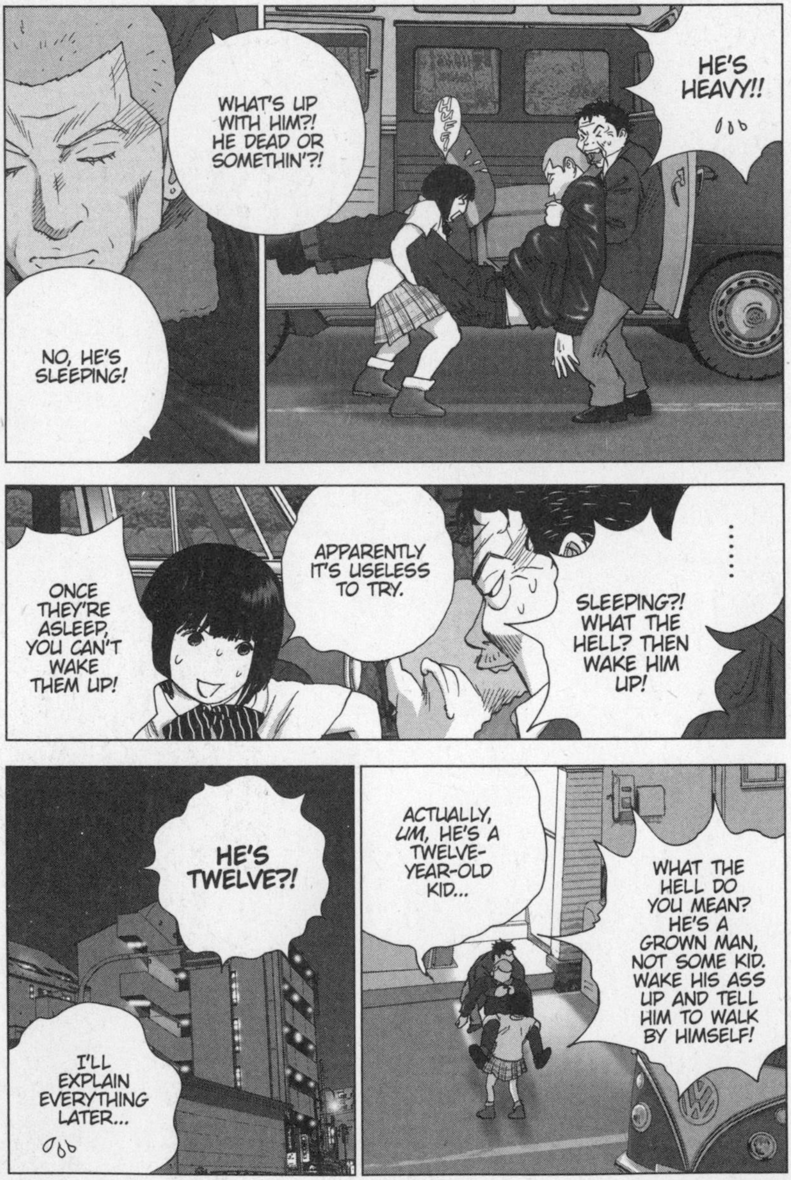
HE'S HEAVY!!
HUFF
WHAT'S UP WITH HIM?! HE DEAD OR SOMETHIN'?!
NO, HE'S SLEEPING!
......
SLEEPING?! WHAT THE HELL? THEN WAKE HIM UP!
APPARENTLY IT'S USELESS TO TRY.
ONCE THEY'RE ASLEEP, YOU CAN'T WAKE THEM UP!
WHAT THE HELL DO YOU MEAN? HE'S A GROWN MAN, NOT SOME KID. WAKE HIS ASS UP AND TELL HIM TO WALK BY HIMSELF!
ACTUALLY, UM, HE'S A TWELVE-YEAR-OLD KID...
HE'S TWELVE?!
I'LL EXPLAIN EVERYTHING LATER...

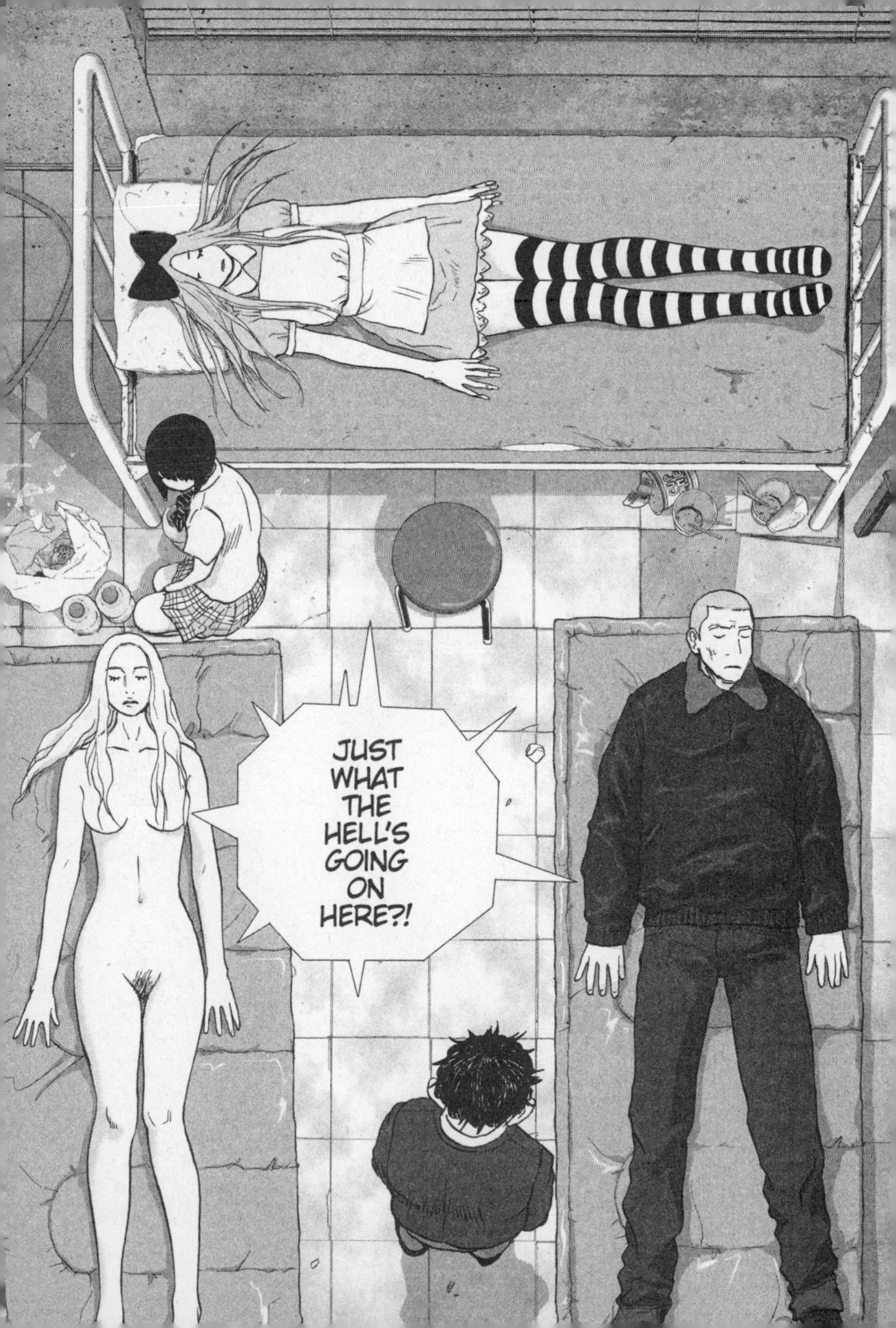
JUST WHAT THE HELL'S GOING ON HERE?!

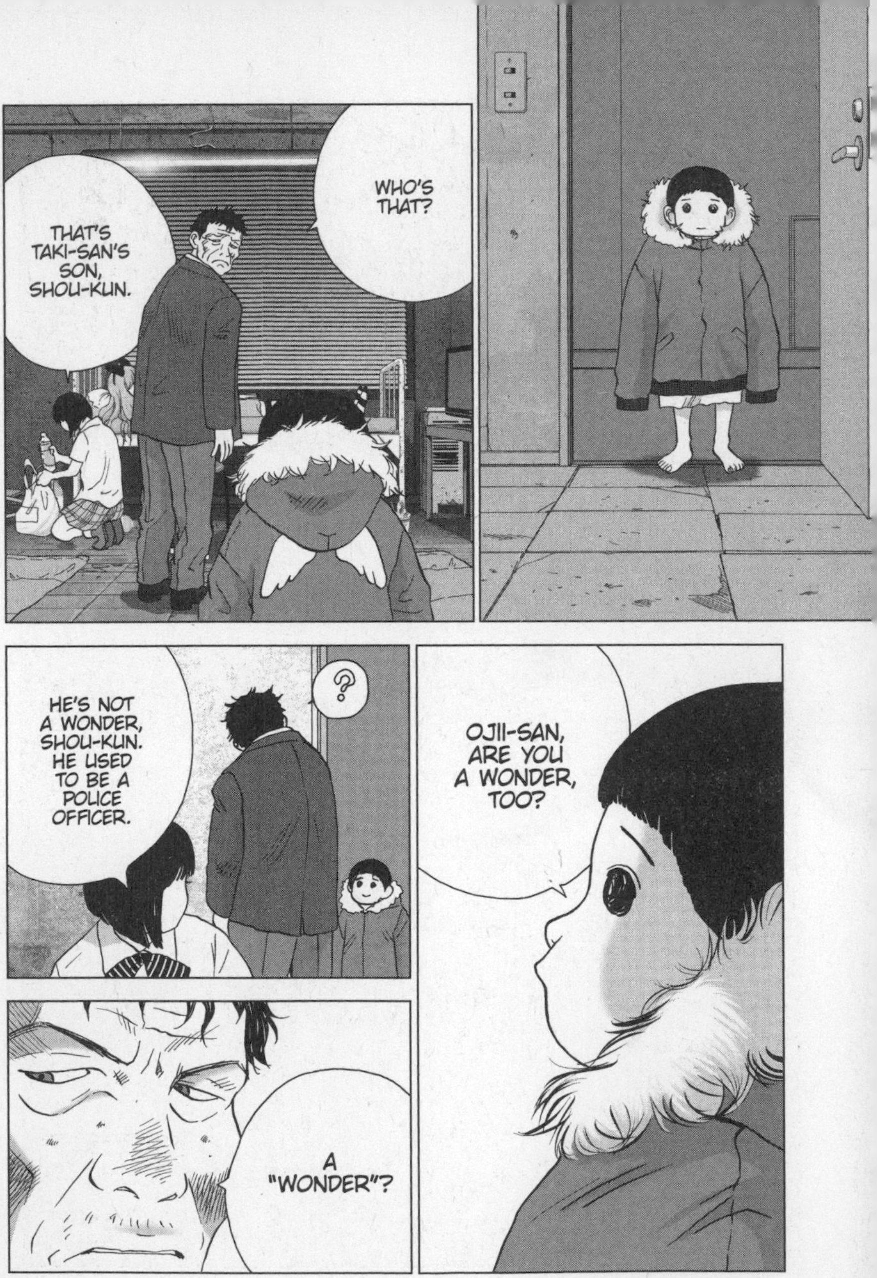
WHO'S THAT?
THAT'S TAKI-SAN'S SON, SHOU-KUN.
OJII-SAN, ARE YOU A WONDER, TOO?
?
HE'S NOT A WONDER, SHOU-KUN. HE USED TO BE A POLICE OFFICER.
A "WONDER"?

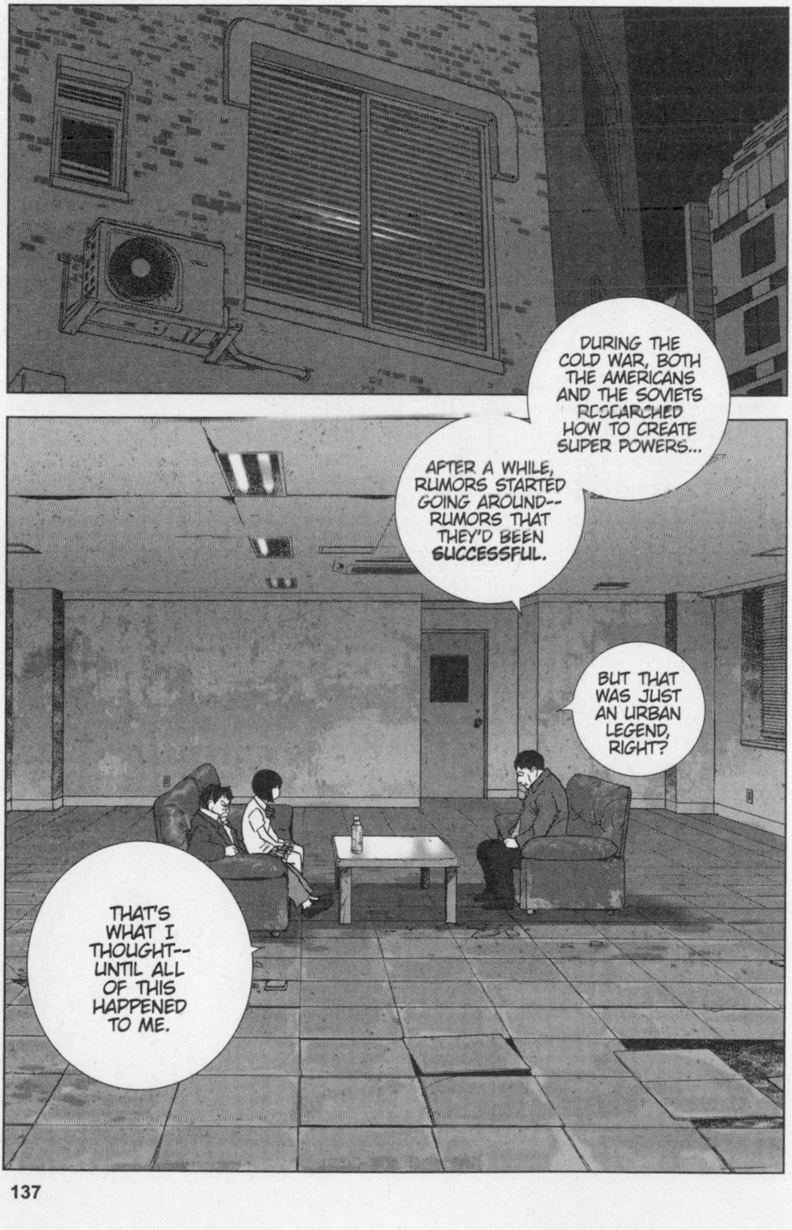
DURING THE COLD WAR, BOTH THE AMERICANS AND THE SOVIETS RESEARCHED HOW TO CREATE SUPER POWERS...
AFTER A WHILE, RUMORS STARTED GOING AROUND-- RUMORS THAT THEY'D BEEN **SUCCESSFUL.**
BUT THAT WAS JUST AN URBAN LEGEND, RIGHT?
THAT'S WHAT I THOUGHT-- UNTIL ALL OF THIS HAPPENED TO ME.

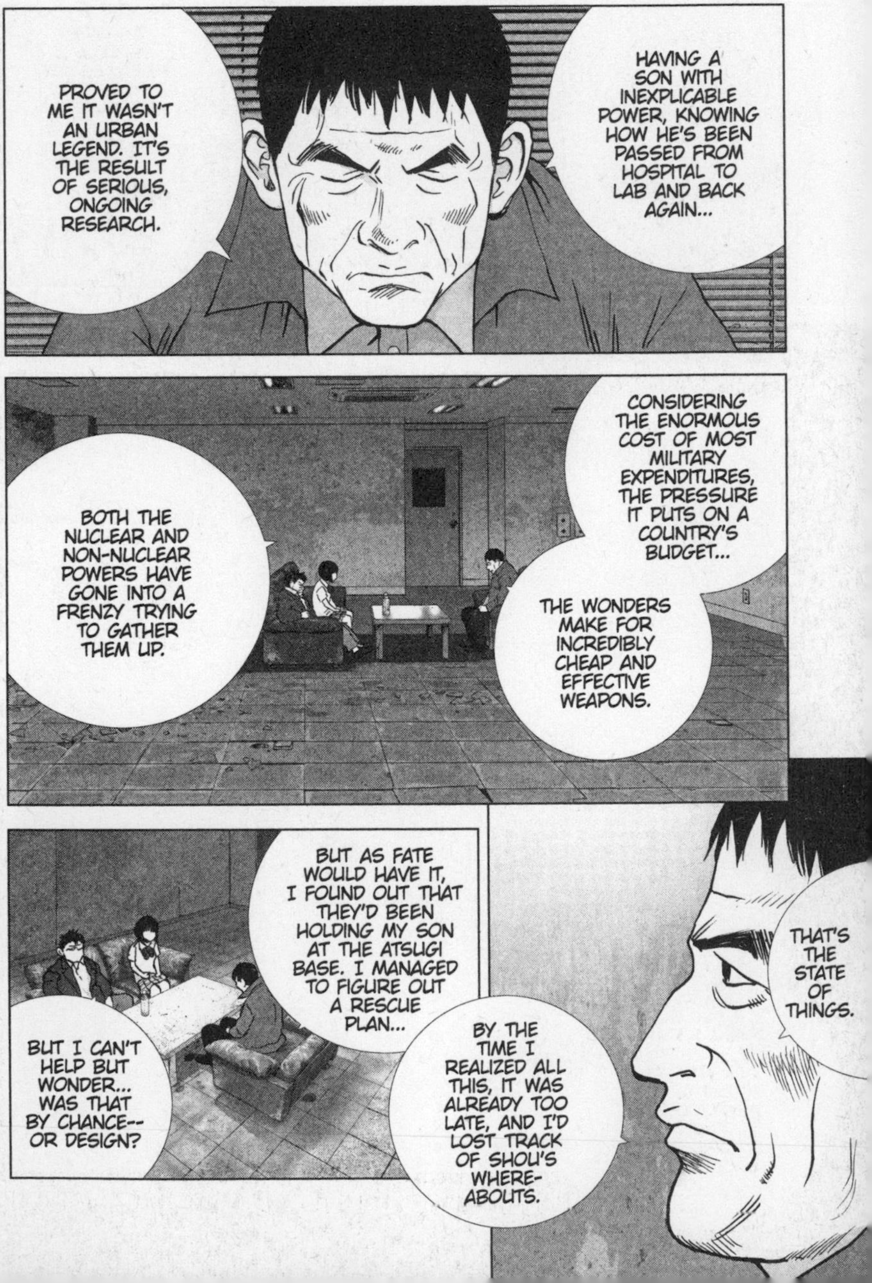
HAVING A SON WITH INEXPLICABLE POWER, KNOWING HOW HE'S BEEN PASSED FROM HOSPITAL TO LAB AND BACK AGAIN...
PROVED TO ME IT WASN'T AN URBAN LEGEND. IT'S THE RESULT OF SERIOUS, ONGOING RESEARCH.
CONSIDERING THE ENORMOUS COST OF MOST MILITARY EXPENDITURES, THE PRESSURE IT PUTS ON A COUNTRY'S BUDGET...
THE WONDERS MAKE FOR INCREDIBLY CHEAP AND EFFECTIVE WEAPONS.
BOTH THE NUCLEAR AND NON-NUCLEAR POWERS HAVE GONE INTO A FRENZY TRYING TO GATHER THEM UP.
THAT'S THE STATE OF THINGS.
BUT AS FATE WOULD HAVE IT, I FOUND OUT THAT THEY'D BEEN HOLDING MY SON AT THE ATSUGI BASE. I MANAGED TO FIGURE OUT A RESCUE PLAN...
BUT I CAN'T HELP BUT WONDER... WAS THAT BY CHANCE--OR DESIGN?
BY THE TIME I REALIZED ALL THIS, IT WAS ALREADY TOO LATE, AND I'D LOST TRACK OF SHOU'S WHERE-ABOUTS.

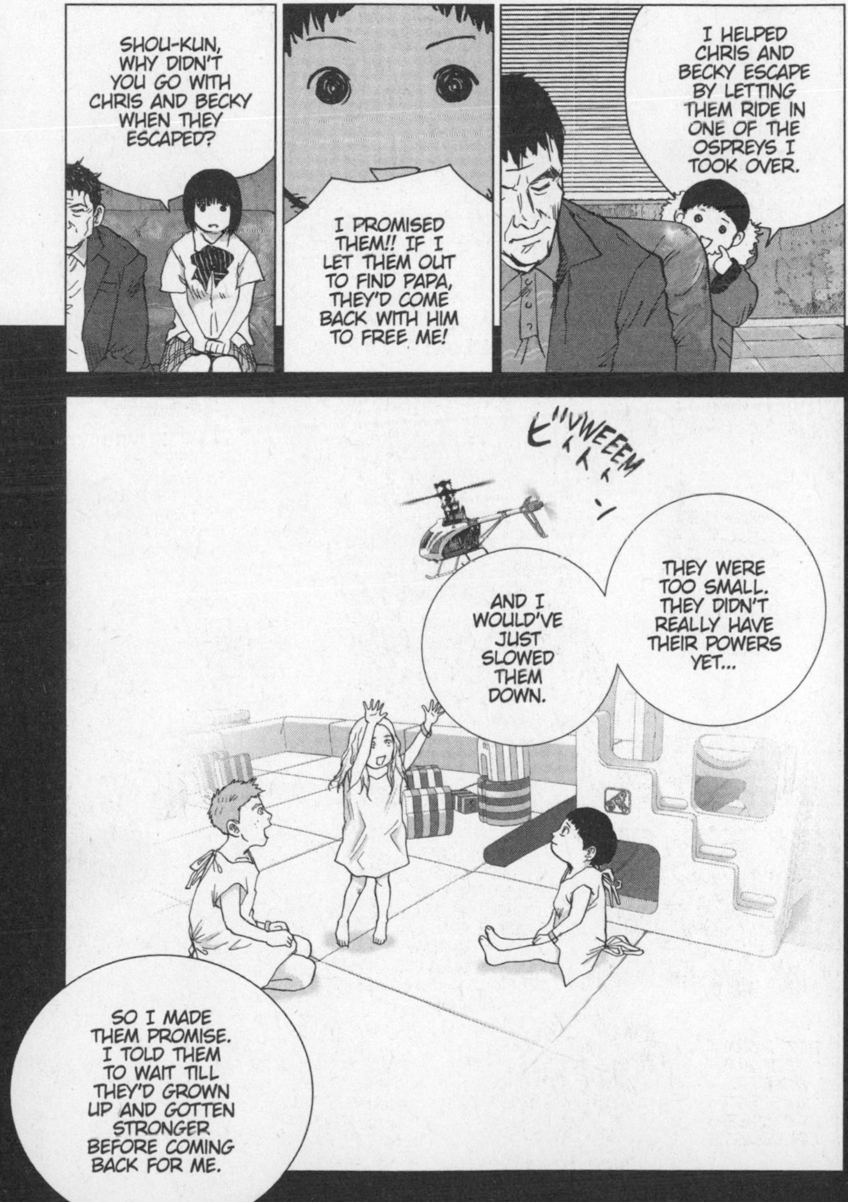
I HELPED CHRIS AND BECKY ESCAPE BY LETTING THEM RIDE IN ONE OF THE OSPREYS I TOOK OVER.
I PROMISED THEM!! IF I LET THEM OUT TO FIND PAPA, THEY'D COME BACK WITH HIM TO FREE ME!
SHOU-KUN, WHY DIDN'T YOU GO WITH CHRIS AND BECKY WHEN THEY ESCAPED?
VWEEEM
THEY WERE TOO SMALL. THEY DIDN'T REALLY HAVE THEIR POWERS YET...
AND I WOULD'VE JUST SLOWED THEM DOWN.
SO I MADE THEM PROMISE. I TOLD THEM TO WAIT TILL THEY'D GROWN UP AND GOTTEN STRONGER BEFORE COMING BACK FOR ME.

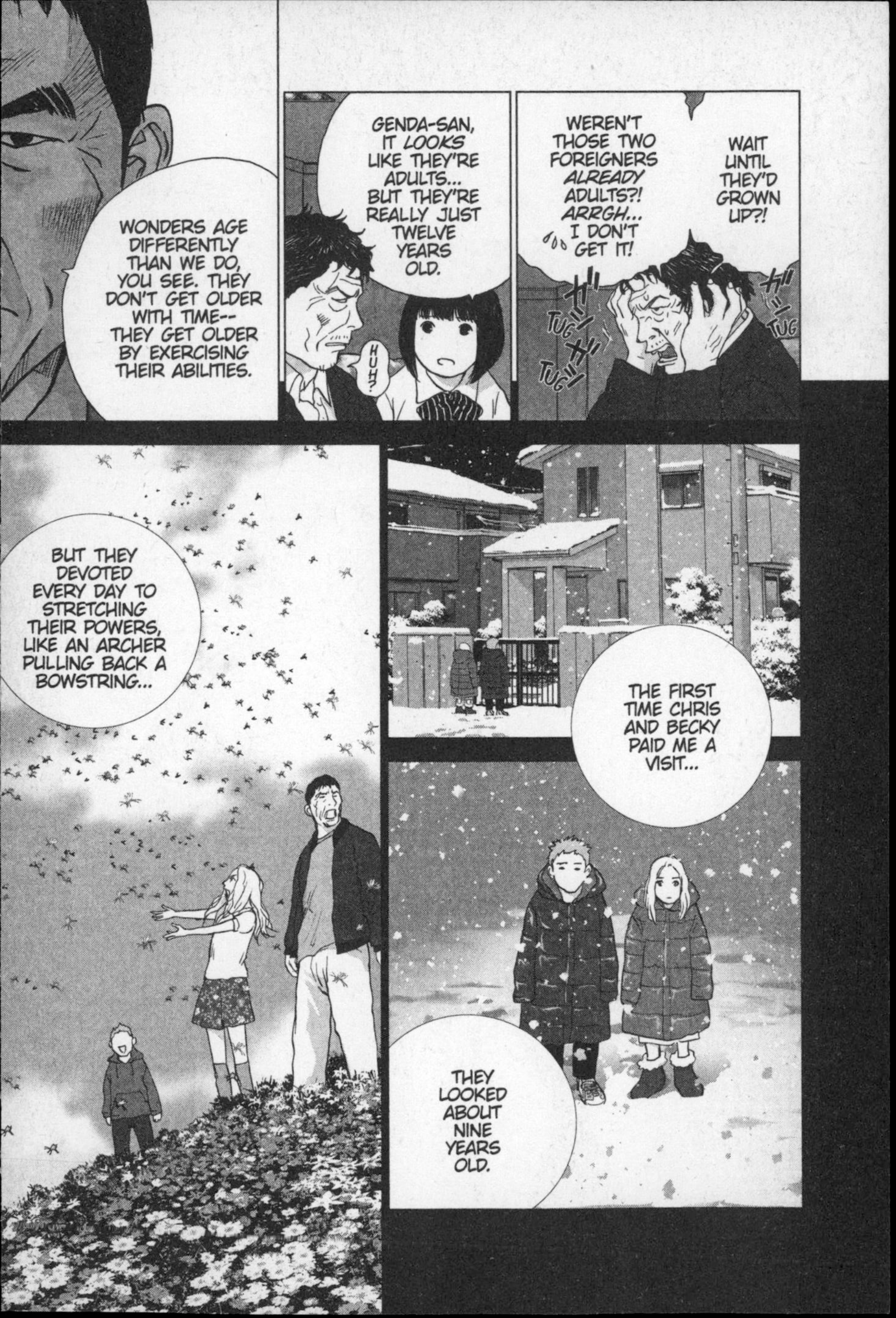
WAIT UNTIL THEY'D GROWN UP?!
WEREN'T THOSE TWO FOREIGNERS ALREADY ADULTS?! ARRGH... I DON'T GET IT!
TUG
TUG
TUG
TUG
GENDA-SAN, IT LOOKS LIKE THEY'RE ADULTS... BUT THEY'RE REALLY JUST TWELVE YEARS OLD.
HUH?
WONDERS AGE DIFFERENTLY THAN WE DO, YOU SEE. THEY DON'T GET OLDER WITH TIME--THEY GET OLDER BY EXERCISING THEIR ABILITIES.
THE FIRST TIME CHRIS AND BECKY PAID ME A VISIT...
THEY LOOKED ABOUT NINE YEARS OLD.
BUT THEY DEVOTED EVERY DAY TO STRETCHING THEIR POWERS, LIKE AN ARCHER PULLING BACK A BOWSTRING...

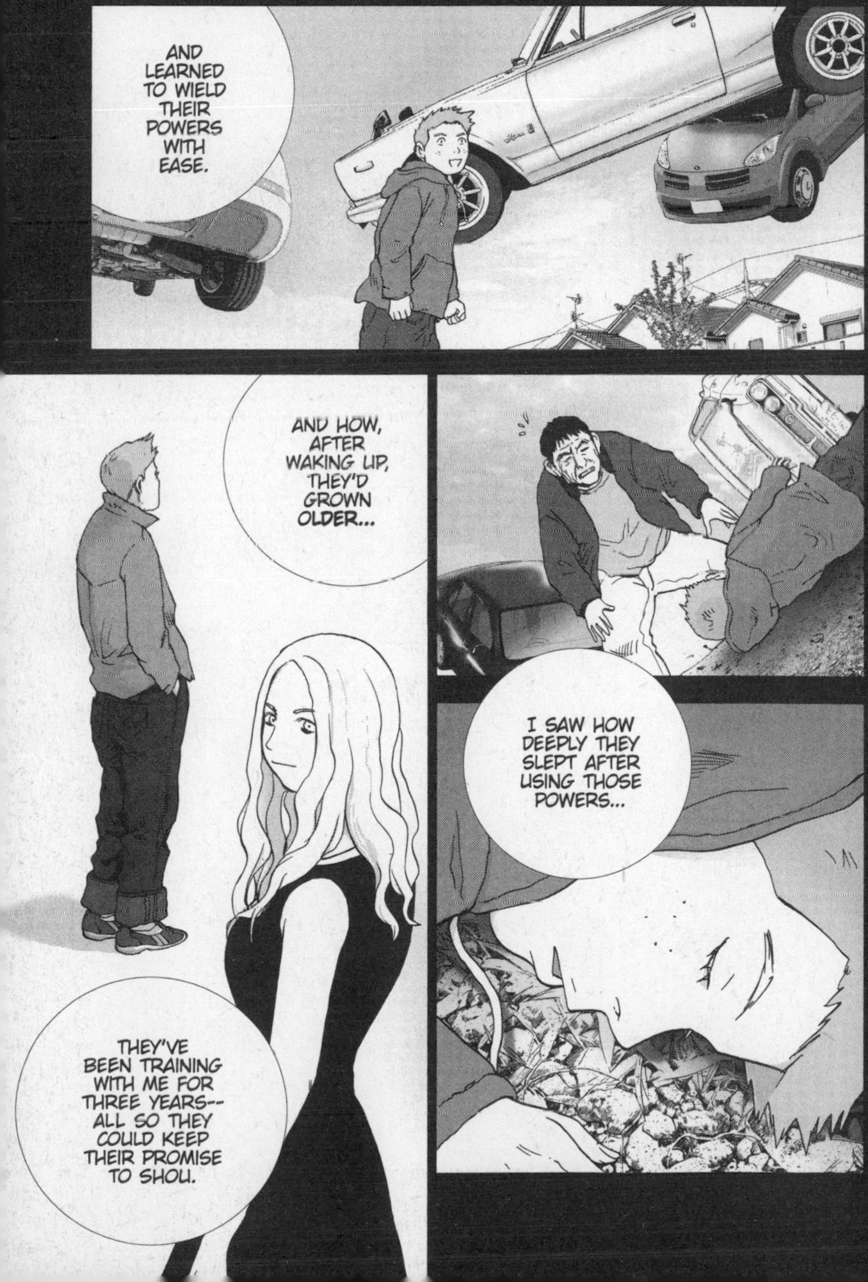
AND LEARNED TO WIELD THEIR POWERS WITH EASE.
I SAW HOW DEEPLY THEY SLEPT AFTER USING THOSE POWERS...
AND HOW, AFTER WAKING UP, THEY'D GROWN OLDER...
THEY'VE BEEN TRAINING WITH ME FOR THREE YEARS-- ALL SO THEY COULD KEEP THEIR PROMISE TO SHOU.

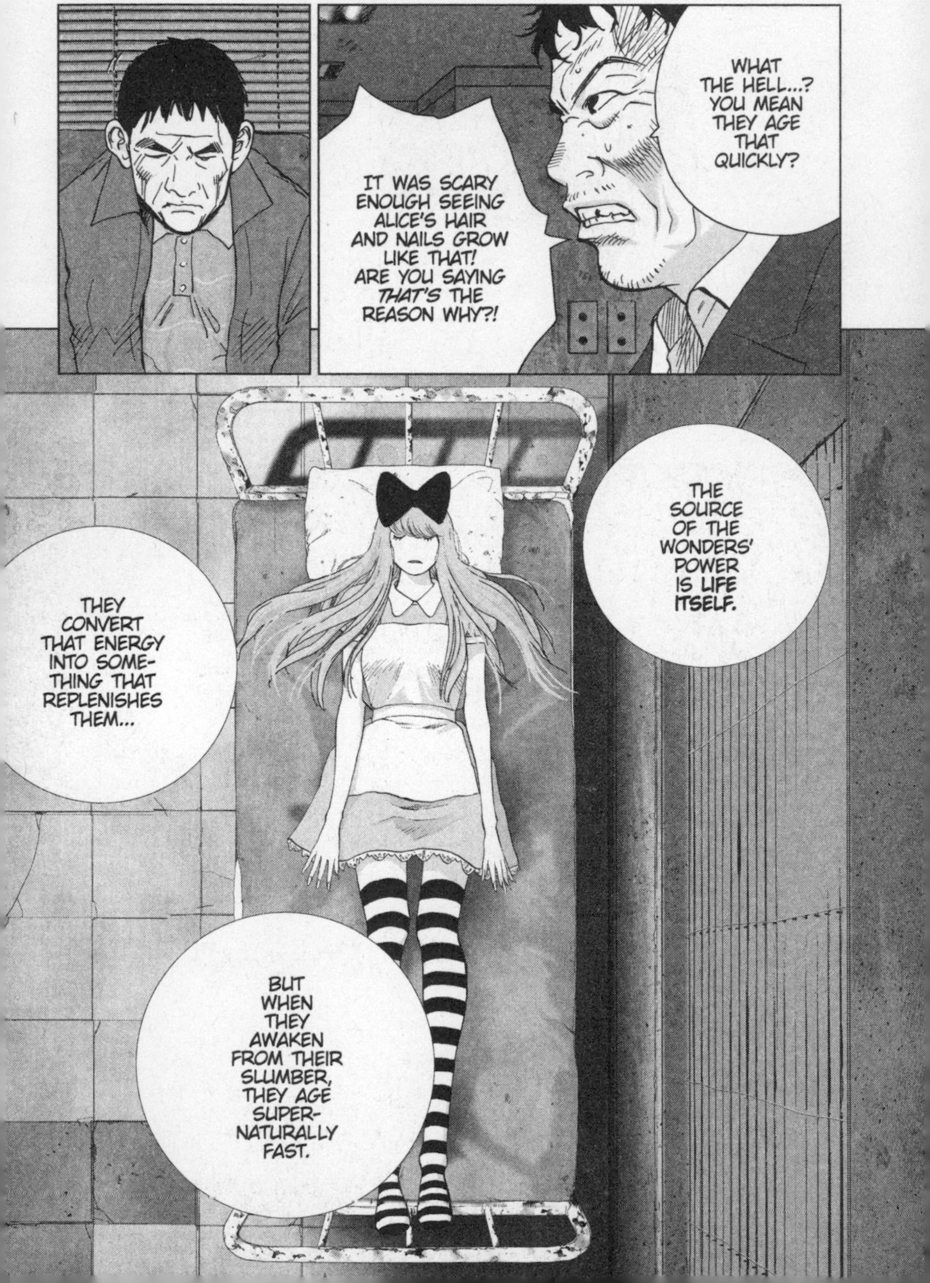
WHAT THE HELL...? YOU MEAN THEY AGE THAT QUICKLY?
IT WAS SCARY ENOUGH SEEING ALICE'S HAIR AND NAILS GROW LIKE THAT! ARE YOU SAYING *THAT'S* THE REASON WHY?!
THE SOURCE OF THE WONDERS' POWER IS LIFE ITSELF.
THEY CONVERT THAT ENERGY INTO SOME-THING THAT REPLENISHES THEM...
BUT WHEN THEY AWAKEN FROM THEIR SLUMBER, THEY AGE SUPER-NATURALLY FAST.

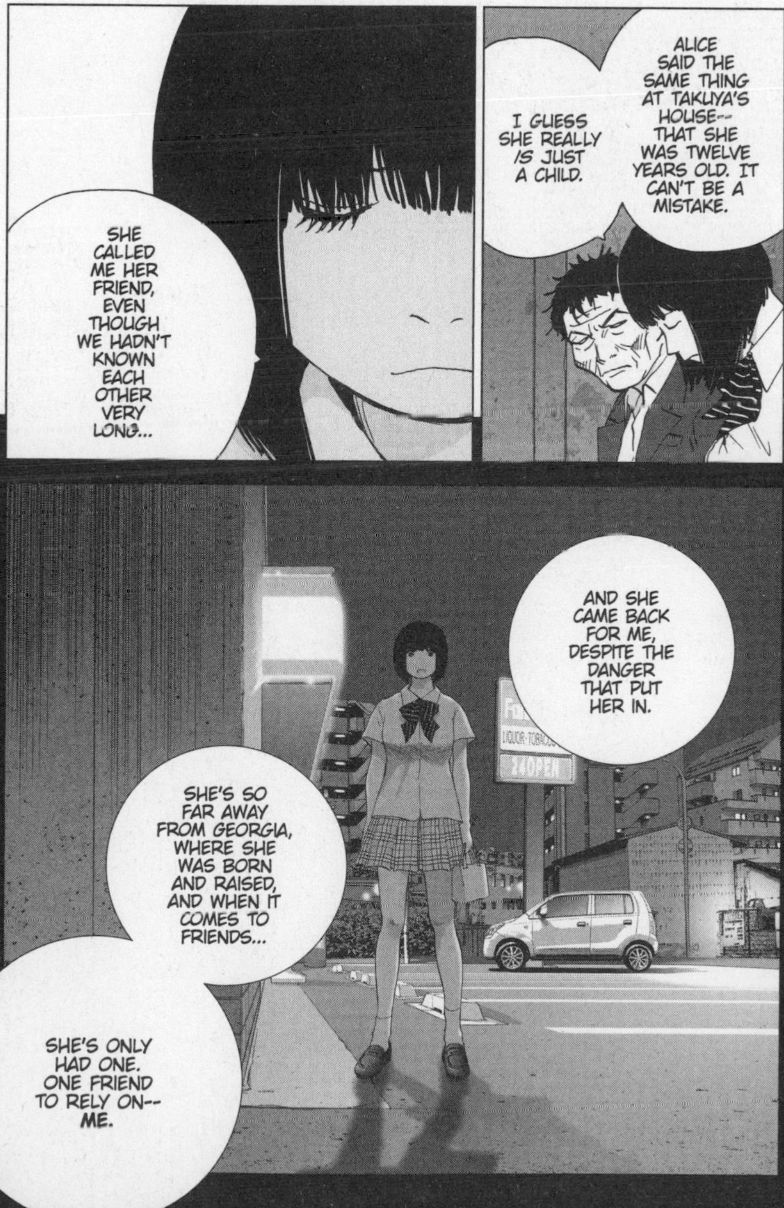
ALICE SAID THE SAME THING AT TAKUYA'S HOUSE-- THAT SHE WAS TWELVE YEARS OLD. IT CAN'T BE A MISTAKE.
I GUESS SHE REALLY IS JUST A CHILD.
SHE CALLED ME HER FRIEND, EVEN THOUGH WE HADN'T KNOWN EACH OTHER VERY LONG...
AND SHE CAME BACK FOR ME, DESPITE THE DANGER THAT PUT HER IN.
SHE'S SO FAR AWAY FROM GEORGIA, WHERE SHE WAS BORN AND RAISED, AND WHEN IT COMES TO FRIENDS...
SHE'S ONLY HAD ONE. ONE FRIEND TO RELY ON-- ME.

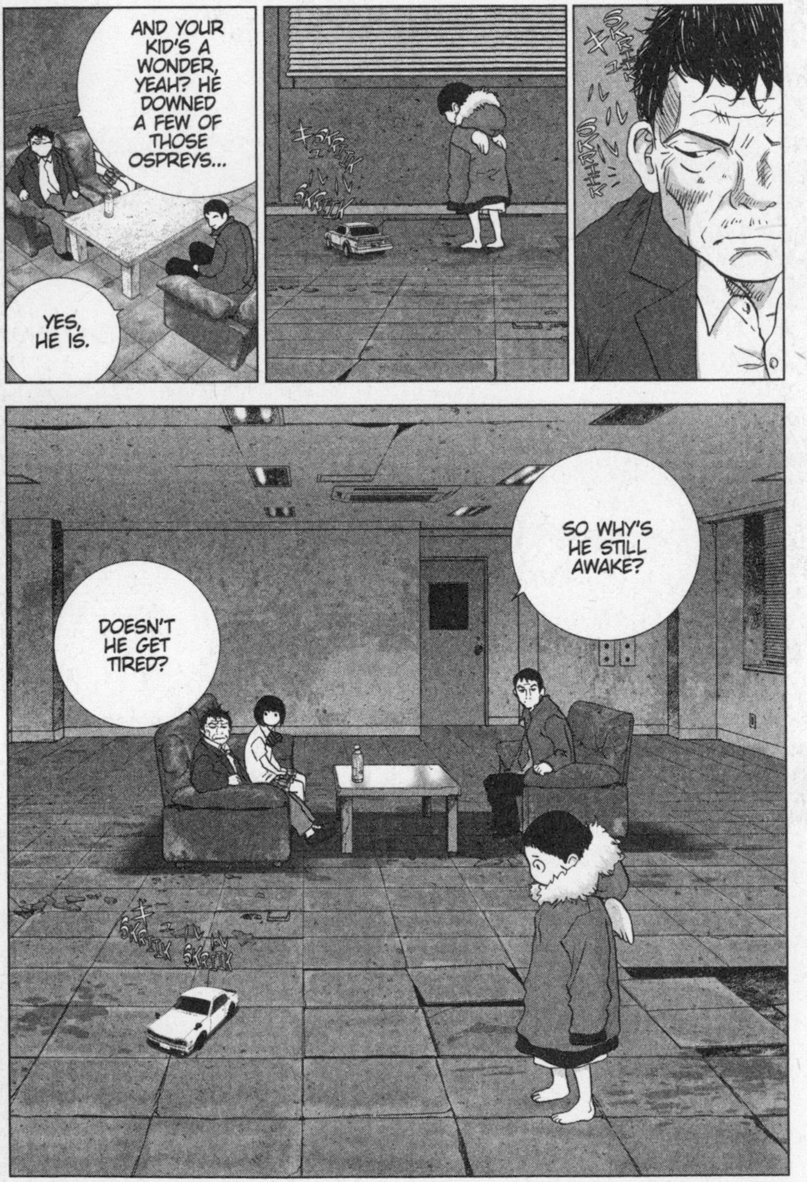
SKRIIK
SKRIIK
SKRIIK
SKRIIK
AND YOUR KID'S A WONDER, YEAH? HE DOWNED A FEW OF THOSE OSPREYS...
YES, HE IS.
SO WHY'S HE STILL AWAKE?
DOESN'T HE GET TIRED?
SKRIIK SKRIIK

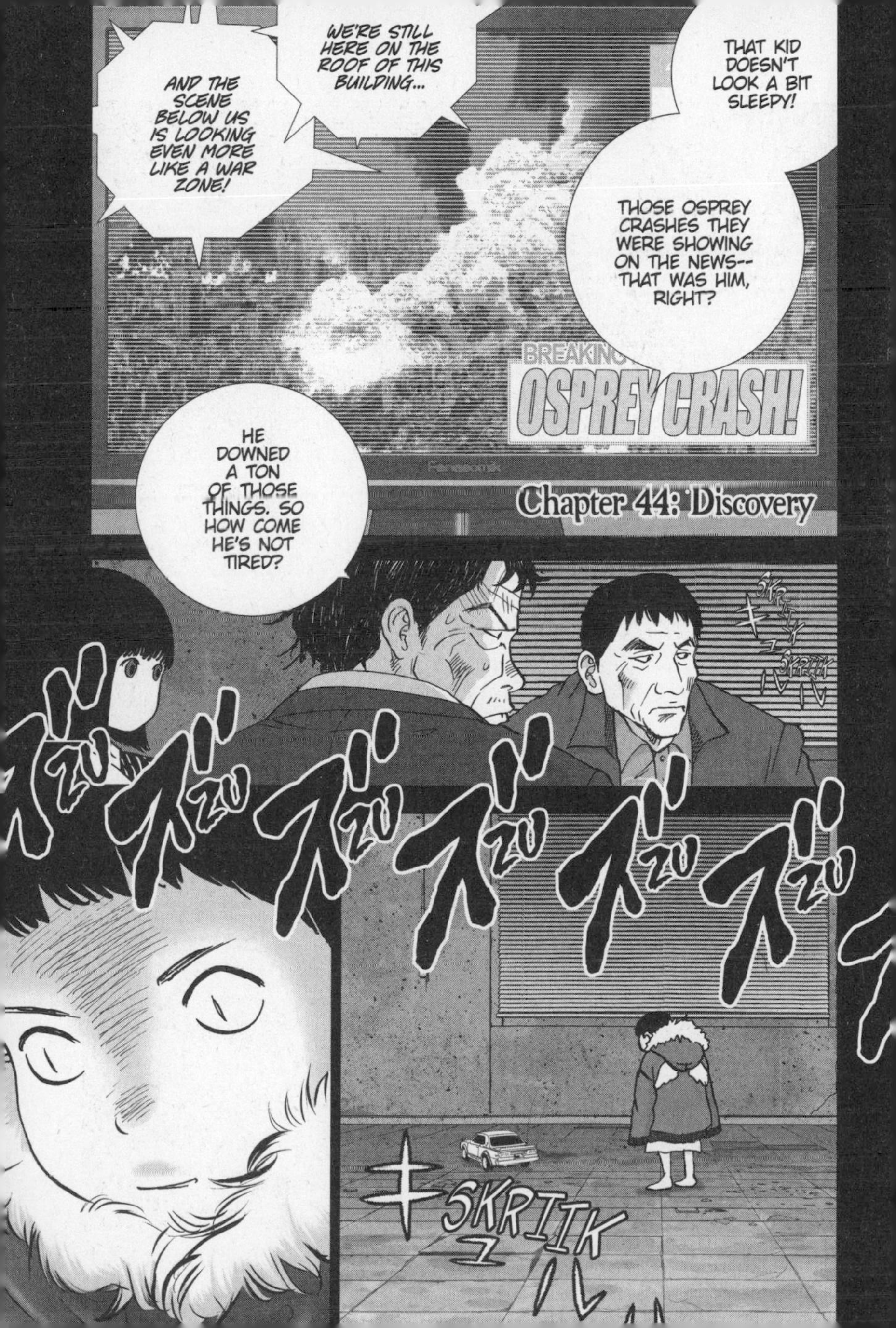
THAT KID DOESN'T LOOK A BIT SLEEPY!
WE'RE STILL HERE ON THE ROOF OF THIS BUILDING...
AND THE SCENE BELOW US IS LOOKING EVEN MORE LIKE A WAR ZONE!
THOSE OSPREY CRASHES THEY WERE SHOWING ON THE NEWS--THAT WAS HIM, RIGHT?
BREAKING
OSPREY CRASH!
HE DOWNED A TON OF THOSE THINGS. SO HOW COME HE'S NOT TIRED?
Chapter 44: Discovery
SKRIIK
SKRIIK
ZU ZU ZU ZU ZU ZU
SKRIIK

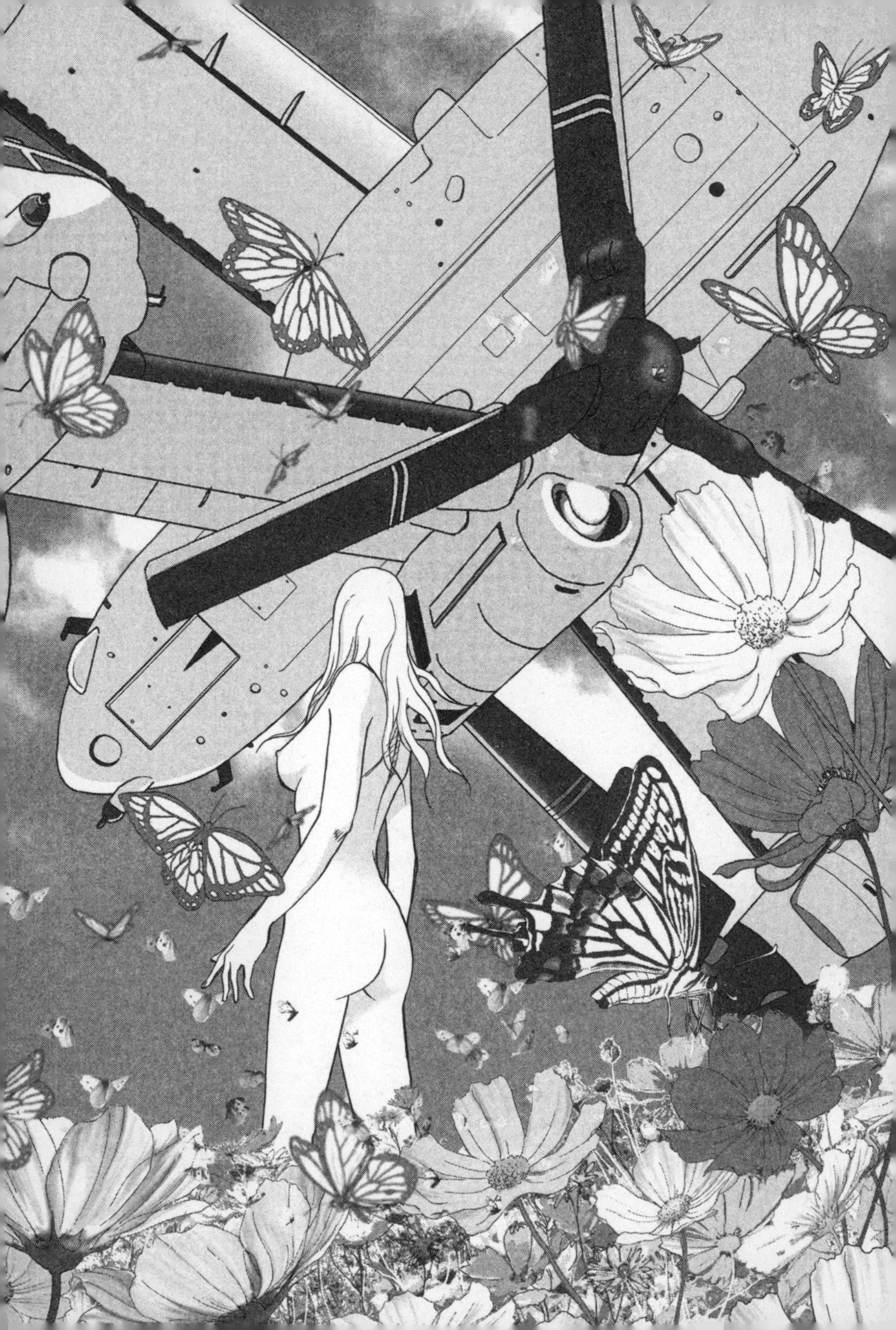

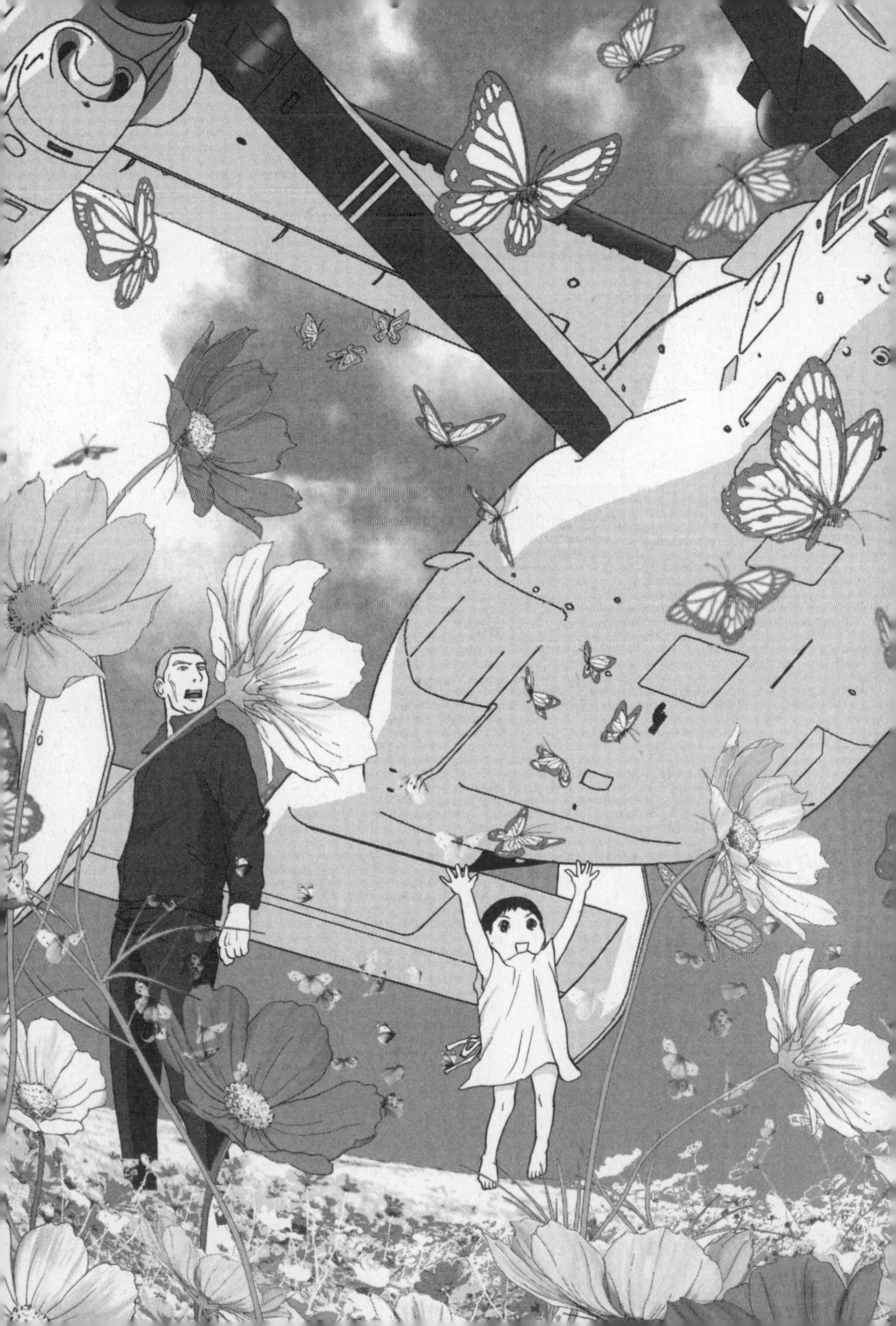

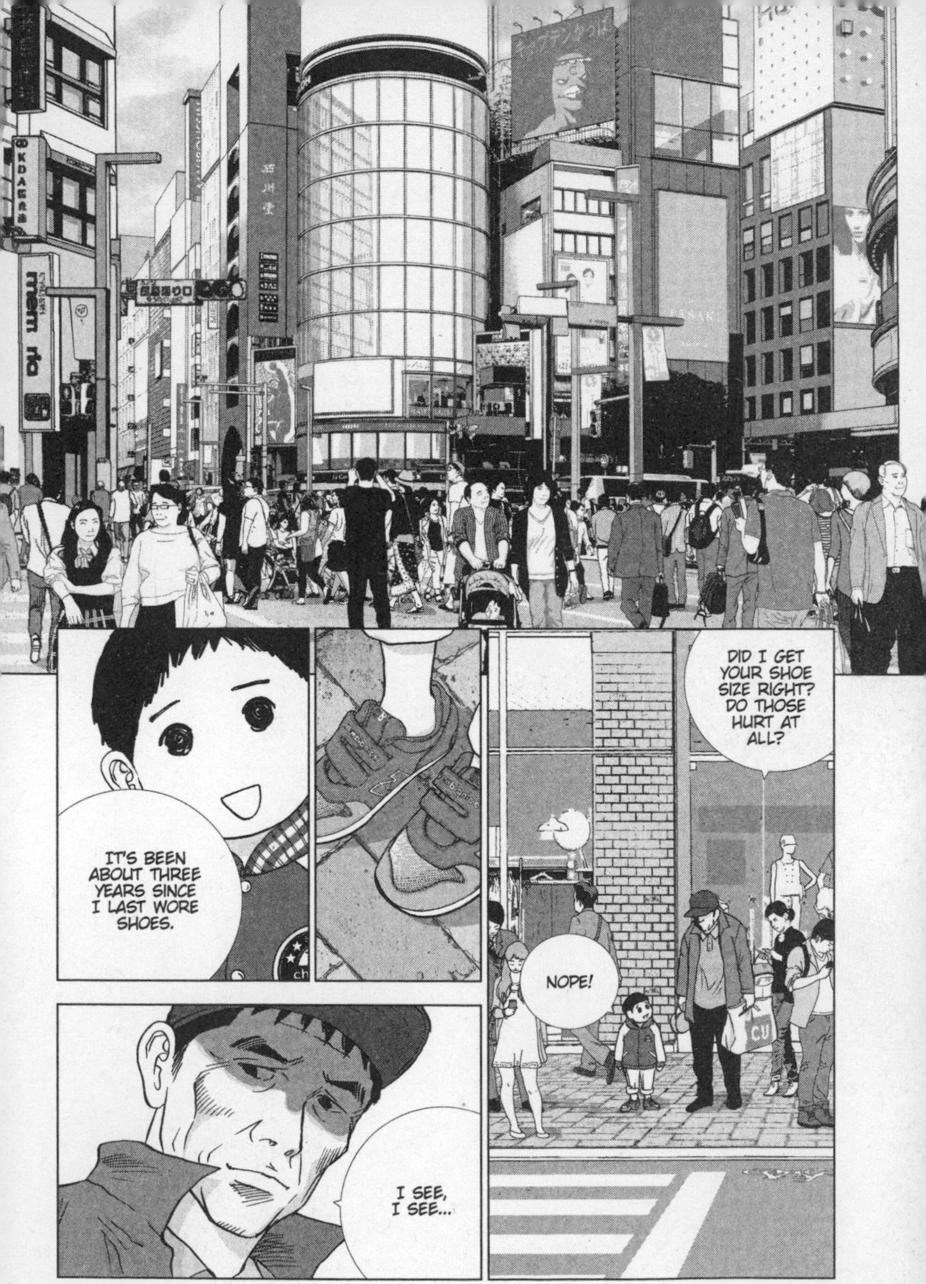
DID I GET YOUR SHOE SIZE RIGHT? DO THOSE HURT AT ALL?
NOPE!
IT'S BEEN ABOUT THREE YEARS SINCE I LAST WORE SHOES.
I SEE, I SEE...

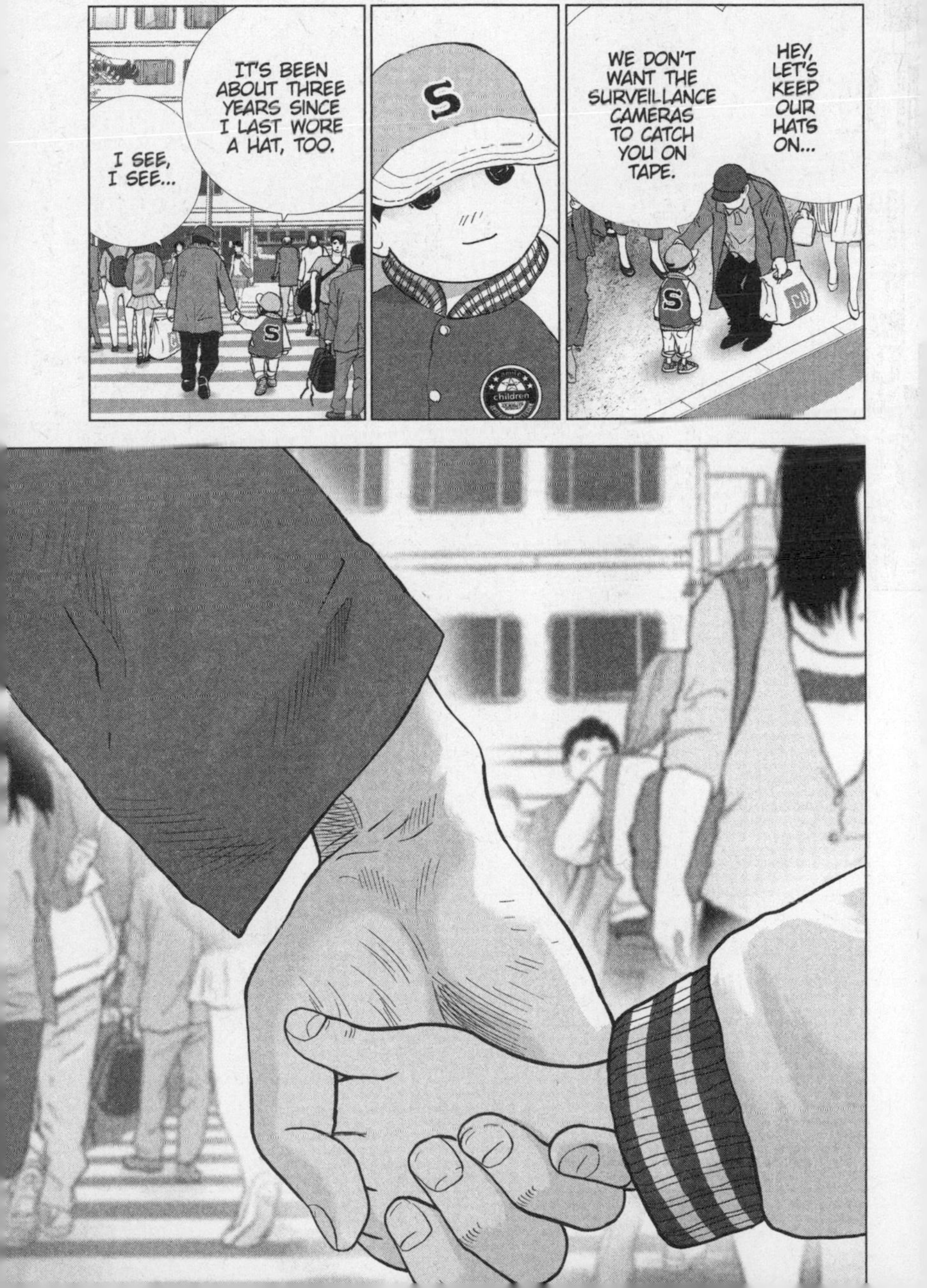
HEY, LET'S KEEP OUR HATS ON...
WE DON'T WANT THE SURVEILLANCE CAMERAS TO CATCH YOU ON TAPE.
IT'S BEEN ABOUT THREE YEARS SINCE I LAST WORE A HAT, TOO.
I SEE, I SEE...

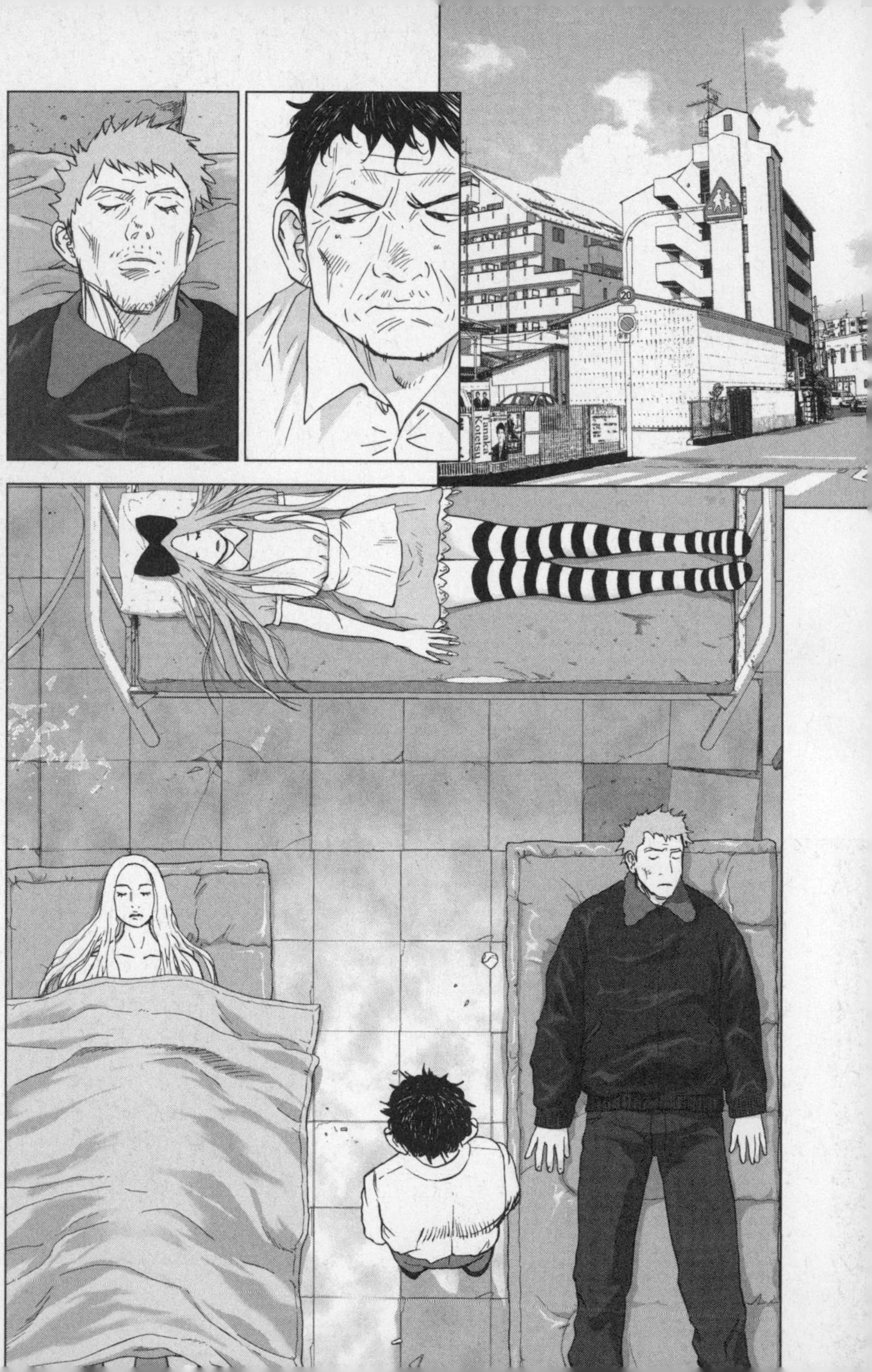
Tanaka
Kotetsu

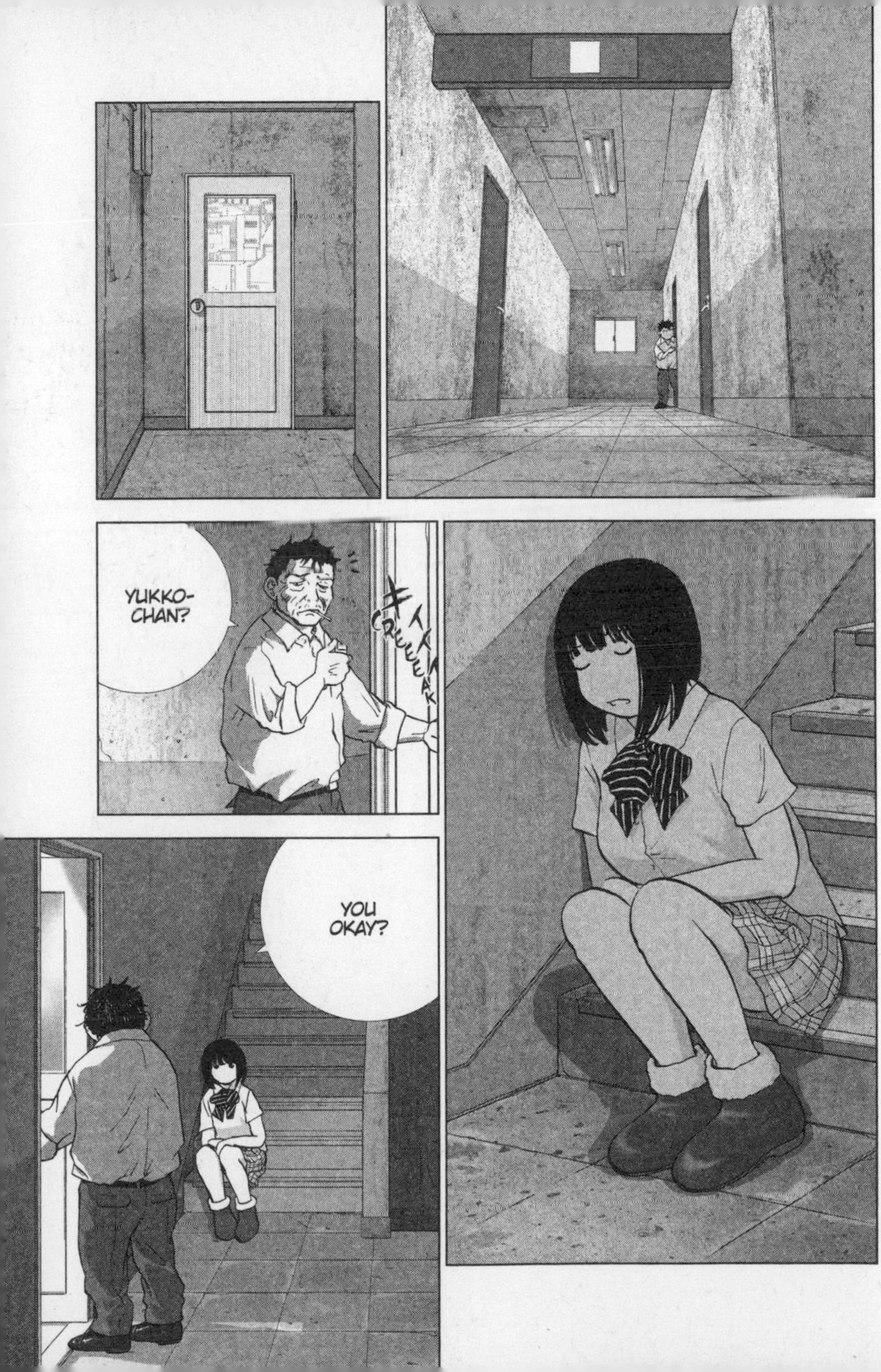
CREEEEAK
YUKKO-CHAN?
YOU OKAY?

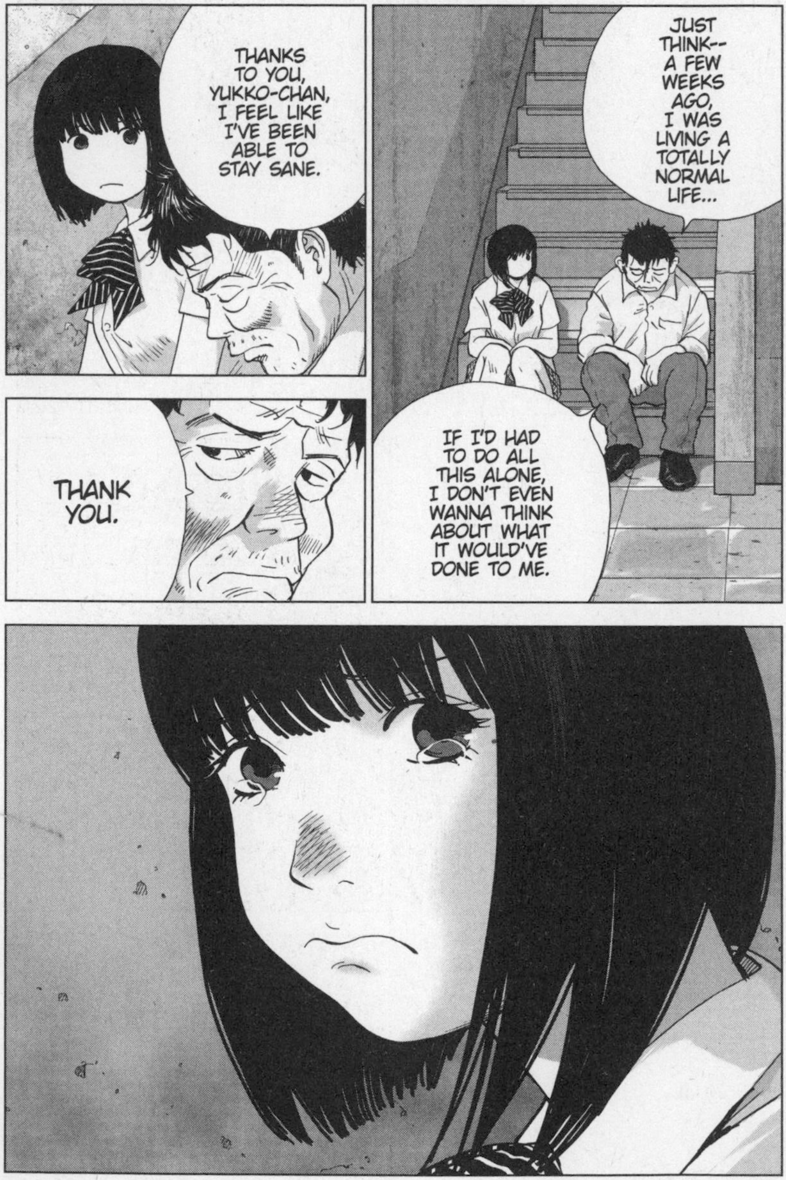
JUST THINK-- A FEW WEEKS AGO, I WAS LIVING A TOTALLY NORMAL LIFE...
IF I'D HAD TO DO ALL THIS ALONE, I DON'T EVEN WANNA THINK ABOUT WHAT IT WOULD'VE DONE TO ME.
THANKS TO YOU, YUKKO-CHAN, I FEEL LIKE I'VE BEEN ABLE TO STAY SANE.
THANK YOU.

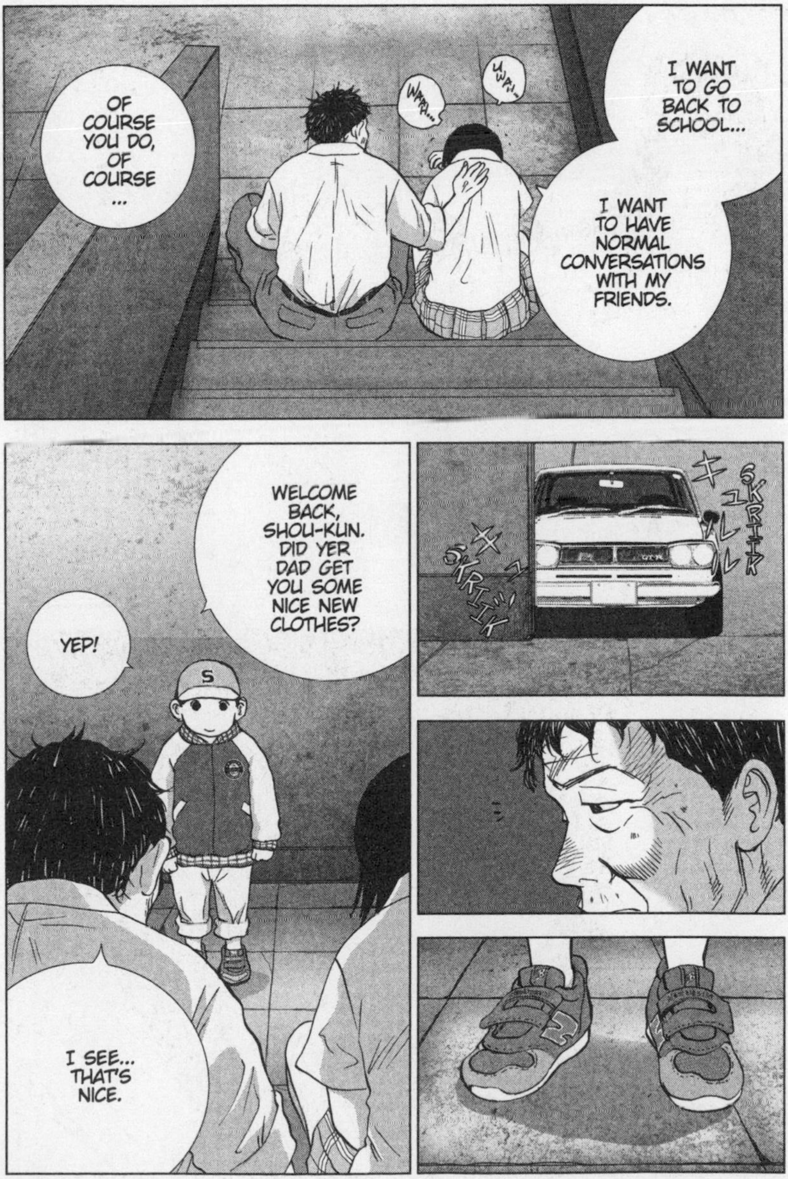
I WANT TO GO BACK TO SCHOOL...
I WANT TO HAVE NORMAL CONVERSATIONS WITH MY FRIENDS.
UWAH...
WAAH...
OF COURSE YOU DO, OF COURSE ...
SKRIIK
SKRIIK
WELCOME BACK, SHOU-KUN. DID YER DAD GET YOU SOME NICE NEW CLOTHES?
YEP!
I SEE... THAT'S NICE.

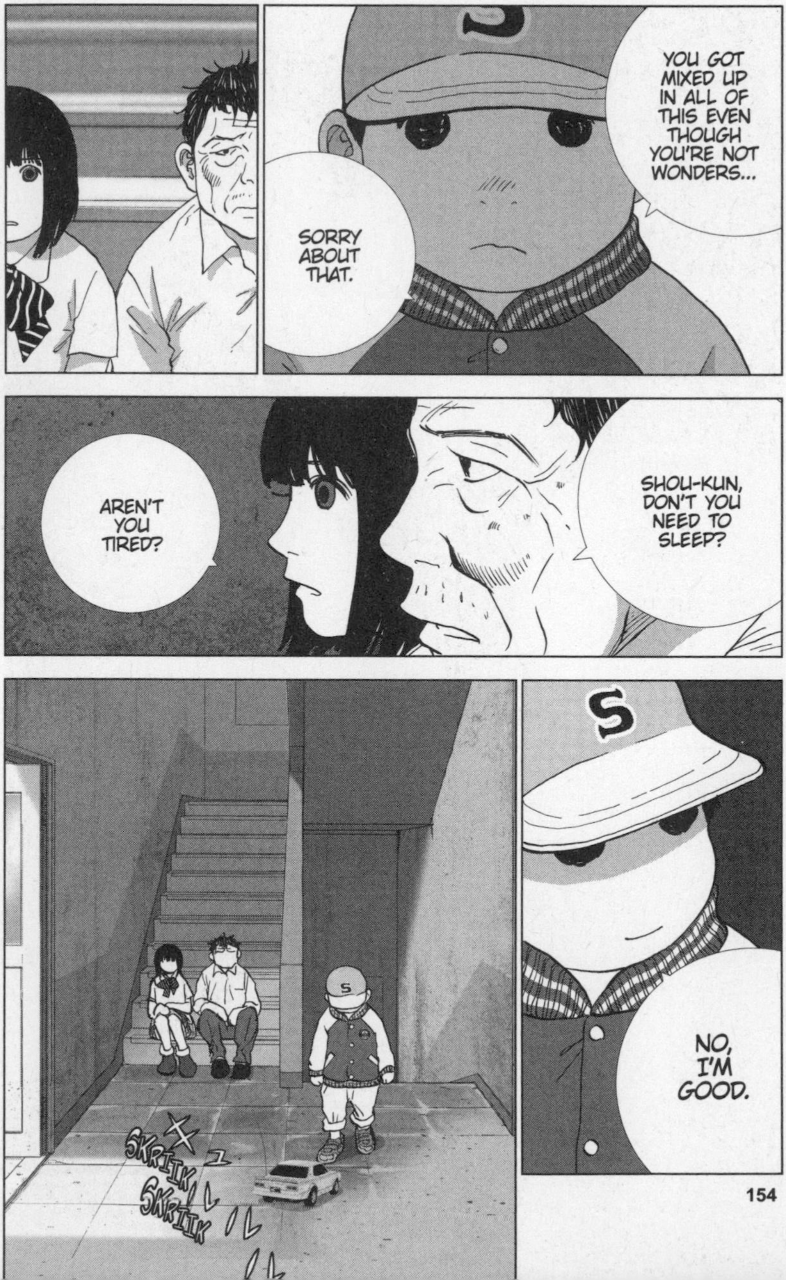
YOU GOT MIXED UP IN ALL OF THIS EVEN THOUGH YOU'RE NOT WONDERS...
SORRY ABOUT THAT.
SHOU-KUN, DON'T YOU NEED TO SLEEP?
AREN'T YOU TIRED?
NO, I'M GOOD.
SKRIIK
SKRIIK

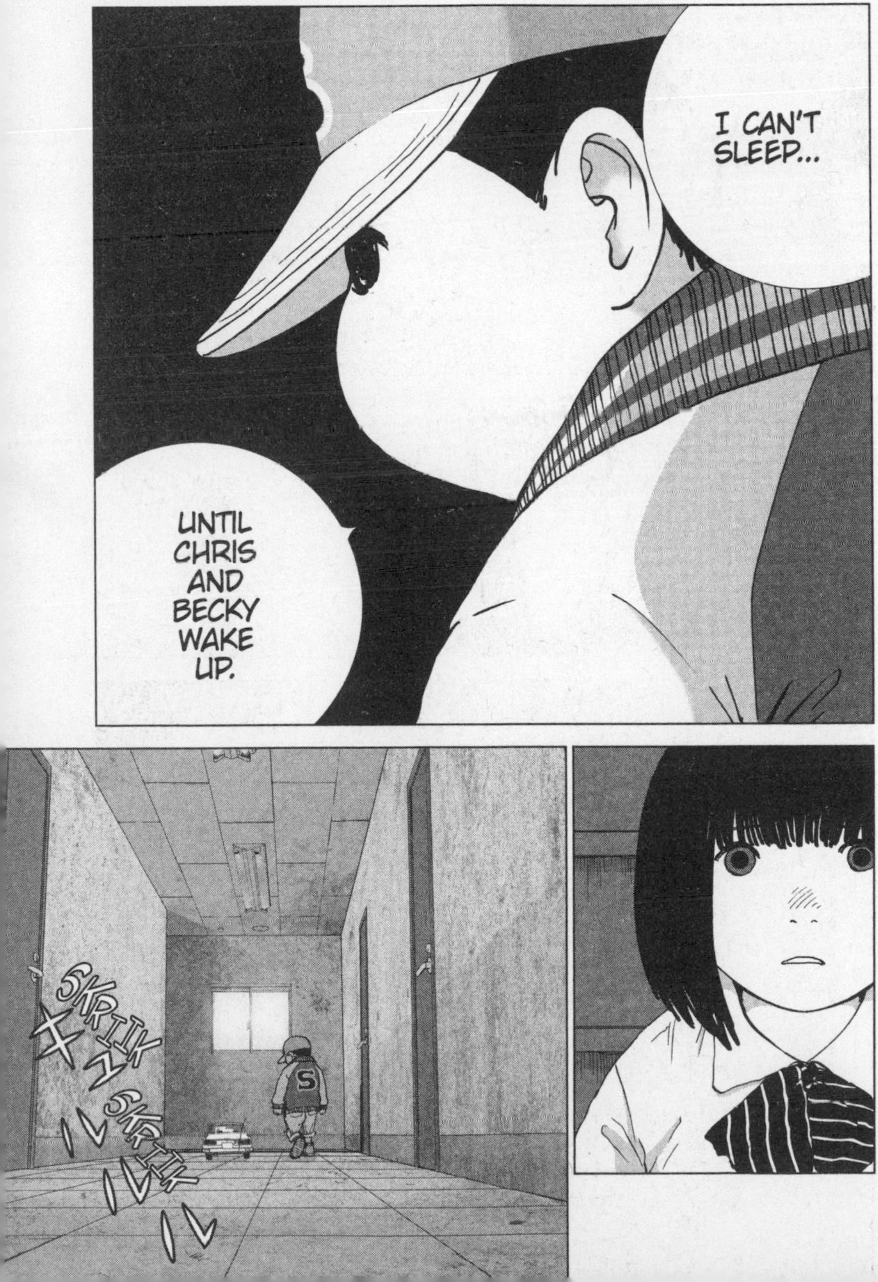
I CAN'T SLEEP...
UNTIL CHRIS AND BECKY WAKE UP.
SKRIIK
SKRIIK

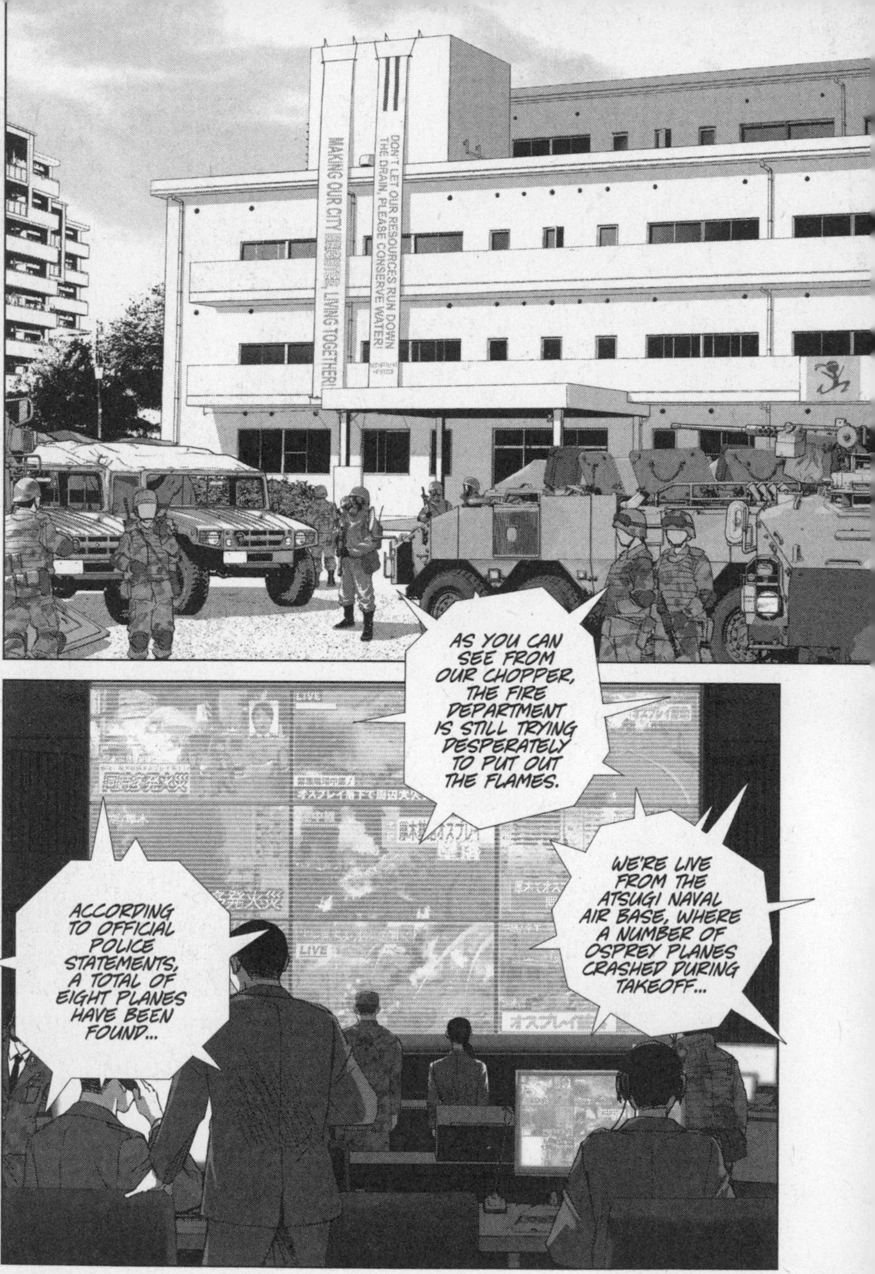
MAKING OUR CITY LIVING TOGETHER!
DON'T LET OUR RESOURCES RUN DOWN THE DRAIN, PLEASE CONSERVE WATER!
WE'RE LIVE FROM THE ATSUGI NAVAL AIR BASE, WHERE A NUMBER OF OSPREY PLANES CRASHED DURING TAKEOFF...
AS YOU CAN SEE FROM OUR CHOPPER, THE FIRE DEPARTMENT IS STILL TRYING DESPERATELY TO PUT OUT THE FLAMES.
ACCORDING TO OFFICIAL POLICE STATEMENTS, A TOTAL OF EIGHT PLANES HAVE BEEN FOUND...

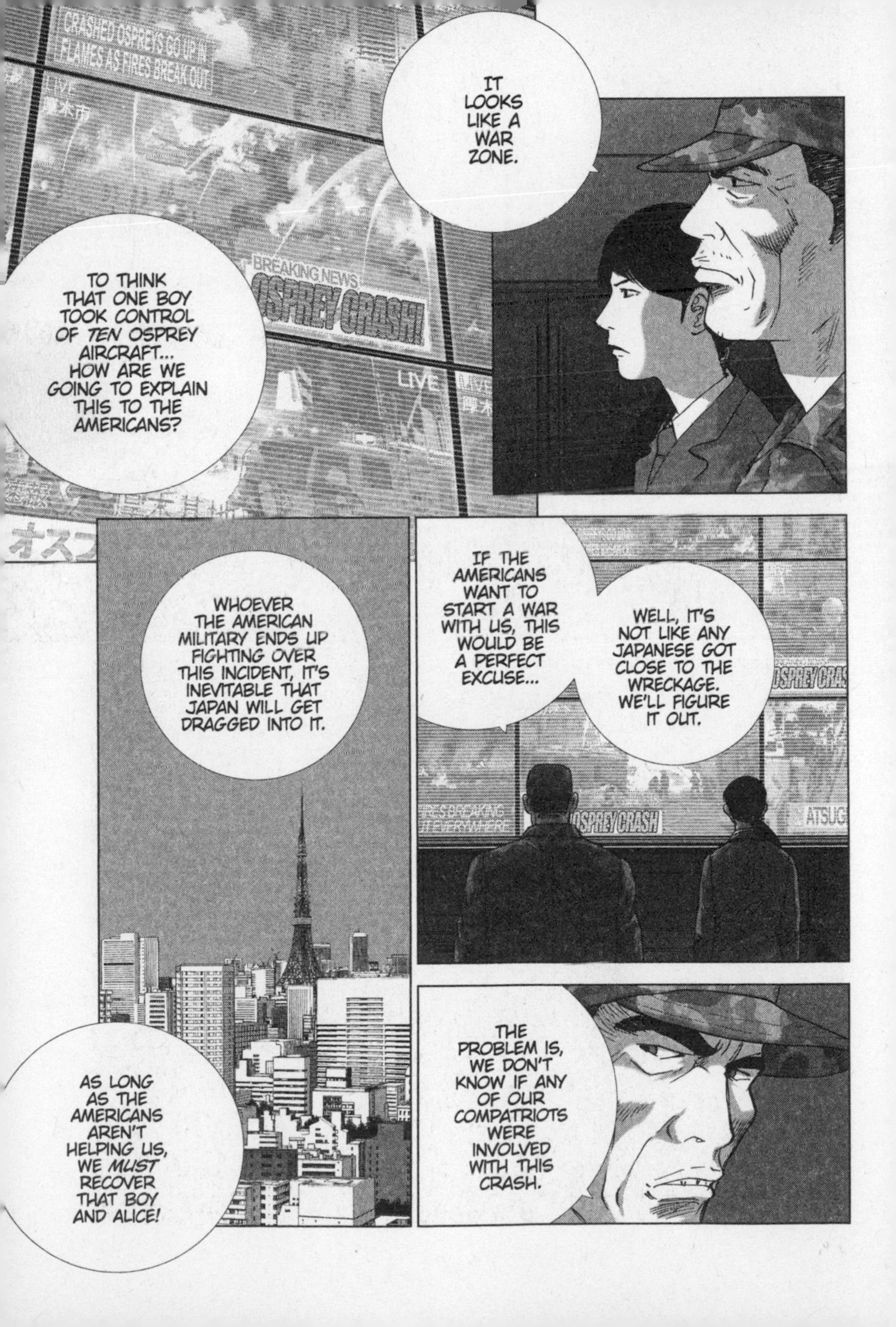
IT LOOKS LIKE A WAR ZONE.
CRASHED OSPREYS GO UP IN FLAMES AS FIRES BREAK OUT
LIVE
BREAKING NEWS
OSPREY CRASH!
LIVE
TO THINK THAT ONE BOY TOOK CONTROL OF *TEN* OSPREY AIRCRAFT... HOW ARE WE GOING TO EXPLAIN THIS TO THE AMERICANS?
IF THE AMERICANS WANT TO START A WAR WITH US, THIS WOULD BE A PERFECT EXCUSE...
WELL, IT'S NOT LIKE ANY JAPANESE GOT CLOSE TO THE WRECKAGE. WE'LL FIGURE IT OUT.
OSPREY CRASH
THE PROBLEM IS, WE DON'T KNOW IF ANY OF OUR COMPATRIOTS WERE INVOLVED WITH THIS CRASH.
WHOEVER THE AMERICAN MILITARY ENDS UP FIGHTING OVER THIS INCIDENT, IT'S INEVITABLE THAT JAPAN WILL GET DRAGGED INTO IT.
AS LONG AS THE AMERICANS AREN'T HELPING US, WE *MUST* RECOVER THAT BOY AND ALICE!

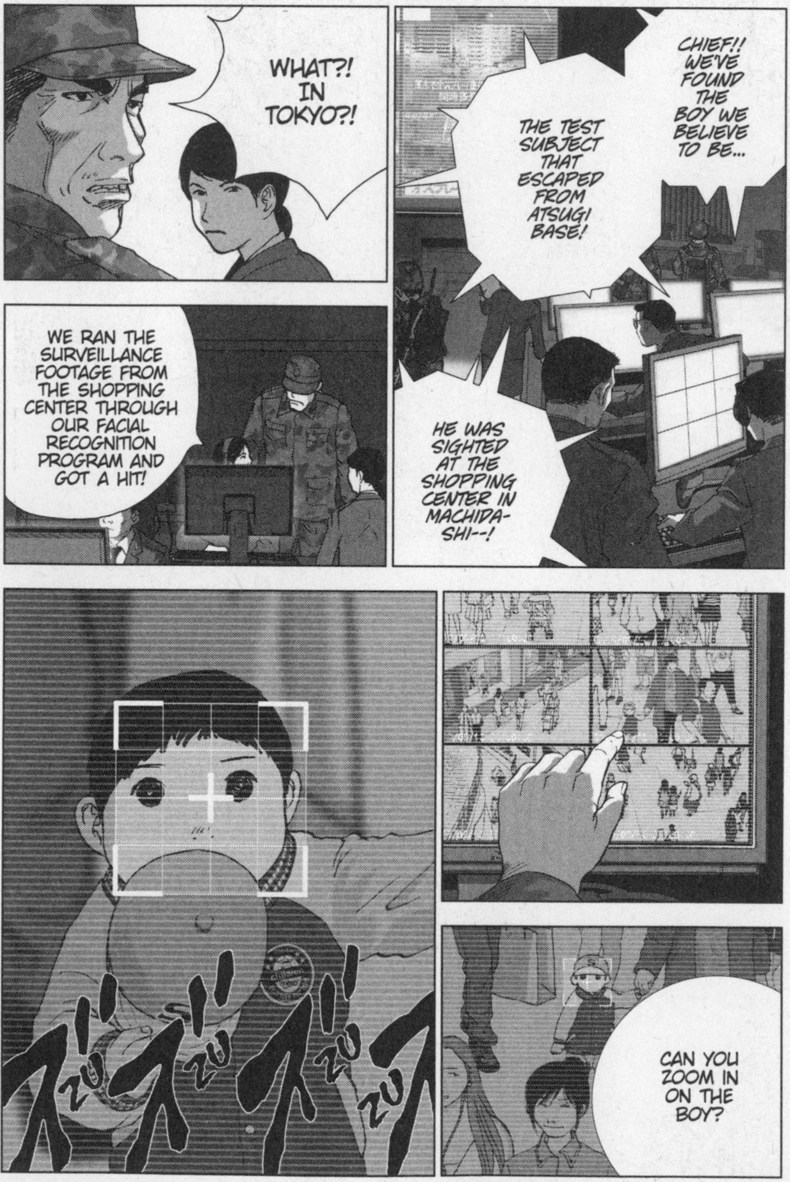
CHIEF!! WE'VE FOUND THE BOY WE BELIEVE TO BE...
THE TEST SUBJECT THAT ESCAPED FROM ATSUGI BASE!
HE WAS SIGHTED AT THE SHOPPING CENTER IN MACHIDA-SHI--!
WHAT?! IN TOKYO?!
WE RAN THE SURVEILLANCE FOOTAGE FROM THE SHOPPING CENTER THROUGH OUR FACIAL RECOGNITION PROGRAM AND GOT A HIT!
CAN YOU ZOOM IN ON THE BOY?
ZU ZU ZU ZU

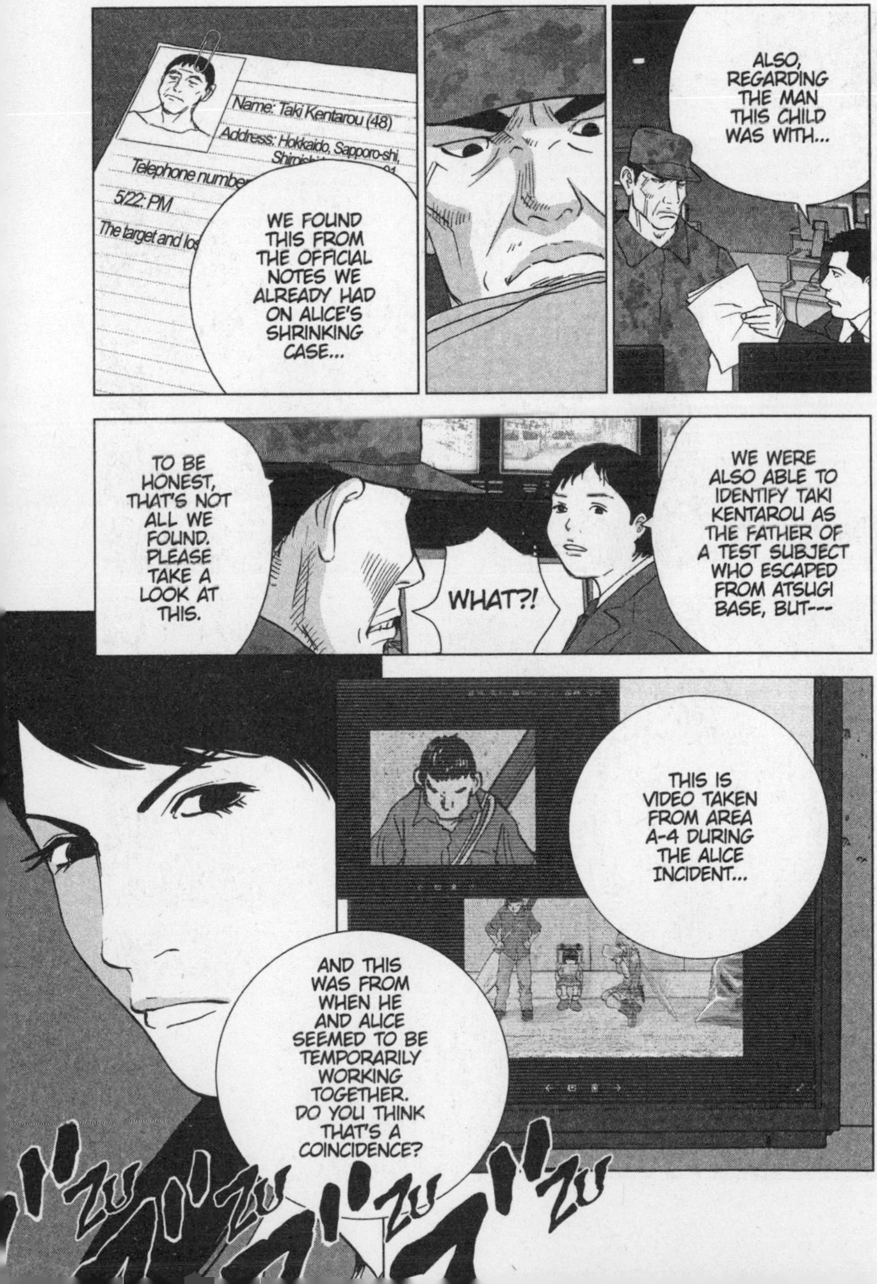
ALSO, REGARDING THE MAN THIS CHILD WAS WITH...
Name: Taki Kentarou (48)
Address: Hokkaido, Sapporo-shi,
5/22: PM
WE FOUND THIS FROM THE OFFICIAL NOTES WE ALREADY HAD ON ALICE'S SHRINKING CASE...
WE WERE ALSO ABLE TO IDENTIFY TAKI KENTAROU AS THE FATHER OF A TEST SUBJECT WHO ESCAPED FROM ATSUGI BASE, BUT---
WHAT?!
TO BE HONEST, THAT'S NOT ALL WE FOUND. PLEASE TAKE A LOOK AT THIS.
THIS IS VIDEO TAKEN FROM AREA A-4 DURING THE ALICE INCIDENT...
AND THIS WAS FROM WHEN HE AND ALICE SEEMED TO BE TEMPORARILY WORKING TOGETHER. DO YOU THINK THAT'S A COINCIDENCE?
ZU ZU ZU ZU

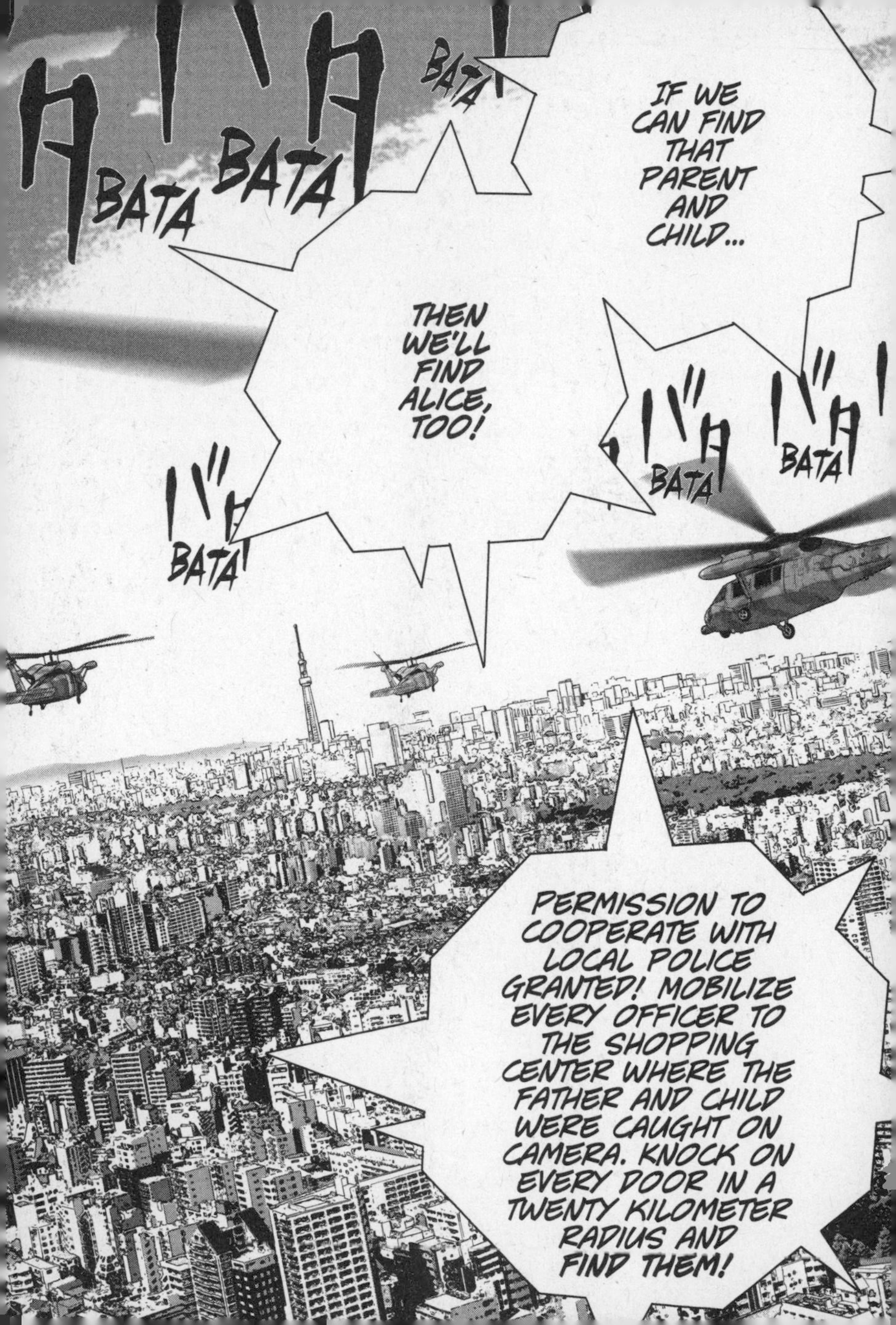
IF WE CAN FIND THAT PARENT AND CHILD...
BATA
BATA
BATA
BATA
BATA
THEN WE'LL FIND ALICE, TOO!
BATA
PERMISSION TO COOPERATE WITH LOCAL POLICE GRANTED! MOBILIZE EVERY OFFICER TO THE SHOPPING CENTER WHERE THE FATHER AND CHILD WERE CAUGHT ON CAMERA. KNOCK ON EVERY DOOR IN A TWENTY KILOMETER RADIUS AND FIND THEM!

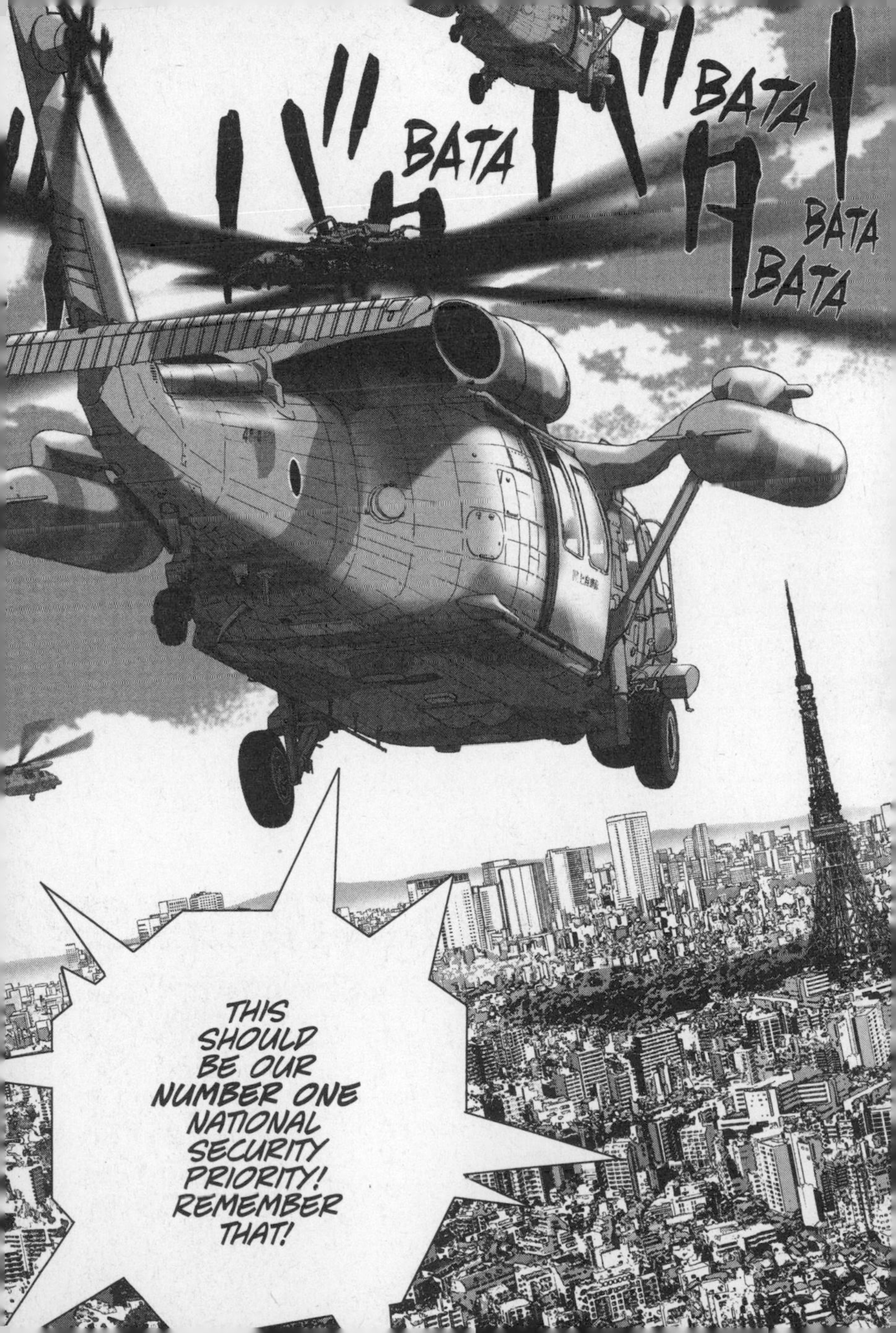
BATA
BATA
BATA
BATA
THIS SHOULD BE OUR NUMBER ONE NATIONAL SECURITY PRIORITY! REMEMBER THAT!

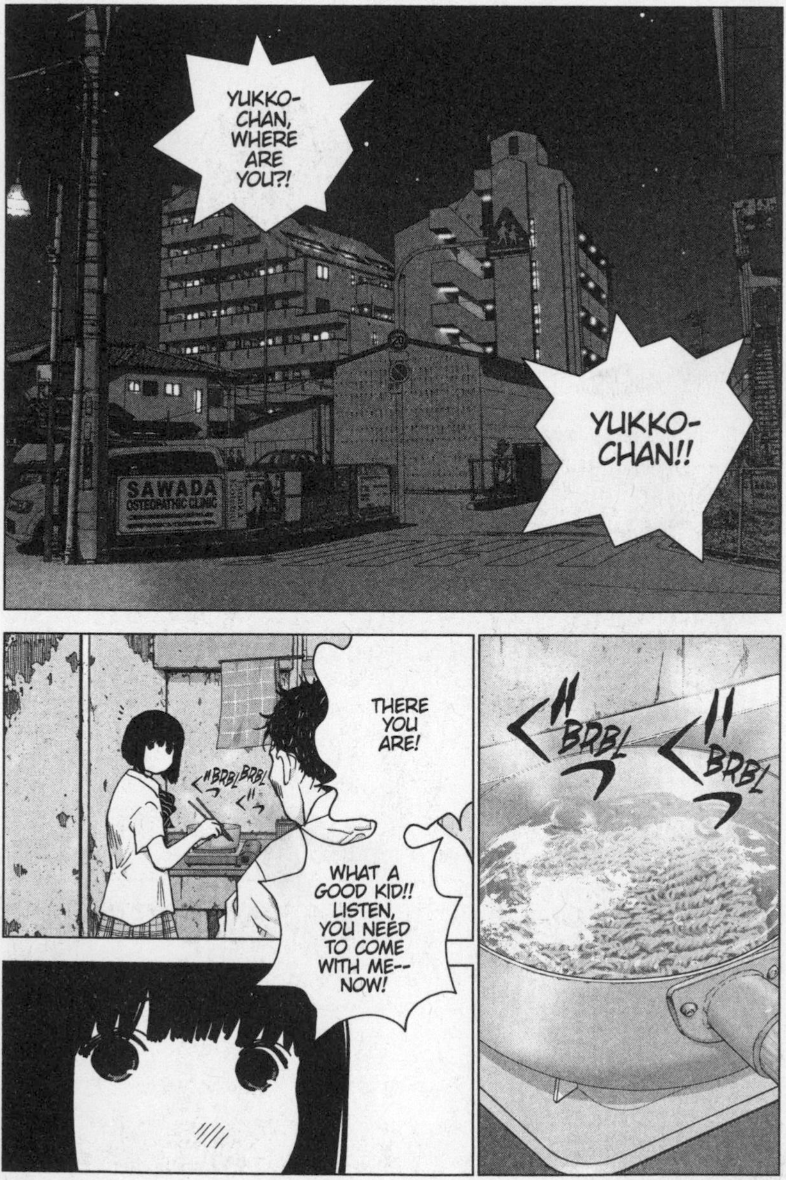
YUKKO-CHAN, WHERE ARE YOU?!
YUKKO-CHAN!!
SAWADA OSTEOPATHIC CLINIC
BRBL
BRBL
BRBL BRBL
THERE YOU ARE!
WHAT A GOOD KID!! LISTEN, YOU NEED TO COME WITH ME-- NOW!

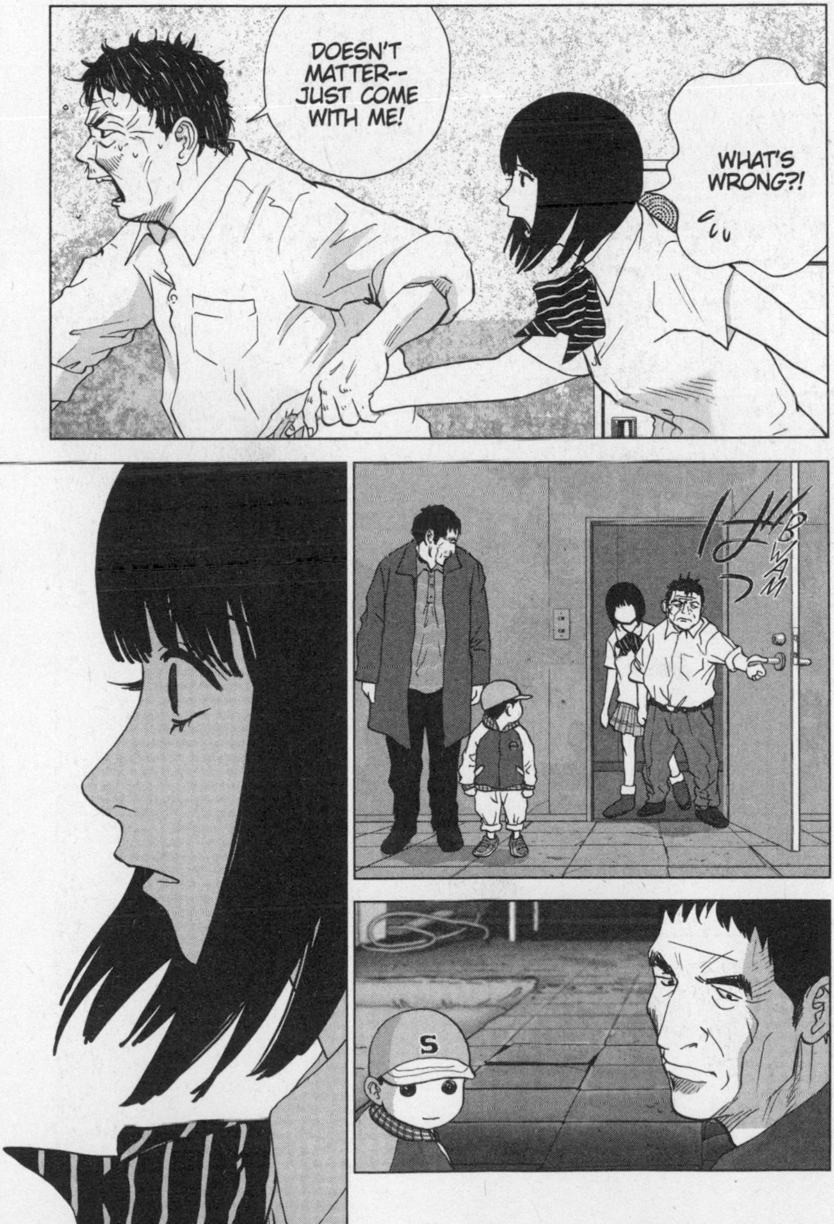
WHAT'S WRONG?!
DOESN'T MATTER-- JUST COME WITH ME!
BWAM

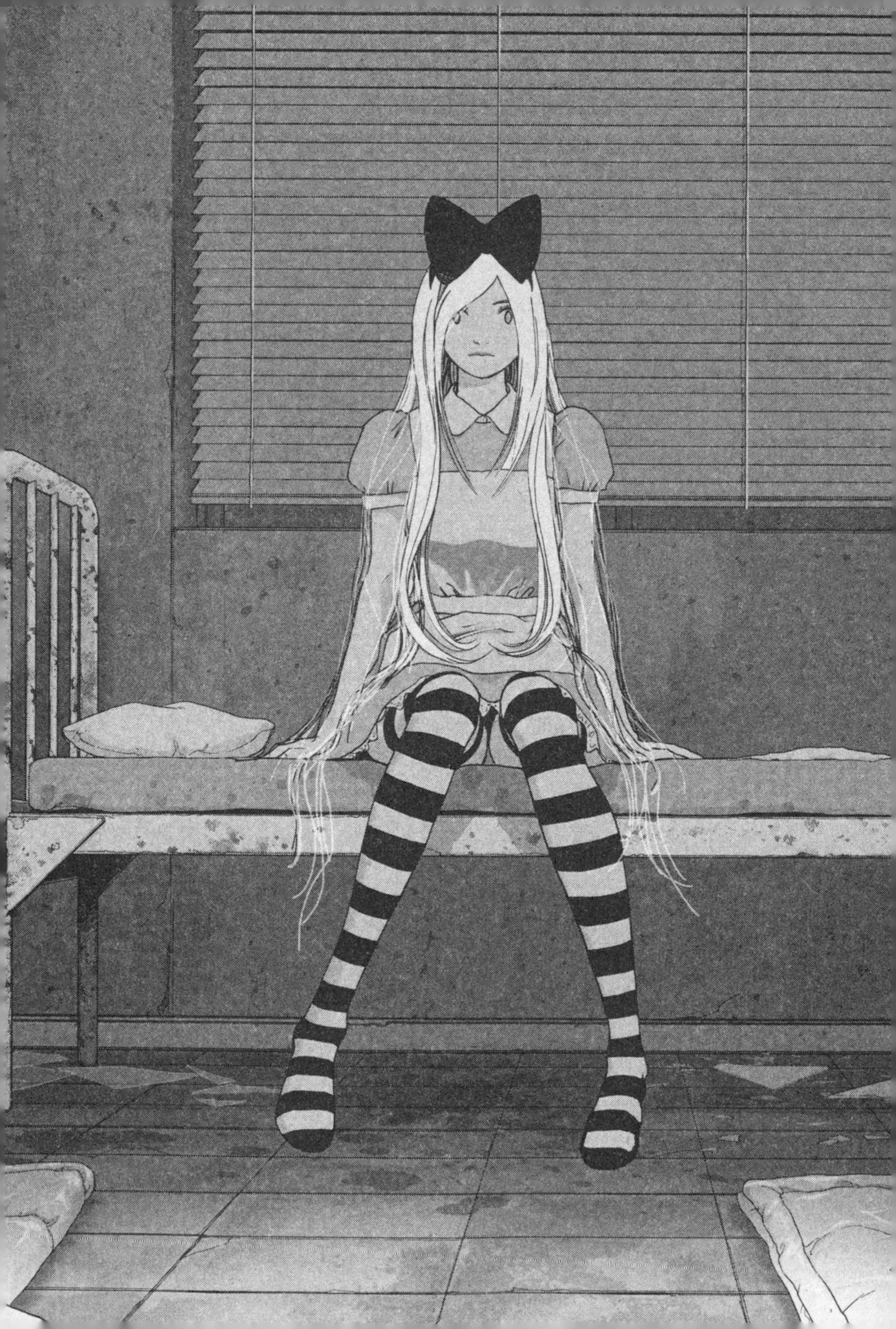

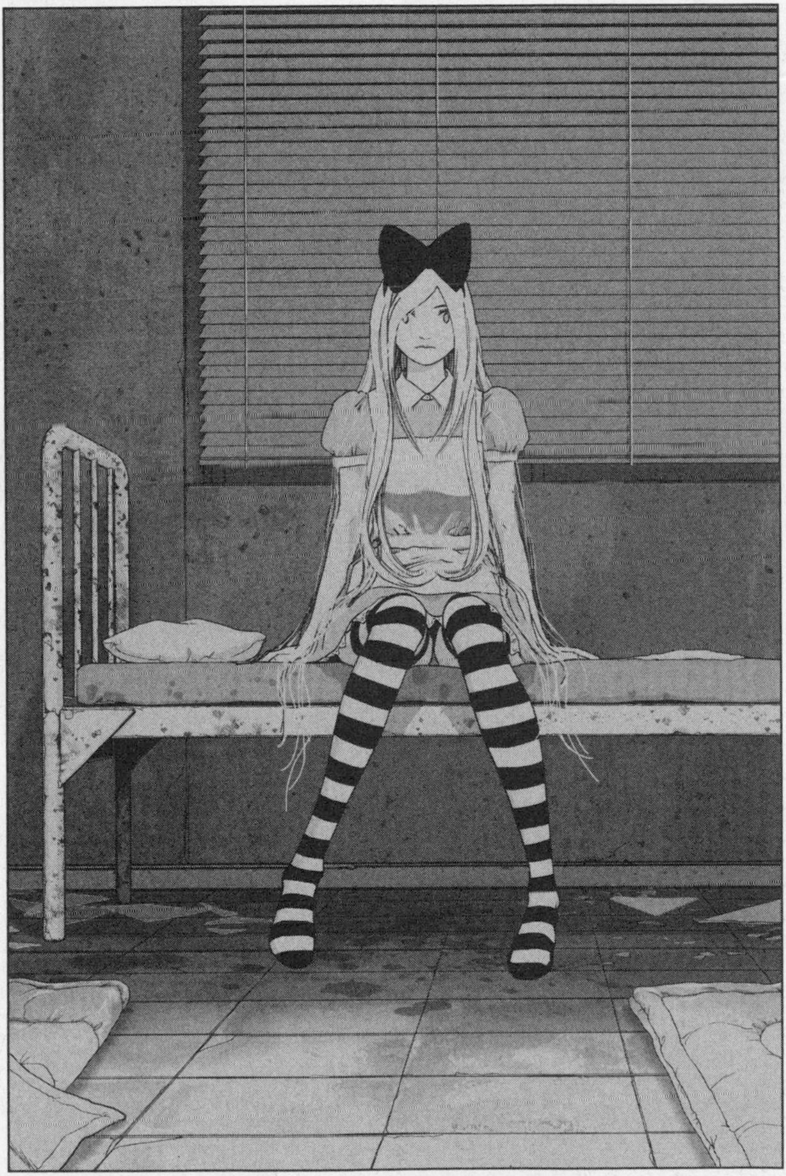

Chapter 45: A Special Power

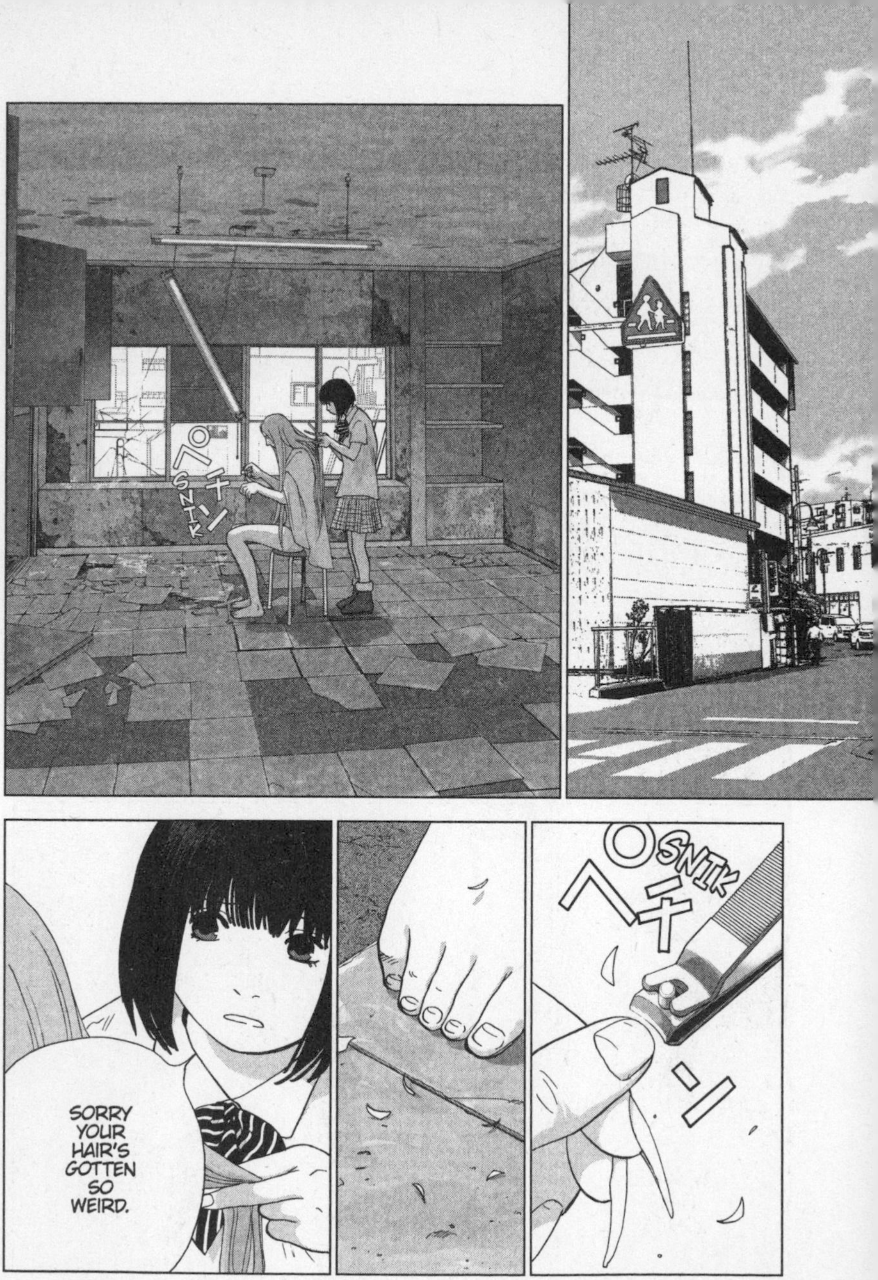
SNIK
SNIK
SORRY YOUR HAIR'S GOTTEN SO WEIRD.

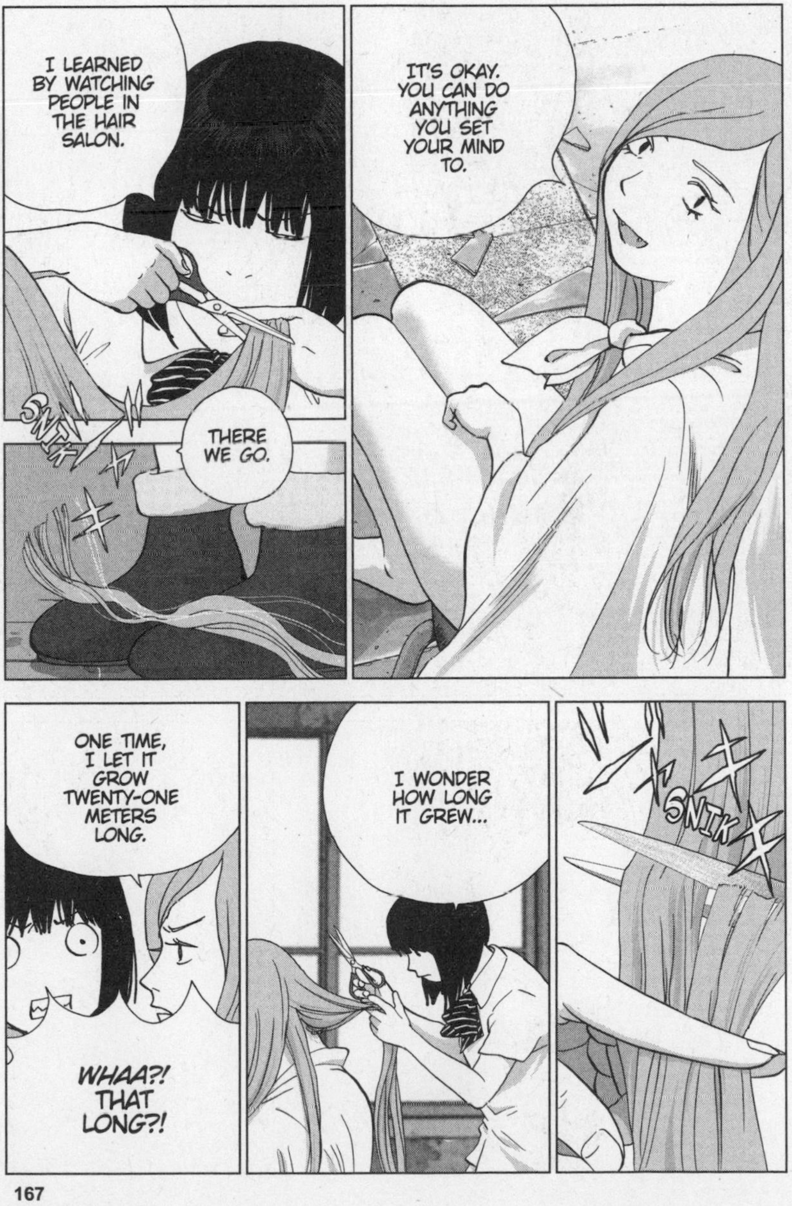
IT'S OKAY. YOU CAN DO ANYTHING YOU SET YOUR MIND TO.
I LEARNED BY WATCHING PEOPLE IN THE HAIR SALON.
SNIK
THERE WE GO.
SNIK
I WONDER HOW LONG IT GREW...
ONE TIME, I LET IT GROW TWENTY-ONE METERS LONG.
WHAA?! THAT LONG?!

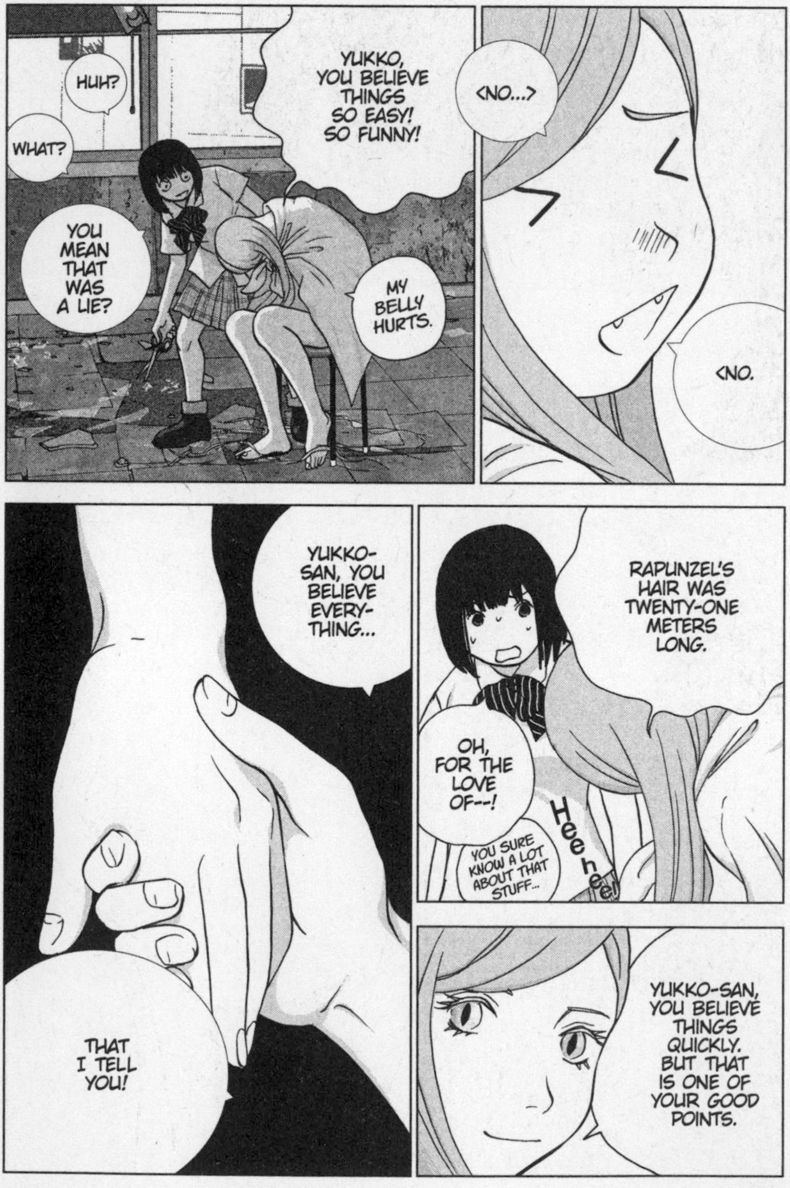
<NO...>
<NO.
YUKKO, YOU BELIEVE THINGS SO EASY! SO FUNNY!
HUH?
WHAT?
MY BELLY HURTS.
YOU MEAN THAT WAS A LIE?
RAPUNZEL'S HAIR WAS TWENTY-ONE METERS LONG.
Heehee!
OH, FOR THE LOVE OF--!
YOU SURE KNOW A LOT ABOUT THAT STUFF...
YUKKO-SAN, YOU BELIEVE THINGS QUICKLY. BUT THAT IS ONE OF YOUR GOOD POINTS.
YUKKO-SAN, YOU BELIEVE EVERYTHING...
THAT I TELL YOU!

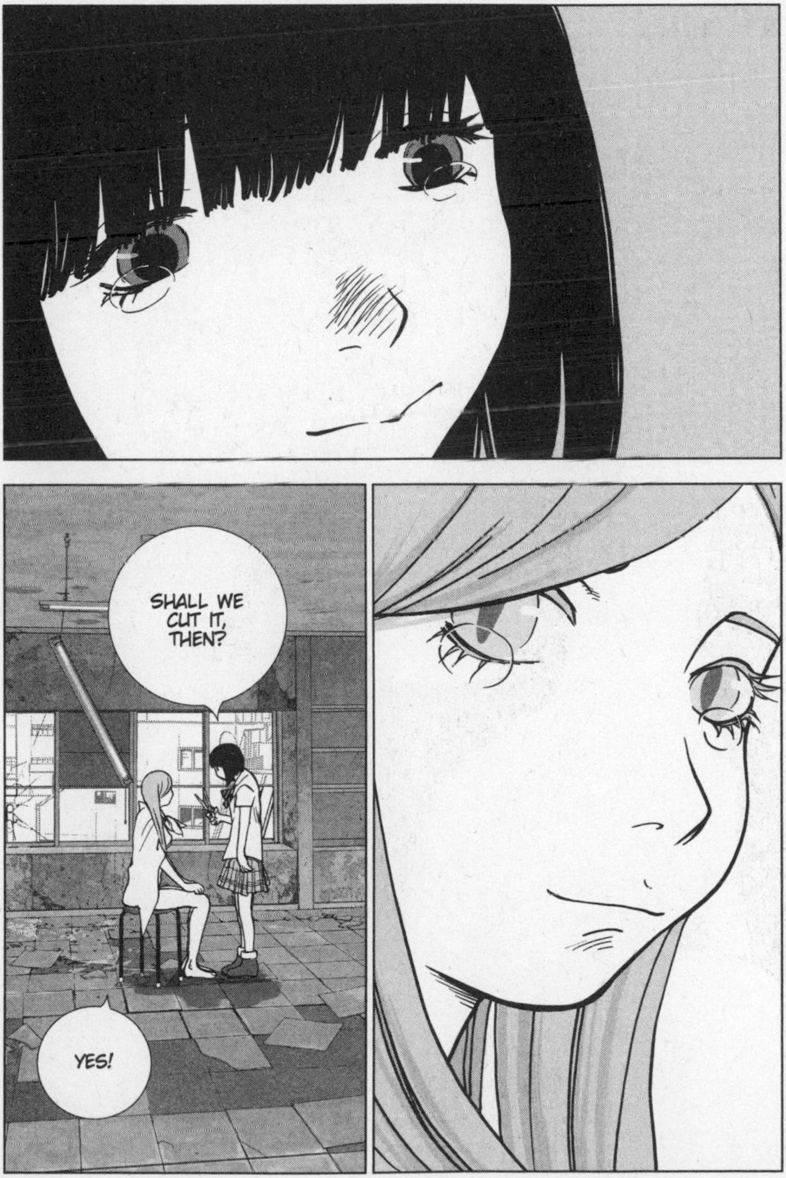
SHALL WE CUT IT, THEN?
YES!

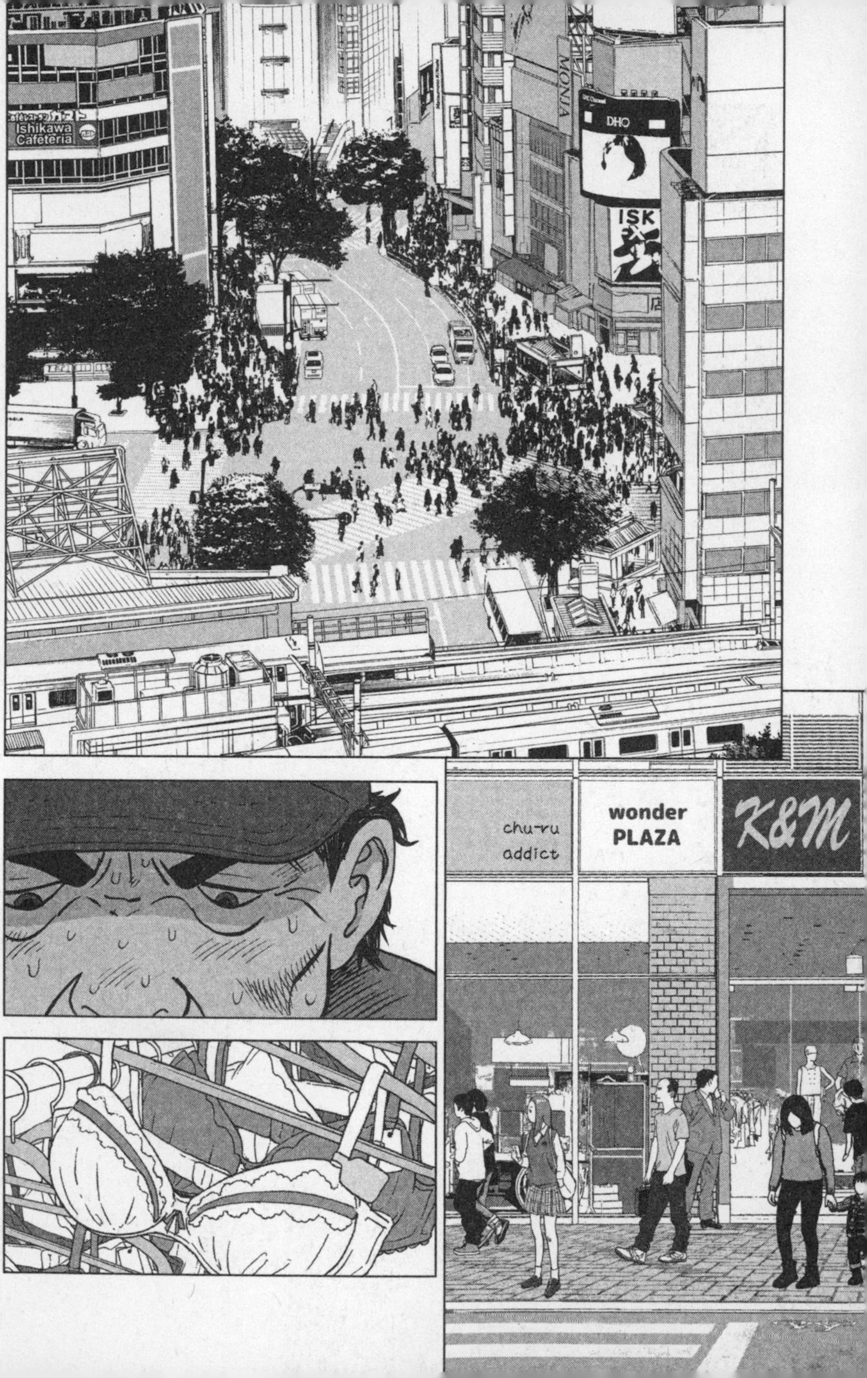
MONJA
DHO
ISK
Ishikawa Cafeteria
K&M
wonder PLAZA
chu-ru addict

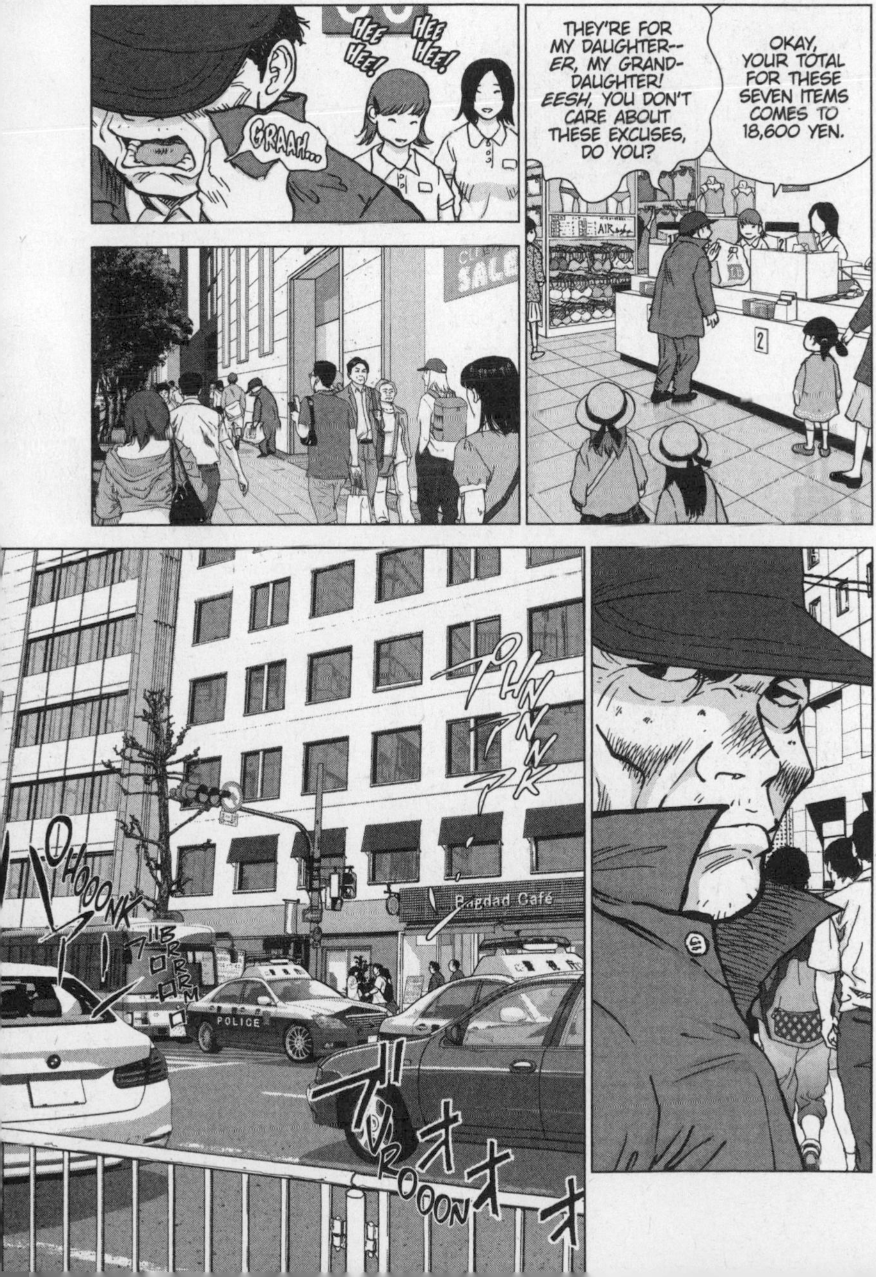
OKAY, YOUR TOTAL FOR THESE SEVEN ITEMS COMES TO 18,600 YEN.
THEY'RE FOR MY DAUGHTER-- ER, MY GRAND-DAUGHTER! EESH, YOU DON'T CARE ABOUT THESE EXCUSES, DO YOU?
HEE HEE!
HEE HEE!
GRAAH...
PHNNNNK
OHOOONK
BRRRRM
Bagdad Café
POLICE
VROOON

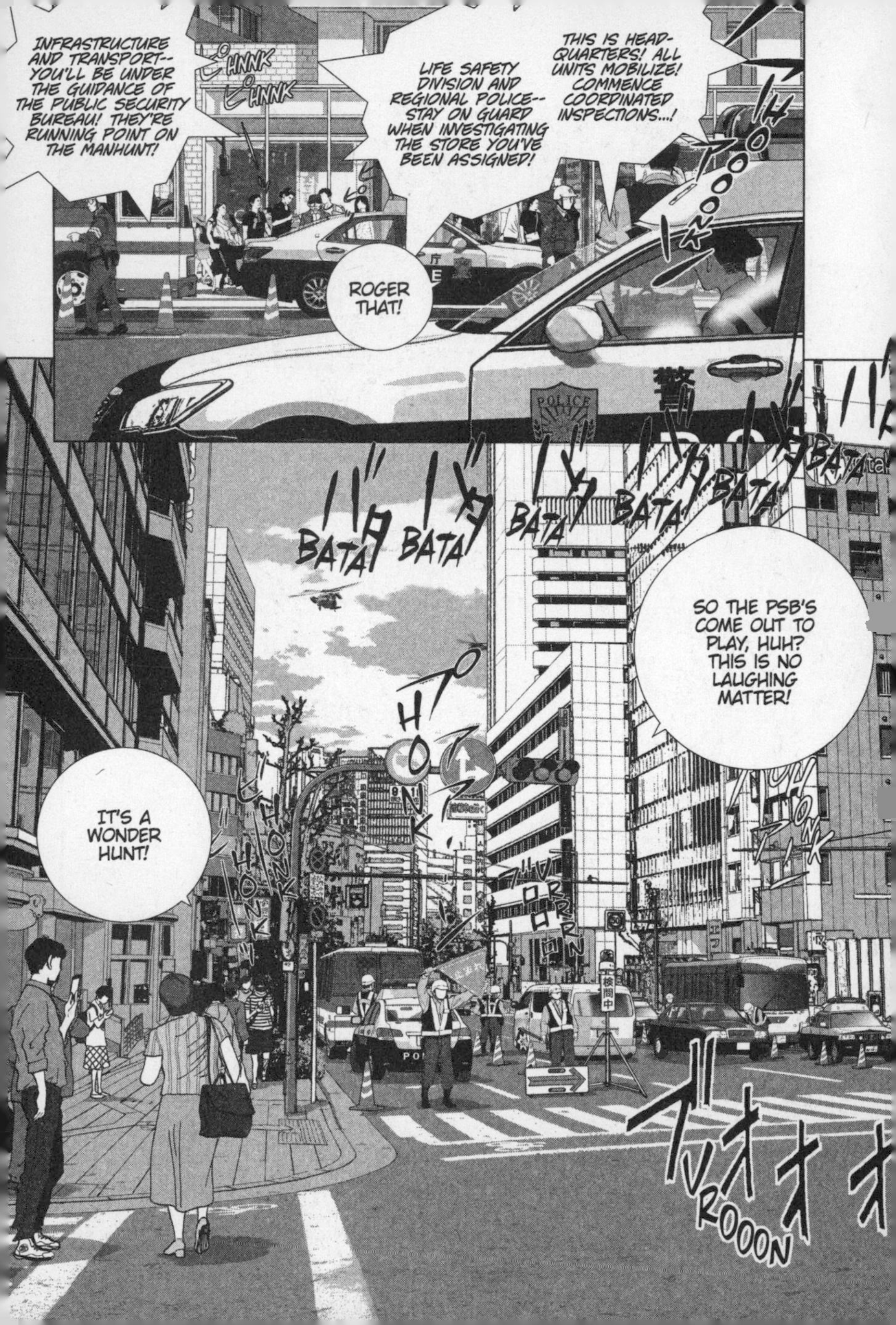
THIS IS HEAD-QUARTERS! ALL UNITS MOBILIZE! COMMENCE COORDINATED INSPECTIONS...!
HOOOONK
LIFE SAFETY DIVISION AND REGIONAL POLICE--STAY ON GUARD WHEN INVESTIGATING THE STORE YOU'VE BEEN ASSIGNED!
HNNK
HNNK
INFRASTRUCTURE AND TRANSPORT--YOU'LL BE UNDER THE GUIDANCE OF THE PUBLIC SECURITY BUREAU! THEY'RE RUNNING POINT ON THE MANHUNT!
ROGER THAT!
BATA
BATA
BATA
BATA
BATA
BATA
SO THE PSB'S COME OUT TO PLAY, HUH? THIS IS NO LAUGHING MATTER!
HONK
VROOOON
HONK
VRRRRN
HONK
HONK
HONK
IT'S A WONDER HUNT!

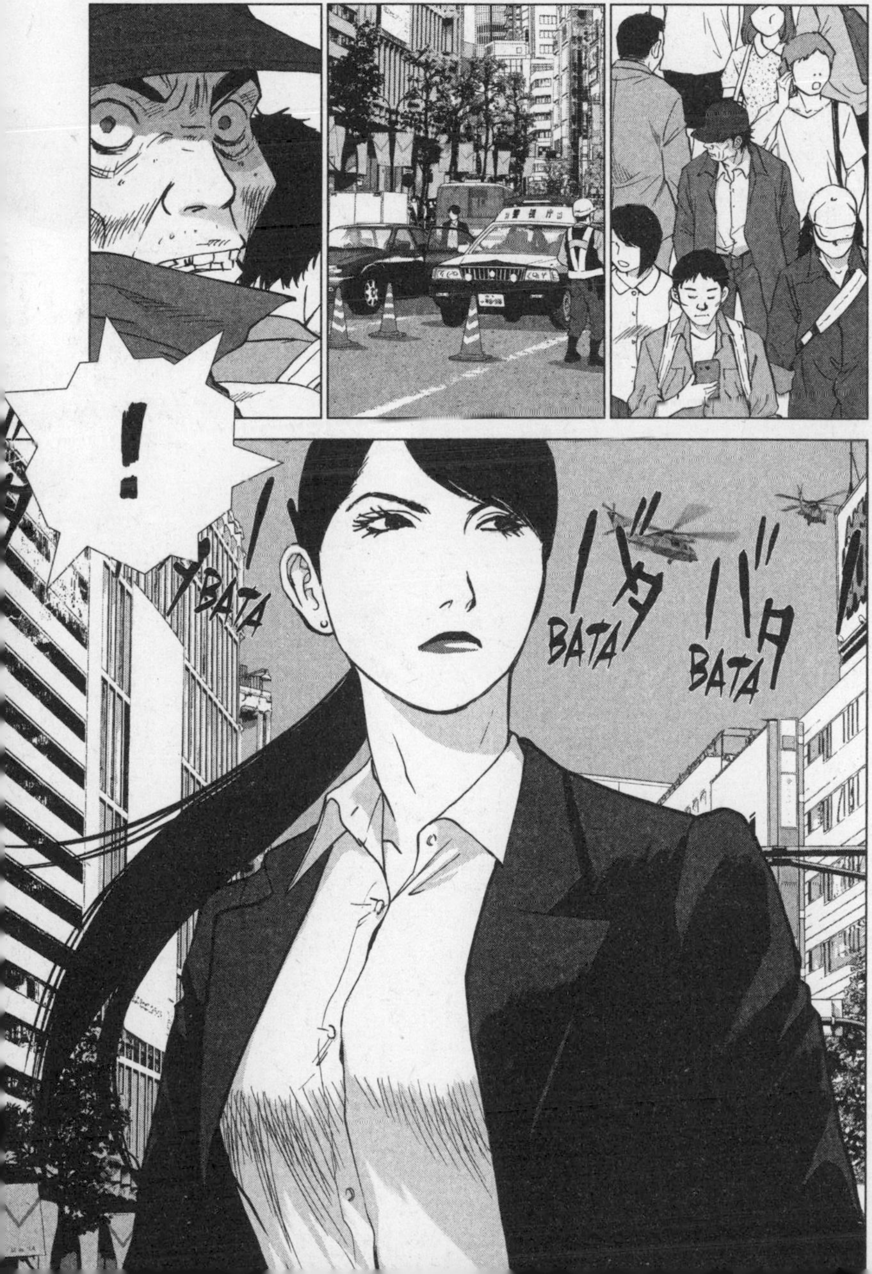
!
バタ
BATA
バタ
BATA
BATA

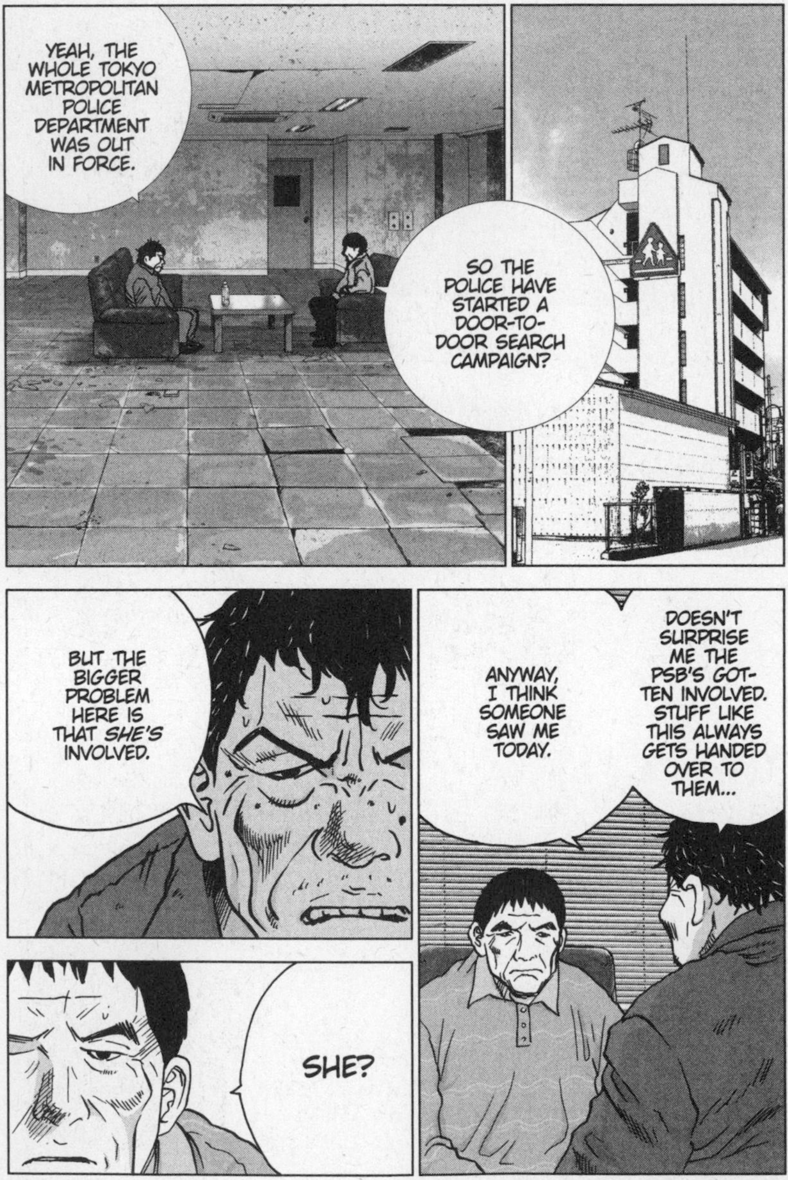
SO THE POLICE HAVE STARTED A DOOR-TO-DOOR SEARCH CAMPAIGN?
YEAH, THE WHOLE TOKYO METROPOLITAN POLICE DEPARTMENT WAS OUT IN FORCE.
DOESN'T SURPRISE ME THE PSB'S GOTTEN INVOLVED. STUFF LIKE THIS ALWAYS GETS HANDED OVER TO THEM...
ANYWAY, I THINK SOMEONE SAW ME TODAY.
BUT THE BIGGER PROBLEM HERE IS THAT *SHE'S* INVOLVED.
SHE?

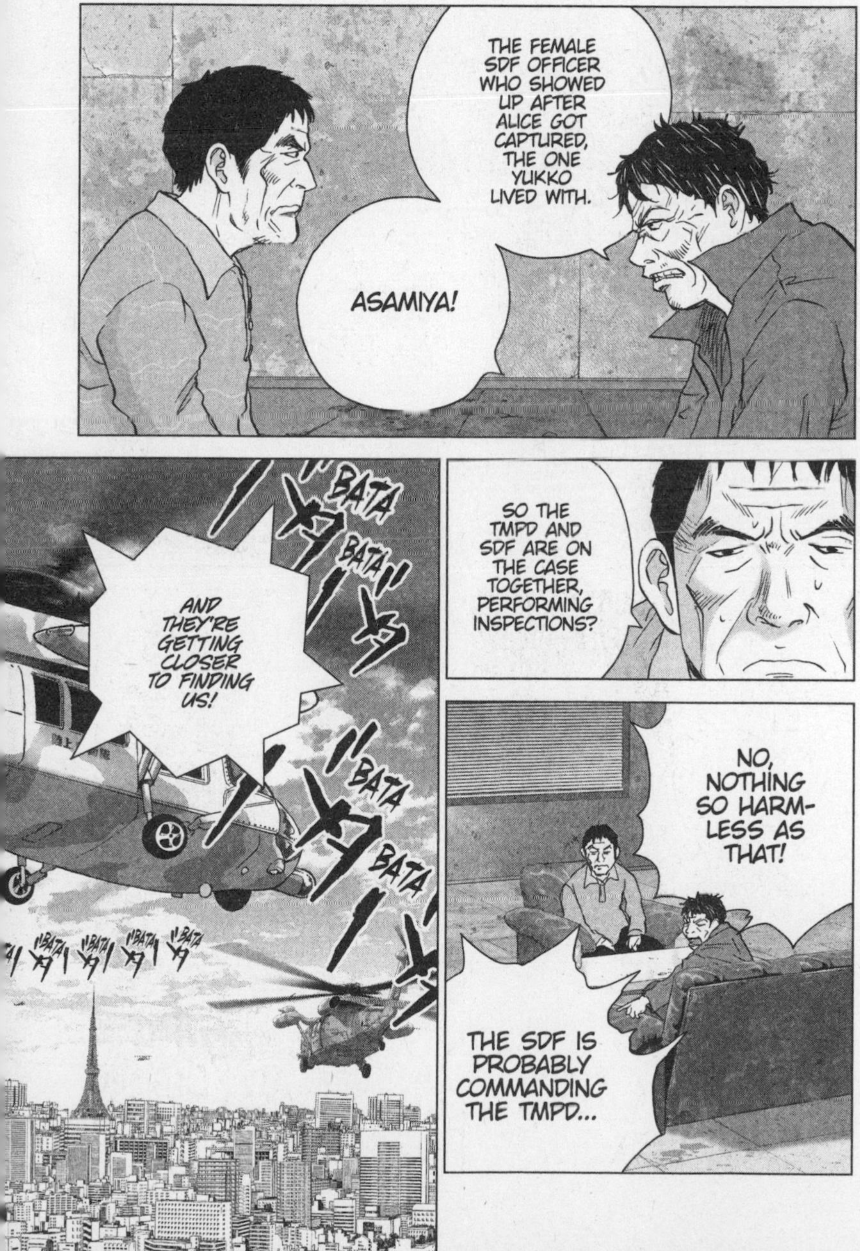
THE FEMALE SDF OFFICER WHO SHOWED UP AFTER ALICE GOT CAPTURED, THE ONE YUKKO LIVED WITH.
ASAMIYA!
SO THE TMPD AND SDF ARE ON THE CASE TOGETHER, PERFORMING INSPECTIONS?
NO, NOTHING SO HARM-LESS AS THAT!
THE SDF IS PROBABLY COMMANDING THE TMPD...
BATA BATA
AND THEY'RE GETTING CLOSER TO FINDING US!
BATA BATA
BATA BATA BATA BATA

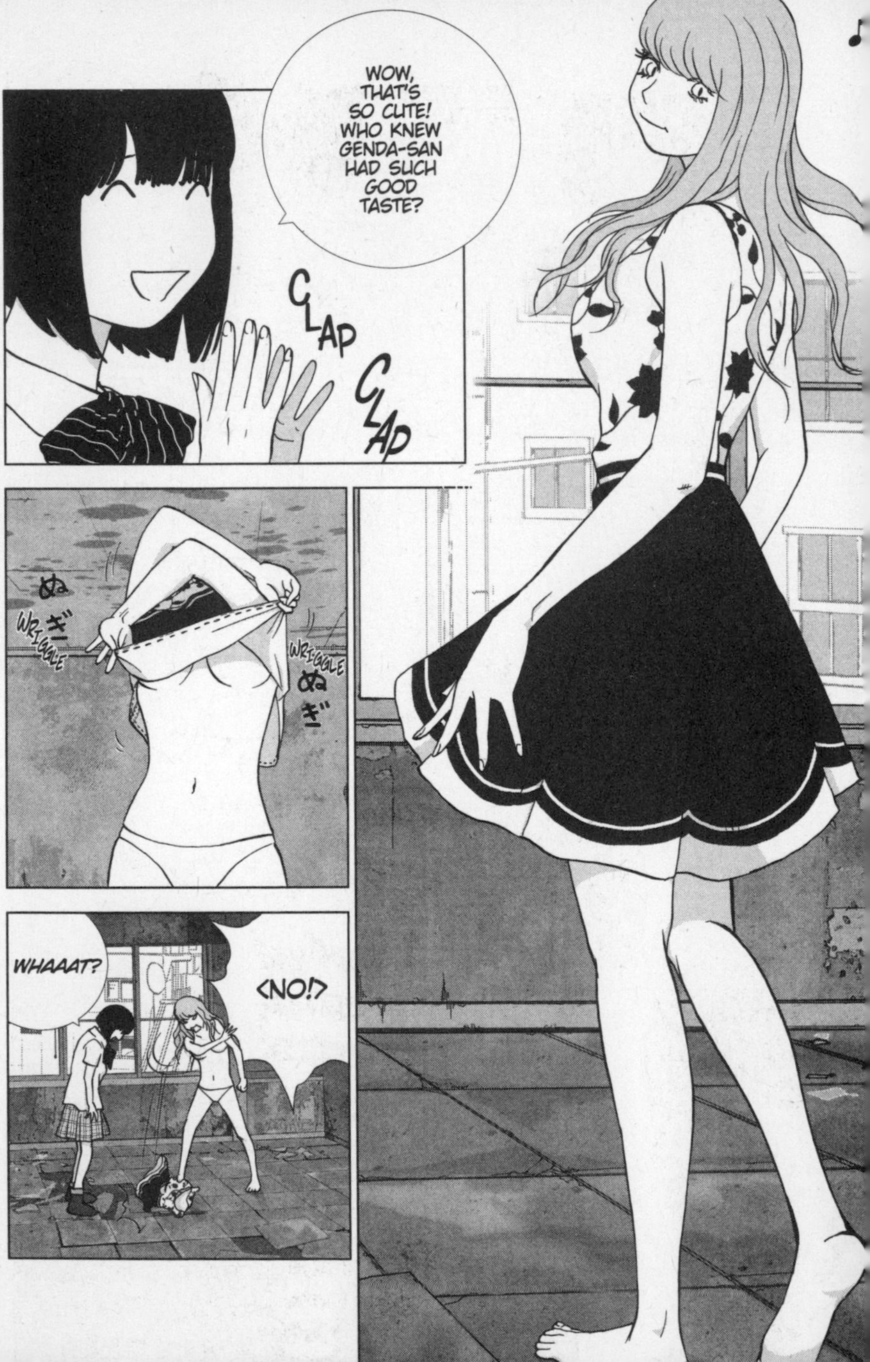
♪
WOW, THAT'S SO CUTE! WHO KNEW GENDA-SAN HAD SUCH GOOD TASTE?
CLAP
CLAP
ぬぎ
WRIGGLE
ぬぎ
WRIGGLE
<NO!>
WHAAAT?

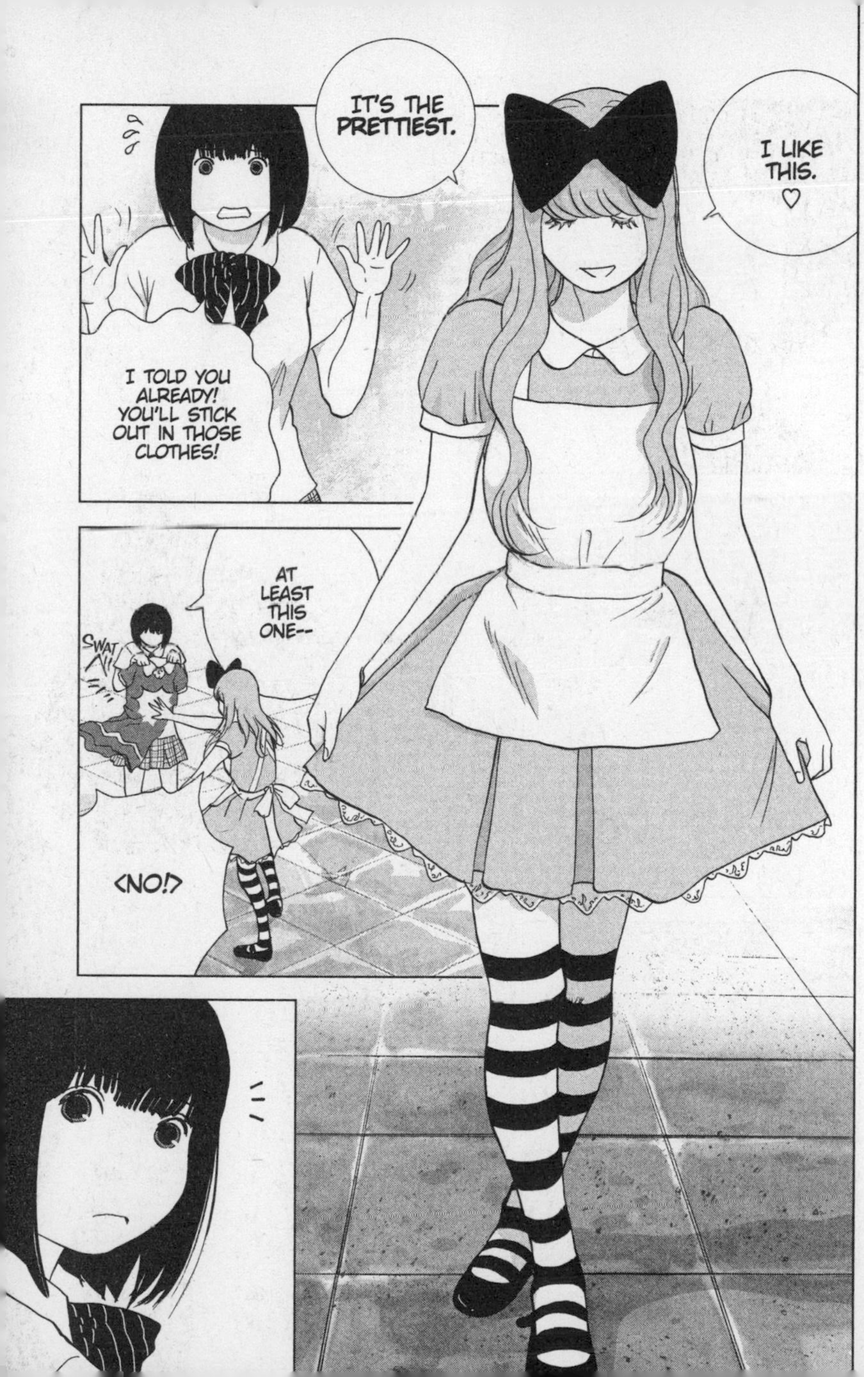

I LIKE THIS. ♡
IT'S THE PRETTIEST.
I TOLD YOU ALREADY! YOU'LL STICK OUT IN THOSE CLOTHES!
AT LEAST THIS ONE--
SWAT
<NO!>

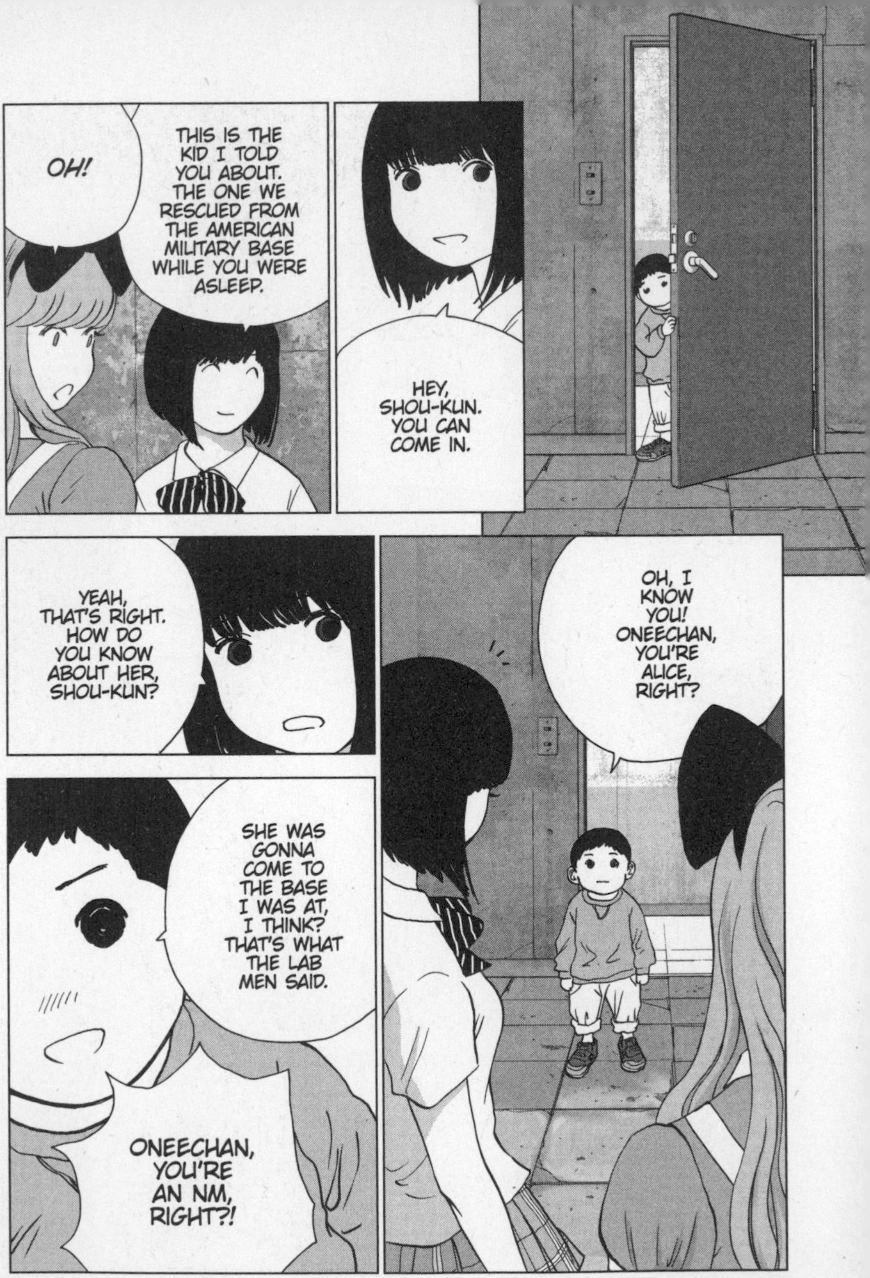
HEY, SHOU-KUN. YOU CAN COME IN.
THIS IS THE KID I TOLD YOU ABOUT. THE ONE WE RESCUED FROM THE AMERICAN MILITARY BASE WHILE YOU WERE ASLEEP.
OH!
OH, I KNOW YOU! ONEECHAN, YOU'RE ALICE, RIGHT?
YEAH, THAT'S RIGHT. HOW DO YOU KNOW ABOUT HER, SHOU-KUN?
SHE WAS GONNA COME TO THE BASE I WAS AT, I THINK? THAT'S WHAT THE LAB MEN SAID.
ONEECHAN, YOU'RE AN NM, RIGHT?!

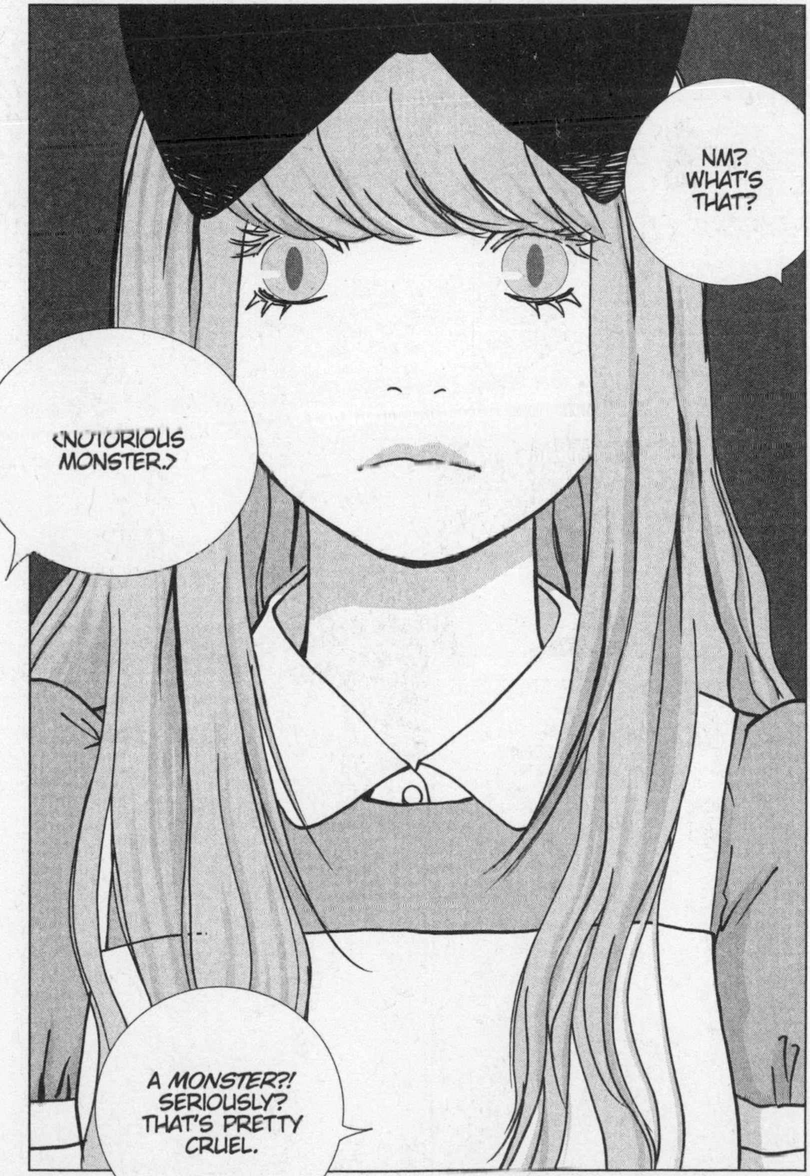
NM? WHAT'S THAT?
<NOTORIOUS MONSTER.>
A *MONSTER?!* SERIOUSLY? THAT'S PRETTY CRUEL.

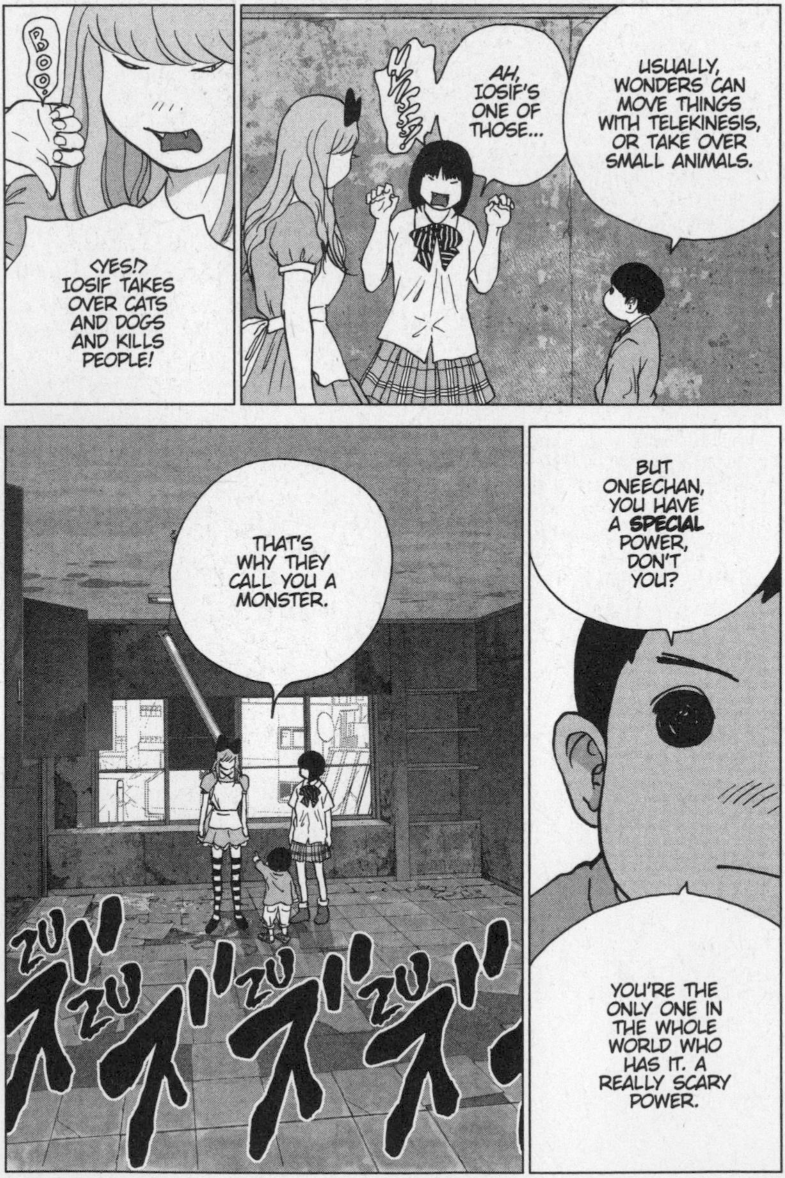
USUALLY, WONDERS CAN MOVE THINGS WITH TELEKINESIS, OR TAKE OVER SMALL ANIMALS.
AH, IOSIF'S ONE OF THOSE...
BOO.
<YES!> IOSIF TAKES OVER CATS AND DOGS AND KILLS PEOPLE!
BUT ONEECHAN, YOU HAVE A **SPECIAL** POWER, DON'T YOU?
YOU'RE THE ONLY ONE IN THE WHOLE WORLD WHO HAS IT. A REALLY SCARY POWER.
THAT'S WHY THEY CALL YOU A MONSTER.
ZU ZU ZU ZU

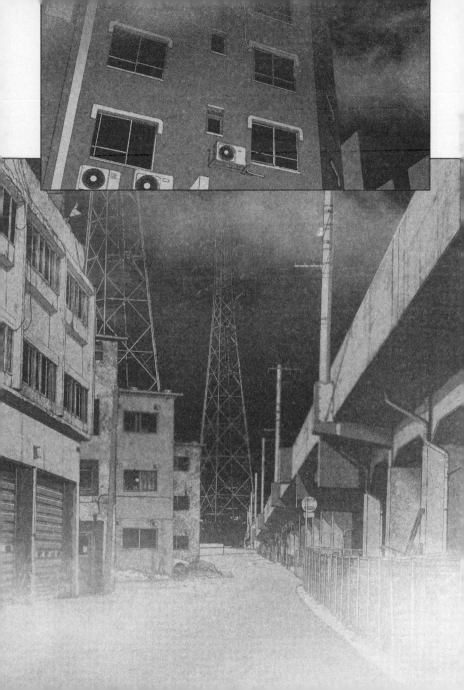

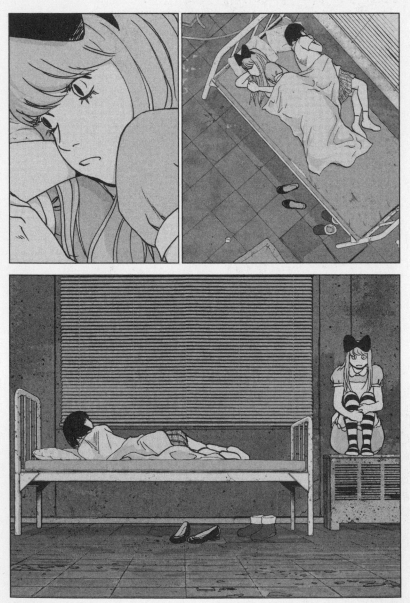

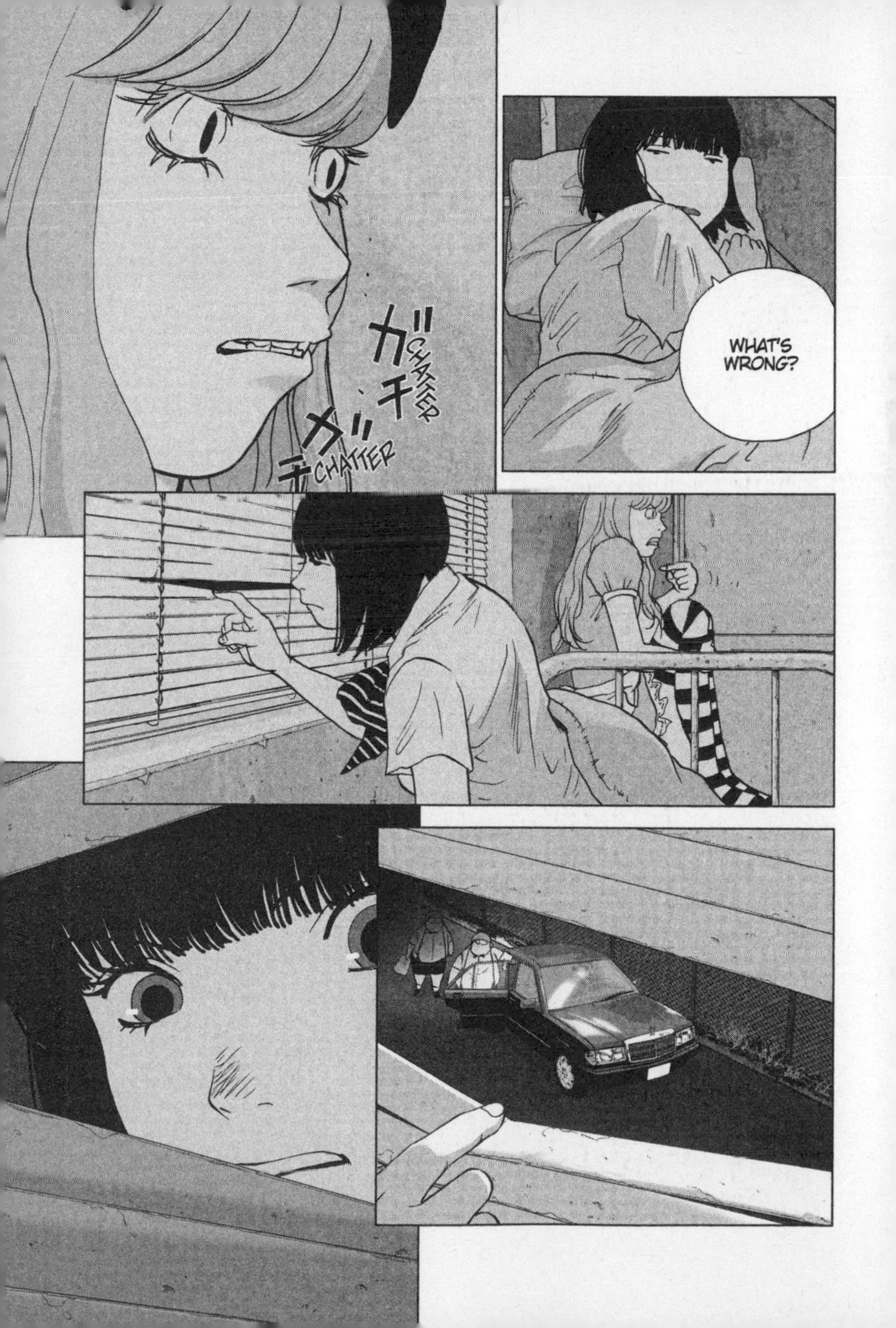
WHAT'S WRONG?
ガチ CHATTER
ガッチ CHATTER

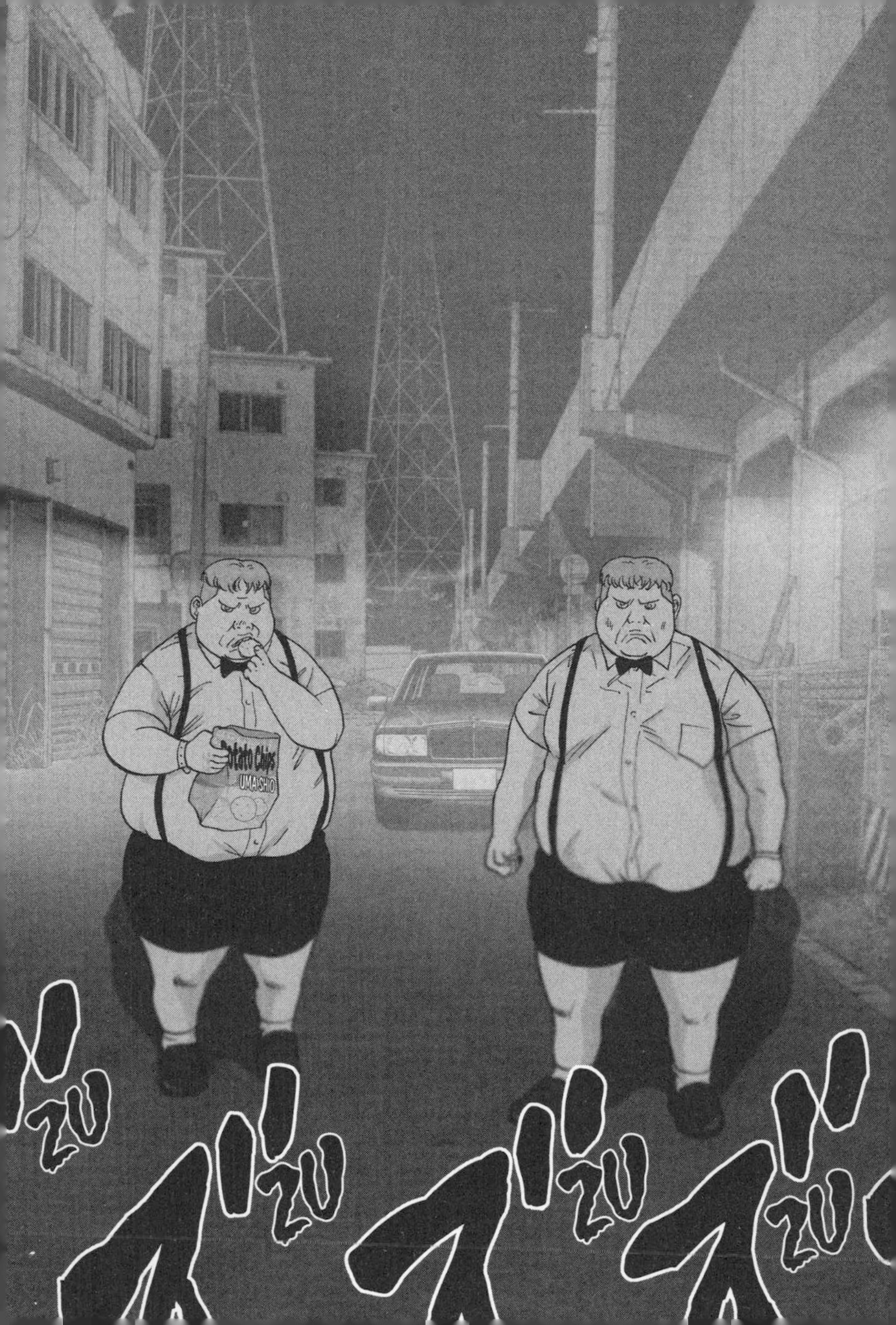

Potato Chips
UMA SHIO
ZU
ZU
ZU
ZU

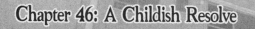

Chapter 46: A Childish Resolve

IT'S THOSE TWINS FROM BEFORE ...

AND THEY'VE GOTTEN REALLY FAT!

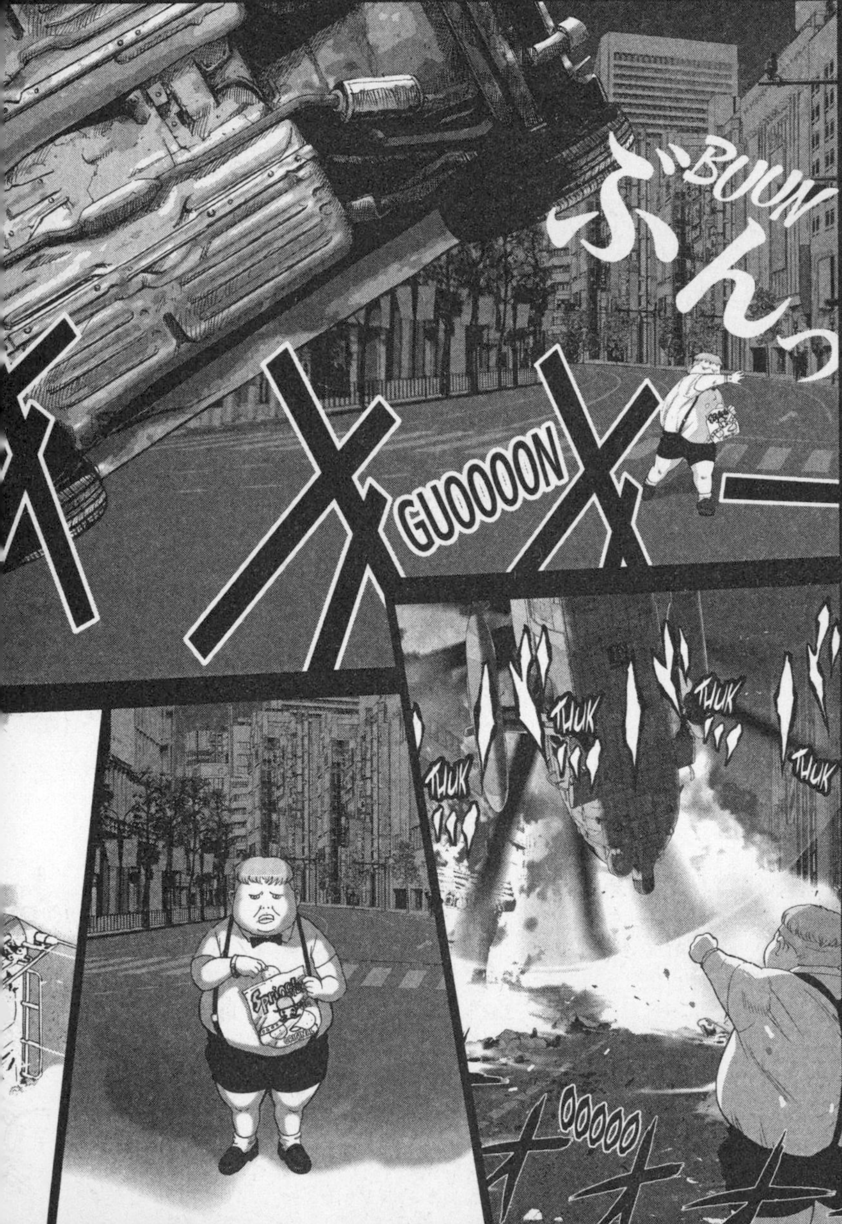
ぶんっ
BUUN
GUOOOON
THUK
THUK
THUK
THUK
OOOOO

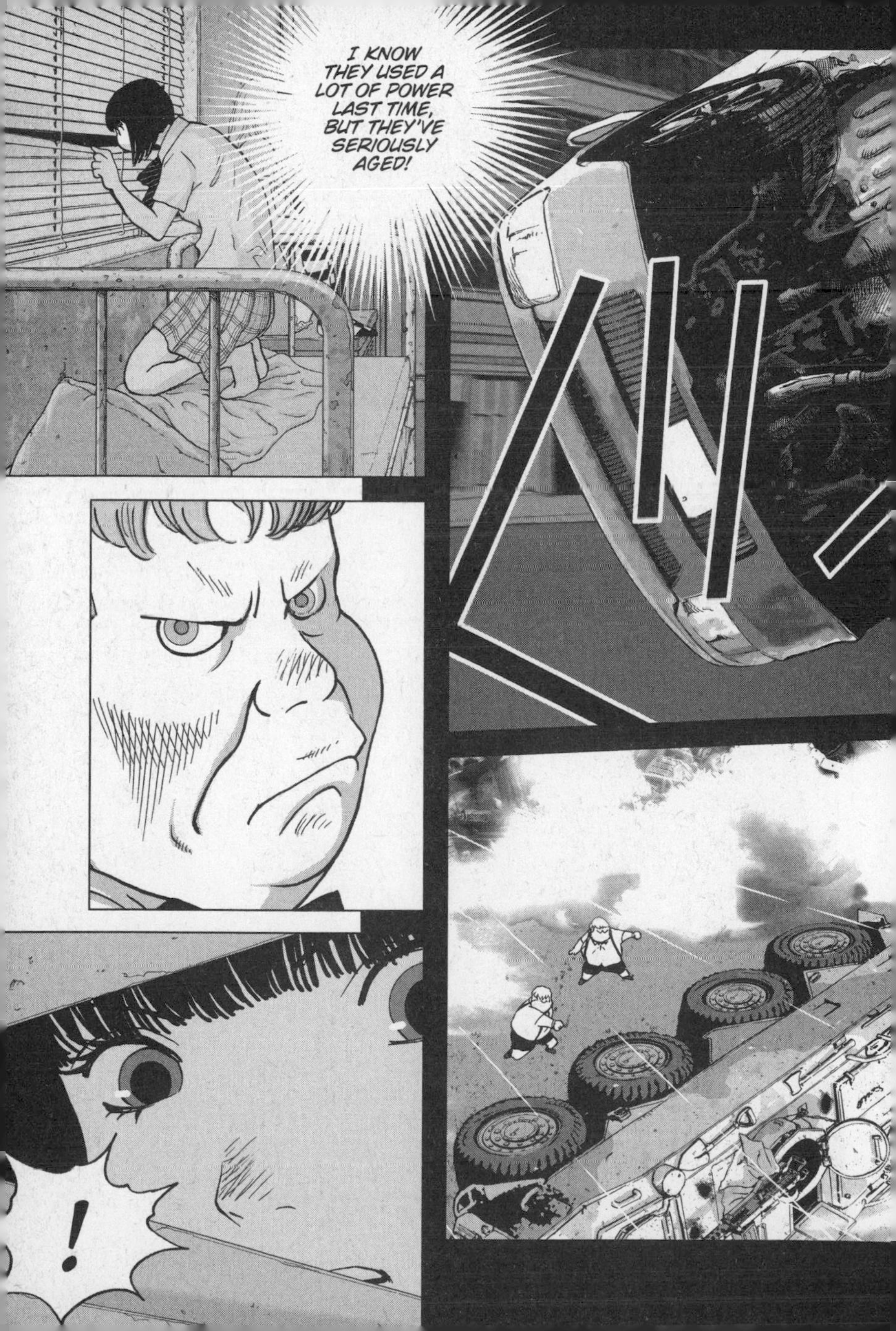
I KNOW THEY USED A LOT OF POWER LAST TIME, BUT THEY'VE SERIOUSLY AGED!
!

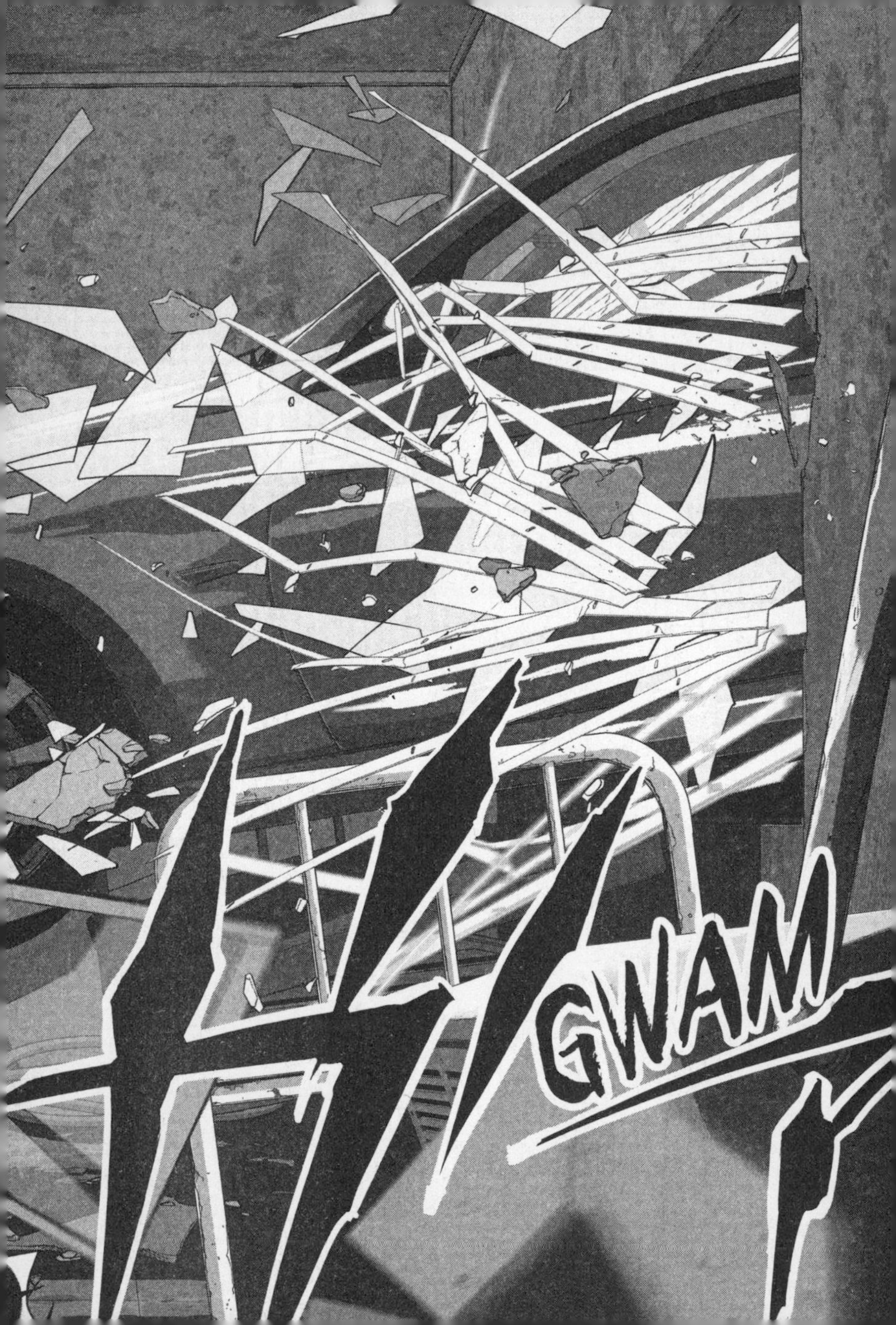
GWAM

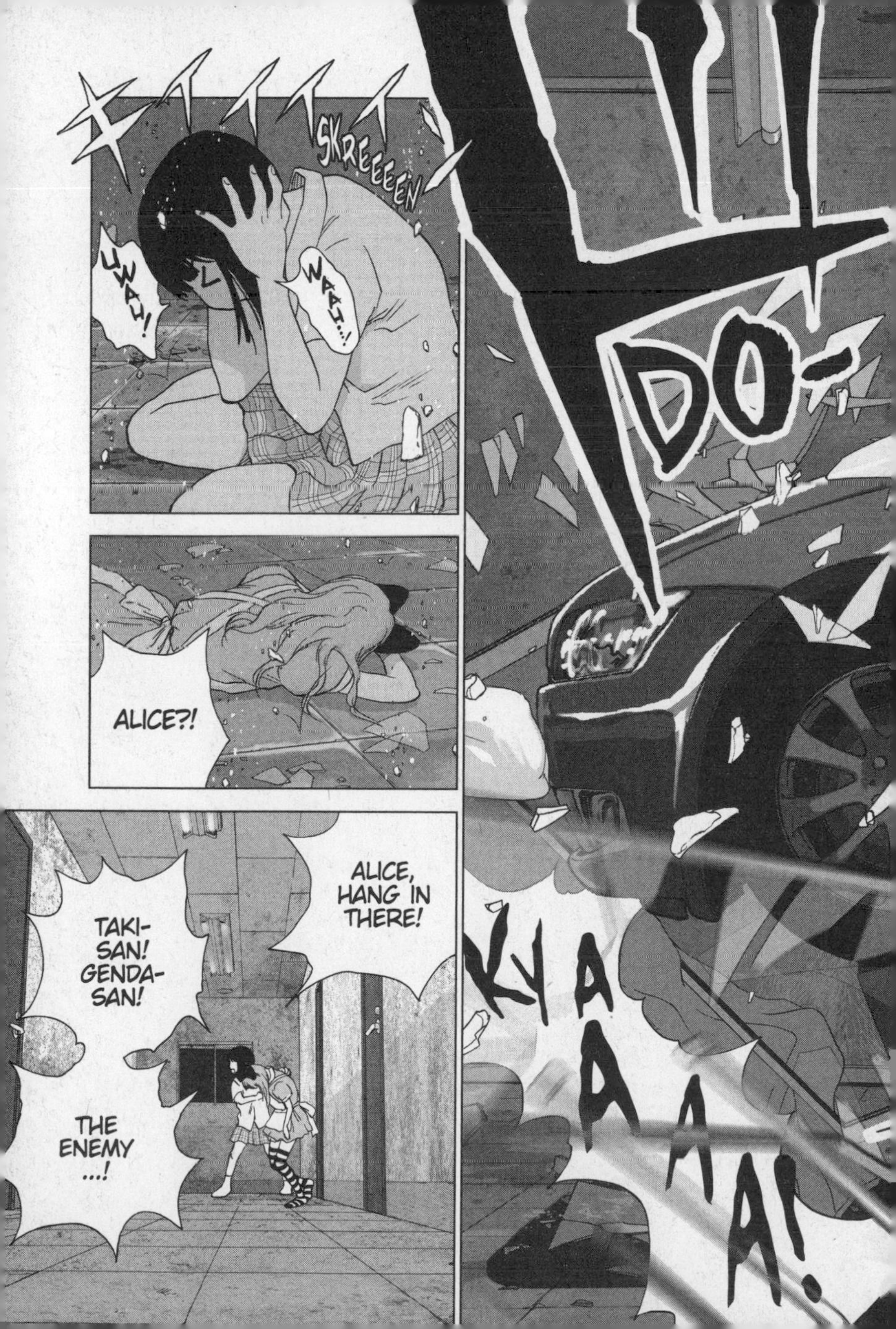
DO-
KYAAAA!
SKREEEEEN
UWAH!
WAAH...!
ALICE?!
ALICE, HANG IN THERE!
TAKI-SAN! GENDA-SAN!
THE ENEMY ...!

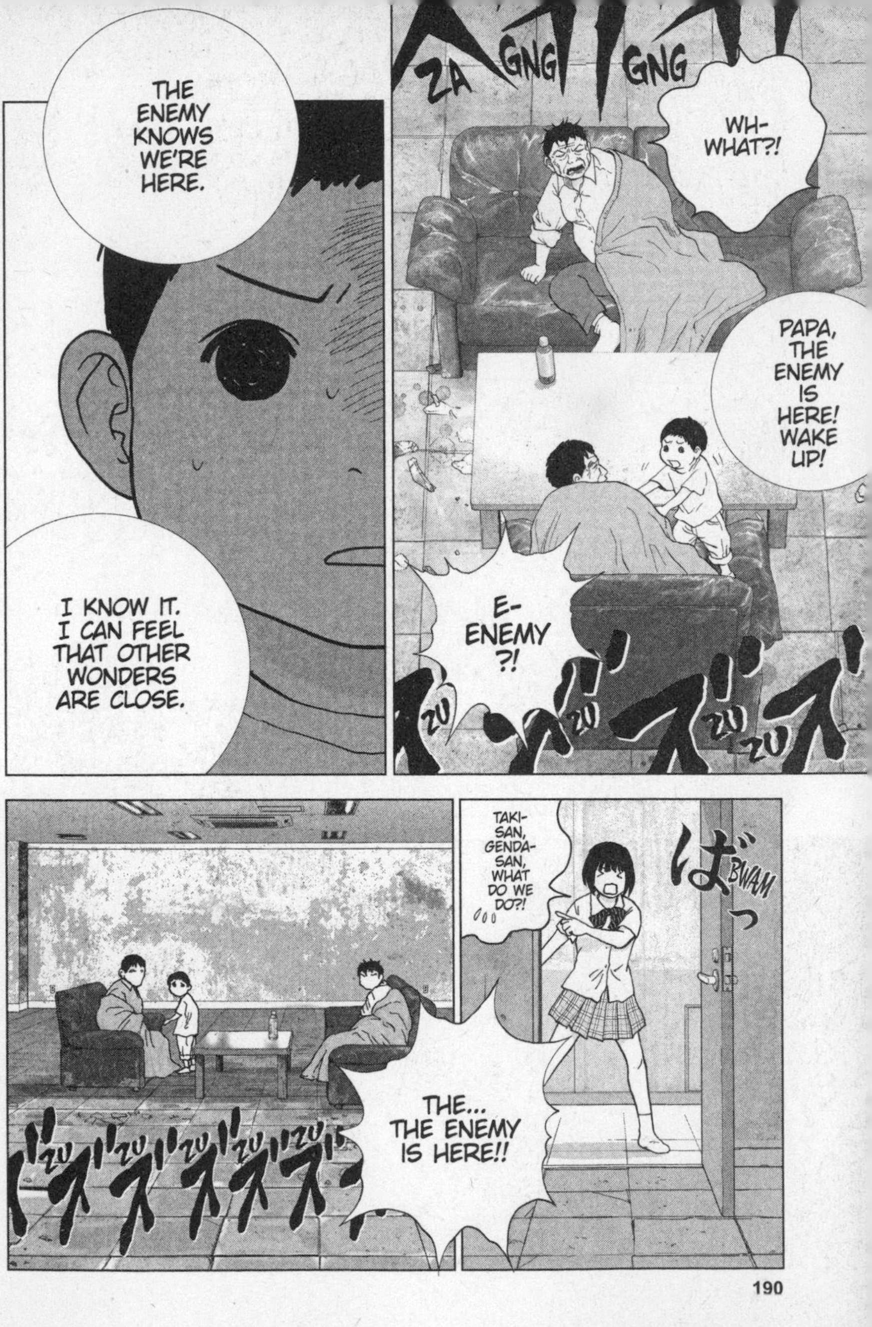
ZA GNG GNG
WH- WHAT?!
PAPA, THE ENEMY IS HERE! WAKE UP!
E- ENEMY ?!
ZU ZU ZU ZU
THE ENEMY KNOWS WE'RE HERE.
I KNOW IT. I CAN FEEL THAT OTHER WONDERS ARE CLOSE.
TAKI-SAN, GENDA-SAN, WHAT DO WE DO?!
ばっ BWAM
THE... THE ENEMY IS HERE!!
ZU ZU ZU ZU ZU

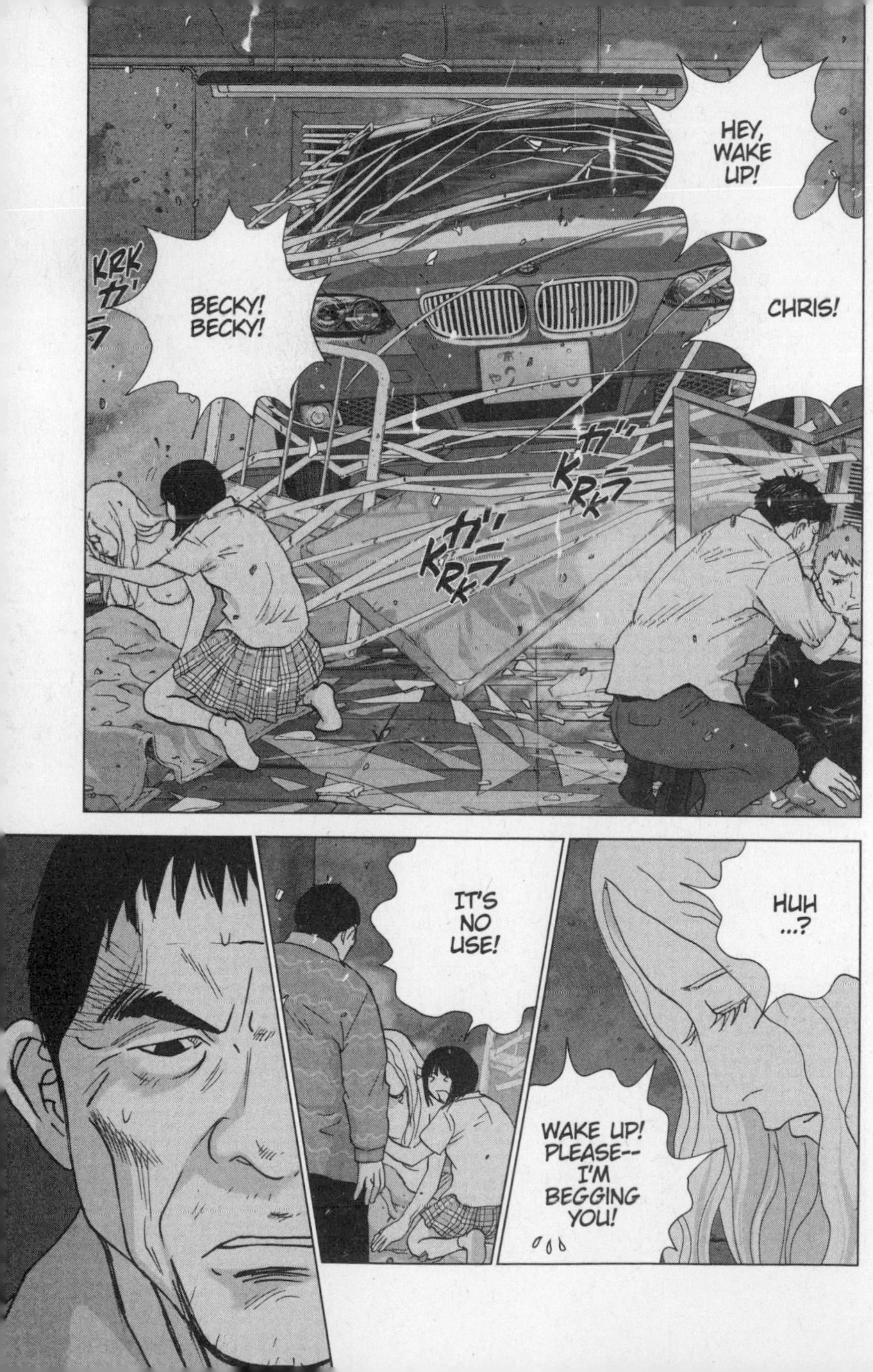
HEY, WAKE UP!
CHRIS!
KRK ガラ
KRK ガラ
BECKY! BECKY!
KRK ガラ
HUH ...?
WAKE UP! PLEASE-- I'M BEGGING YOU!
IT'S NO USE!

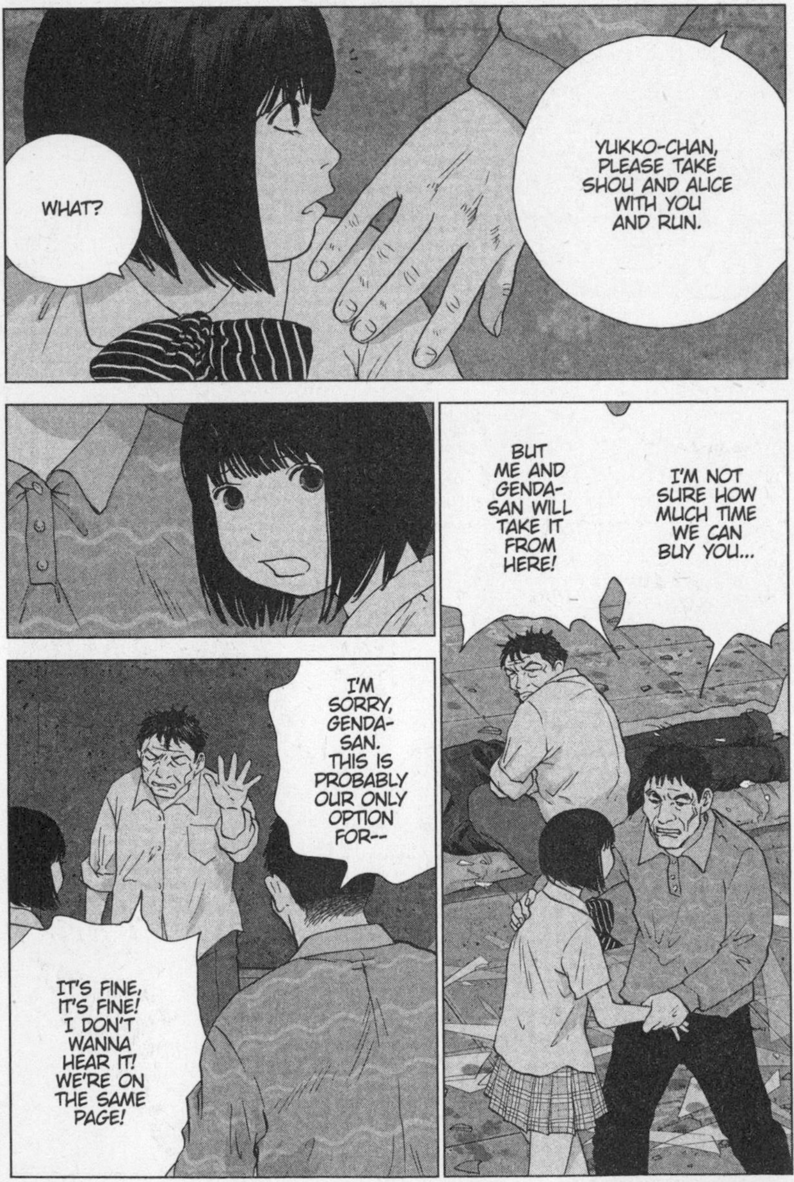
YUKKO-CHAN, PLEASE TAKE SHOU AND ALICE WITH YOU AND RUN.
WHAT?
I'M NOT SURE HOW MUCH TIME WE CAN BUY YOU...
BUT ME AND GENDA-SAN WILL TAKE IT FROM HERE!
I'M SORRY, GENDA-SAN. THIS IS PROBABLY OUR ONLY OPTION FOR--
IT'S FINE, IT'S FINE! I DON'T WANNA HEAR IT! WE'RE ON THE SAME PAGE!

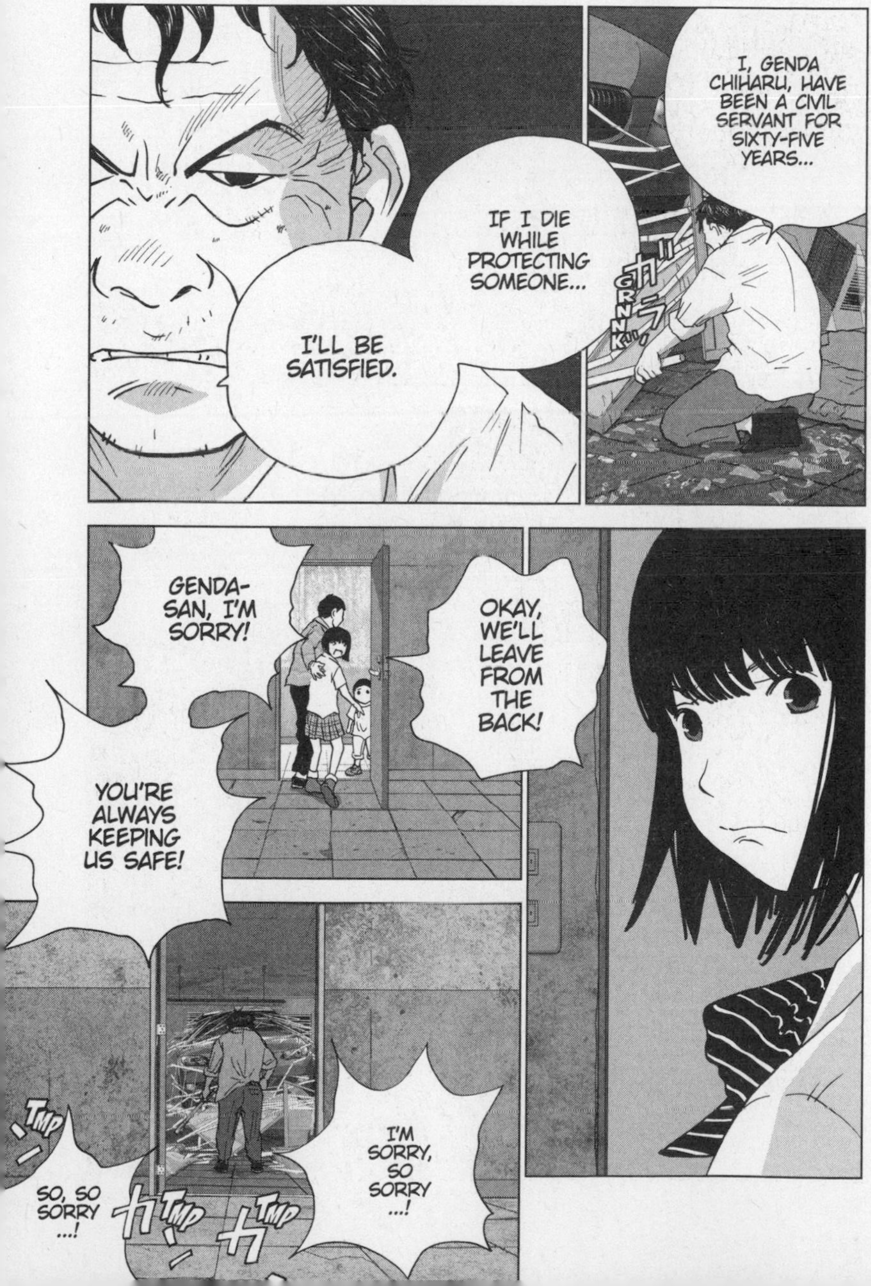
I, GENDA CHIHARU, HAVE BEEN A CIVIL SERVANT FOR SIXTY-FIVE YEARS...
GRNK
IF I DIE WHILE PROTECTING SOMEONE...
I'LL BE SATISFIED.
OKAY, WE'LL LEAVE FROM THE BACK!
GENDA-SAN, I'M SORRY!
YOU'RE ALWAYS KEEPING US SAFE!
I'M SORRY, SO SORRY ...!
TMP
TMP
SO, SO SORRY ...!
TMP

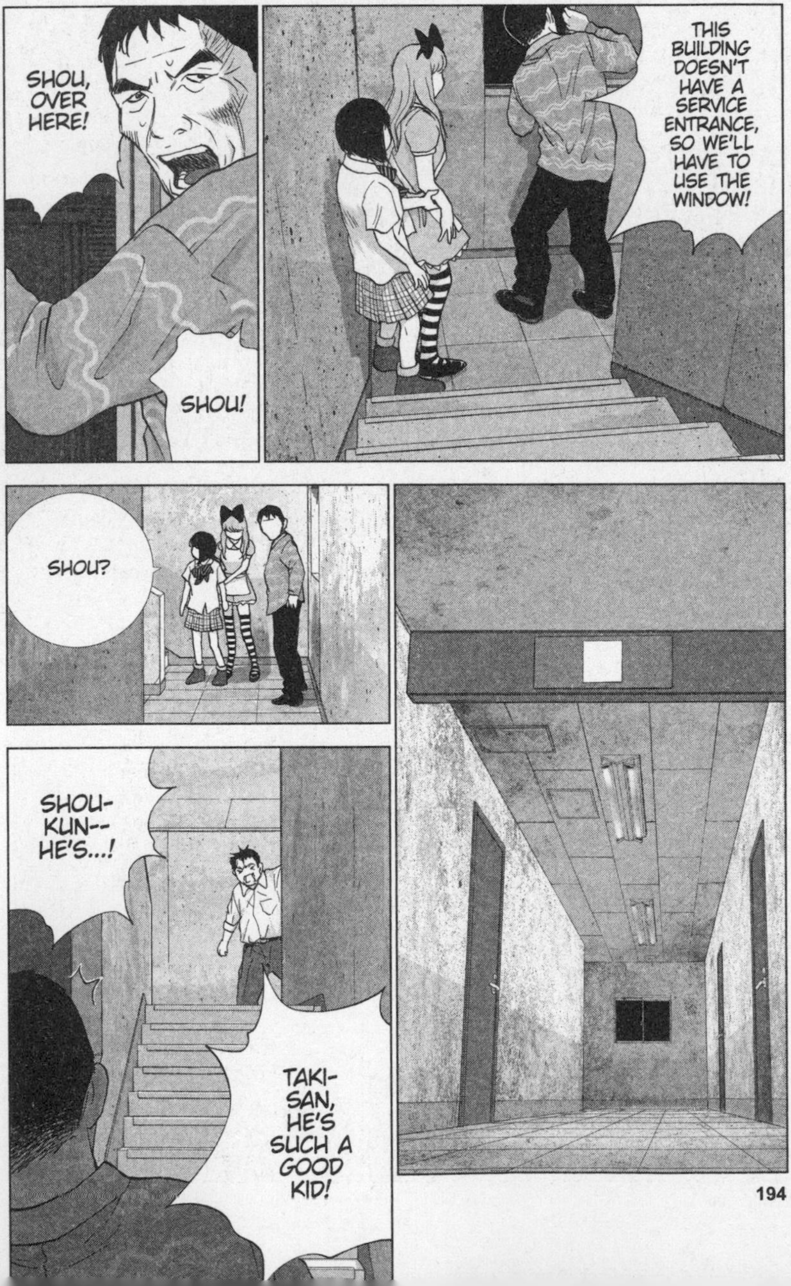
THIS BUILDING DOESN'T HAVE A SERVICE ENTRANCE, SO WE'LL HAVE TO USE THE WINDOW!
SHOU, OVER HERE!
SHOU!
SHOU?
SHOU-KUN-- HE'S...!
TAKI-SAN, HE'S SUCH A GOOD KID!

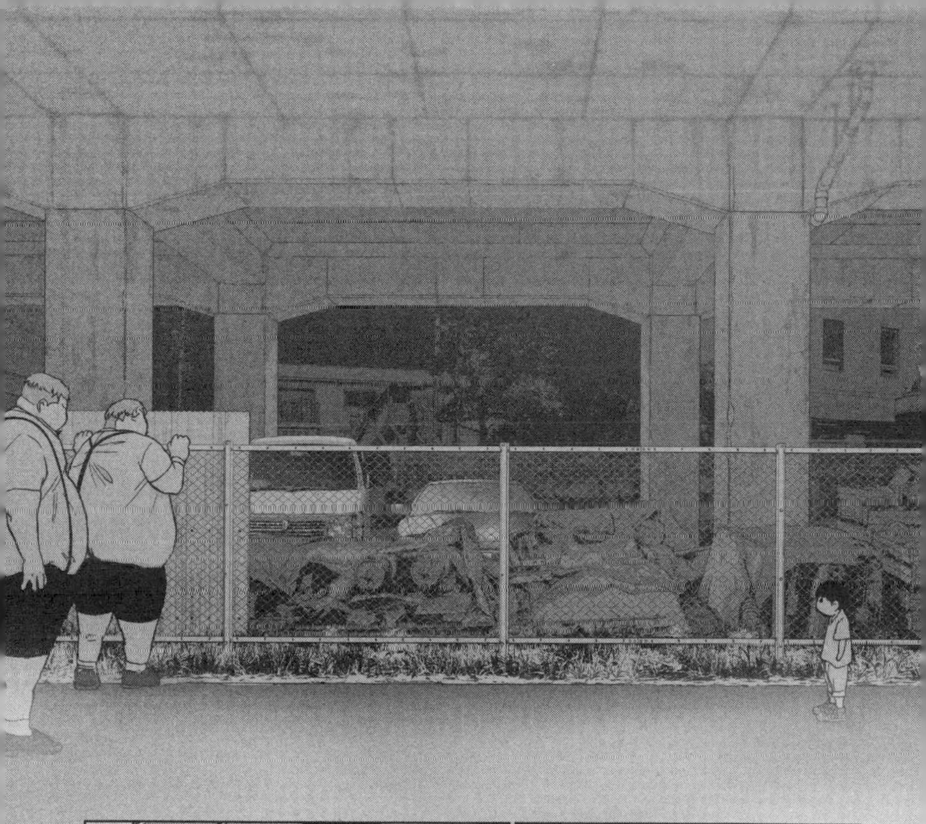

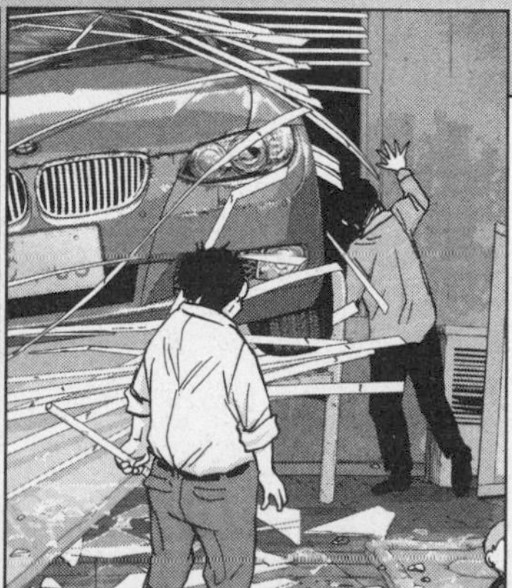

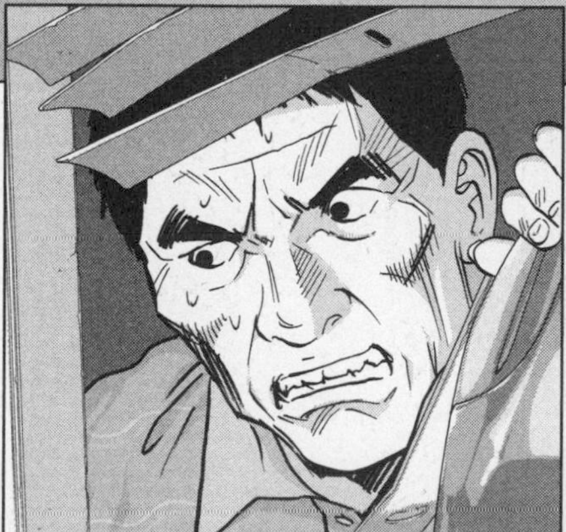

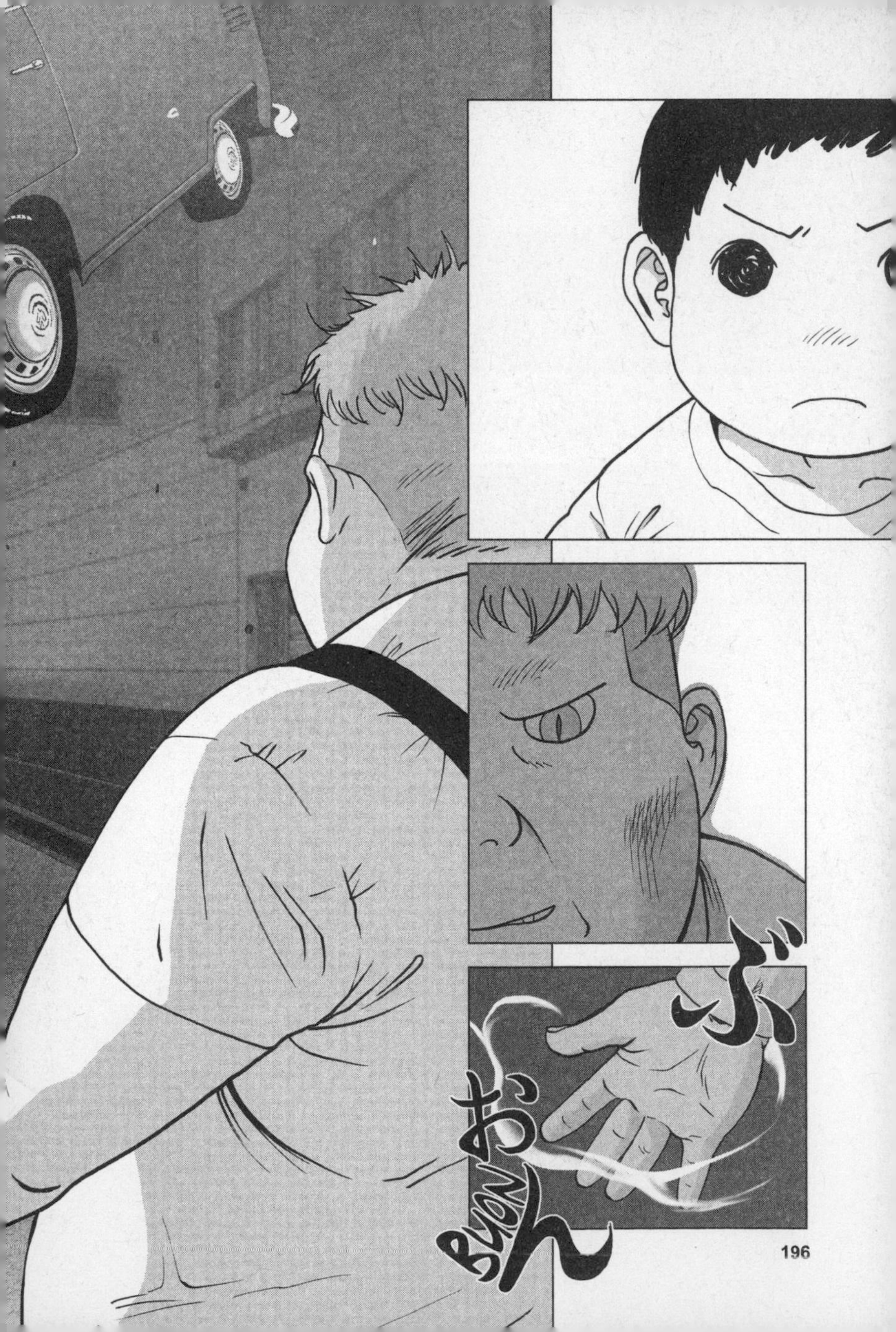
ぶおん
BUON

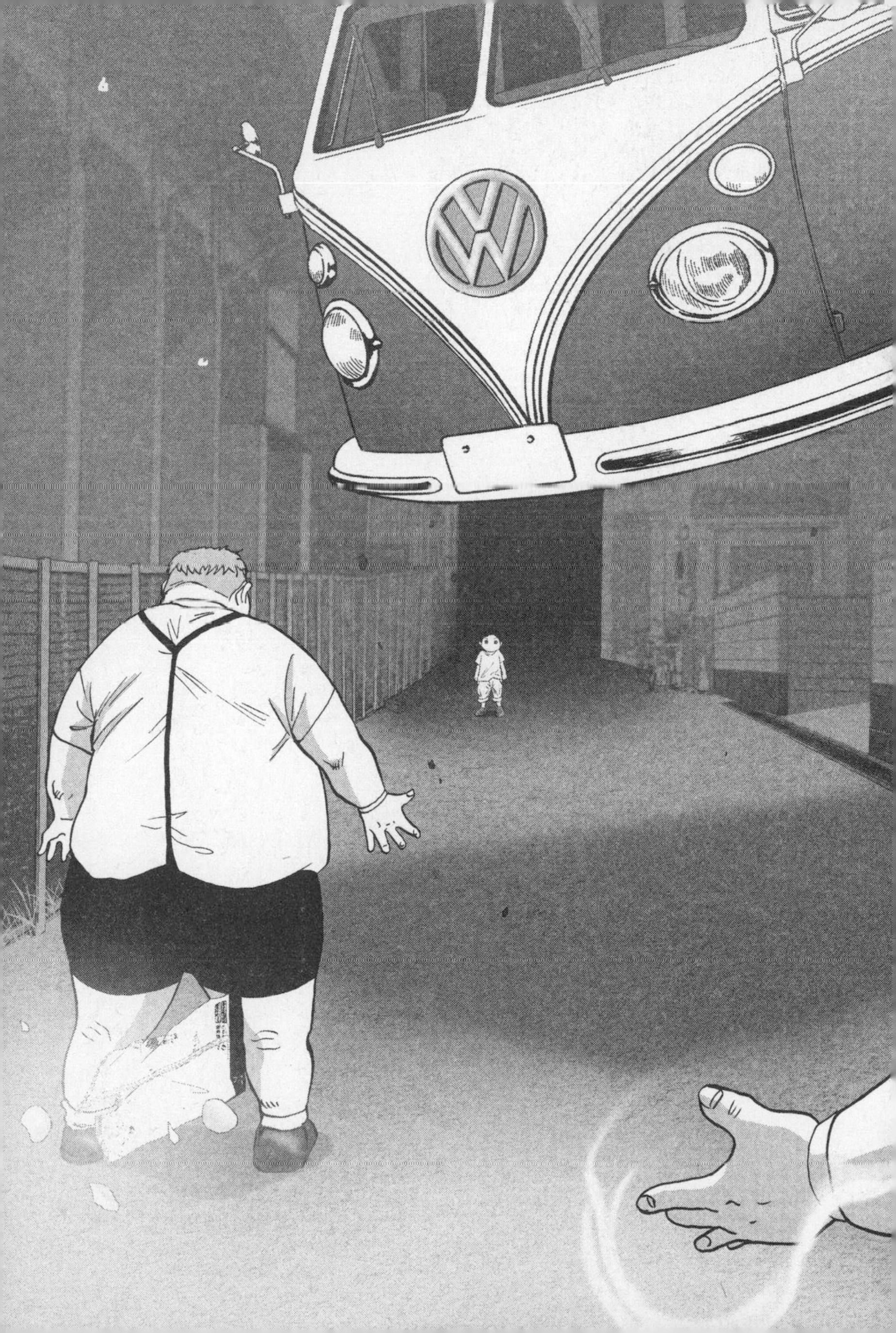

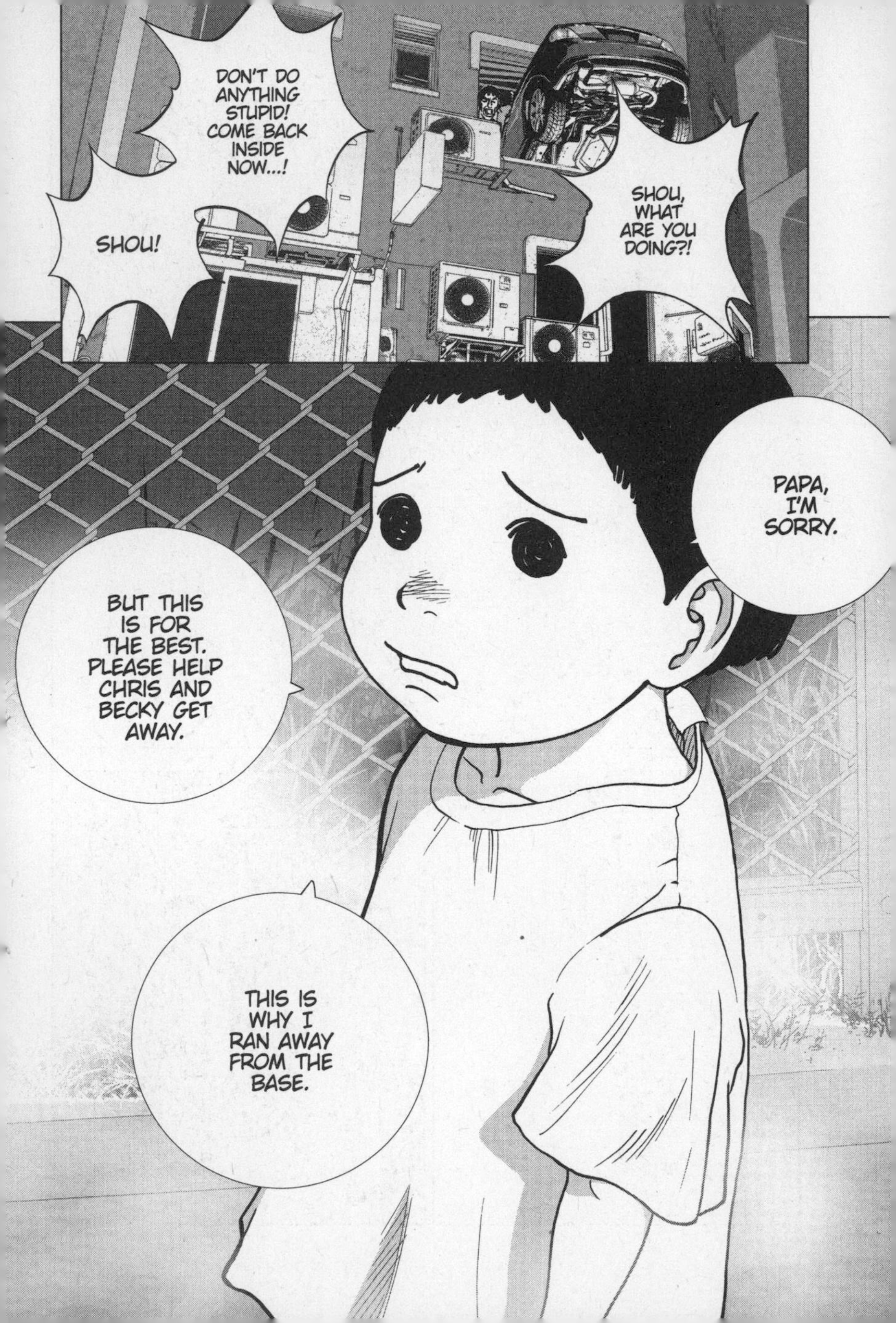
SHOU, WHAT ARE YOU DOING?!
DON'T DO ANYTHING STUPID! COME BACK INSIDE NOW...!
SHOU!
PAPA, I'M SORRY.
BUT THIS IS FOR THE BEST. PLEASE HELP CHRIS AND BECKY GET AWAY.
THIS IS WHY I RAN AWAY FROM THE BASE.

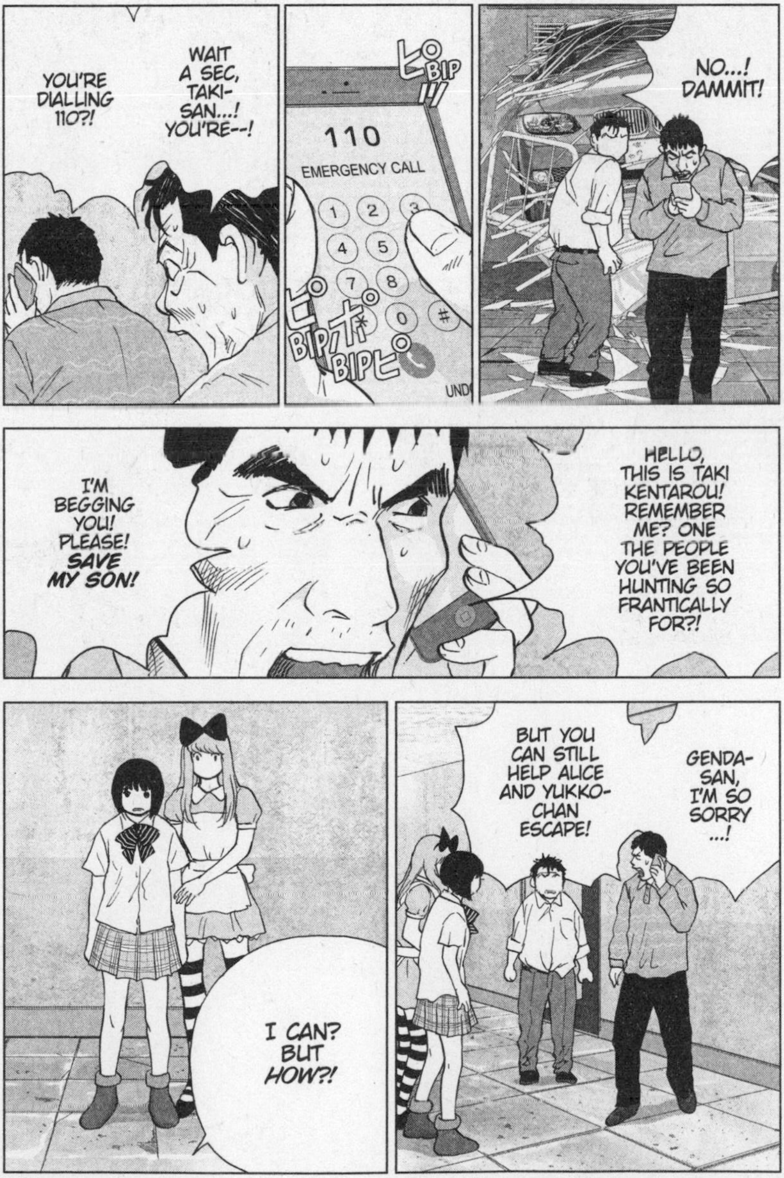
NO...! DAMMIT!
BIP
110
EMERGENCY CALL
BIP BIP BIP
WAIT A SEC, TAKI-SAN...! YOU'RE--!
YOU'RE DIALLING 110?!
HELLO, THIS IS TAKI KENTAROU! REMEMBER ME? ONE THE PEOPLE YOU'VE BEEN HUNTING SO FRANTICALLY FOR?!
I'M BEGGING YOU! PLEASE! *SAVE MY SON!*
GENDA-SAN, I'M SO SORRY ...!
BUT YOU CAN STILL HELP ALICE AND YUKKO-CHAN ESCAPE!
I CAN? BUT *HOW?!*

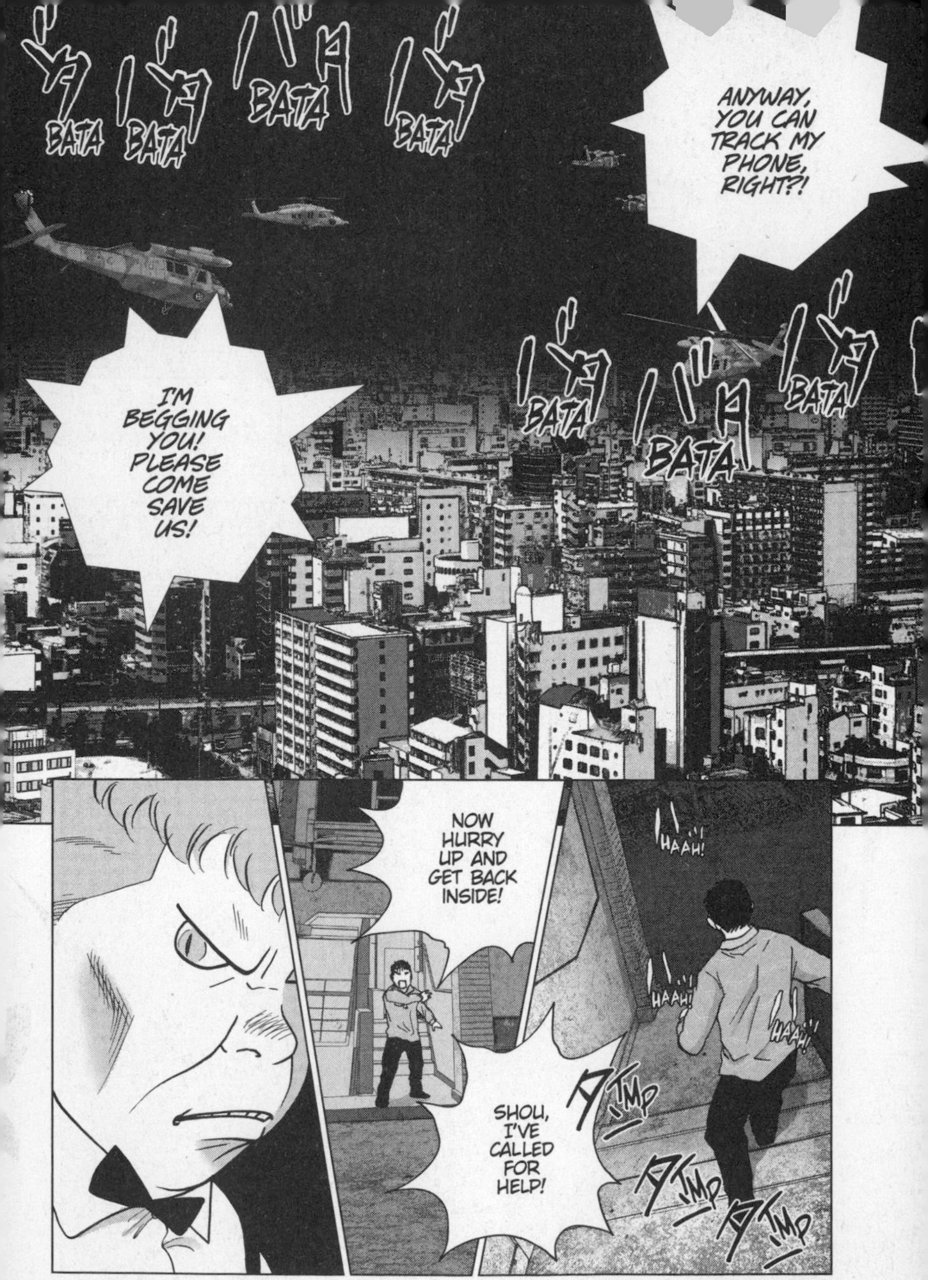
BATA BATA BATA BATA
ANYWAY, YOU CAN TRACK MY PHONE, RIGHT?!
BATA BATA BATA
I'M BEGGING YOU! PLEASE COME SAVE US!
BATA BATA BATA BATA
HAAH!
HAAH!
HAAH!
TMP TMP TMP
SHOU, I'VE CALLED FOR HELP!
NOW HURRY UP AND GET BACK INSIDE!

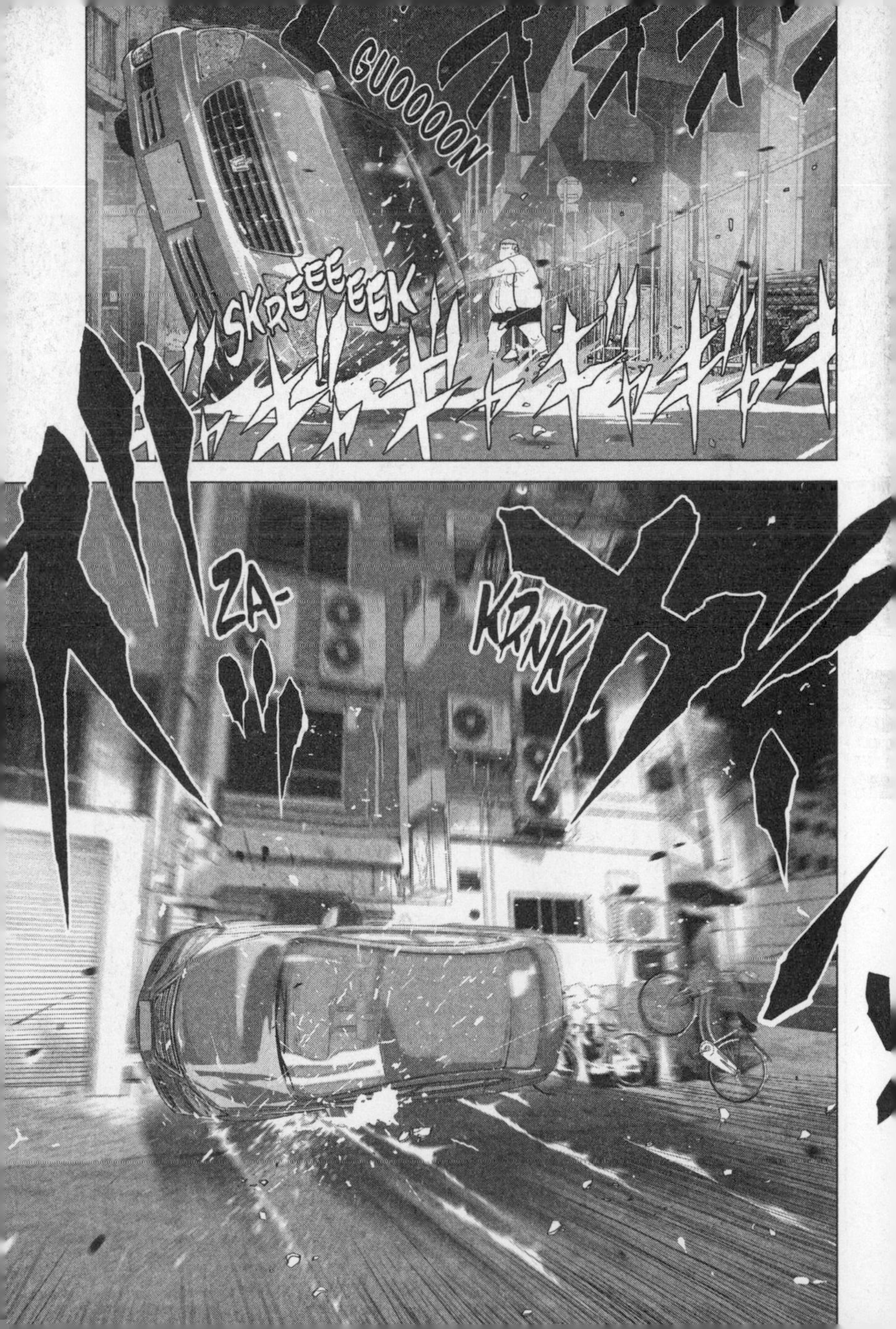
GUOOOOON
SKREEEEEEK
ZA-
KONK

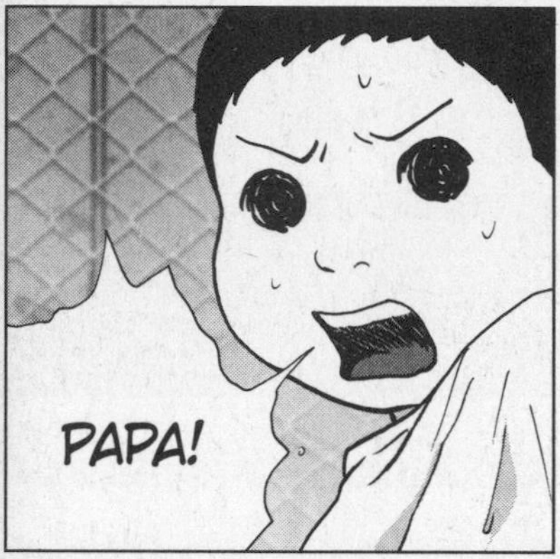
PAPA!
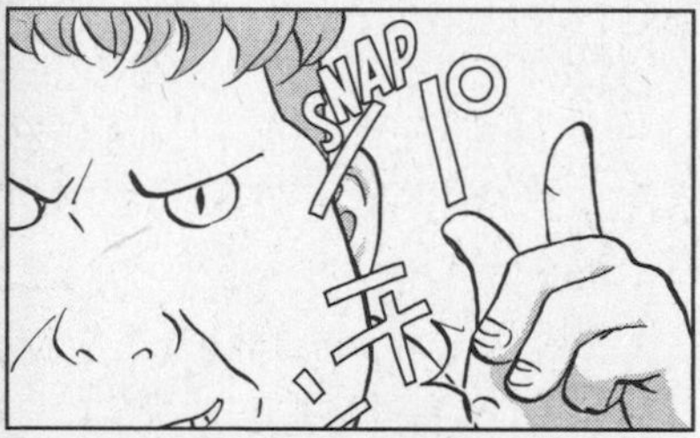
SNAP
パキ
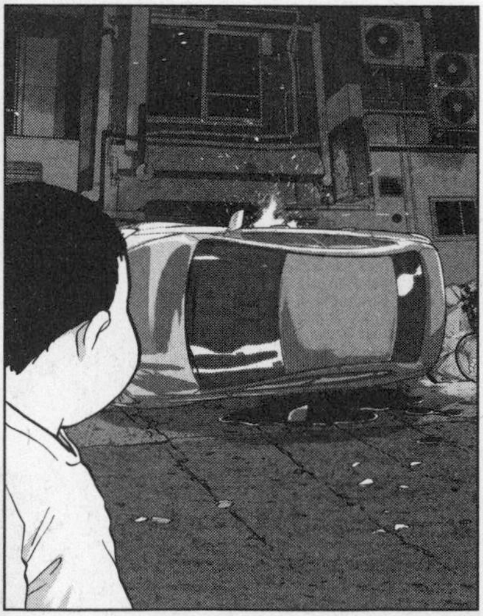
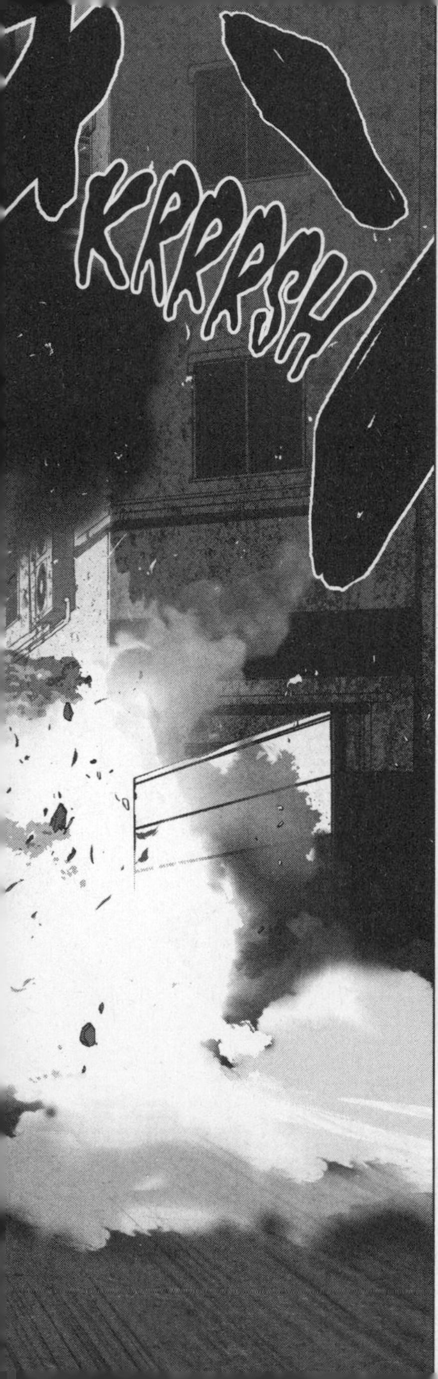
KRRRSH

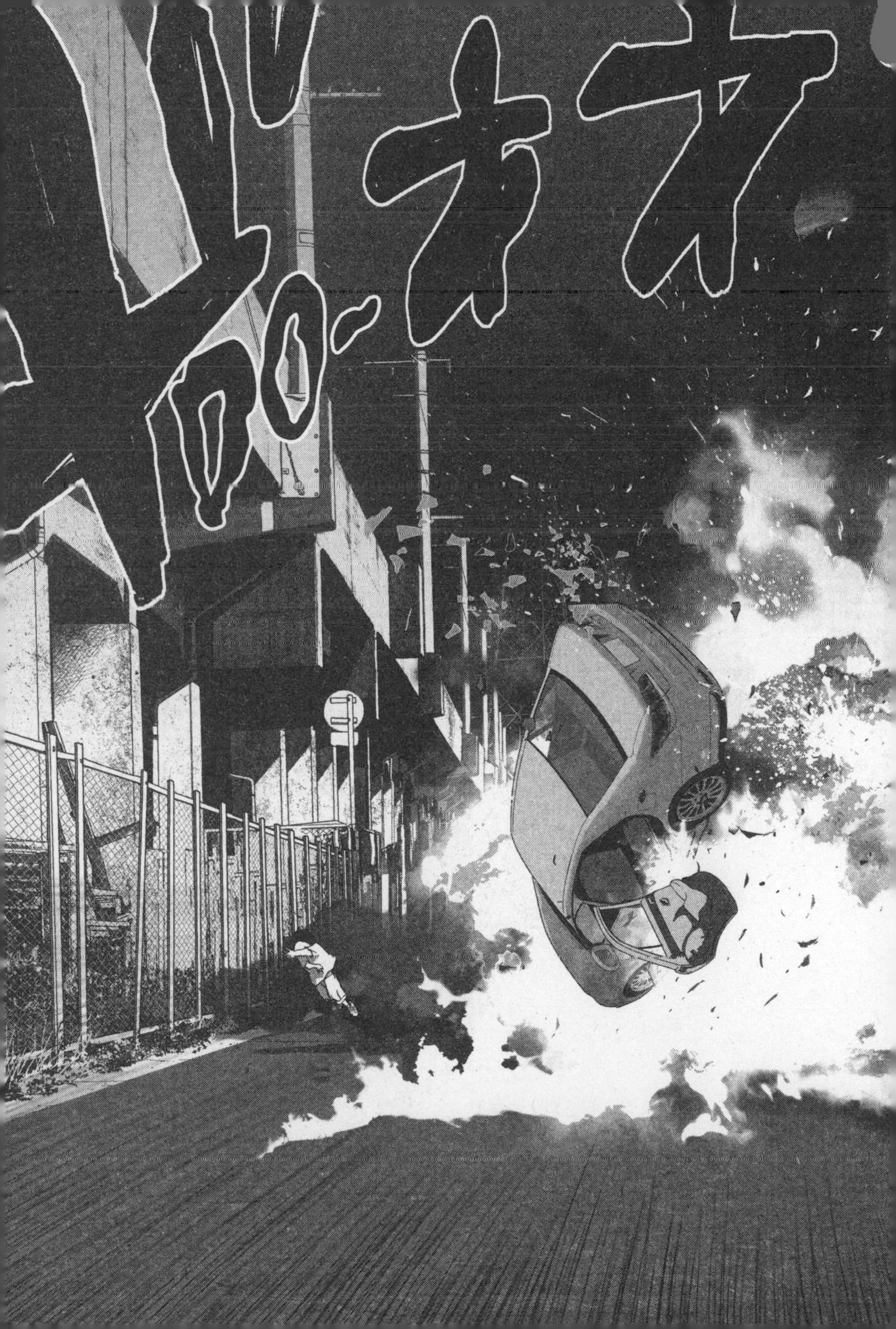

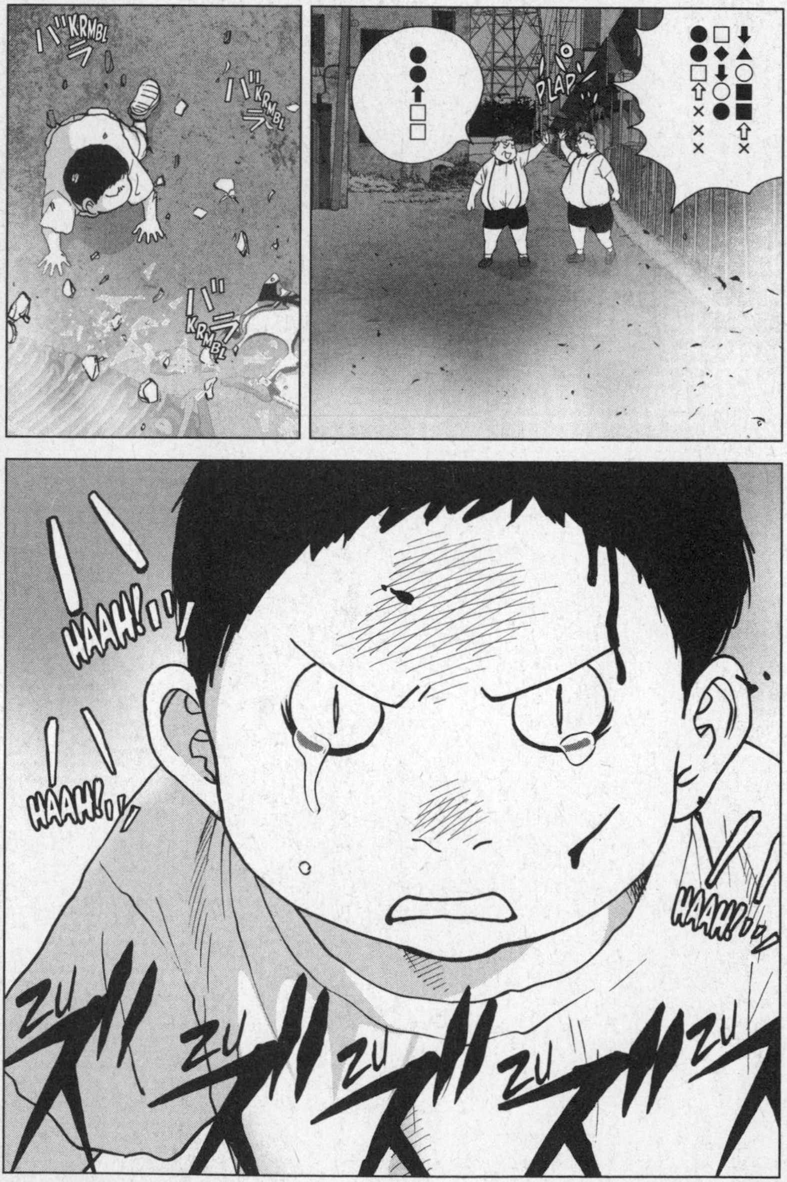
⬇▲○■■⇧×
□◆⬇○●
●●□⇧×××
PLAP
●●⬆□□
KRMBL
KRMBL
KRMBL
HAAH!
HAAH!
HAAH!
ZU
ZU
ZU
ZU
ZU

Wonderland

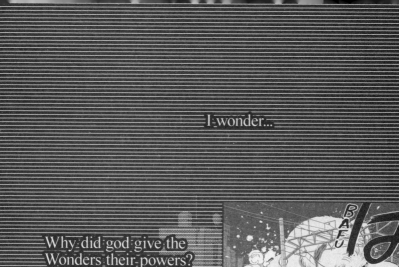

I wonder...

BAFU

Why did god give the Wonders their powers?

BUON
Уандер нельзя бороться!
ワンダーは戦ってはダメ！
А почему использоваться такая способность в качестве оружия!?
そのせっかくの能力をなぜ兵器として使わなきゃなんないの!?

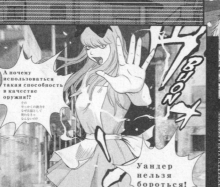

Shou, who just lost his father, loses himself in his fight against the telekinetic Russian twin Wonders.

ZU
ZU.
ZU
ZU

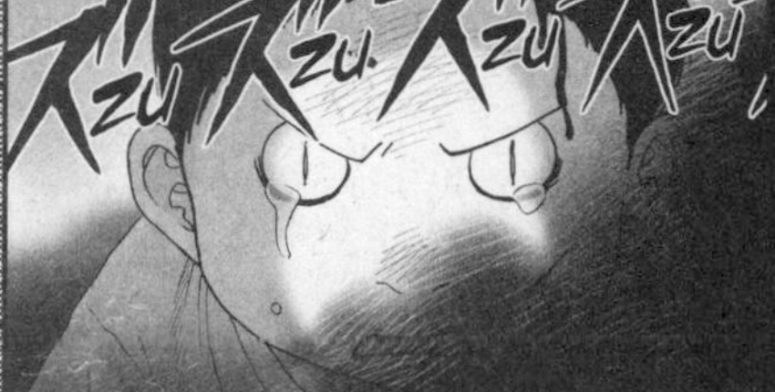

Wonders shouldn't be fighting each other!

Why do you have to weaponize your powers?

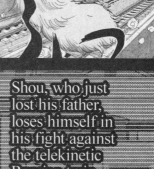

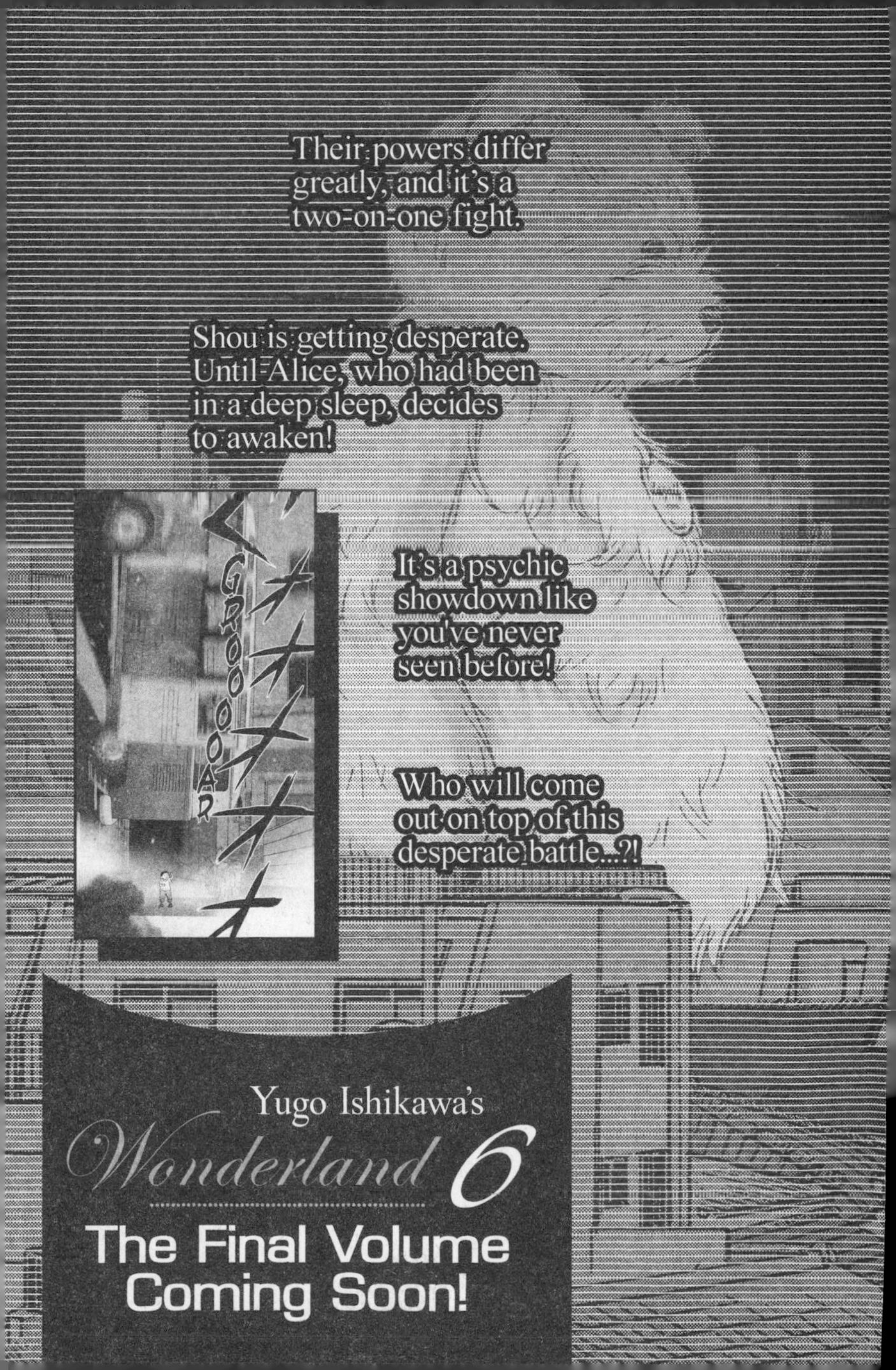
Their powers differ greatly, and it's a two-on-one fight.
Shou is getting desperate. Until Alice, who had been in a deep sleep, decides to awaken!
GROOOOOAR
It's a psychic showdown like you've never seen before!
Who will come out on top of this desperate battle...?!
Yugo Ishikawa's
Wonderland 6
The Final Volume Coming Soon!

SEVEN SEAS ENTERTAINMENT PRESENTS

Wonderland Vol. 5

story and art by YUGO ISHIKAWA

TRANSLATION
Molly Rabbitt

ADAPTATION
Marykate Jasper

LETTERING AND RETOUCH
James Gaubatz

ORIGINAL COVER DESIGN
Mikiyo Kobayashi＋Bay Bridge Studio

COVER DESIGN
KC Fabellon

PROOFREADER
**Kurestin Armada
B. Lana Guggenheim**

EDITOR
Jenn Grunigen

PREPRESS TECHNICIAN
Rhiannon Rasmussen-Silverstein

MANAGING EDITOR
Julie Davis

ASSOCIATE PUBLISHER
Adam Arnold

PUBLISHER
Jason DeAngelis

Seven Seas press and purchase enquiries can be sent to Marketing Manager
Lianne Sentar at press@gomanga.com. Information regarding the distribution
and purchase of digital editions is available from Digital Manager CK Russell
at digital@gomanga.com.

Seven Seas and the Seven Seas logo are trademarks of
Seven Seas Entertainment. All rights reserved.

ISBN: 978-1-64505-227-2

Printed in Canada

First Printing: March 2020

10 9 8 7 6 5 4 3 2 1

FOLLOW US ONLINE: www.sevenseasentertainment.com

READING DIRECTIONS

This book reads from *right to left*, Japanese style.
If this is your first time reading manga, you start
reading from the top right panel on each page and
take it from there. If you get lost, just follow the
numbered diagram here. It may seem backwards at
first. but you'll get the hang of it! Have fun!!

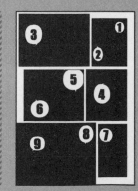